THE GENERAL
AGAINST
THE KREMLIN

THE GENERAL AGAINST THE KREMLIN

Alexander Lebed: Power and Illusion

HAROLD ELLETSON

LITTLE, BROWN AND COMPANY

A *Little, Brown* Book

First published in Great Britain in 1998
by Little, Brown and Company

Copyright © 1998 by Harold Elletson

PICTURE CREDITS
1, 4, 13, 27, 38: Frank Spooner/Gamma; 2, 3, 5, 11, 16, 18,
24, 30, 31, 33, 34, 39: Popperfoto; 6, 10, 19: AP/Topham;
7: R. Bossu; 8, 12, 14, 15, 21, 26, 28, 29, 32, 35, 36: Sygma;
9, 17, 22, 23, 37: Magnum; 20, 25: Network

A CIP catalogue record for this book
is available from the British Library.

ISBN: 0 316 64477 3

Typeset in Stempel Garamond by M Rules
Printed and bound in Great Britain
by Clays Ltd, St Ives plc

Little, Brown and Company (UK)
Brettenham House
Lancaster Place
London WC2E 7EN

For Fiona, Alexander and George

CONTENTS

ACKNOWLEDGEMENTS

My greatest thanks must go to my wife, Fiona, for all her help, enthusiasm and long-suffering forbearance during my work on this book. I am also grateful to my two sons: Alexander ensured that my mind did not go stale by repeatedly interrupting me for games of football, and George had the good sense and tact to bless us with his arrival only as I reached the last chapter.

Many people were very generous with their time and with advice, information, suggestions and encouragement. I am especially grateful to Alexander Ivanovich Lebed for giving me so much of his time, and to his press secretary Alexander Yakushenko. I am also deeply indebted to Halil Akinci of the Turkish Foreign Ministry; Bruce Anderson; the incomparable Maggie Blair, whose computer skills saved days of work from disappearing for ever; Justin Bodle; Vitaly Bondarenko; Lt.-Col. Jonathan Bourne-May; Colonel Roger Brooks; Dr Marie Benningsen Broxup; Alexei Chaplygin; Howard Chase of British Petroleum; Charles Chkotoua; Lt.-Col. Dr Viorel Cibotaru; Eugen Colac; Dr Wolfgang Danspeckgruber of Princeton University; Merric Davidson, for his advice and commitment to the project; Dzhokhar Dudayev; Leyla Ecin; Hermi and Ian Ferguson; General John Galvin of the Fletcher School of

Diplomacy at Tuft's University; Edward Garnier MP; Andrew Gordon; Hannah and Jack Grove; Professor Steve Grigg; Parvin Guliev; Dr Rasul Guliev; Dr Robert Halfon; Dr Kinga Hazai; Anders Hellner of the Swedish Foreign Affairs Institute; Professor John Hiden and the Department of Modern European Studies at Bradford University; the Rt. Hon. Douglas Hogg MP, for an interesting adjournment debate; Lisa and Jamie Jameson; Vitaly Kozlikin; Michael Lowy; Igor Markov; Ambassador Richard McCormack; Svetlana Mingulia; Chet Nagle; Boris Nemtsov; Igor Oleynik; Ambassador Boris Pankin; Sergei Paramonov; the Rt. Hon. Michael Portillo; Seda Poumpianskaya; Donna Richmond, for all her dedication; the Rt. Hon. Malcolm Rifkind; Richard Ritchie; Lennart Roslund; Arne Runske; Alan Samson and all the team at Little, Brown; Shery Shahnavaz, who provided amusing stories and astonishing contacts; Colonel John Smith; Crocker Snow; Artyom Tarasov; Heather Taylor, who produced a large amount of detailed research and some excellent analysis; Frau Grete Urban; Richard Ware; Susannah Waldo Wood; Thomas Wood; Gennady Yanayev; Shamseddin Alaedin Yusuf; and numerous friends in Russia, Chechnya, Georgia, Azerbaijan and Moldova, whose assistance I will not forget.

Staff of the following institutions were also very helpful, and I am most grateful to them: the Ministry of Defence; the Department of Modern European Studies at Bradford University; the Fletcher School of Diplomacy at Tuft's University; the Foreign and Commonwealth Office; the House of Commons Library; the London Library; Princeton University; the School of Slavonic and East European Studies; the Caucasus and Central Asia Departments of the Turkish Foreign Ministry in Ankara; and the Weidener Memorial Library at Harvard University.

PREFACE

*'Well, you know, everyone in Russia's baptised,
they're even Orthodox believers, but they've all got
rotten morals and absolutely no sense of right and
wrong.'*

N. S. LESKOV, 'A Winter's Day'[1]

Modern Russia is not a democracy. It has some of the characteristic features and attributes of a democracy; some of its institutions appear democratic; its constitution pays lip-service to the concept of democracy and some of its political leaders use the language of democracy; but still, it is not a democratic country.

Does it matter? Having hailed Mikhail Gorbachev as the man who would democratise the Soviet Union, the West then trumpeted the triumph of Boris Yeltsin, who overthrew him, as a victory for democracy in Russia. In the dark days of the August 1991 *putsch*, when he preached defiance from the top of a tank outside the Moscow 'White House', Yeltsin was cast as the heroic champion of Russia's liberals and the beacon of hope for its nascent democracy. In the years since his victory, however, his instinct, common to all his predecessors in the Kremlin, has been to do whatever is necessary to preserve power rather than to nurture democracy. This instinct has led him to order an armoured assault on the Russian Parliament, as it sat in the same White House building where he had so stirringly resisted tyranny only two years earlier; it has led him also into the bloody chaos of a brutal war in Chechnya, where a people whom he claimed as citizens of his own republic, entitled to the protection of its constitution, were bludgeoned to death by the repeated aerial and artillery bombardments of his armed forces. Whatever the truth of his claim to have renounced his Communist past, the myth of Yeltsin the democrat lies buried beneath the rubble of Grozny.

To the West, such concerns seem to have mattered little. The initial evangelistic zeal for spreading democracy into the lands of the former Soviet Union soon disappeared beneath a tide of investment *realpolitik* and panic-stricken wishful thinking. As President Clinton preached about human rights in Bosnia he turned a blind eye to the carnage in Chechnya, and European parliamentarians cravenly voted to allow Russia to join the Council of Europe. Clearly, there were more important strategic considerations: the West felt that Yeltsin was another man with whom it could do business, and it was prepared to ignore his democratic shortcomings. Yet, in the twilight of Yeltsin's rule, as he has veered from heart attack to heart by-pass, the Kremlin has been dominated by a small group of presidential advisers and their commercial supporters whose intrigues have become Russia's most significant political activity. Whilst the threat of a return of communism has receded, this Kremlin *apparat* seems as strong as ever, but Yeltsin has no obvious successor and the powerful commercial and political alliance that delivered his last election victory is unlikely to survive his passing.

In the struggle to succeed him, one leading contender will be Alexander Lebed. A gruff but charming former paratroop General, who chain-smokes from an aristocratic cigarette-holder and beguiles his listeners with folksy aphorisms, Lebed despises Russia's 'pseudo-democracy' and cultivates a faintly sulphurous aura. 'I am not a liberal, I am a General,' he says. Yet he is far from the anti-democratic bogeyman of his enemies' caricatures. A professional soldier, his political views have been moulded by his experience of serving the Kremlin during some of the greatest crises in the last quarter-century of its history. Indeed, Lebed's story is interwoven with modern Soviet and Russian history. As a small boy, he witnessed the first stirrings of public discontent with Soviet rule and observed their brutal suppression. As a junior officer in Afghanistan, he saw the mujahideen struggle against Moscow's 'fraternal assistance', giving the first serious shock to the Soviet system. In the Caucasus, he watched the Soviet empire begin to unravel. In Moscow in 1991, he played a crucial role in ensuring Yeltsin's victory. And in Moldova and Chechnya, he brought to an end two of the bloody conflicts that followed the fall of the Soviet Union.

Lebed's experience has led him to believe that the foundations of democracy and the rule of law have never been properly laid in Russia. He is deeply cynical about the former Communist Party officials, the *apparatchiks* who have learned the language of democracy but never forgotten the corrupt power-politics of the old elite, the *nomenklatura*. Despite his scepticism about 'pseudo-democracy', Lebed may have more genuinely democratic instincts than his rivals. That will not stop them portraying him, however, as the next big threat to Russian 'democracy'. In any event, whether Russia is capable of reaching democracy on its present course, and whether Lebed constitutes a threat to it or the best hope of it, are questions that are in many ways best answered by a consideration of the events of his lifetime.

THE GENERAL AGAINST THE KREMLIN

I

NOVOCHERKASSK

'You'll have the look of a knight
And the soul of a cossack.'

M. Y. LERMONTOV,
'A Cossack Lullaby'[1]

Novocherkassk, in the Rostov region, is unlike other Russian towns. The capital of the Don Cossacks, it was founded on the banks of the river Don by Cossack auxiliaries of Tsar Ivan IV of Muscovy, on their return from a victorious campaign against the Turks in 1570. In 1805, when the river Don broke its banks and flooded once too often, the town was moved to its present site, on higher ground at the confluence of the smaller, less turbulent Tuzlov and Aksay rivers.

Throughout its history, Novocherkassk has had an independent, frontier spirit and a certain rebelliousness. Its inhabitants are proud of their Cossack tradition. Their ancestors are the same Cossacks who fought in the uprising against Peter the Great in 1707 and joined the armies of later Tsars to defend Russia's Circassian borderlands, carrying *natraika* whips, brandishing sabres and wearing the dark-blue trousers and black sheepskin caps of imperial Cossack troops. A regiment of Don Cossacks formed part of the Imperial Guard, and the Tsar's heir, the Tsarevich, was their colonel or 'Ataman-in-chief'.

In return for their military service to the Russian state, the Don Cossacks received special privileges and greater freedom. As a consequence, they supported the old regime to the end, and

Novocherkassk was a centre of opposition to the Bolsheviks in the civil war of 1917–20. Soviet life never quite managed to destroy the Cossack heritage, though, and in modern Novocherkassk, home of factories producing electric locomotives, machine tools and mining machinery, 80 per cent of the population of 180,000 is of Cossack descent – and some of the surrounding villages are as much as 100 per cent Cossack. With the end of Soviet rule, local people have begun to return to their Cossack past, and there was even an attempt in 1993 to re-establish the 'Don Republic', which had been proclaimed by local 'white' anti-Bolshevik commanders in 1918.

It was into this Cossack world, with its military traditions and a strong folk memory subdued – but never eradicated – by the Communists, that the future Lieutenant-General Alexander Ivanovich Lebed was born on 20 April 1950. His family were poor, and without influence or connections in the Party. They lived in a converted stable building. There were no career officers among his relatives, and those who had served in the Soviet Army had done so in the ranks. Lebed's maternal grandfather, Grigory Vasilievich, had held the highest rank, serving at the front throughout the Second World War as a Sergeant-Major in the sappers. Lebed later complained about the treatment his grandfather received from the Soviet authorities after the end of the war: 'He didn't live very long at all, and died from his wounds in 1948. But because he didn't die on the field of battle and only passed away later in a hospital ward, my grandmother, Anastasiya Nikiforovna, was left without a pension for the rest of her life. The law is strict, but it's the law! So the man was at fault because he didn't die at once but passed away from his wounds.'[2]

Lebed's father, Ivan Andreevich, a quiet, unassuming carpenter who could hardly read or write, lived longer than Grigory Vasilievich but suffered perhaps even more. In 1937 he was sentenced to five years in a labour camp for twice being five minutes late for work. When war broke out in 1939 between Finland and the Soviet Union, he was conscripted into a 'punishment battalion' and sent to attack the Mannerheim Line. Lebed remembers his father describing conditions at the front: 'He experienced the impenetrability of the Mannerheim Line. He froze, he starved, he sawed bread with a hand-saw in the frost, he often took part in attacks (and everyone knows that punishment soldiers never got any cover), but God saved him from the bullet and the bayonet. He did not shed his blood.'³

In theory, it was possible for a *shtrafnik* (punishment soldier) with a good record at the front to transfer from a punishment battalion to the regular army – but only if he had been wounded. The transfer had to be seen to be paid for, in blood. At the end of the Finnish war, Ivan Lebed's commanders recognised that he had not been a coward and, indeed, had shown his bravery, but the transfer rule was strict. And Ivan Lebed had not been wounded. Eventually, however, reason prevailed, and he was transferred to a construction detachment where he was able to make use of his civilian skills. He stayed there for almost two years, until Germany invaded the Soviet Union in 1941. Then, together with the forces of the western front, he fell back on Moscow and later took part in the winter counter-offensive.

In 1942 Ivan was wounded, and just missed having his leg amputated. 'He got a crazy notion that he was immune from death and the enemy bullet,' says his son.

In the summer of forty-two, the battalion in which he served went to the front. A tank battalion moved there. The tank men suggested throwing infantry against armour. And so, from somewhere or other, a single stray shell splinter played havoc with his right hip . . . He didn't remember how he got to the medical unit, but he spent a year in hospital beds. They managed to save his leg but it was shortened by five centimetres. My father hobbled around the hospital courtyard and gradually got himself back into shape.

Just then, however, Stalin ordered that the shortening of the lower extremities by five centimetres or less was not to be considered an obstacle to continuation of service. Ivan Lebed was sent back to his construction detachment and then again to the front. He finally got back to Novocherkassk, after ten years away, in 1947.

The harsh years away from home, in labour camps and hospital beds, had made Ivan Lebed even more reserved and silent. They had not, however, taken away from him his enjoyment of work or his good nature. 'He always spoke briefly and concisely,' his son, who has a similar characteristic, remembers. 'If he saw that someone needed help – an elderly neighbour who wanted to repair a fence, for example – he just took his saw and his axe and did it. In silence. Without payment.'

He was a good craftsman, who took care over his work and never hurried it. 'All his handiwork had a stamp of quality, thoroughness and completeness about it.'[4]

The affection and admiration with which Alexander Lebed remembers Ivan is very similar to the way in which Boris Yeltsin writes of his father, Nikolai. Their fates were similar, both suffering arrest and detention in the labour camps, returning weary and full of quiet despair, hoping to lose themselves in their families. Their experiences had a profound effect on their sons. Indeed, Yeltsin's earliest memory is of the night of his father's arrest in 1934:

> I was only three years old at the time of my father's arrest, but I remember to this day all the horror and fear. One night people came into our barracks room. I remember my mother shouting and crying. I woke up and also began to cry. I was crying not because my father was going away – I was still too young to understand what was happening to him – I was crying because I saw my mother crying and saw how frightened she was. Her fear and her tears were transferred to me. My father was taken away, and my mother threw herself at me, hugging me until I calmed down and fell asleep. Three years later, my father returned from the camps.[5]

The suffering of both Ivan Lebed and Nikolai Yeltsin in Stalin's camps, a fate shared by millions of Russians, has never been forgotten by their sons.

Unlike Nikolai Yeltsin, however, Ivan Lebed had no wife and children waiting for him when he returned to Novocherkassk. Yet, shortly after his return, he met and married Lebed's mother, Yekaterina Grigoryevna, who worked at the town's Post Office. They had two sons – Alexander, and his younger brother, Alexei. They were good parents who tried to do the best for their children in difficult circumstances, and despite his disability, which had made him a virtual invalid, Ivan Lebed never took his frustration out on the boys.

'He never shouted. He never beat us. Neither I nor my brother ever received so much as a slap from him, although at times we must have deserved it.'[6] Although violence was not a part of Alexander Lebed's home life, his later childhood was marked by a bloody event which he witnessed in Novocherkassk. The brutal suppression of a worker's demonstration by armed troops in the summer of 1962 sent a tremor through the Soviet system. The twelve-year-old Alexander watched events unfurl with childish bewilderment as Novocherkassk, normally a quiet Soviet backwater, was gripped by anarchy, becoming the scene of the largest anti-Soviet riots in Russia since the civil war. Ironically, details of the riots were first published in a Russian newspaper in 1989, just after Soviet paratroops were ordered to attack civilian demonstrators in Tbilisi.

On the morning of 1 June 1962, following Khrushchev's agricultural reforms, national radio announced a 'temporary' rise of about 30 per cent in the price of milk, meat, eggs and other food products. At the same time, the management at the Budenny locomotive works in Novocherkassk raised the piecework norms, effectively lowering wages. The factory boss, Kurochkin, and the Communist Party secretary held a meeting with workers' representatives in one of the workshops. They flatly rejected the workers' protests and Kurochkin, noticing a woman outside carrying a tray of pastries filled with liver sausage, even joked: 'If you don't have money for meat, then eat sausage rolls.'[7]

The factory's 11,000 workers were so incensed by these callous remarks that they chased Kurochkin out of the plant. They then downed tools and walked out into the yard, where they held a meeting. Some of them covered the factory building with placards and graffiti, saying 'Down with Khrushchev!' and 'Cut up Khrushchev for sausages!'[8] Others spilled over on to a nearby railway line and ripped up some of the track, stopping a passenger train going from Saratov to Rostov.

In the evening, the regional Party boss tried in vain to address the workers from a balcony. Unarmed soldiers were sent to the factory, but they started to fraternise with the workers and their officers had trouble restoring discipline. Armoured personnel carriers appeared briefly and then withdrew. At dawn the next morning, 2 June, tanks ringed the factory and soldiers with automatic weapons advanced up the railway line. Thirty people, who were suspected of being the ringleaders, were arrested and taken to KGB headquarters in Bataisk.

The arrests prompted workers at nearly all the other factories in Novocherkassk to join the strike. Workers from the Budenny plant and other factories poured into the town centre. As they filed past troops on the bridge over the river Tuzlov, they shouted, 'Make way for the working class!'[9] By the afternoon, huge crowds had converged on police headquarters and on the 'Gorkom' (city Party committee) building. The crowds included many women, who were furious at the food price rises, and children, including Alexander Lebed, who were attracted by the noise and excitement. Some small boys had climbed up into the branches of nearby trees to get a better view.

A tank by the statue of Lenin on the main square fired a blank round as the workers swept into Party headquarters and overwhelmed the soldiers there. However, the violence began at the town's main police station, when a worker tried to snatch an automatic weapon from a soldier and was shot dead. Then the order was given to open fire on the crowds outside Party headquarters. One officer, who refused to pass on the order, tore up his Party card and shot himself instead. Lebed later praised the heroism of this man, saying that he was a true Russian officer.

At first the troops fired into the air, but they hit some of the children in the trees. Anger and panic seized the crowds when the soldiers started firing. One witness later remembered the horrific scene: 'A middle-aged man ran past a concrete container with flowers. A bullet hit him in the head, and his brains spilled out over the concrete. A mother carried a dead baby in her arms. A hairdresser was wounded in her shop. A girl lay in a pool of blood. A Major, half-crazed, stepped into the blood. When people screamed, "You bastard, look where you're standing," he shot himself in the head.'[10]

The troops continued shooting even when the crowd turned and started to flee. Accounts differ as to how many people died. The official figure, confirmed by the senior military procurator, Yuri Bagrayev, was twenty-four,[11] although witnesses recall many more corpses. Some accounts claim that more than seventy lost their lives. Many more were wounded and hundreds were imprisoned.

When the shooting stopped, the Party moved quickly to remove all traces of the tragedy. A high-level delegation headed by Anastas Mikoyan and Frol Kozlov, both members of the

Politburo, flew into the Don region to supervise the aftermath of the affair. Corpses were loaded into lorries and buried in secret locations. According to a recent report in *Izvestiya*, 'The bodies of the victims were distributed around three derelict cemeteries near Taganrog, Novoshakhtinsk and in the Tarasov region, many kilometres from Novocherkassk, and tipped straight from the lorries into specially dug pits.'[12] Doctors who treated the wounded were forced to sign statements swearing to remain silent, and some of the wounded were exiled with their families to Siberia to keep them quiet. People who inquired at the mortuary about missing relatives were arrested.

The authorities had difficulty covering all traces of the massacre. One witness, an instructor at the local police academy, remembers how they tried to hide the event: 'They tried hard to wipe the blood from the square. First they hosed it from fire-engines, then they used brushes and a road-roller. Finally they put asphalt over the top.'[13]

Slowly, the situation calmed down. Kozlov and Mikoyan ordered special supplies to be rushed in, so that for a while the food shops in the Don were well stocked. New blocks of flats were hurriedly built. The dual policy of improvements in local conditions combined with severe penalties for those involved in the demonstration managed to contain the damage to the Party, but the memory of the summer of 1962 is still strong in Novocherkassk. For Alexander Lebed, who witnessed the events from his hiding-place in the branches of a birch tree, it must have made a deep and lasting impression.

It did not, however, prevent him from enjoying the usual rough and tumble of boyhood and youth in Novocherkassk. One report describes him as a bit of a ruffian who lived mainly on the street. 'Impatient and restless, always ready to argue and fight, he was afraid of no one. Least of all his parents. Even as a child, he took up "arms". In his trouser pocket he always carried a home-made catapult. He hit sparrows with little stones with astonishing accuracy. Bigger birds were not safe from him either.'[14]

At school, Lebed's behaviour was little different: 'He found it difficult to subordinate himself to anyone else. If he had to, then it was only until the moment came when he could regain the upper hand. Fellow pupils who tried to tease him came to regret it. He liked to try it on with the teachers too. Some of them forgave his cheekiness because they appreciated his thirst for knowledge and his lightning-quick ability to pick things up. Others found him unforgivably arrogant. But even they paid him a grudging respect and avoided arguments.'[15]

When he reached his fourteenth birthday, the young ruffian decided to take up boxing. His teachers encouraged him, no doubt in the knowledge that the discipline and commitment involved would channel his energy in a more appropriate direction and knock off some of his rougher edges. The young Lebed was heavy, well-built with long arms, and not afraid of getting hit. He soon mastered the technique and began to do well in the ring. One day, however, there was a long training session which involved leaping over a vaulting horse. Lebed began to tire, and when he jumped the vaulting horse too slowly, he landed awkwardly and broke his collar-bone.

'It was Saturday. The medical centre was closed. They took me to hospital straight away. Either the doctor was in a hurry or the nurse was inexperienced, but they said the usual words: "It'll be all right until you get married." Then they hung my arm in a sling and tied it up.'[16]

The experience somehow made Lebed think seriously for the first time about what he wanted to do with his life. He claims that the physical blow he suffered turned into a unique psychological stress, which manifested itself in a subconscious attraction to the sky. 'The profession of fighter pilot became a symbol of virility for me. I was ready to endure any ordeals.' He did not have to wait long. When his broken collar-bone set a week later, it had grown shorter by three centimetres. He could neither lift his arm nor move it to the side. 'I had to agree to have it broken again. After all, I thought an officer can't have a collar-bone like this. I'll have to put up with it. And I did.'[17]

His collar-bone had just healed when Lebed sustained another injury, this time a broken nose, which he got in a fight after a football match against another local team. 'As a result, my nose was bent to the side, but I didn't mind much. I'm not a girl. At about that time, I learned that a man has to be just a little better-looking than an ape and that his true worth is not determined by the prettiness of his face.'

As a result of his injuries, his doctor refused to approve further visits by him to the gymnasium. His protests did not help, nor did threats. The doctor was insistent. Lebed took his revenge, though, on the doctor's window with his catapult.

When he told his father that he wanted to become an officer, he was disappointed by the reaction. Lebed felt that the gentle old man, who had probably begun to despair of his son's adolescent antics, showed by his lack of enthusiasm his doubt that his son was officer material. 'When I first told my father that I wanted to become an officer he took the news calmly, but I could tell by his reaction that he didn't believe in my dream, although he didn't argue about it.'[18] Perhaps it was just that having experienced the most unpleasant form of Soviet military life himself, he could not wish a similar fate on his son.

The remainder of Lebed's turbulent school career was spent preparing himself for the selection board of the Kachinsky Air Force Academy. He made his application and was summoned to the selection board, where everything seemed to go well until he reached the medical examination. His sporting injuries let him down. To his extreme consternation, an elderly female doctor, who examined him, wrote the words 'unsuitable for pilot training' on his medical record, mainly because of breathing difficulties resulting from his broken nose. Lebed refused to accept the doctor's verdict and decided to go and have an operation on his nose at the local hospital. Within two weeks the bridge of his nose had been rebuilt, and he presented himself again at the selection board. He was not greeted with much enthusiasm. 'Eat porridge and get ready for next year,' he was told.

Seventeen and a half years old, Lebed had focused all his hopes on entry into the academy. He had no other plans, and now, having left school in a fit of enthusiasm for the idea of training as a fighter pilot, he was left stranded, with a year to wait until the next selection board and little chance of finding work at any of the local factories until he reached his eighteenth birthday. Everywhere he went to look for work, he was told that he was too young. His mother, who hoped he might become an engineer, started trying to persuade him to apply for a place at the Polytechnic. To placate her, he attended a few classes at the faculty of mechanics, and even sat an exam in mathematics. His heart was not in it, though, and he soon stopped going. All he could think about was flying.

Eventually, he managed to find a job at a factory in

Novocherkassk, making magnets. At the end of his first day at work, a pretty girl introduced herself to him as the secretary of the Komsomol (Communist youth league) in the factory. She told him bossily to tidy up his work-bench. Untidiness would not be tolerated, she said. Her name was Inna, and whatever irritation he may have felt at his first meeting with her was soon forgotten as he began a four-year campaign to win her heart.

In the meantime, his application to join the Kachinsky Air Force Academy was once again turned down. This time, it was suggested that he might apply to the academy for interceptor pilots at Armavir. On the strength of this suggestion, Lebed's despair of becoming a pilot disappeared. He was swept away by a new tide of enthusiasm for the idea of flying, and immediately handed in his notice to the factory manager, Vishnevsky, who tried to persuade him that it might be more sensible simply to take some leave for the entrance board. Lebed rudely disagreed and left the factory, swearing at Vishnevsky because the manager could not understand his enthusiasm. 'When you are eighteen years old and your head is full of Napoleonic plans, you don't want to listen to common sense,' Lebed admitted later.[19]

Lebed again tried to pass the medical board and again failed. He repeated his tour of hospital wards and operating theatres in an attempt to get himself fit. By now his situation was becoming desperate. His pride would not allow him to return to the factory, even though Inna had called and tried to persuade him. Instead he worked in a warehouse for a year, as a packer. When he returned to the medical board in early 1968, the doctor who examined him was satisfied that his broken nose was not a problem, but now began to express concern about his collar-bone. Lebed lost his temper and began to shout at the head of the medical commission, cursing him with every conceivable Cossack oath. The doctor merely waved his hand dismissively and said: 'Go to Armavir – let them decide your fate there.'

Unfortunately, the answer was the same at Armavir. Lebed found the head of the medical service, a dreary Lieutenant-Colonel who initially seemed prepared to help. Having listened to Lebed's story, he summoned a surgeon, who agreed that although the collar-bone had not set well, there were no complications. When an ear, nose and throat specialist examined him, however, he was once again told that he was 'unfit for pilot training'. He returned to the Lieutenant-Colonel, who shook his head and said: 'Well, there's nothing I can do. It's an order from the minister of defence.'

By the time Lebed had finished raging at the head of the medical commission and left the academy at Armavir, he was 'crazy'. He wandered for a long time along the road and lost all his money. He was hungry and angry, and for the first time in his life had no idea what he was going to do. So he hitched back to Rostov and went straight to the enlistment office, where everyone was sympathetic to his plight. A Major who interviewed him said, 'Well, what's so good about being a pilot? You want to be an officer, so let's find you somewhere just as good.'

Lebed and the Major discussed the various possibilities – tanks, submarines, artillery. None of them appealed. Then, right at the end of the list, was an institution whose name was a rich example of the grandiose but absurd titles which the Communist Party liked to bestow – the 'Twice Red Banner Leninist Komsomol Officer Training School for Airborne Troops', at Ryazan. 'I decided to risk it,' said Lebed. 'It was nearer to the sky than the others.'[20]

He returned to Novocherkassk and told his father what he had decided to do. The old man was, no doubt, pleased that he had finally been dissuaded from joining the air force, and without much enthusiasm gave Lebed's new venture his blessing. As his son had no idea what it was like to jump out of an aircraft in a parachute, however, he suggested that it would be worth trying a jump before he joined up, to see if he liked it. Lebed agreed that this was an eminently sensible idea, as the notion had recently begun to fill him with some horror. He made for the Donskoi airfield, ten miles outside Novocherkassk, where there was a small flying club. When he approached a group of men hanging around at the airfield and asked them if they would mind letting him jump out of their aeroplane with a parachute, they all roared with laughter. Eventually they pointed him towards an instructor, a thick-set, rather coarse-looking man who gave him a very unfriendly welcome.

'What are you doing loafing about here? Did you want to jump? Well go away . . . there are lots of people like you who come here.' I went back to my new friends. They laughed.

From a distance they had already understood the instructor's reaction.

'Go and get some vodka,' one of them advised me, 'and everything will be all right. Three bottles should do it.' I got four bottles. They only cost kopecks in those days. The instructor turned his head. 'All right, now go and learn how to pack a parachute.'

After some rudimentary parachute training, Lebed went for yet another medical. This time things were easier, and for the first time luck was on his side. An attractive young female doctor was sitting in the surgery, reading a book. She looked up lazily, smiled, pointed at a notice board and asked if he could see the top two letters, which were easily visible in clear, bold print. When he replied that he could, she said, 'That's good. Go and jump, then.' With that she gave him his first authorisation to go into the air.

The night before the jump he took Inna to the theatre, and when he returned to the airfield, he stayed up talking late into the night. The mixture of nerves and excitement made it difficult to sleep. During the night, a light breeze started to blow and a thin May mist settled over the airfield. At dawn, an Antonov aircraft was ready for take-off, but Lebed's instructor and the airfield meteorologists were arguing about the weather, since parachute jumps were to be cancelled if it was too windy. The argument was unsettling and compounded Lebed's nervous tension. As the weather calmed down, however, so did the instructor and the meteorologists. When it was at last announced that they had been cleared for take-off, Lebed was wild with excitement. 'A leap into the infinite, the unknown, the future. I already imagined myself to be a cadet of the Ryazan academy, jumping behind enemy lines.'[21]

He jumped from the aeroplane a little awkwardly but without any great difficulty. The most dangerous part of any parachute jump is not the moment of departure from the plane, however, but the landing. On the way down towards the ground, Lebed felt a little disappointed. The view was magnificent, but not as spectacular as he had hoped. The anticipation of an event is always better than the event itself, he thought. As he approached the ground, at a distance of about 200 metres, there was a sudden gust of wind which caught him unawares and blew him off-course. He landed on his coccyx and cracked his spine.

The pain was intense, and he feared that his spine was broken, but he eventually managed to wave his arms and stand up. He shouted for help, but there was silence, and nobody came. At the flying club buildings in the distance, they must have assumed that he was shouting with the exhilaration of a successful parachute jump. Somehow, he managed to walk with his parachute the 500 metres to the flying club, where he handed in the parachute and went to the doctor's surgery. It was the same young girl who had given him permission to jump. She was horrified at his condition and immediately called an ambulance, which eventually arrived and took him over the long, bumpy roads to the hospital in Novocherkassk.

Yet another visit to a hospital ward. This time, however, it was much more serious than before. A cracked spine was very dangerous. He might not walk again. He would certainly have to lie immobile for months on the hard wooden board which he had been given instead of a mattress. As he lay there gazing at the ceiling, he must have felt that there was very little chance of him becoming an officer of the Airborne Forces now.

It was the late spring of 1968. Outside, the sun shone on the streets of Novocherkassk. The massacre six years earlier was already a distant memory, and people were looking forward to a long, hot southern Russian summer of modest picnics, country walks and bathing in the river Don. And while Alexander Lebed lay on his back, the Airborne Forces, whom he dreamed of joining, were busying themselves without him, bringing the spring to an end far away in Czechoslovakia.

2

RYAZAN

'He wished to fix each pallbearer
in his memory:
young recruits
from Ryazan and Kursk,
so that later he might
collect enough strength for a sortie,
rise from the grave,
and reach these unreflecting youths.'

YEVGENY YEVTUSHENKO,
'The Heirs of Stalin'[1]

As Alexander Lebed lay motionless in hospital throughout the summer of 1968, hoping that his disastrous parachute jump would not leave him permanently crippled, the Soviet Airborne troops whose ranks he sought to join were playing a leading role in Moscow's campaign to crush the independence of Czechoslovakia. The success of their operation was to make them an indispensable part of the Kremlin's response to future crises, eventually ensuring that they developed a political importance unrivalled by any other branch of the armed forces.

In early 1968, the new Czechoslovak Communist Party leader Alexander Dubček had promised 'socialism with a human face' and begun a programme of reforms which had angered and alarmed Moscow. The Kremlin feared a weakening of Czechoslovakia's commitment to the Warsaw Pact, and saw the danger of liberalisation in Prague spreading to Warsaw, Budapest and Berlin. The problem was that Dubček was popular. If military action was to be taken to prevent reform in Czechoslovakia, it would be necessary to knock out the Czechoslovak leadership quickly and prevent it from becoming a focus of popular discontent. The Airborne troops were the Kremlin's choice for the task.

Soldiers of the 7th Guards Airborne Division arrived at Ruzyne airport near Prague just before dawn on 21 August 1968. One group of them moved quickly to Hradcany Castle, seat of the Czechoslovak government, and arrested the President, Ludvik Svoboda. Another group made for the Party headquarters, where they found Dubček, Smrkovsky and virtually the entire Czechoslovak leadership, all of whom had been taken completely by surprise by the speed of the operation. At the same time, paratroopers seized key communication centres in Prague and captured the Czechoslovak General Staff headquarters, preventing the co-ordination of resistance by the army.

Other units from the regular army, tank crews and infantrymen, began arriving in Prague later the same day to secure the paratroopers' gains. The 'Prague Spring' was soon snuffed out, and the Kremlin leadership realised that its Airborne troops were the main reason for the swift, decisive and almost bloodless defeat of 'socialism with a human face'.[2] Henceforth, Airborne troops became the Kremlin's most trusted elite, called upon repeatedly in times of crisis and destined, during the next quarter-century, to play a crucial role in the bitter conflicts and power struggles marking the end of the Soviet Union and the birth of the Russian Federation.

The growing political importance of the Airborne troops was not a matter of any significance to the young Alexander Lebed when he finally rose from his hospital bed and made his way to the Airborne Forces Academy at Ryazan. However, he would quickly have begun to appreciate the role which the Airborne troops were increasingly required to play and the fact that, as a consequence, they were now able to demand a much higher class of recruit than other branches of the armed forces. Under Khrushchev, the Strategic Missile Force had clearly been the Kremlin's favourite service, but now the Airborne Forces, with their distinctive blue berets, were fast becoming the most respected. Soon they were given first choice of personnel, and their friends in the Kremlin made sure that not only were they staffed with the best troops in the Soviet Army, but they were also kept up to their full wartime complement. Their commander, Vasily Margelov, a veteran of the Finnish campaign and the Second World War, also had a unique position in the Soviet armed forces. Although he only commanded eight divisions, he was a

General of the Army, the same rank as the Commander-in-Chief of the Land Forces, who had one hundred and seventy divisions under his command.[3]

The Ryazan Airborne Forces Academy was one of over a hundred officer training colleges throughout the Soviet Union. Each one served a particular armed service and aimed to produce up to five hundred technically competent and politically loyal lieutenants every year. Cadet officers in the colleges were expected to master all aspects of modern tactics. Most of their training took place in the field, with winter and summer exercises, practice alerts, cross-country movements and manoeuvres at night or under conditions of poor visibility. They studied enemy weapons, military topography and field works. They practised measures to reduce casualties from enemy use of napalm and fought mock battles under the simulated conditions of a nuclear battlefield.[4]

For young officer cadets at the Ryazan academy, the training was much more intensive than it would have been in similar infantry establishments. Ryazan cadets could also count on better training facilities and staff. Whereas ordinary infantry cadets might have been expected to train with old or out-of-date equipment, nothing was too good for the Airborne Forces.

The cadets at Ryazan were organised into companies, and the company commander was responsible for their training. Lebed's first company commander was senior Lieutenant Nikolai Pletnev, a small, smartly dressed officer who placed particular emphasis on physical fitness. He expected his cadets to march or run between training sessions, never to walk, and in physical sessions he led by example, often completing a round of exercises without even taking off his overcoat. At first, Lebed found the training at Ryazan hard, but there was no bullying (a very common problem throughout the Soviet Army) and he enjoyed the competitive, soldierly atmosphere. With long route marches and runs in full combat gear, his skin was never dry from sweat and he seemed to be permanently hungry, but he knew that the experience was a crucial test in which he had to prove his worth to the army. Seventeen cadets in his company dropped out in the first six weeks. 'Those who remained,' he says, 'had the hide and the heels of a rhinoceros.'[5]

The toughest exercise took place in the autumn of Lebed's first year as a cadet, after a weapon disappeared from one of the ranges during the third-year cadets' small-arms training. For twenty-four hours the entire battalion had to look for it, until it was eventually found back at the camp. The culprit never owned up, and Lieutenant-Colonel Karpov, the battalion commander, ordered all the cadets to do a seventy-kilometre *marshbrosok* (speed march) in twenty-four hours as a punishment. The cadets had to carry full packs, rifles and gas masks. They completed part of the march in anti-radioactive body suits, which became unbearably hot as they ran. The exercise helped to develop team spirit and comradeship though, as the stronger soldiers helped their weaker colleagues by giving them a lift or carrying a piece of kit. When Lebed arrived back at camp, he had two automatic rifles and a grenade launcher on his shoulders.

Although hard physical training was an important part of life at Ryazan, particularly in the first year, there were other activities which were considered equally important. As in any Soviet military college, political education was given the highest priority, often at the expense of purely technical training. Any Soviet Army recruit's training schedule included a period of political education but, in the officer training colleges, it was much more substantial. Cadets in the officer colleges would soon be Lieutenants, and the Party saw them as having a key role in providing political leadership to the other ranks.[6] As Lieutenants, they would be expected to spend a great deal of their time in lengthy training sessions with their men and, as part of the younger element of the population which the Party was committed to winning over, their role in political preparation and psychological training of troops was of great importance. Their own political education and reliability were, therefore, a top priority.

Much of the basis of Lebed's political education and development as an officer would have been formed by his study of *The Officer's Handbook*, which was first published during his third year as a cadet at Ryazan. Its main objective was to 'assist officers in broadening their outlook and in resolving many practical problems related to the training and education of subordinates'. *The Officer's Handbook* was the result of a determined effort by the Central Committee of the Soviet Communist Party to 'improve' party political work in the armed forces. A resolution to that effect had been passed in 1967, and the Party was quite clear that political and moral instruction were vital to combat readiness. Officers were expected to instil a high level of political consciousness and psychological preparedness into their men, because the Cold War was largely a war of ideas.

The Officer's Handbook instructed junior officers that their subordinates should learn from them enthusiasm for the Communist Party; an attachment to the rudiments of Marxism–Leninism; and 'a selfless devotion to the socialist homeland'. It even suggested that without a high level of political consciousness, the Soviet Army would be unable to guarantee the security of the motherland. Officers were also told that the success of communism was demonstrated by its military strength, and that the Soviet victory in the Second World War was of 'universal importance' as it proved the invincibility of the socialist system. The *Handbook* left its readers in no doubt about the enemy and his evil intentions:

> The ruling circles of the USA are feverishly stepping up the arms race, reinforcing aggressive blocks by every possible means and aggravating international tension. By implementing the policy of 'local conflicts' and 'small wars' elaborated in Washington, they try to hold on to their positions in different parts of the globe and insolently interfere in the internal affairs of sovereign states. For several years now, the American imperialists have been conducting a shameful, murderous war against the Vietnamese people. They have unleashed bloody military adventures against the people of Laos and Cambodia in order to suppress the liberation movement in Indochina. The American military clique directly sponsored and orchestrated the military–fascist revolution in Greece; with the covert and overt encouragement of imperialist circles in the USA and Britain, the rulers of Israel unleashed a war of conquest in the Near East against the United Arab Republic and other Arab countries . . .

Officers were also told that, although bourgeois societies had their own individual doctrines, they were united in their political objectives, which were 'forcible seizure of foreign territory and the enslavement of other peoples'. The intentions of the Soviet Union were, of course, very different. The *Handbook* quoted

Leonid Brezhnev: 'Being well aware of the aggressive nature of imperialism, our Party considers it essential to support the peaceful policy of the Soviet Union with its invincible defensive might. The interests of the Soviet people and of world peace demand this. Therefore, one of the constant concerns of the Central Committee, the Soviet Government and the entire nation is the strengthening of our glorious armed forces.'[7]

The Officer's Handbook was not one of the many turgid tracts of propaganda which were laboriously churned out by the Party's publishing houses and usually ended their days unread and gathering dust on the shelves of obscure reading rooms. It was an important part of the junior officer's military training, and it reflected the turbulent relationship which for over fifty years the Communist Party had had with the armed forces.

The Party leadership's relations with the Red Army had been in a state of flux since the earliest days of the revolution, hurtling in a series of terrifying reversals between pride and fear. At the centre of Communist concern about the army had always been the Party's attitude towards the officer corps. The early Bolsheviks had envisaged a Workers' and Peasants' Red Army, where there were no insignia or ranks, and each unit was run by an elected committee which chose its own officers. Trotsky soon reversed this policy and appointed a former Tsarist, General Bonch-Bruevich, to head the Supreme Military Council and create a new army on more traditional lines. When Stalin came to power, however, his paranoia and obsessive fear of 'Bonapartism' caused him to set about destroying the best part of the officer corps in a programme of brutal purges. The break-up of the Molotov–Ribbentrop Pact brought about the abandonment of this policy, and victory over Germany established the Soviet Army's position at the heart of a highly militarised society, with Stalin as Generalissimo and Marshal of the Soviet Union. In the Khrushchev era, the army began to flex its political muscles, eventually helping to force the General Secretary out of power in 1964.

With Leonid Brezhnev in the Kremlin, the army and the Party were bound more closely together than ever before. There seemed to be almost an unofficial social contract, in which the army accepted that its prestige and influence depended on its relationship with the Party, whilst the Party realised that the guarantor of its hold on power was the army. During the fifty years of Soviet power, the army had moved from a position where it was treated with suspicion and distrust to one where it was effectively the backbone of the Communist Party. It is hardly surprising that *The Officer's Handbook* was able to boast in 1971 that more than 80 per cent of all armed forces personnel were members of the Communist Party or its youth wing, the Komsomol.

So, as a member of the Soviet armed forces, Alexander Lebed was part of a highly politicised institution. As part of the Airborne Forces, he was in possibly the most politically significant part of the Soviet Army. And as an officer cadet, he was being trained for a crucial role in the Party's political education work. It is unlikely, in such circumstances, that he could have escaped joining the Communist Party, and there is no evidence that he sought to do so. Although his personal background suggests that he might have had good reason to hate the Party which jailed his father and killed many of his fellow citizens in Novocherkassk, he made no attempt to avoid the embrace of Marxism–Leninism. Despite his recent attempts to distance himself from the Communist Party, and his protestations that he has 'never served Tsars or Commissars or Presidents',[8] he was prepared to accept that membership of the Communist Party was essential to a successful career in the armed forces.

Lebed's image-makers today carefully try to cultivate an impression of resistance by the young soldier to Communist attempts to indoctrinate him. According to one version, he was contemptuous of the Party's role in the army, believing that all that was needed was good discipline. His attitude was seemingly one of cautious mockery of the system: 'Once, when he had to deliver a political lecture to his soldiers, he made them fall in and stand to attention. For this, the political officer gave him a black mark. Orders at the time instructed that soldiers should be "at ease" when listening to political education.'[9]

Such minor acts of bloody-mindedness hardly constituted a challenge to Communist orthodoxy. However, Lebed probably did join the Party simply from expediency and an understandable desire to further his career, but his readiness to entertain the army's Communist connection led much later to such a level of intimacy with the Party that, as a senior officer, he was elected one of the military delegates to the CPSU Congress. As a young cadet in Ryazan, though, his intention was probably no different from that of millions of other Soviet citizens who joined the Party or the Komsomol to gain promotion at work, a better flat or a place at university. It was, however, in sharp contrast to the uncompromisingly anti-Party attitude of one of Ryazan's most celebrated residents, the writer Alexander Solzhenitsyn, who was thrown out of the local branch of the Writer's Union at almost the same time as Lebed entered the academy.

At the end of Lebed's first year, one of the Soviet Army's greatest celebrities, General Vasily Margelov, the father of the Airborne Forces, paid a visit to the academy. Such was his legendary reputation, and so great was the cadets' awe of him, that Lebed described the moment when the doors of the sports hall opened and the General strode in as being like Christ's appearance before the people. This was the man who had commanded the 1st Naval Infantry Regiment and carried out daring raids behind German lines during the siege of Leningrad. Indeed, Margelov's naval connection was the reason the Airborne troops now wore a striped sailor's shirt as part of their uniform. He had been commander of the 49th Guards Rifle Division too, and had forced a bridgehead over the river Dnieper near Sadovy in March 1944, winning himself the order of Hero of the Soviet Union for his bravery. He was a true soldier and a charismatic leader whom Lebed hero-worshipped, identifying strongly with his humble Belorussian roots and modest upbringing in the industrial towns of eastern Ukraine. Lebed knew also that it was Margelov who had given the Airborne Forces their motto, 'No task is too great for us.'

All the cadets wanted to impress the General as he watched them doing their gymnastics, and no one was more keen to catch his eye than Lebed. When the General asked if they could jump over the vaulting horse, they all said that they could, even though they had never practised it before. The first three cadets successfully vaulted the horse, and Lebed, next in line, was about to begin his run towards it when Margelov suddenly asked, 'And how about a somersault over the horse, can you do that?'

Lebed remembers how two cadets ran forward and immediately somersaulted over the horse. 'Then it was my turn. All my thoughts were concentrated on one thing: "I have never done a somersault over the horse but I can't get out of it now." I raced up and jumped. I well remember how I did one somersault and started to turn into the second when the floor hit me – the shock was so great that I lost consciousness. I ended up in hospital with concussion. That was how my first meeting with the Commander of the Airborne Forces ended.'[10] Such reckless courage and a reluctance to admit the possibility of failure have been discernible characteristics of Alexander Lebed throughout his career, constituting both a powerful advantage and, at times, a serious impediment.

The pain of his encounter with General Margelov was soon replaced by the joy of a much more significant event. On 20 February 1971, Lebed married Inna, his old sweetheart from Novocherkassk. He was given twelve days' leave from the academy and returned to Novocherkassk for the ceremony, which was attended by all his old classmates from the local school, some of them perhaps a little jealous that he was the first of them to marry. Young though he was, Lebed was fortunate in his choice of bride and has never regretted his decision.

'I was lucky with my wife,' he said recently. 'She is my one-and-only, and for all my life. Now we already have three grown-up children, but my feelings towards her have not faded. She was and still is my darling little swan. Time has neither blunted nor changed my feelings.' Lebed's love of his wife appears genuine, despite rumours put about recently by his political opponents that he frequently beats her up.[11] The fact that the marriage has lasted for so long, however, surely gives the lie to such slurs. And in Russian terms, a marriage lasting for nearly thirty years is very much the exception rather than the rule.

Not long after Lebed's marriage to Inna, Lieutenant Pletnev left the Ryazan academy for a posting as a Captain in an Airborne regiment. He was replaced by a series of new company commanders, none of whom stayed for long. Lebed's opinion of them as commanders varied. First there was Captain Anatoly Ilyin, who was soon recruited by the 'Spetsnaz' special forces because of his good command of English. He was replaced by Captain Zaitsev, a war correspondent who was working on a grandiose novel about the Airborne Forces and had asked to be allowed to command a company so that he could get some authentic background material. Lebed despised him and thought him a ridiculous figure, rather like a character in the nineteenth-century satirist Saltykov-Shchedrin's *History of the Town of Fools*. 'He was of medium height, thirty years old and absolutely bald as a globe.'[12] Zaitsev had originally been given command of a company in the 105th Division at the Airborne Depot in Fergana. He proved so incompetent though that he was transferred to Lebed's cadet company, where it was felt that he would cause less damage. During his eight months with the company, he sentenced Lebed, whom he soon came to regard as an insubordinate trouble-maker, to a total of twenty-three days in the guardhouse, despite the fact that Lebed was by now a senior Sergeant and deputy commander of a platoon. Lebed, however, did not serve one day behind bars, so little attention did he pay to Zaitsev's orders. In Lebed's view, there was only one advantage in having Zaitsev as company commander: he was a perfect example of what an officer should *not* be.

At the end of Lebed's third year at the academy, a young Lieutenant arrived from the Baltic to take over command of the platoon. He was dynamic, energetic and intelligent. Within a month he had replaced Zaitsev as company commander. His name was Pavel Grachev and, for the rest of his military career, his destiny was inextricably linked with that of Alexander Lebed, their paths crossing repeatedly over the next twenty years until the moment when their old friendship counted for nothing and they turned on each other in a final, rancorous power struggle.

Lebed's first impression of Grachev, however, was very positive. 'At that time, Grachev was the complete opposite of Zaitsev. In a short space of time, we had returned to the system established by Pletnev. Grachev was an expert at skiing, a smart, strict officer, who knew how to lead the cadets. The company led a sporting life and a spirit of competitiveness developed.'[13]

By the end of Lebed's fourth year, after a long battle camp at Fergana in Uzbekistan with the 345th Regiment of the 105th Airborne Division, and a period of intensive winter parachute training back at Ryazan, the cadets were as fit as they had ever been. Under Grachev's leadership, they were even considered to be as good as the 9th company of the Spetsnaz, 'the elite of the elite'.

Lebed's relationship with Grachev at the time, although not one of close personal friendship, was certainly based on a healthy mutual respect. Lebed admired the way his bright young commander had transformed the company, and Grachev, in his turn, recognised that Lebed was one of his best cadets. When Lebed graduated as an officer in 1973, Grachev invited him to stay on at the academy and serve under him. Lebed had intended transferring to a posting in Kaunas with the 7th Airborne Division, and was furious at being made to stay. Eventually, though, he accepted the position and was, no doubt, secretly pleased that he had been recognised as one of the best. With chin up and shoulders back, he marched with pride through pouring rain at his passing-out parade on 29 July. As the occasion was being filmed, the parade took place not once but five times until the cadets, in their best uniforms, were soaked through by the unrelenting downpour.

Lebed's first posting as a newly commissioned officer was as a platoon commander in Grachev's company, the first-year cadets. Grachev had been determined to keep Lebed with him and had fixed his appointment with the battalion commander. For the next two and a half years, Lebed shared a room with Grachev and another officer, Vladimir Krotik. The accommodation in the officers' mess was like a hotel in comparison to Lebed's previous barracks, but their room was quickly nicknamed 'the zoo' because of the names of its inhabitants. In Russian, *lebed* is a swan, *grach* is a rook and *krot* is a mole.

Shortly after Lebed's appointment, Grachev arranged a strange, peculiarly Russian initiation into life as an officer, in which Lebed was deprived of sleep for three consecutive nights and forced to play cards with his brother officers. The first night, he was already exhausted after a long drive into the country with Grachev and the battalion commander, but the officers insisted that he play cards with them. The game eventually ended at a quarter to six in the morning, with Lebed owing Grachev eighteen roubles and Krotik seventeen. Grachev said he could wait until pay-day to collect his debt, stretched out on his bed and said that he was going to sleep for a few hours. Just as Lebed began to do the same, Grachev told him that he was in charge of the morning PT session, beginning in fifteen minutes' time at six o'clock. When he arrived at the gymnasium, the smartly turned-out Sergeant-Major Oskin gave him a suspicious look but did not object to him taking the session.

For the next two nights, Grachev repeated the exercise, forcing Lebed to play cards until dawn and then ordering him to take the morning PT session. By the fourth night, Lebed, whose only consolation was that he had won back some of the money he had lost to Grachev and Krotik, swore at his brother officers and told them exactly what he thought of them. Instead of taking offence, however, they applauded him, and Grachev admitted that the sleepless nights were his initiation test and that he had passed with flying colours. 'Just as not every bird can fly to the middle of the river Dnieper,' remarked Lebed, 'so not every swan [*lebed*] can keep going for three days.'[14]

In his new position as platoon commander, and later as company commander, Lebed began to appreciate how disorganisation and lack of discipline undermined military effectiveness, and how they were usually the result of weak leadership by senior officers. On one occasion, Lebed was blamed for a large fight that broke out between Interior Ministry Forces (MVD) cadets and the Airborne cadets. He actually managed to stop the fight but a warrant officer, who had warned him not to go near it, reported his presence and, when a special commission investigated the incident, Lebed took the blame for allowing the fight to continue. It was obvious that there was not going to be a proper investigation into its causes and it was easier simply to be the unprotesting scapegoat for more senior officers.

More serious incidents, this time showing the disorganisation soon to become endemic in the army, took place during parachute training exercises. On the first occasion, in the spring of 1976, Lebed's cadets, together with another company, were ordered to make the first parachute jumps in the academy's history from a new Soviet military aircraft, the Antonov (An) 22. Previous jumps had been from the much smaller An-12, and there was some confusion about how many cadets should jump in any one drop. At first, they decided groups of twenty-one, then seventeen and finally nineteen should jump through the aircraft's two doors. Lebed protested that it was better to keep to platoon formation, but he was overruled and told that it would take too long. There would be thirty-eight men in each drop.

As the argument continued, the weather began to change and a small cloud appeared on the horizon. The first thirty-eight men, including Lebed, jumped successfully and assembled on the edge of the airfield but, just as the second group jumped, an enormous gale began to blow, making it difficult for observers on the ground to remain standing. As the troops neared the ground, their parachutes turned into sails and they were dragged across the airfield at high speed. Four men were killed: one was strangled by a parachute rope; another smashed his head against a rock; and a third was dragged into a fence in a small hamlet nearly four kilometres away, where a metal stake impaled him in the eye. The fourth man was Sergeant-Major Oskin, whose skull was cracked open when he hit an electricity pylon.

To make matters worse, the fact that the soldiers had not jumped in their usual formations made it much more difficult to identify the dead and injured. Rumours began to spread that over half of those who had jumped were dead. Two expectant mothers, wives of soldiers in the jump, miscarried, and the grandmother of one of the deceased had a heart attack when she heard the news. When the tragedy was investigated later, it became clear that the wind measurement had been wrong and that the wind speed at the time had been much higher than the maximum permissible limit.

A few months later, Lebed realised that, despite the terrible tragedy, its lessons had not been learned. It was the summer of 1976, and he had taken a group of cadets to Pskov for an exercise with the 237th Regiment of the 76th Guards Airborne Division. The cadets and their fellow parachutists in the 237th were part of a combined arms exercise with a tank regiment. The plan was that, as they landed, the tanks would start up their engines and launch an attack.

When the paratroops' air transport approached the jump zone, however, a warning came through: the wind was very strong, but just below the maximum limit. They were told to proceed with the jump. Whilst Lebed was still in the air, he could see that a group which had jumped earlier were being dragged along the ground by the wind. No one appeared to have remembered the tragedy of a few months previously. Lebed made a reasonably soft landing on a dusty track, but was dragged for nearly two hundred metres, tangled in his parachute ropes. His colleagues had a much worse time, though. Three men broke both legs, twenty broke one leg, and several others broke their arms or collar-bones. Everyone else had scratches or abrasions, and a Major had his lip torn off.

In the chaos of the paratroops' landing, the tanks started up their engines, moved forward and began to fire their guns. There was so much smoke that visibility was reduced to fifty metres and it was a miracle that no one was run over. The chaos was the result of a combination of gung-ho foolhardiness and disorgan-isation, a feature of many later active-service operations, particularly in Afghanistan and Chechnya. It hardly enhanced the reputation of the Kremlin's Airborne elite.

The cadets who had taken part in the exercise graduated the following year and, as Lebed watched them pass out and leave the academy to join their various Airborne regiments, he realised that he was becoming bored with the job of teaching and applied for active service. Typically, his first application was lost in the system and he had to spend another year training cadets, a short time without any post at all and many months as a member of a mili-tary inspection team, scrutinising the work of the 98th Airborne Division in Bolgrad.

Despite occasional breakdowns of discipline, the Soviet armed forces were still in comparatively good shape during Lebed's period in Ryazan. Cracks were beginning to appear, however, in the Soviet political edifice. Widespread alcoholism, growing levels of petty crime and hideous environmental pollution all helped to undermine the credibility of the Party's promises of a brighter Soviet future. This was the dark heart of the 'era of stagnation', and there was a growing sense of despair that, in the hands of the Kremlin's ailing gerontocracy, the Soviet Union was losing its way. The army listened with contempt and puritan disapproval to rumours of corruption in the higher echelons of the Party. There were stories that some members had become multi-millionaires, with their own palaces, hunting reserves and even, in one instance, a private racetrack.[15]

Meanwhile, on the Soviet Union's borders, the first serious threats for more than a decade to the monolithic empire were beginning to appear. Hungary, under János Kádár, had begun a cautious but successful programme of economic liberalisation, much to Moscow's annoyance. Czechoslovakia was sullen and resentful after the crushing of its revolution. Romania and Yugoslavia stubbornly resisted attempts to make them conform. And Poland was dangerously volatile – even on the verge of mil-itary dictatorship as the only means of protecting the Party.

Yet it was not in Eastern Europe but just over the Soviet Union's southern border that the first major shock finally came. In Afghanistan, where the Soviet leadership, through its local Communist puppets, had been arrogantly trying to impose its will on a reluctant Muslim population, the Kremlin found itself sucked into an ill-conceived military intervention which rapidly escalated into an embarrassing guerrilla war. Alexander Lebed's years of boredom and fruitless attempts to apply for active service duties were about to end. Soon the Soviet Union would need all the volunteers for Afghanistan that it could get.

3

AFGHANISTAN

'When you're wounded and left on Afghanistan's
    plains,
And the women come out to cut up what remains,
Jest roll to your rifle and blow out your brains
An' go to your Gawd like a soldier.'

RUDYARD KIPLING[1]

'Have you an enemy?'
'Yes, I do have a cousin.'

AFGHAN PROVERB[2]

On 25 December 1979, Soviet forces invaded Afghanistan. The 356th and the 66th motor-rifle divisions crossed the border and moved quickly to capture Herat, then Shindand, Farah and Kandahar. The 201st made for Kunduz, Badakhshan and Baghlan. A forward command centre was established at Bagram by Lieutenant-General Mikhailov, advance force commander of the 40th Army under Colonel-General Tukharinov. The capture of Kabul itself was successfully achieved on 26 and 27 December, with a continuous airlift of 5,000 troops who linked up with a 'Muslim battalion' and other Soviet forces, infiltrated during the previous month into the Afghan capital. A combined force of some 15,000 men set about paralysing Kabul. The 105th Guards Airborne Division, under the command of Colonel Ivan Ryabchenko, captured the Interior Ministry. The 'Muslim battalion' attacked the Defence Ministry and the KGB's Spetsnaz unit 'Zenit' took control of the post office, the radio station and the Pul-i-Charki prison. By the next day Kabul had been secured, and Soviet military police were even directing the rush-hour traffic. The Soviet Union's Afghan war had begun on a deceptively auspicious note.

It is unlikely that many members of the Soviet Politburo at the end of the 1970s would have been familiar with the works of Kipling or the details of the British General Elphinstone's ill-fated nineteenth-century expedition into Afghanistan. Had they studied the history of Britain's two Afghan wars, they might have concluded that Afghanistan had a proud history of resistance to imperialism and was unlikely to be easily subdued by an invading Soviet Army. Instead, their reading of history was more likely to have been influenced, though they may not have realised it, by Tsar Nicholas I, who said, 'Where the Imperial Flag has flown, it must never be lowered.'

Leonid Brezhnev had precisely such sentiments in mind when he gave the order for Soviet troops to provide 'fraternal assistance' to Czechoslovakia in 1968. At that time, eleven years before the invasion of Afghanistan, *Pravda* had published a declaration that, 'The Soviet Union and other socialist states, in fulfilling their internationalist duty to the fraternal peoples of Czechoslovakia and defending their gains, had to act and did act in resolute opposition to the anti-socialist forces in Czechoslovakia.'[3] The statement, less concise and elegant than the Tsar's version, became known as the 'Brezhnev Doctrine'. Its apotheosis was in Afghanistan.

The process by which the Soviet leadership came to apply the Brezhnev Doctrine, and thus to throw its armed forces into an Afghan quagmire, is long and complicated. Afghanistan had enjoyed a limited form of democracy with a constitutional monarchy since 1946. In 1953, when Lieutenant-General Mohammed Daoud Khan became Prime Minister, he started to extend Afghanistan's international economic ties by making overtures to the Soviet Union. Soviet military assistance followed, and in 1956 Daoud signed an agreement with Moscow providing for the re-equipping of the Afghan army and an extensive training programme by Soviet specialists. A large number of Afghan cadets and officers were trained in the Soviet Union from 1961 onwards and, by 1963, Soviet officers were highly visible in Kabul as military instructors to the Afghan armed forces. There was also substantial economic assistance. The Soviets built the Salang tunnel and a highway from Kabul. By the mid-1970s, they had provided over a billion dollars of aid.

In 1973, Daoud seized power for himself in a successful coup against the monarchy. He brought into his government a number of advisers with strong ties to the pro-Soviet People's Democratic Party of Afghanistan (PDPA), which began to build a power base for itself in the officer corps and the civil service. When Daoud finally became concerned about the growing power of the PDPA and began to round up its leaders, the PDPA, in true Leninist style, retaliated by launching a coup in April 1978. Daoud and his advisers were captured and butchered in the presidential palace. Suddenly, much to the Kremlin's surprise, Afghanistan was in the hands of the avowedly pro-Soviet Nur Mohammed Taraki, Chairman of the Revolutionary Council, and Hafizullah Amin, his Prime Minister. The new situation was not altogether one for which the Kremlin would have wished. Daoud's regime had been quite acceptable to Moscow, ensuring that Afghanistan gradually became a compliant client state, which was no longer the cause of trouble on the Soviet Union's southern frontier. Now, however, Moscow was faced with a socialist government with a radical programme in a traditional Islamic country. Its precarious hold on power was bound to be difficult to maintain, and soon it would inevitably turn to Moscow for assistance.

In December 1978, Nur Mohammed Taraki visited Moscow and signed a friendship pact. In a joint communiqué with the Soviet leadership he agreed to pursue long-term co-operation with the USSR. At the same time, a high-level Soviet military delegation, led by General Ivan Pavlovsky, deputy Minister of Defence and Commander-in-Chief of the Land Forces, and General Alexei Yepishev, a senior commander during the invasion of Czechoslovakia in 1968, visited Kabul to evaluate the situation. They had considerable cause for concern.

The PDPA was increasingly split between two internal factions, the *Khalq* ('Masses') faction, to which Amin and Taraki belonged, and the *Parcham* ('Banner'), led by Babrak Karmal. The Khalq wing was the more extreme, driven by crude Marxist ideology, veneration of Stalin and a determination to reorganise Afghanistan along Soviet lines. The split was particularly evident inside the Afghan army, the PDPA's main source of support, where there was open discrimination against Parchamis. When the government attempted to introduce education for women, it was confronted with a tide of Islamicist opposition, a major public-order problem and a mutiny inside the army. In March 1979, when Muslim rebels launched a revolt in Herat, calling for a jihad (holy war) against the Kabul regime and the infidel Russians who lurked behind it, they were joined by the army's 17th Infantry Division.

In the ensuing disturbances, as enraged mobs rampaged through the streets, nearly 5,000 people died. Among the dead, hacked to pieces by the mob, were one hundred Soviet citizens, including the families of military advisers. It was becoming impossible for Moscow to ignore the situation. On 17 March, Leonid Brezhnev called a senior Politburo member, Kirilenko, from his *dacha* and told him that events in Afghanistan could no longer be pushed to one side. The Politburo would meet to discuss the situation the following morning, at the Central Committee offices on Staraya Ploshchad.

Despite the worsening situation in Herat, however, the initial reaction of leading Politburo members was cautious, and unenthusiastic about greater involvement in Afghanistan. The KGB Chairman, Yuri Andropov, and the Soviet Foreign Minister, Andrei Gromyko, both spoke out firmly against any intervention, setting out the political and ideological case against it.

'It is completely clear to us that Afghanistan is not ready for a socialist solution to its problems,' said Andropov. 'The pressure of religion is enormous there. There is almost total illiteracy amongst the rural population and the economy is retarded. We know Lenin's teaching about a revolutionary situation. And no such situation exists in Afghanistan. Therefore, I consider that we could only secure the revolution in Afghanistan with the aid of our bayonets, and that is completely unacceptable to us. We cannot take such a risk.'

Gromyko agreed. 'I fully support the conclusion of Comrade Andropov that we should exclude measures such as the intervention of our armed forces in Afghanistan,' he said. 'The army there is hopeless. In which case, our army, going into Afghanistan, would be an aggressor. Against whom would it fight? Above all against the Afghan people, and it would have to fire at them. Comrade Andropov has rightly noted that the correct conditions for revolution have not developed, and everything we have worked so hard to achieve over the past few years, with a lessening of international tension, a reduction of armaments and much more, would all be thrown back.'[4]

The initial caution of Gromyko and Andropov, however, was

soon overtaken by the rush of events, by Brezhnev's ill-judged attachment to the Afghan Communist leader Taraki and, ultimately, by his enthusiasm for a revolutionary imperial adventure. The Politburo meeting was perhaps the last chance to stop the juggernaut rolling towards intervention and set the Soviet Union on a more rational course. If the advice of Gromyko and Andropov had been followed, the history of the last few years might have been very different. For there is little doubt that the reckless adventure upon which the Soviet leadership now embarked caused a massive, unsustainable shock to the political system of the USSR; a shock comparable in its ultimate effect to the blow to Tsarist autocracy from the Russo-Japanese war of 1905.

In the event, however, Leonid Brezhnev, who was reportedly unable by the end of the 1970s to take a serious decision or to sustain an intellectual conversation for longer than twenty minutes, found himself besieged by desperate requests for help from the Afghan regime. On 20 March, Taraki flew to Moscow and cajoled Brezhnev into agreeing to supply technical support, arms, ammunition and a small number of Soviet troops. Brezhnev's intention at this stage was most likely simply to provide the maximum support available to enable Taraki to stabilise the situation after Herat, and to counter whatever assistance the rebels were receiving from Pakistan and Iran. When Taraki left Moscow, Brezhnev hugged and kissed him.

However, despite the increased level of support extracted by Taraki, which included Mi-24 helicopters and an expanded corps of 3,000 military advisers, the Afghan regime's position became more and more precarious.[5] Desertions halved the size of the government army from 90,000 to 40,000, and whole brigades went over to the rebels.[6] The Soviet Embassy passed on requests for yet more assistance. In July, the Kremlin sent a battalion from the 345th Guards Airborne Regiment (later to be commanded by Alexander Lebed) to Bagram military airport near Kabul, to establish a secure airhead and provide extra protection for the Soviet An-12 transport regiment, which was bringing in regular supplies of equipment.[7] Even so, by the autumn, the north-east of the country was completely beyond Kabul's control.

The political situation was also deteriorating rapidly. Taraki's paranoia and intolerance of opposition led to purges in the major cities which killed more than 17,000 people. At the same time, a split developed within the Khalq faction itself, and Hafizullah Amin, Taraki's main rival, began to plot a seizure of power. According to one Western diplomat, the Afghan leadership at this time resembled 'a bottle full of angry scorpions all intent on stinging each other'.[8]

The Soviet government was growing more and more concerned about the situation. Its commitment to the PDPA regime was now so intense as to make withdrawal difficult and humiliating. In Moscow, those who favoured military intervention began to gain the upper hand. Their motives may have been 'expansionist', seeing Afghanistan as an important step towards the long-term objective of capturing Iran's oil supplies and securing a strategic position on the Persian Gulf; or they may have been dominated by a fear of Islamic fundamentalism, which they felt could seep through the USSR's southern border and infect Soviet Central Asia. More likely, however, the Kremlin simply became convinced by the rapidly increasing level of its own commitment to its client regime in Kabul that to abandon the PDPA would set a dangerous precedent. The commitment had been made; the flag of socialism had fluttered, however unconvincingly, over Kabul, and the Brezhnev Doctrine had to be applied.

What finally convinced Brezhnev that full-scale military intervention was justified, however, was the brutal murder of Taraki, who was smothered with a pillow by agents of Amin's secret police. Following his death, Kabul sank into even deeper turmoil as civil war broke out between the various factions of the PDPA and, in early December, a plot by Taraki's supporters to assassinate Amin almost succeeded. It was clear to Moscow that the Khalq faction was irreparably split and that the legitimacy of the PDPA had been almost fatally damaged by it. The Politburo decided that only a leader from the Parcham faction stood any chance of restoring order. However, since Parcham had been so weakened by both Taraki and Amin that it was incapable of staging a coup on its own, Brezhnev agreed to send a 'limited contingent of Soviet forces' (*Ogranichenny Kontingent Sovietskikh Voisk* – OKSV) to install the Parchami Babrak Karmal as head of a new government in Kabul.

And so it was that the Soviet Union began to fight a long, bitter and costly war which ultimately helped to destroy it. At the time, the Politburo could not have imagined that Afghanistan would prove such a dangerous and fatal entanglement. The Soviet Defence Minister Marshal Dmitry Ustinov, in common with many Generals and politicians before and after him, probably imagined that his 'limited contingent' would secure its objectives quickly and easily. There were indeed some early successes. The initial infiltration of Afghanistan was achieved without upset, and the Spetsnaz operation 'Shtorm-33' to assassinate Hafizullah Amin after a poisoned dinner at the Taj-Bek palace in Darul-Amman proceeded with brutal thoroughness.[9] The day afterwards, the 345th Guards Airborne Regiment escorted Babrak Karmal into Kabul. The scene on that day cannot have been wholly dissimilar to one a hundred and forty years earlier, when the British General Keane and Sir William Macnaghten led their puppet ruler, Shah Shuja, into the Afghan capital. At the time, one observer wrote that 'the jingling of money-bags and the gleaming of the bayonets of the British had restored him to the throne which, without these glittering aids, he had in vain striven to recover'. Shah Shuja's arrival was apparently greeted 'more like a funeral procession than the entry of a king into his dominions'.[10]

Babrak Karmal would have been fortunate if his entry into Kabul had been greeted merely with such sullen resentment. Instead, it fanned the flames of rebellion. In a singularly tactless broadcast on television and radio, he gave a traditional Islamic blessing and then invited the Soviet Army to invade the country. The faithful were insulted, Afghanistan was gripped by the fever of war, and a bloodthirsty call to jihad echoed from the mosques up to the mountains of the Hindu Kush, where the mujahideen guerrillas gathered and prepared to harry the invader.

The Soviet invasion of Afghanistan was already in its second year when Alexander Lebed grew bored with life in Ryazan and began to apply for new postings. At the beginning of November 1981, he spoke to a senior officer at the Ryazan academy and demanded to know why his requests for a new posting had been ignored. The officer assured him that he had made several telephone calls on his behalf and that the matter was being given due consideration. In time, no doubt, there would be an answer. Lebed was unable to control his impatience at this and, with typically insubordinate impulsiveness, demanded to use the telephone himself.

Eventually he found a Colonel Kamolov, who was responsible for recruitment for Afghanistan. According to Lebed, their conversation went as follows:

> 'Who are you?' he asked.
> 'Captain Lebed, former company commander of the cadets.'
> 'How long have you been commanding the company?'
> 'Five years and two months.'
> 'Do you want to command a battalion in the south?'
> 'Yes, I do.'
> 'Well, why don't you ask me whereabouts?'
> 'It's all the same to me.'
> 'Call me back in two hours.'[11]

It was clearly not a desire to fulfil his internationalist duty to his fraternal Afghan comrades that motivated Captain Lebed. He was more like a junior officer in the nineteenth century, bored with life in the provinces, the endless monotony of the barracks routine and the Officers' Mess, longing for adventure in the mountains and deserts of the south. Like most Russian officers, Lebed was familiar with the works of the poet Lermontov, who as a subaltern over a hundred years earlier had also yearned for action just to relieve the boredom:

> And, restless, he begs for storms,
> As though in storms there is rest.[12]

He soon found the storms he was seeking. He was appointed to command the 1st battalion of the 345th Guards Airborne Regiment, which had been in Afghanistan since July 1979, when it had arrived at the request of Hafizullah Amin to secure the military airport at Bagram. When he flew from the regimental depot in Fergana to Bagram, it was the first time in his life that he had left Soviet soil. It was November 1981, and although the Afghan mujahideen had not yet acquired American 'stinger' missiles, Lebed's An-12 transport aircraft flew high. From it, the earth was distant and the mountains seemed almost artificial. The land had a beautiful, mystical quality to it. He remembers feeling that it was almost like becoming part of some eastern fairy tale:

It was quite a dangerous feeling because I had to keep my feet firmly on our sinful earth and make sure I didn't get lost in the heavens. It is interesting that this sensation was not mine alone. And it often happened that someone who didn't manage to come out of this fairy-tale perception of the surrounding reality would be sent home in a zinc-lined coffin – in a 'black tulip'. Just like the song: 'In Afghanistan / In a "black tulip" / With vodka in the glass / We float in silence above the earth.'[13]

When Lebed came down to earth, he had quite a shock. The regiment was in bad shape and its irascible commander, Lieutenant-Colonel Yuri Kuznetsov, did not welcome the new arrival, fresh from the military academy, which he despised. He told Lebed that his arrival was unexpected and a thorough nuisance. Nevertheless, he gave him command of the 1st battalion, whose duties for two and a half years had consisted entirely of guarding the eighteen-kilometre perimeter fence around the aerodrome. The troops were restless, bored and ill-disciplined. Their living conditions were primitive and they spent their days in small groups spread out around the airport, rarely coming into contact with other platoons. There was no *esprit de corps*, no pride in the regiment and no sense of comradeship.

Throughout the Soviet Army, soldiers' living conditions were poor and hygiene was a problem. Dysentery, hepatitis and other infectious intestinal disorders, caused by inadequate sewerage, poor food handling and contaminated water, were common amongst conscripts. On several occasions the army had been forced to establish Extraordinary Anti-epidemic Commissions as an emergency measure. In Afghanistan, these typical problems were magnified. Lebed's first days in command were spent trying to improve the men's living conditions, reorganising the field kitchens, the bath-house and the laundry. He understood that bad conditions had left their mark on his men, making them resentful and difficult to command. 'If a soldier lives like a human being, he will serve like a human being. And if he lives like a pig . . .'[14]

He was faced with a much greater threat to discipline, however. Bullying of recruits, *Dedovshchina*, had long been a problem in the Soviet Army. It still continues today in the Russian Army, and a recent report concluded that twenty-five people are killed every day in non-military activity in the armed forces. Lebed, however, soon realised that in a theatre of war it was particularly damaging. He determined to stamp it out and to impress his authority on the men.

His opportunity came when he set about trying to improve his soldiers' level of physical fitness, which had fallen dramatically during the long years of sentry duty at Bagram. He ordered his men to build a small gymnasium, which was equipped with weights made from tank tracks, parallel bars and a horizontal bar. Despite its rough and ready appearance, the gymnasium helped to improve the men's level of fitness. However, one soldier had a problem with some of the exercises. He was approached by a group of eleven more senior soldiers in his company, who asked if he could somersault backwards over the horizontal bar. When he replied that he could not, they tied him to the bar with a belt, attached a lead from a T-57 tank to his legs, and cranked it up with the handle of a field telephone. The shock was so great that the soldier's body jolted up towards the ceiling. When Lebed found out, he was furious. Deeply angry at the bullying he had already seen in the battalion, he determined to make an example of those responsible for the latest incident.

The punishment he meted out to the culprits has become part of Lebed's legend. He lined up the eleven bullies and punched them all in the face. He hit the ringleader so hard that he was unconscious before he fell to the floor. His deputy fell alongside him and, moments later, the others landed in a crumpled heap in the corner. Only one of them needed more than one punch from the furious former boxer; he had to be hit twice before he too landed on the pile. Afterwards, Lebed remembers that his conscience tortured him all evening: 'I have rejected the use of violence as a means of education all my life. I always believed and taught my subordinates that if an officer had come to the point where he had no arguments left, only his fist, they should report him and leave the army. But here my well-worn theory suddenly came up against the ugly reality.'[15]

Despite Lebed's reservations, though, his aggressive response to the bullies transformed his relationship with his men. On parade the next morning, there was a completely different atmosphere. As he inspected the battalion, he was greeted with looks of admiration from his men. The ones he had punched were the most impressed of all. Everyone seemed concerned to listen to him attentively and, above all, not to annoy him.

He decided to capitalise on the improved atmosphere in the battalion with a rigorous programme of training, which was designed to get the men fully fit for combat in two weeks. When he told the commanding officer, Kuznetsov, of his plan, the gruff colonel told him to do it in ten days. Lebed set about the task with vigour at four o'clock the following morning, when his men left camp on a long march with full equipment. They spent the day in extensive combat training and returned to camp late in the evening. Lebed told them that no one would be allowed to sleep until all the weapons and equipment had been cleaned and checked. The order was very unpopular and, to show their disapproval, the men deliberately carried it out slowly. Lebed ignored them and let them do the work as slowly as they liked. The following morning, however, he ordered them to be woken up after only two and a half hours' sleep. Once again, they were marched out of camp for another full day's combat training, from which they returned exhausted. This time, however, they cleaned their weapons and equipment at high speed, knowing that the sooner they finished, the sooner they would get to bed. After ten days, Kuznetsov agreed that they were ready for combat.

Lebed's battalion was about to join active combat operations at a difficult time for the Soviet Army in Afghanistan. After some initial successes during the first phase of the Soviet occupation, it soon became clear that the Limited Contingent of Soviet Forces (OKSV) was unable to subdue resistance for any significant period. The pattern for large-scale offensives by the OKSV was first set in February 1980, when a force of 5,000 men, backed by armour and air support, moved into the Kunar Valley. Although the mujahideen were powerless to stop the advance, Soviet troops were unable to hunt down the guerrillas, who quickly disappeared into the mountains and lateral ravines. When the Soviet troops withdrew, the mujahideen returned.[16]

Similar large-scale operations in 1981 in the Panjshir Valley were equally unproductive. The mujahideen had learned that large armed groups soon attracted the attention of the Soviet forces and presented easy targets. Instead, they operated in smaller, more flexible partisan detachments of 20 to 200 men. The success of the mujahideen's tactics was soon clear in one of the

Panjshir offensives, when 15,000 Soviet and Afghan government soldiers, backed by 150 Mi-24 gunships, suffered 3,000 casualties.[17] Despite its ever-expanding efforts to crush resistance, it was clear to Soviet field commanders that attempts to use large military formations were without effect. Instead, they began to undertake battalion-size manoeuvres with helicopter support. Soviet strategy at this time was to revive the Afghan government army and help it to attack the resistance. At all times, the Soviet Union aimed to limit the level of its military commitment. The nature of the Afghan army, however, made this a forlorn hope.

Lebed's first major combat role was a large-scale operation in January 1982, when his 345th Guards Airborne fought alongside the '444th Regiment of Afghan Commandos'. The two regiments were part of a sweep to comb the Bagram Valley, which led into the Panjshir Valley to the north and then on to the Soviet border. The area straddled the main road north from Kabul and provided the mujahideen with good cover from which to ambush Soviet columns coming south from the USSR. Although at times split between several factions, most mujahideen groups accepted the command of Ahmad Shah Massoud, a Tajik who proved himself early in the war to be one of the most effective guerrilla leaders, capable of organising a highly motivated, disciplined resistance movement keen to prosecute a bloody jihad against the Soviets.

There were six types of mujahideen fighters, according to Lebed, each with different motives and characteristics. The first type were genuine patriots; proud, freedom-loving, independent people for whom the mere presence of foreign occupying forces on their native soil was unbearable. The second were people who had lost out as a result of the kaleidoscopic changes in Afghan politics from the Shah to Babrak Karmal. They hoped, by fighting in the war, to secure a return of their possessions or to acquire new ones. The third category were religious fanatics who were insulted by the presence of non-Muslims in their country, and who had declared a holy war. They were ready to fight for decades until the body of the last unbeliever had been torn up and scattered to the wind.

The fourth group were mercenaries, who were drawn from many nationalities but were often courageous and well-trained. They all shared the same Achilles heel, however. As their overriding motivation was money, they were less prepared to take risks and wanted at all times to ensure that they were safe. They would carry out attacks on Soviet columns in full if there was no resistance, but if they encountered opposition they would disappear, leaving everything, including their own dead and wounded, behind them. The fifth category were poor Afghanis who were offered enough money to marry, buy a home and raise a family in return for a year's service with the mujahideen. Often they developed a taste for blood and wanted to continue fighting. If, however, at the end of the year they asked for payment, they would simply be told to 'go in peace'. Few of them ever went more than a kilometre in peace.

The sixth type were fighters, for whose motivation the Soviet forces were responsible – they were people whose villages, homes and families had been destroyed. Lebed describes the motivation of this type with particular sympathy: 'A man who is completely removed from the war and does not want to fight returns home and finds that he has no wife, no children, no mother. His blood boils in him. He is no longer a man but a wolf, ready to cut and shred and kill for eternity. And the longer the war lasts, the more there are of these wolves.'[18]

Lebed's Afghan allies were not driven by such motives. They were made of much less stern stuff than the mujahideen. Yet the 40th Army was under strict orders that all operations had to be conducted jointly with Afghan government troops. Lebed's opinion of his Afghan allies in the 444th Afghan 'commandos' was contemptuous. 'The regiment consisted of the usual rabble, it had completely lost its *esprit de corps* and discipline. They were all basically slippery. They weren't soldiers. There were no leaders.'[19]

The plan which Lebed and his allies were to carry out involved encircling a large area and gradually tightening the ring so that, as the Soviets and their Afghan allies moved through the villages of the Bagram Valley, they could liquidate the Islamic committees and comb out the mujahideen guerrillas, killing those who resisted as they moved. The remainder of the population were supposed to be 'vetted' in 'filtration camps'. In practice, however, to Lebed's exasperation, the Afghan commandos were so lax that the mujahideen guerrillas easily managed to escape.

Lebed grew particularly irritated with the Afghan battalion's habit of stopping for tea in every village. He was greeted with incomprehension when he tried to explain that he had nothing in principle against tea, but that the operation should be completed first; then it might be possible to take tea. Furthermore, the Afghan battalion had a gang of batmen, who appeared to have no other purpose than to make life as comfortable as possible for their officers. In the evening, they would 'scuttle off in all directions like cockroaches' and gather up an enormous collection of blankets, pillows and cushions with which to make a comfortable place for their commanding officer and his comrades to spend the night. They were not prepared to share even the dirtiest blanket with their Russian allies. Eventually, Lebed grew so irritated by their attitude that he marched into the house they had occupied for themselves, thanked them for making such comfortable accommodation ready for him, and drove them all out of it. The Afghans spent the night shivering outside in the cold, but, says Lebed, 'they drew the right conclusions. The most important of these was that he who wants most receives least.' In future, the Afghans made sure they looked after their allies – and particularly the commander of the Soviet battalion.

By the sixth day of Operation Kol'tso, the 'ring' had been closed to a size of five kilometres in diameter and they had rounded up a huge number of local people who were supposed to be taken to the filtration camps. There were 211 men in Lebed's battalion, and they were now guarding 1,750 prisoners. There were no clear instructions as to what to do with them and no means of transporting them. The situation was chaotic, and could quickly have become dangerous, but Lebed persuaded two mullahs to instruct the crowd to sit down and wait patiently. At nine o'clock in the evening, three extra companies, including an intelligence company, arrived to take the prisoners to the village of Charrikar, nine kilometres away. Lebed handed them over to the commander of the intelligence company and prepared to continue with the operation. On the way to Charrikar, however, many of the prisoners escaped and, on arrival, the Governor of Charrikar announced that the 'filtration' system to check if the remaining prisoners were mujahideen or civilian was not yet ready. There were only a few policemen and no Afghan government security agents at all. The governor gave all the prisoners certificates to say that they had passed through a filtration point and released them. The following morning, Lebed's men were attacked from the rear by forty well-armed mujahideen. Only the concentrated fire of two machine-guns enabled the battalion to continue its advance to the river Gorband.

Operation Kol'tso was not a success. It had involved a huge amount of effort but yielded little of real significance. The theory behind the operation was clear enough; to block off a region in which a guerrilla force was located and then comb the area until it could be found and destroyed. Operation Kol'tso showed that the mujahideen were able simply to disappear in the villages or as they were being taken to filtration camps. They wriggled through the 'ring' which had been thrown around them, and then regrouped to carry on the attack from the rear.

The difficulties encountered by Lebed's men were not unique, but they returned to camp feeling frustrated and angry. Other problems included the mujahideen's impressive intelligence-gathering and their ability to ambush Soviet forces with a concentration of heavy fire. One officer, Major S. N. Petrov, described a similar search by an Airborne battalion of the village of Sherkhankhel in early 1982:

> Intelligence reports indicated that a well-armed group of approximately forty mujahideen were operating out of Sherkhankhel village . . . The 3rd Airborne Battalion commander planned to move his battalion secretly to the Sherkhankhel region and to seal it off with two companies of paratroopers while a third company would search the village. One airborne company would remain in reserve. An artillery battalion and four Mi-24 helicopter gunships would provide support with the initiation of combat.
>
> In the pre-dawn hours of 20 March, the battalion moved out from Bagram to Sherkhankhel. A reconnaissance patrol moved 300 metres in front of the column. The approach march moved on a wide, straight road. Along the left side of the road stretched a thick, high, long adobe wall while on the right side lay a concrete lined canal . . . Suddenly, through an embrasure cut in the adobe wall, and practically at point-blank range, the enemy opened fire on the reconnaissance patrol. The survivors scrambled for safety into the canal. A machine-gun opened fire from a house 150 metres further north from the ambush site . . .

The battalion finally began to manoeuvre its reserve company in an effort to encircle the enemy, but only after the mujahideen ceased fire. However, even this attempt was stopped by a veritable hurricane of enemy fire ... There was no thought of conducting a pursuit or continuing the action. The 3rd Airborne Battalion lost eight men killed and six wounded. Two of the dead were officers. The battalion did not search the village since the mujahideen were already gone.[20]

Lebed's troops were soon involved in a similar operation in the village of Argankheil. This time, however, the result was much more encouraging for them. The battalion found a large pack of interesting documents and took several dozen prisoners. For the first time Kuznetsov congratulated Lebed. What pleased Lebed most, however, was that there were no casualties and no wounded. He claims that, throughout his service in Afghanistan, his main priority was to keep his soldiers alive: 'Grief came into the homes of few mothers on my account, but there were casualties all the same. However much you dodge or trick or manoeuvre, there is no such thing as a war without casualties.'[21] And one of the main causes of death in war, particularly in Afghanistan, was not military action but carelessness: by the end of his tour of duty in Afghanistan, Lebed calculated that 42 per cent of all casualties were the result of negligence or stupidity. As he prepared to leave Argankheil, his joy at seeing his men complete an action without taking any casualties was marred by just such an incident.

The three companies under his command were preparing to leave the village in an armoured column. His driver had just poured him a cup of tea when there was an explosion and the sound of screaming from the front of the second company's column. When Lebed reached the site of the explosion, he saw a soldier's body from which the head and the left arm had been detached by the force of the blast. It soon became clear that the victim of the explosion, a stocky, cheerful Siberian called Petrov, had died because of the negligence of his company commander. What had apparently happened was that another soldier had presented two captured anti-personnel mines to the company commander, who ordered Petrov to put them in his rucksack without first checking that they had been disarmed. Later the company radio was packed on top of the mines. When the order was given to mount up into the armoured vehicles, Petrov slipped as he was climbing on board and fell on to the rucksack. The mines exploded and Petrov's body was ripped apart and scattered across the road, along with fragments of the radio transmitter.

Later, Lebed watched the deputy company commander and two soldiers carefully gathering up Petrov's remains. As they worked, the other soldiers in the company, who had grown accustomed to such scenes of violent death, got out their mess tins and began to eat.

When the battalion returned to barracks, Lebed was in no mood for the welcome he received. A military band was playing a triumphal march, 'Let the thunder of victory roll'. When Lebed ordered the conductor to stop it, he was told, 'I can't! The commanding officer ordered that you should be greeted with an orchestra, comrade Captain!'[22]

Life in Lebed's battalion returned briefly to the usual routine of garrison duties at Bagram. Despite occasional mujahideen attacks, the main problem for any garrison was boredom. Conditions were still bad, with the soldiers living in overcrowded, makeshift quarters and often under canvas. Yet life in Afghanistan had its advantages for Soviet soldiers. Indeed, there were some special opportunities such as hard-currency bounties and a limited selection of Western goods in the *voentorg* (military shop), which could often be sold at a profit to local Afghans. And some soldiers found that when a Kalashnikov rifle could be sold for 100,000 afghánis and a woman could be bought for the night in Kabul for 100, the situation was not without its attractions.[23]

Lebed's men did not have long, however, to reflect on their position. As a paratroop battalion, they led a much more active existence than ordinary Soviet infantry soldiers. The army often used them to spearhead attacks or to lead a rapid response to rebel incursions. On 25 February, the battalion deployed to the Nidzhrab Valley for a major operation, involving the entire army group rather than just the division. Lebed's orders were to take his men through the long, narrow valley to a point at the far end where they could begin to search the villages and ravines for mujahideen. The long march through the valley passed without any major opposition, although the driver and some of the passengers of a BTR armoured personnel carrier were killed when it fell from a bridge into the river below. The driver had fallen asleep. Lebed added another incidence of negligence to his list of casualty statistics.

When Lebed's men reached the point in the valley where they were supposed to part company with the 3rd Battalion of the regiment in order to begin a search of one of the lateral ravines, they were unable to move forward because their rations had not been delivered. The entire battalion had only one pack of army rations. When Lebed had finished complaining about this latest incidence of incompetence and the commanding officer had agreed to fly the rations in by helicopter, the order was given to move forward. The Afghan government troops who were accompanying them went first, which Lebed felt was a considerable advantage, if only because they were a good barometer of danger, moving straight ahead if it was safe and looking anxiously from side to side or hiding behind rocks if it was not. For the first kilometre, there was a deathly, oppressive silence, broken only by the sound of a dog barking somewhere in the distance.

'It is only in the cinema that weapons fire all the time and bullets always hit the target with amazing accuracy – and even if the heroes die, they do it beautifully and with a story-book correctness, accompanying their death or victory in the right time and place with appropriate cries or shouts,' Lebed observes. 'In reality, it is not like that. War is hard, dirty, bloody work. And, most of all, it is work. The periods of fighting themselves, those that might actually be considered war, pass quite quickly. The rest of the time you are moving out, crawling, digging in, operating and repairing your equipment, or organising the supply of ammunition and provisions. It is routine work and there is not much that's heroic in it.'[24]

Suddenly, the Afghan troops began to look worried. Their heads turned rapidly from side to side, nervously seeking out danger behind the rocks. They were not mistaken. Soon they were under fire from four places. Lebed's men and the 3rd Battalion, still on the slopes above them, returned fire and the fighting ended as rapidly as it had begun. However, despite the rapidity of the exchange, there were casualties. A young Afghan soldier, only sixteen years old, who was almost the mascot of the Afghan battalion, had been killed. As he was so young and treated like everyone's son, he had been given a helmet and a flak jacket to protect him, but a bullet had gone straight through the jacket and hit his heart.

The incident, which upset Lebed as he had recently had a conversation with the young soldier, drew attention to the poor quality of much Soviet equipment. Lebed's colleague, Major Vostrotin, commander of the 3rd Battalion and a future Hero of the Soviet Union, had tried to convince his men that the flak jackets worked by hanging one up from a tree and shooting at it from a distance of 100 metres. Bullets easily passed through the front and back of the jacket. The same thing happened from 200 and 300 metres. Major Vostrotin only spared his blushes in front of his men by explaining how good Soviet bullets and rifles were.

In general, Soviet field kit was thoroughly inadequate for the Afghan campaign. Much of it was designed for motor-rifle troops and was unsuitable for long infantry operations in rugged, mountainous terrain. Until the Soviet Union began to manufacture reasonable equipment late in the war, many soldiers were forced to buy surplus British or Pakistani rucksacks, sleeping bags and other gear at local bazaars. The standard army boot, the most important item for any soldier, was almost useless in the mountains, so many paratroopers soon started wearing Kimris, a type of locally manufactured sneaker.[25]

Soviet operations in Afghanistan were often impeded not only by the mujahideen and the mountainous terrain of much of the country, but also by the extreme weather conditions, which could change suddenly and make any movement impossible for days. The baking heat could become driving rain without warning, and almost immediately hard, dry ground would become a deep, muddy swamp. As Lebed advanced up the ravine, a blizzard got up. Soon it became thick and swirling. His men could hear the sound of machine-gun fire but they could see nothing. The blizzard lasted for three days, and there was no chance for helicopters to bring in the men's rations. However, there was no alternative but to try to move forward. The men gradually inched their way through deserted villages, where the only living creatures were black billy-goats whose devilish, blood-red eyes stared at them through the swirling snow. The men's hunger was so great that the billy goats were soon killed and eaten.

When the blizzard had died down, Lebed's men entered a village near the end of the valley. They were greeted by a group of elders who swore that the village was entirely peaceful. There were women and children of all ages, some of whom were frightened by the sound of gunfire nearby. The presence of so many women and children might well have persuaded any mujahideen group in the vicinity to pass by the village and not to stay. It was important to be sure, though. Lebed assured the elders that he would not harm the women and children but demanded to inspect all the men of the village. Altogether, there were about seventy, of whom fifty were young, strong and healthy. When Lebed had satisfied himself that there were no rebels amongst them, the Afghan commander and his political officer informed him that they were under orders to recruit villagers for the government army. To Lebed's surprise, when the Afghan commander gave the order that all those who wished to volunteer should take two paces forward, the entire group stepped forward. Later, Lebed realised the problems that such recruitment procedures could create. Many of the recruits from the countryside soon deserted, taking with them rifles, ammunition, documents and even 'hostages' to give to the mujahideen. Often they would try to take their officers with them, and the most impressive bounty they could carry off was the Russian liaison officer attached to an Afghan battalion.

As dusk fell, Lebed led his men to the end of the valley, where they stayed overnight in an abandoned village. Outside, from somewhere in the surrounding darkness, they could hear the sound of gunfire, and occasional rounds ricocheted against the walls of the houses. In the morning, to Lebed's annoyance, he received an order to return at once through the valley. They had reached their present position only with a great effort and in considerable danger. Although they had not yet searched the area, they were being told to withdraw. Inevitably, the order led to another angry clash between Lebed and his superior, Lieutenant-Colonel Kuznetsov.

The weather had improved, however, and the return journey was much easier and faster. Back at Bagram, everyone expected a brief period of rest, but the following morning the battalion was ordered to deploy immediately to the village of Makhmudraki, which was known to be one of the mujahideen's main bases. Lebed's orders were to cover the withdrawal of the rest of the army from the Nidzhrab Valley and to wait until the last soldier had left before returning to Bagram.

The journey to Makhmudraki was slow and difficult. It was raining heavily and the dusty ground of a few days earlier had become a sea of mud. The soldiers were soaking and covered in mud up to their waists. The heavy going made it impossible to reach Makhmudraki before nightfall. When they eventually arrived the next day, the village was unusually quiet. As Lebed's men filed through the deserted streets, there was no sign of any occupants. They had expected that their arrival would provoke a response from the mujahideen, but not a shot was fired, and the very calm filled Lebed with alarm. The silence continued into the night but the enveloping womb of darkness made his men begin to feel safer. Lebed noticed that the sentries were half asleep though, and swore at them rudely to wake them up.

At dawn, the mujahideen attacked. Lebed was taken by surprise and, fearing imminent disaster, angrily responded to their rocket-grenade attack with heavy machine-gun fire. When he asked each of his company commanders for a situation report, he expected to be given details of heavy losses. Instead, only one company, the second, appeared to have been badly hit. However, although several men were seriously wounded, only one was killed.

A short while later, Lebed himself had a lucky escape. From the turret of an armoured personnel carrier, he noticed a small group of soldiers in the distance, silhouetted against the skyline. In such an isolated position, they were in real danger, and he began to shout at them furiously to come back. Just as he began to demand the name of the officer who had allowed them to wander off, he realised that they were not his soldiers but mujahideen. His shouting had drawn their attention to him and, before he could take cover, they began to fire. Although he was completely unprotected and his APC was hit several times, he was unharmed. After the incident, he felt a strong sense of fatalism and remembered Jaroslav Hašek's words: 'A man born to be hanged will not drown.'[26]

Lebed's men maintained their position until the last regiment of the army had been withdrawn from the Nidzhrab Valley. The return to garrison duties at Bagram after the excitement and danger of field operations in the valley soon began to take its toll on the men's morale, however. Discipline had been easy to maintain in the field but, amidst the boredom of barracks life, it began to slip again. Two peculiarly Russian incidents of indiscipline nearly cost Lebed his military career at the end of March 1982. The first, so absurd that it could almost have been scripted by Vladimir Voinovich, involved the 3rd company of his battalion, which was on sentry duty near a bakery, run by a soldier who was considered a master of his trade. His bread was extremely popular with all the men. When the sergeant of the company sent some of his men to fetch bread from the bakery, the master baker refused them. The sergeant's men then started to fight with the bakers. The sergeant himself became so incensed at the news that his men had been refused bread that he ordered an armoured personnel carrier to point its guns at the bakery. The bakers responded by reverting to their secondary, combat role as anti-aircraft gunners and pointed an anti-aircraft gun at the sergeant's armoured personnel carrier. Unsure what to do next in their fortified positions, the two sides began to shout a whole catechism of swear-words at each other. It was at this moment that Lebed appeared on the scene.

'It's difficult to say who would have won this duel. The armaments were spread out over a completely open space only 120 metres from each other, but there is a general principle: he who shoots first, laughs last. Fortunately, the duel did not take place.'[27] At Lebed's approach, everyone fled. The sergeant was stripped of his rank and for the next three months became a private again.

The second incident occurred two days later. One of the soldiers in the first company was absent without leave at the eight o'clock parade. He was a diligent soldier, who had served a year in the regiment, so his absence was particularly worrying. Lebed informed Kuznetsov, who told him to drop everything and look for the missing man. By eleven-thirty he still had not been found, and Kuznetsov ordered that the search area should be extended with the help of the 2nd Battalion, which had arrived two days earlier from Bamian after almost two weeks without proper rations because of the bad weather.

Eventually, the missing soldier was found by the second-in-command of the regiment, Lieutenant-Colonel Slava Zhukov. Lebed had just begun to interview the soldier when he was ordered to report to Kuznetsov's office, together with Major Livensky, the adjutant of the 1st Battalion, and Zhukov. As they sat waiting in the Colonel's tiny office, with the soldier nervously cowering in the corner, the door was flung open and Kuznetsov shouted 'attention' as he entered the room. He complained that soldiers were 'running about all over the place like hares' and announced that he would take over the investigation, telling Lebed and the other officers in the room to 'fuck off'. The coarse, bad-tempered Kuznetsov was immediately confronted by the naturally insubordinate Lebed, who asked him three times what he wanted them to do. Each time, the Colonel repeated his command to 'fuck off'. Lebed remembers that, each time the Colonel uttered the words, Zhukov looked shocked and the soldier in the corner appeared to have stopped breathing. Lebed asked Kuznetsov once more what they should do and again he told them to fuck off. Lebed walked out of the office and slammed the door so hard that it came off its hinges, a picture fell off the wall, smashing the glass in its frame, paint flaked off the door and the Colonel's glass kerosene lamp was shattered on the floor.

For a long time, Lebed waited outside the Colonel's office for an apology, but the Colonel never came out. Lebed returned to his quarters with Major Livensky. The truth about the missing soldier began to emerge and Lebed realised that he was not at fault. He had had intense stomach pains during the night, a common complaint in Afghanistan, and after the morning gymnastics he had gone to the regimental surgery, where he was told that he should have made an appointment. So the soldier went instead to the divisional surgery, hoping that they would see him, but he was given the same answer. His stomach was now so bad, however, that he decided to wait for the chief medical officer of the division. He hid at the back of the surgery, frequently rushing to the lavatory, which is where he was found by Lieutenant-Colonel Zhukov. Lebed's attitude towards him, when he discovered the true story, was sympathetic.

'Such things were widespread in Afghanistan. The military elite and the political officers had stomach aches. So did those who disturbed military discipline, the drunkards and the idlers. So did the Communists and the non-Communists. Everyone did. I don't know a single person in Afghanistan who didn't have the pleasure of a stomach ache.'[28]

Lebed and Livensky waited for a whole day and the following night to hear from Kuznetsov, but they heard nothing. Nobody called on them, and they began to consider themselves relieved of their command. Lebed gave command of the battalion to a junior officer and ordered him to take the parade the following morning, whilst he and Livensky stayed in their quarters, playing dominoes to kill time. The new battalion commander returned from the parade with the news that they had been summoned to the Colonel's office. Lebed replied that they had been told to 'fuck off', so they had done. A little while later, the Colonel's ADC arrived and asked if they were mutinying. They explained that they were simply waiting for an apology. The message was relayed and Lebed continued his game of dominoes with Livensky. Suddenly the door was flung open and the Colonel stood on the threshold, shouting at them that disobedience during wartime could lead to a court-martial. Lebed did not reply but picked up the domino board and threw it to the floor, accidentally hitting the Colonel's leg as he did so.

As he limped around the room, nursing his leg, the Colonel seemed to calm down. His tone suddenly changed and he began to blame his temper on his nerves. Lebed and Livensky were silent, and began to feel a little guilty as they listened to the Colonel. When he asked them to follow him to the parade ground, they walked behind him on to the platform and listened in astonishment as he apologised to them in front of the regiment and ordered them to take back command of the 1st Battalion.

The two incidents are interesting for a number of reasons. They are a good example of the poor quality of many Soviet staff officers and of the endemic lack of discipline among Soviet combat troops. They also show some of Lebed's strengths and weaknesses. He is deeply concerned about the welfare of his men, is held in great respect by them and can quickly restore order in a crisis, but he is also insubordinate, quick to take offence and quite prepared to use violence to get his way.

In the spring of 1982, Soviet and Afghan government troops tried to assert their strength with large-scale offensives in the Panjshir Valley, Farah province and the Gorband Valley. On each occasion the mujahideen were ready to meet the Soviet advance. Their intelligence was good and they often appeared to have been informed of impending attacks, enabling them to evacuate non-combatants and to prepare appropriate firing positions. The movement of Soviet armoured columns was easy to track, and preparations for their deployment were soon identified. In consequence, the rebels managed to launch at least one pre-emptive strike against the air base at Bagram before the start of an offensive. In addition, the Soviets were increasingly aware that their control of any area could only last as long as they could maintain a physical presence in it. Whenever they left, the mujahideen reappeared.

Lieutenant-Colonel Kuznetsov was, therefore, determined that the battle should be taken to the mujahideen in a quieter, less obvious way. He summoned Lebed, Major Vostrotin, commander of the 3rd Battalion, and the new regimental second-in-command, Lebed's old colleague from Ryazan, Lieutenant-Colonel Pavel Grachev, to his quarters for a briefing. He told them that he wanted to launch an attack against the mujahideen but, this time, the regiment would be deployed in a lighter and more flexible formation. The 3rd Battalion would lead the attack and Lieutenant-Colonel Grachev would have overall command of the operation. Lebed would remain in the rear, in command of an armoured company, whose role was to cover any withdrawal, if necessary.

Despite all the careful planning, however, things soon started to go wrong. The battalion managed to deploy in total silence, but the mujahideen were waiting for them. As Lebed sat in the turret of his armoured personnel carrier, watching the daylight gradually pierce the darkness, the silence of dawn was suddenly broken by the sound of machine-gun fire and grenades. Vostrotin's men were under attack. Lebed called up Lieutenant-Colonel Kuznetsov, who told him to wait and hold his position. Typically, though, Lebed's impatience got the better of him and he disobeyed the Colonel's order, telling his company to move forward to assist Vostrotin. He justified his decision to ignore the Colonel's order on the grounds of his own supposed experience and intuition. In the event, he was proved right. The mujahideen, who had attacked Vostrotin from several positions, scattered when they heard the approach of Lebed's armoured company. Two Mi-26 helicopters flew overhead and fired into the mountains, but without any hope of hitting the mujahideen, who had long since disappeared.

When Lebed reached the 3rd Battalion's position, he found Major Vostrotin and Lieutenant-Colonel Grachev sitting on the ground, smoking cigarettes and staring gloomily at a soldier's body. There was a black hole in his head where his right eye should have been. Nearby two soldiers were carrying the body of a young lieutenant, Astakhin. He had served well in Afghanistan, earning himself the Order of the Red Banner, and the operation was to have been his last before he returned home. Five minutes later, another officer, Lieutenant Popov, was carried out by his men, heavily wounded. Popov had been one of the cadets in Lebed's company at the Ryazan academy, and this was his first and last tour in Afghanistan. He died of his wounds three days later. Altogether, the operation that morning resulted in three dead and seven wounded. The number of casualties increased on the way back to Bagram, however, when an armoured personnel carrier drove over a mine. Another soldier was killed in the explosion and Lebed himself was injured by the blast, which left him with severe bruising on his shins.

When the field hospital failed to cure Lebed's legs, which soon became badly swollen, making it almost impossible for him to walk, he was sent to the divisional hospital in Fergana and then back to Ryazan. His legs still failed to heal, however, and he was told to take some leave at home in Novocherkassk. There he sat on the veranda, enjoying the southern Russian spring and soaking his legs in a basin of hot water and herbs prepared by his mother. The old lady's simple country remedy was better than anything Lebed had been given in hospital. In three days the swelling disappeared and his legs were completely cured. By the middle of May, he was able to return to Afghanistan, where his regiment was taking part in another offensive in the Panjshir Valley. In his absence, the battalion had been split up and its various companies had been assigned to other battalion commanders.

As Lieutenant-Colonel Grachev was in the field, Lebed was ordered to replace him temporarily as Kuznetsov's second-in-command at regimental headquarters, where he was made responsible for a range of tedious and exhausting administrative duties. No doubt the experience taught him that there was more to the gruff old Colonel of the regiment than he had imagined. Indeed, the Colonel's accomplishments were soon recognised by a higher-ranking authority than Captain Lebed.

In early June, as Lebed sat in his office working on some papers, the Colonel appeared at the door, grinning uncharacteristically. He demanded that Lebed follow him to his quarters, where the regimental political officer informed a group of officers, who had been hastily rounded up, that a decree of the Presidium of the Supreme Soviet of the USSR had just been published, honouring Lieutenant-Colonel Kuznetsov with the title of Hero of the Soviet Union. The Colonel was beaming with pride, and his usual choleric temper had vanished. The table in his office was covered with bottles of vodka. There were speeches, reminiscences and toasts in his honour. The party went on until the middle of the night, when the political officer, Lieutenant-Colonel Kudinov, suggested that the men should be told of the Colonel's award. Lebed was ordered to assemble them. It was half-past midnight and all the officers were so drunk that they could hardly speak. Kudinov read out the text of the decree of the Supreme Soviet. He managed to pronounce the words without difficulty, but there was a gap of three or four seconds between each word. The Colonel, who had tears in his eyes, was swaying from side to side in the background. The men realised that all their officers were drunk, but they understood and forgave them. They seemed genuinely proud of the Colonel's honour, perhaps feeling that it was partly theirs too. A few days later, Lebed's battalion had another cause for celebration when he was promoted to the rank of Major.

There was little time to celebrate, however. The battalion was soon back in combat again. At the beginning of June 1982, as part of an attempt to extend the defensive ring around Bagram air base, Lebed's best company, commanded by Major Livensky, was ordered to set up a fortified position near Makhmudraki. After a month and a half living in the worst possible conditions in the heat of the Afghan summer, and without enough lightweight uniforms, the strain began to tell on Livensky's company. Lebed asked for permission to withdraw them and, after repeated refusals, his request was eventually granted. The withdrawal of a company from a forward position was a complicated and dangerous operation, though. Lebed, at the head of an armoured Airborne company, collected Livensky's men from their post and began the journey back to Bagram.

Travelling in Afghanistan was a nerve-wracking business because of the risk of a sudden ambush or a minefield. Lebed's column contained a team of sappers and two tank transporters. They also had clear instructions to stay away from main roads because of the risk of mines. Nevertheless, as they rounded the bottom of a hill just after collecting Livensky's men, there was a loud explosion. The sixth vehicle in the column, an armoured personnel carrier, had been hit by a mine. One soldier was killed and several others were injured. There was nothing left of the dead soldier's body, just his head, still intact, inside its helmet. A column of smoke and dust from the explosion rose up into the sky as Lebed's men gathered up the soldier's remains, mounted up once more and made their way back to camp.

The operation was Lebed's last in Afghanistan. His tour had been a short one because he had been selected to continue his military education at the Soviet Army's staff college, the Frunze Academy. He left behind the 345th Guards Airborne Regiment, with its new commanding officer, Lieutenant-Colonel Pavel Grachev, who was eventually made a Hero of the Soviet Union for his service in Afghanistan.

A few days later Lebed was on a military transport aircraft back to Fergana. No one on the aeroplane seemed relieved or pleased to be leaving. Everyone was subdued, engrossed in their own thoughts and memories, gloomily looking out at the endless succession of Afghan mountains below.

'We brought Afghanistan with us – in our souls, in our hearts, in our memory, in our customs, in everything and at every level,' Lebed remembers. 'This feeble political adventure, this attempt to export a still unproved revolution, marked the beginning of the end. Our bureaucratic state, rotten to the core, took no serious measures to rehabilitate the veterans and so it aggravated the situation. In the majority of towns, officials just pouted, tucked in their satiated bellies, grandly puffed themselves up and, like pharisees, began to pronounce, "We didn't send you to Afghanistan."'[29]

The Afghan adventure did indeed mark the beginning of the end for the Soviet state. It spawned a whole class of disaffected veterans, the *afgantsy*, who returned home to a state which was embarrassed to acknowledge them and reluctant to offer support. They were a new underclass but a powerful one, which felt that it had been betrayed by the politicians in Moscow. Lebed's own sense of betrayal was marked by a belief that the army had been thrown carelessly into an unnecessary war and a conviction that, despite the eventual, ignominious withdrawal, the soldiers who fought in Afghanistan had not disgraced themselves.

Afghanistan is pain. Afghanistan is tears. Afghanistan is a memory. It is everything but it is not a disgrace. There were politicians who took certain decisions, reasonable, unreasonable, advisable, inadvisable. History will judge and set everything out on the bookshelves. For the unreasonable decisions, it was the soldiers who paid with their lives, their health, their wounds and their blood. Those who have begun wars and continue to organise them know full well that it is not they themselves, nor their children, nor their grandchildren, nor their friends, nor their acquaintances who will fight . . .

In Afghanistan, the Red Army of workers and peasants fought. The children of workers and peasants. It was not important who someone was there: a private, a major, a colonel. No one ever saw the sons of well-off parents there. And yet the soldiers did their duty to the letter. They didn't win that war and they couldn't win it – it wasn't that sort of situation. Moscow wasn't behind them, nor was Russia, but they didn't lose it – because they are the descendants of Suvorov's and Zhukov's soldiers.[30]

The lessons of the Afghan war have still not been learned. Thousands more descendants of Suvorov and Zhukov were to be thrown carelessly into the numerous brutal conflicts that marked the end of the Soviet Union and the tortured birth of its successor states. It is perhaps ironic that it was to be a distinguished *afganets*, Lebed's close colleague Pavel Grachev, who would later order Russian troops into a similarly bloody and disastrous campaign in Chechnya. And it was, no doubt in part, Lebed's memory of the cynical misuse of the army in Afghanistan by politicians that made him so ready to oppose Defence Minister Grachev's decision to launch the Chechen war.

Lebed left the Afghan war early. It staggered on for another six years, laying waste to Afghanistan, pock-marking its valleys with craters, killing or wounding thousands of its people and scattering over a million anti-personnel mines across the country. When the last Soviet column, followed by the last commander of the 40th Army, General Boris Gromov, left Afghanistan and returned across the Amu Darya bridge into the Soviet Union on 15 February 1989, the last arrogant foreign adventure of an empire on the verge of collapse came to an end. Afghanistan was but one of the symptoms of decay but, by the time Lebed left, the rot had set in and the Soviet state had begun to crumble.

In the Kremlin, the Brezhnev regime, derided in the Western press as an ailing gerontocracy riven by scandal and rivalry, was on its last legs. Yuri Andropov, Konstantin Chernenko and others were vying for the position of Brezhnev's heir. In the spring of 1982, the General Secretary's closest ally, the party ideologue Mikhail Suslov, died. As diplomats started to whisper about Brezhnev's increasing isolation and rumours about his poor health began to circulate, his daughter and son-in-law became involved in an exotic sexual and financial scandal, involving a circus performer, 'Boris the Gypsy'. The bizarre details, which quickly leaked and fuelled Moscow gossip, showed that Brezhnev could not even control his own family, let alone the state.

By October 1982 it was clear that Brezhnev's health had seriously deteriorated. He appeared on Lenin's mausoleum on 7 November for the parade on the anniversary of the revolution. Three days later, however, Gosteleradio interrupted its normal programming to play solemn music as the members of the Politburo hurried to form a 'funeral commission', which was usually headed by the man most likely to emerge as the new General Secretary of the Soviet Communist Party.

A formal announcement was made. Leonid Brezhnev was dead. The head of the funeral commission was the KGB Chairman, Yuri Andropov, a man reputedly keen to begin to reform the Soviet system. The 'era of stagnation' was over, and the pace of change was about to quicken until it overwhelmed those who sought to control it.

4

THE FRUNZE ACADEMY

'"It is all over!" said someone near him.
He caught the words and repeated them in his soul.
"Death is all over," he said to himself. "It is no more."
He drew in a breath, stopped in the midst of a sigh,
stretched out and died.'

COUNT TOLSTOY, *The Death of Ivan Ilyich*[1]

Leonid Brezhnev's corpse was escorted on a gun-carriage to the Hall of Columns in the former Assembly of the Nobility, now known as the House of Trade Unions. Inside the elegant, pale green building with its classical stucco pilasters, the corpse lay in state. It had been washed, powdered and painted with cosmetics to remove traces of the personal excesses of the last years of the dead leader's life and the worst ravages of the illness that had killed him. As the body lay on a bed of red cushions, amidst a sea of red carnations, tucked up under a red flag, the grandees of the Party, the state and the army filed slowly past, paying their last respects to the man whom, secretly, many of them had disliked and few had admired. There were members of the family too, even those who had been the cause of such disquieting gossip during the last few months.

The grim-faced leaders of the fraternal socialist bloc and the most senior members of the Soviet government, all wearing black and red armbands as a sign of their comradely mourning, took it in turns to form a guard of honour around the corpse, watching over it through the dark hours of the night, as though to ensure that the soul of their godless colleague remained for ever trapped in its lifeless shell and was not somehow spirited away to face its

final reckoning. On the faces of those waiting by the corpse for
the moment when army officers, dressed in their finest parade
uniforms, arrived to take it to its last resting-place, there was no
trace of the tears which had run freely down the cheeks of those
present at the obsequies of earlier dictators. Leonid Ilyich
Brezhnev was a man who had inspired neither love nor fear; so, as
his colleagues gazed at his corpse, they felt neither grief nor relief
at his passing, merely anxiety about the future.

On the morning of the funeral, the General Secretary's remains
were mounted on a gun-carriage and officers with sabres drawn,
slow-marching in the traditional Russian goose-step, led a military
parade from the House of Trade Unions, past the Gosplan building and the National Hotel into Red Square, which had been
decorated with red and black banners for the occasion. On the history museum at the entrance to the square, opposite St Basil's
Cathedral, there was a huge portrait of the dead leader. To the
repeated strains of Chopin's *Marche funèbre*, the military parade –
a fitting tribute to the man who had done more than any of his
predecessors to confirm the army's position at the heart of Soviet
society – made its way towards the Kremlin walls, coming to a halt
in front of Lenin's mausoleum. There were dull speeches, devoid
of any personal affection for the dead leader, and the carefully
selected groups of workers listening to them on platforms around
the square looked bored. When the speeches ended, the atmosphere changed. Brezhnev's widow, Viktoria, and his daughter,
Galina, kissed the corpse's forehead in the old Russian Orthodox
fashion. At the sight of this unplanned gesture, tears at last began
to run down the cheeks of some of Brezhnev's closest Politburo
colleagues, Chernenko, Tikhonov and Marshal Ustinov. When
the widow, overcome with grief, had turned away from the corpse,
it was taken behind the mausoleum and buried by the Kremlin
wall, not far from the place where Stalin had ended up in 1961
after his dramatic, nocturnal removal from the mausoleum, which
he had shared with Lenin for eight years. When it was lowered
into the ground, one of the straps gave way and the dead leader
was jolted on his bed of red silk as the coffin landed a second too
early on the cold, hard earth at the bottom of the grave.

The new General Secretary and his Politburo colleagues threw
handfuls of soil on to the coffin. When they returned to the
mausoleum, army officers filled in the grave. At the sound of a

siren from a nearby factory, everyone in Red Square stood to attention and observed three minutes of silence; sirens sounded as the pre-arranged signal for silence at similar ceremonies and parades all over the Soviet Union. At the end of the funeral, a military band of fifteen hundred men struck up marching tunes and troops from each branch of the armed forces paraded past the new General Secretary. It was the biggest and most elaborate funeral ceremony Moscow had seen since the death of Stalin nearly thirty years before.

At the Frunze Military Academy, which Alexander Lebed had entered in July, funeral parades had a special significance. The academy provided a 'funeral team' which organised and carried out much of the ceremonial for important funerals. Soon after he entered the academy, Lebed became part of the funeral team, which was traditionally made up of Airborne officers.

'I am reminded that I studied at the academy from 1982 to 1985,' he remembers. 'During this period, no less than three General Secretaries departed this life. And there were Marshals of the Soviet Union Bagramyan and Ustinov too; as well as Pelshe, a member of the Politburo. And a mass of other less well-known but no less significant figures. We certainly had our work cut out. We rushed around from funeral to funeral like the fire brigade.'[2] On the orders of Colonel Makarov, deputy commandant of the Moscow garrison, Lebed was often given the job of carrying the deceased's portrait. This task, with such obvious overtones of destiny, was certainly appropriate to the Napoleonic ambition of Alexander Lebed. Yet, his friend Valery Vostrotin joked that he had been chosen for it 'because of the natural gentleness of his face'.[3]

From his vantage point behind the photograph of the deceased, Lebed watched how the Soviet Union bade farewell to the Brezhnev era, as it paid its last respects to some of the Soviet leader's closest colleagues and most senior subordinates. It was not a pleasant sight. Lebed was revolted by the petty jealousy and hypocrisy which often surrounded the funeral ceremonies. People would comment snobbishly on the number of wreaths that were displayed, how many medals had been pinned to the deceased's chest, or the fact that some important organisation or other had not sent a message of condolence. Often the most important facts of the deceased's life were forgotten in the tributes that were paid to him. At the funeral of Lieutenant-General Germashkevich, who had fought through the Second World War and been decorated nine times, Lebed was ashamed when none of the tributes mentioned the General's outstanding war record. Instead, they concentrated on his fondness for hunting expeditions, a fact which was clearly of much greater significance to the *nomenklatura* who attended state funerals.

As Lebed began his studies at the Frunze Academy, the new General Secretary, Yuri Andropov, settled into his post and began the process of reform which disturbed the cosy existence of the *nomenklatura*. Andropov's main concern was not military reform but the elimination of corruption, which had become such an evident characteristic of the Brezhnev years. His aim was to shake up the old Brezhnevite social contract, the essence of which is best summed up in a phrase, often repeated at the time: 'We pretend to work and they pretend to pay us.' Although the KGB portrayed its former boss as a whisky-drinking, jazz-loving liberal, Andropov was in fact a strict disciplinarian who believed that good order was the solution to the Soviet Union's problems. 'Introducing good order doesn't require any capital investment whatever, but it can produce great results,' he told machine-tool workers in January 1983.[4]

He had begun his campaign to crack down on corruption during his period as head of the KGB. It was he who had insisted, partly perhaps as a means of applying pressure on the ailing Brezhnev to make him his heir-apparent, that corruption investigations should even include the General Secretary's own family. When he himself became General Secretary, he sacked several ministers who were suspected of running black-market businesses.

Andropov's fundamental goal was to make the Soviet system work properly according to its own laws. This required him to be relatively authoritarian, but it also implied a radical shift from the prevailing concept of 'socialist legality' to a less overtly partisan concept of legality, where the law meant what it said and a citizen might begin to rely on a more objective interpretation of it. It was not until the emergence of Mikhail Gorbachev as General Secretary that this idea was pushed to its logical conclusion but already, under Andropov, it helped to increase the pressure for change and to constitute a threat to the Party's hegemony.

Whether Andropov could have squared the circle and preserved the Party's power in a Soviet Union based on the rule of law is doubtful. There had already been a fundamental challenge to the Party's legitimacy. In Afghanistan, Alexander Lebed and his brother officers had watched the destruction of the notion of the historical inevitability of communism, upon which the Party's legitimacy was based. If the forward march of socialism was not inevitable – and clearly in Afghanistan, where it had been brought to an abrupt halt, it was not – then the basis of the Party's legitimacy, together with its position as final arbiter and the vanguard of history's most progressive class, the proletariat, was under direct threat.

It was not just Afghanistan, either. In Poland, General Wojciech Jaruzelski had imposed martial law to save the Polish comrades from a trade union-led challenge to their authority. As the cracks in the Soviet system began to grow bigger, the Soviet leadership was growing less and less able to deal with them. The Soviet Union was passing from the 'era of stagnation' to an era of funerals; the old men of the Party were dying off. Even Andropov himself, who perhaps had a better understanding than most of the challenges that awaited the Soviet Union in the years ahead, was dead in little more than a year after taking office.

With the Party's legitimacy under threat, the role of the army and particularly the Airborne Forces was likely to be ever more crucial in preserving the Kremlin's authority in the future. Whether or not the officers and lecturers at the Frunze Academy understood this, they had now entered the most critical decade in the Soviet Union's history. The lessons they learned in the academy's classrooms and on its training grounds would be vital in determining whether or not Moscow could preserve its empire. Perhaps those officers like Lebed and his friends Valery Vostrotin and Ivan Babichev, who entered the academy after service in Afghanistan, were in the best position to understand that the tides of history were beginning to turn away from the Soviet Communist Party.

As Lebed stepped off the train at Narofominsk, near Moscow, and strode into the main hall of the Frunze Military Academy, he was entering a Russian military institution which predated the Bolshevik period. Under the Tsars, it had been known as the *Alexandrovskoye Uchilishche*, the Alexandrov Academy, which was renowned as one of the most elite military establishments in the Russian empire. It remained staunchly loyal to the Romanovs for as long as it could hold out during the revolution, but in 1918 the Bolsheviks took it over, and Stalin later changed its name to honour one of the 'heroes of the civil war', M. V. Frunze.

The new choice of name was a strange one. Frunze was one of the earliest of Stalin's military leaders to die in suspicious circumstances. He passed away on the operating table of a clinic to which he had been taken without complaining of any particular illness. The cause of death appeared to have been an overdose of the drugs which had been prescribed to him. In the 1930s, when Stalin's paranoia about his own generals reached its height, other military leaders followed Frunze to an early grave. The academy's name was thus a conspicuous reminder of the darkest days of the Party's troubled relationship with the officer corps.

Nevertheless, despite these sombre associations, the Frunze Academy had managed to preserve its Tsarist predecessor's reputation as one of the most prestigious institutions in the army. Lebed's entry into it was an important career move, offering the promise of access to senior levels of command unavailable to those who had not passed out from it. In this respect, it was roughly the equivalent of the British Army's Staff College at Camberley.

From Lebed's point of view, the most important fact about it was that it was almost unheard of for an officer to be given command of an Airborne regiment without graduating from Frunze. The exceptions to this rule were very rare, and only consisted of officers who had graduated from equivalent colleges which provided specialist training at staff-officer level for other branches of the army. The most prominent example of this type was Vladislav Achalov, a future commanding officer of the Airborne Forces, who was given command of the Ryazan Airborne regiment after graduating from the Malinovsky Academy of Armoured Warfare.

Lebed joined the Frunze Academy with some of the brightest officers of his generation. Many of them had fought in Afghanistan and all of them were exceptional. Lebed's group of sixteen included Yuri Popov, Alexander Kolmakov, Valery Vostrotin, who was already a Hero of the Soviet Union, and Ivan Babichev, who later showed real heroism by refusing to massacre civilians in Chechnya.

Life at the academy was civilised, providing a welcome return to some of the creature comforts which officers serving in Afghanistan had been forced to abandon. For Lebed and other married officers, there was the chance to enjoy time with the family. There was time too to travel to Moscow to visit the theatre and the ballet. The most civilised aspect of the academy, however, was the relatively open environment within which issues affecting the Soviet armed forces were discussed. The Frunze Academy was more than simply a training centre for staff officers, it was also a research facility where problems of military theory and strategic planning for the future of the armed forces were considered. In addition, Lebed's group of Airborne officers knew and trusted each other. They were confident that, among themselves, they could speak openly, without fear of being reported for expressing their opinions. Lebed and his colleagues were able to discuss frankly political problems and the role which the army might have to play in solving them in the future.

This spirit of openness and relative freedom of thought was not a new phenomenon. In 1948, when many army officers were among the millions Stalin had consigned to the labour camps, a rebellion broke out at one of the most notorious camps in the 'Gulag' system – Vorkuta, in the Arctic region of European Russia. It was organised and led by a group of army officers who were all graduates of the Frunze Military Academy and full of the independent spirit that it seemed to encourage. None of them had ever belonged to the Communist Party, and all of them had fought against Germany. They disarmed and killed the KGB troops guarding their camp, liberated a neighbouring camp, and marched on Vorkuta. They were only defeated when paratroopers and dive-bombers were sent in against them.

Lebed may not have been aware of this incident when he went to the academy, but it illustrates both the fierce independence and the close personal loyalty of the tightly-knit community of Frunze graduates. Lebed's own independent spirit, which at times bordered on insubordination and was later to lead him into open conflict with the Defence Ministry and the Kremlin, was thus very much in the Frunze tradition.

His tendency towards insubordination emerged again soon after his arrival at Frunze, during the intensive examination period for new staff officers. Already irritated at the fact that his group of

Airborne officers had been instructed by non-commissioned officers on the staff of the academy to perform a series of humiliating chores, such as picking up litter and cutting grass with a penknife attached to a stick, he eventually made his frustration known during an altercation with a group of more senior officers who were starting a course at the academy as external students.

At the end of the written examinations, the Airborne officers and the external students were ordered to do another chore; this time, roofing two large warehouses with slates. Despite their annoyance at being told to perform yet another menial task, the Airborne officers set about it with vigour, making their own ladder to climb up on to the roof of the warehouse. The external students, who were all at least one rank higher than Lebed and his colleagues, did not show the same initiative. For a while, they flapped about in the branches of a nearby tree, trying desperately to get on to the roof of their building. When they realised that they could not get from the tree to the roof of the warehouse, they came over to Lebed's group, pulled rank and demanded the ladder. Lebed told them that as they were sitting on a different roof, their rank was irrelevant. When one of them, a Lieutenant-Colonel, tried to seize the ladder, Lebed's fellow paratroopers jumped down from their roof, grabbed the ladder back and forcibly explained that stealing was a sin.

Lebed strongly objected to the menial tasks which he was ordered to perform because he felt that they debased the honour of an officer. His concept of an officer's honour is very old-fashioned; almost straight out of the nineteenth century. It may sound faintly ridiculous and not a little snobbish, with a good deal of similarity to the attitudes of the average British Colonel of an Indian Army regiment in the days of the Raj, but it is a very important part of his military and political outlook. Throughout his career, he appears always to have deeply resented being told to do things that he thought unworthy of an officer, whether picking up cigarette ends at the academy or dealing with peaceful demonstrations by Russian civilians during the *putsch* of August 1991.

> An officer must always be an officer. An officer who works on the side guarding the coffers of powerful businessmen, unloading lorries or putting slates on roofs, whether he wants to do it or not, will stop being an officer. If anyone thinks you can

plunge an officer in shit for a month and then pull him out, clean him up a bit and carry on, he is very much mistaken. This sort of operation does colossal moral damage to an officer's dignity. An officer digging a trench – yes! An officer dragging a field gun with soldiers – yes! That's a different matter. Any soldierly task, no matter how hard, is noble in its way. But cigarette ends or the humiliation of cutting grass with sticks – how can you measure the damage done to dignity, self-respect and honour? Where and at what levels of service in the future does this booby-trap work? Isn't it one of the sources of the unbearable caddishness, conceit and arrogance of seniors towards their juniors? Who knows how the former Captain (now a Major-General) pays off his old scores with the Lance-Corporal who was insolent to him back then?[5]

The concept of an officer's dignity should be even more important to the state, according to Lebed, than basic human dignity. 'In theory, everyone has a right to human dignity. In practice, sometimes they don't. But an officer's dignity is a special category. It presupposes the definite presence of human dignity. And, as a minimum, it should be of a higher order than it. Then the state can sleep soundly.'[6] Lebed's views on the officer's dignity were not, therefore, the cantankerous growling of a crusty staff officer but an analysis of an important aspect of *realpolitik* which, in the Soviet context, was particularly prescient. After all, the collapse of the officer corps' self-respect and the readiness of the Kremlin to expect its officers to put up with the most appalling conditions was the cause of serious trouble in the years ahead. When political circumstances began to change at an alarming speed, and Kremlin politicians turned desperately to the military to save money, to curry favour with the West or to help them to hang on to power, the last thing they considered was the dignity of their own officers. Yet, as Alexander Lebed realised, it should probably have been the first.

At ten o'clock on 31 August 1982, Lebed and all the officers who had passed their entrance examinations stood to attention in a corridor on the seventh floor of the academy. A small, grey-haired, rather ordinary-looking Colonel introduced himself and told the assembly to stand at ease. 'I am the director of your course,' he said. 'My surname is the same as that of the last

Russian Tsar – Romanov. My first names are the same as those of Suvorov [the great Russian strategist] – Alexander Vasilyevich.'

Behind the Colonel's unremarkable exterior, Lebed soon recognised considerable wisdom, subtlety and an understanding of human psychology. 'He led the course confidently, strictly and firmly, but no one objected because he was always fair,' says Lebed. 'He knew how to find a way out of any difficult situation. And there were quite a few of those in the early days. He could always manage to melt an obstacle with a smile . . . He always appeared where he was least expected. He was as methodical and scrupulous as a German. He loved grand military order and was able to inculcate a taste for it in us . . . In his hands, the course worked like clockwork. In my view (and not just mine), Alexander Vasilyevich was a sort of officer-tutor.'[7]

The Colonel's tact and diplomacy even helped to ensure, so Lebed says, that the 'political organs' were unable to reach into the course, a fact which must have greatly assisted freedom of thought and discussion. 'We lived and learned as though in the bosom of Christ, as they say.'

Colonel Romanov was popular with his students, who appreciated the sense of discipline, honour and humanity he passed on to them. 'All of us students of Alexander Vasilyevich Romanov remember, love him and are grateful to him for what he instilled in us. And the most important of this is always, everywhere, however high destiny may raise you or however low it may sink you, remain a human being and never, not for any money, squander your honour.'[8] The deep impression that Colonel Romanov made on Lebed, together with his own views on the dignity of an officer, perhaps partly explains the disgust which he later felt at the commercial activities of senior officers.

Lebed's admiration for Colonel Romanov was not, however, matched by a similar feeling for other members of the academy staff. Although several of the lecturers taught clearly and well, demanding a great deal of their students, many were simply not up to the job. The problem was that the academy had all too often become a convenient place in which to deposit officers who did not fit in elsewhere.

'Everyone in the army has their ceiling. Not everyone is aware of it, but we all have it,' says Lebed, who soon recognised a certain type of officer who ended up at the academy:

He was a good battalion commander, went to the academy, left to become deputy commander of a regiment. He worked confidently – good lad. They made him commanding officer of a regiment and here, in the majority of cases, he hit his ceiling. The two most difficult positions in the army are company commander and commanding officer of a regiment. The officer tries, struggles like a fish, comes in early, goes home late – but to no purpose. Things get worse and worse in the regiment. The worse things get in the regiment, the more he gets upset, shouts and swears. The more he shouts and swears, the worse things get in the regiment. He shouldn't shout, he should manage but he can't.

His wise older bosses have a look at him; well, he doesn't drink and he doesn't smoke. He is trying again, he is not a fool and he doesn't cheat. But where shall we send him, such a ne'er-do-well? To be a teacher. And so there is a vicious circle: those who can, do, and those who can't, teach. And those who can't even do that, teach others how to teach.[9]

Lebed's frustration with the poor quality of the teaching staff at the academy was compounded by his belief in the crucial importance of the academy to the army. He believed that military research and training facilities were some of the most vital organs of the army.

The army is a deeply conservative institution and, in the main, this is a good thing. But when the heart of the army, its highest academic institutions, are submerged in conservatism, sink in routine and drown in dogmatism, it can lead to catastrophic consequences. Why are they the heart of the army? We can turn to a generally known truth. The general staff is the army's brains. No one would argue with that. Academia generally, and the Frunze Military Academy in particular, can be compared with the heart because, to anatomise the army again, the academies feed the other parts which make up the military organism, including its brain, with fresh blood.[10]

The academy's innate conservatism worried Lebed. It had an important role to play in the development of military theory and strategic planning for the future, but it was hamstrung by its anachronistic approach. Despite the enormous changes in the nature of warfare since 1918, the basic three-year course at Frunze had not changed. The period since the civil war had brought huge changes in tank warfare and military aviation but also the development of wholly new types of combat, involving aerospace, rockets and airborne troops. Education about these new types of warfare, however, was simply crammed into the same basic course, which still insisted that students should master the detail of classical warfare, such as Hannibal's scheme for the capture of Carthage.

Furthermore, in addition to the plethora of military topics, students at the academy were expected to master an extensive course of *politpredmety*, political subjects, which included scientific communism, Marxist–Leninist philosophy, political economy and the history of the Communist Party of the Soviet Union. They were expected to read and summarise vast amounts of turgid, Communist prose before each seminar and, not surprisingly, most of them either copied or asked their wives to do the work for them.

The problem of a crowded syllabus was aggravated by a lack of information technology and the constantly changing preferences of the academy's principals, who came from different branches of the army and thus attached differing priorities to the study of various types of warfare. In the confusion, the teaching of important concepts of modern warfare, such as the development of automatic command systems, was condensed and almost forgotten.

The weaknesses which Lebed noticed in the academy's programme were part of a much wider malaise in Soviet society and the Soviet economy. The illusion that living standards were rapidly improving and that soon the Soviet Union would overtake America did not last long after Brezhnev's death. Soon it became clear that the crisis was fundamental and that the army was at the heart of it. The deterioration in Soviet–American relations, combined with increasing competition in the development of military technology, had begun to place severe strains on the Soviet economy in recent years. Brezhnev had been determined to win the arms race, telling senior officers and defence industry chiefs at a conference in the Kremlin shortly before he died that 'lagging in this competition is inadmissible'.[11]

Andropov realised, however, that the competition was dangerously straining the Soviet economy and, although Konstantin
Chernenko, who replaced him as General Secretary in 1984,
tried to return to Brezhnev's policy of prioritising the military–
industrial sector, it was clear that change was becoming inevitable.
When Chernenko died in 1985, the Politburo at last decided that
the need for reform was now so urgent that a younger man, capable of taking the job seriously, was needed. Mikhail Gorbachev
was appointed General Secretary of the Communist Party in the
year Alexander Lebed passed out of the Frunze Academy.

Gorbachev knew, just as Lebed suspected from his analysis of
the education staff officers were receiving in modern warfare, that
the West was already vastly superior to the Soviet Union. There
was no chance of overtaking America, and when President Reagan
proposed an expensive new arms race in 'star wars' technology, it
became clear that the Soviet Union would never achieve
supremacy. At the same time, domestic pressure was growing for
improvements in living standards and greater personal freedom.
Gorbachev wanted a *rapprochement* with the West and a dramatic
reduction in military spending commitments. The military was
being squeezed, the role for which it had trained was changing
fundamentally, and the army was about to face a series of new and
very difficult problems. With its anachronistic programme and
uninspiring lecturers, the academy was ill-equipped to introduce
into the military sphere the 'new thinking' of which Gorbachev
spoke with such enthusiasm. Only the relatively liberal environment of the academy and its few good 'officer-tutors', perhaps,
gave Lebed and his Airborne colleagues an opportunity to appreciate, in their discussions together, the enormity of the changes in
the air.

Lebed's time at the academy was not always as comfortable as
it might have been. As a youth he had never been able to stay out
of hospital for long, and now, during a visit to a sports centre on
the banks of the river Nara, his hand slipped from a high bar and
he broke his forearm. When he went to the military hospital, the
army doctor – a Major who had been decorated with the Red
Star for his service in Afghanistan – was drunk. He told Lebed
that he was lucky because he was a surgeon and could operate on
his arm straight away. However, he said that there was only a 50
per cent chance that the operation would be a success with an

anaesthetic. Without anaesthetic, though, there was a 100 per cent chance of success, he said. He told Lebed to choose. Lebed watched the doctor prepare for the operation and wash his hands for what seemed an inordinate length of time. Then he chose the 100 per cent chance of success.

They smoked a cigarette together before the doctor stubbed his out and said, 'Shall we begin?' The operation took forty minutes – forty minutes of unforgettable pain.

The doctor had an original method of testing whether his surgery was working. When the two pieces of broken bone joined together and Lebed screamed, the doctor muttered, 'Good, good.' After about thirty minutes of the torture, during which time Lebed was either in a cold sweat or 'mooing like a cow', he felt an almost uncontrollable urge to box the doctor's ears. At that precise moment, either by intuition or perhaps because it had happened to him before, the doctor told a nurse to hold Lebed's right hand, so that he couldn't punch him. The drunken doctor's manipulation of Lebed's broken bone was altogether more accurate than his attempt to set it in plaster. After a while it began to ache, and Lebed had to visit another doctor to have it reset. He too was drunk, but he did a reasonable job and Lebed's arm began to heal.

It was not just the doctors who were drunk. In those days, almost everyone seemed to be drunk almost all of the time. Vodka was a cure-all, a religion, a friend. It was an escape route, a relief from the monotony of Soviet life. It had been cheap and widely available under Brezhnev, a useful, modern form of 'bread and circuses', but to Mikhail Gorbachev it was the root cause of much that was wrong with Soviet society. Gorbachev believed that vodka was one of the main reasons why the Soviet system was not working and, as Alexander Lebed prepared to graduate from the Frunze Academy, Gorbachev sent his party of *apparatchiks* into the distilleries to smash up vodka bottles. Henceforth, vodka was to be rationed to two bottles per person a month and people were encouraged to drink mineral water instead. The new General Secretary (*generalny sekretar*)'s decision earned him the derisive nickname of *mineralny sekretar* ('mineral secretary') and helped to undermine the little personal popularity he enjoyed. It is difficult to imagine anything that he could conceivably have done to upset and annoy more the normally placid Russian population, which had been cowed into apathy by sixty years of communism. To smash a Russian's vodka bottle is like stealing a Frenchman's wine or shooting his mistress.

On 15 May 1985, the country was still drinking heavily, but on the morning of 16 May, the Politburo expected everyone to have given up. It made it a little difficult for Lebed and his colleagues to celebrate their graduation from the academy. There was much to celebrate, too: Lebed's group of Airborne officers had passed out with unusually high grades. Nine members of the group of sixteen gained a distinction and 'red' diplomas, two (Yuri Popov and Valery Gaidukevich) won gold medals, two became 'candidates of honour', and all were awarded 'excellent' marks for physical training. The exceptional quality of the group was shown by the fact that, subsequently, six of them became Generals – Kolmakov, Popov, Babichev, Gaidukevich, Vostrotin and Lebed. That fact alone perhaps explains the self-confidence, to the point of insolence, that Lebed later showed both to politicians and to other senior officers. The fact that he belonged to such a distinguished group has always been a particular source of pride.

Not surprisingly, after such an impressive performance in their final examinations, Lebed and his friends were keen to celebrate their success in the usual way. Despite the 'mineral secretary's' vodka-smashing campaign, the Airborne officers and two of their favourite lecturers, both Colonels, decided to head for the centre of Moscow to celebrate their results and show what they thought of Gorbachev's *ukaz* (decree). They managed to soak up a large amount of the 'little water' at the Slavyansky Bazaar restaurant and then made towards the Kremlin. At the entrance to Red Square, however, as they began to sing merrily, they were stopped by a policeman, who was unusually polite, addressing the group as 'comrade officers' and telling them that singing in Red Square was not very pleasant. He stepped aside and allowed the officers to make up their own minds. Impressed by the policeman's tact and respect for their uniform, Lebed's group decided not to sing in Red Square. 'Maybe it was for the best,' he said as they parted company and went their different ways to the new commands which awaited them.[12]

To Lebed's great surprise, after only two months as second-in-command of a regiment, he was appointed commanding officer of the 331st parachute regiment in Kostroma. The divisional commander accompanied him to his new posting in an An-2 transport plane. It was drizzling and there was a cold wind blowing as they landed. The regiment was formed up, standing to attention, on a parade ground which had been unevenly covered with asphalt. The divisional commander introduced Lebed to the regiment with the words, 'You've got ten seconds to explain that you're the new commander of the regiment,' before climbing back into the aeroplane and leaving Lebed, for once speechless, to his new command.

When Lebed made a tour of inspection of his new regiment, he was horrified at its condition. His predecessor, Lieutenant-Colonel Bashkevich, had clearly hardly ever visited his men in their barracks. Lebed had asked him to show him round, and Bashkevich had simply pointed at the barrack blocks of the regiment's three battalions, explained that it was impossible to see the depot from where they were standing, climbed into a jeep and left. Lebed set off on his own to inspect the regiment. 'The most cursory inspection yielded the most lamentable results,' he said.

I was staggered by the ignorance and squalor in the regiment. The newest-looking building was certainly no less than forty years old and the exercise area was all cluttered up. It wasn't surprising because I couldn't find a single bin or skip. In the park, metal objects had been deposited, all bunched up together in a completely wild heap with quite a number of battered gates, crooked sheds and vehicles standing in the mud. The depot area was overgrown with weeds. The squalor inside the barracks was particularly shocking. The regiment only had two barracks, and in addition to appalling overcrowding (which is being more or less objective), there was a totally apathetic attitude towards their maintenance. It is enough to say that there were no drying rooms and no everyday living rooms in any company. The lavatories and washbasins presented a shocking spectacle of disintegration . . . In all the sleeping area, there were just two or three lamps hanging from the dust-covered ceiling. Senior recruits slept as authorised, whilst the juniors just slept anywhere they could. Some slept on a mattress, some covered themselves with a mattress. Some had a blanket but no sheets . . . These were barracks in the most vile sense of the word, and everyone who ended up in them felt himself simply bound to do something criminal.[13]

Lebed returned to his quarters in a mood of deep depression. As he sat in his office, thinking about how he could begin to drag the regiment out of such appalling chaos, he heard voices singing drunkenly on the parade ground outside. His first thought was that he was hallucinating, but despite shaking his head he could still hear the voices. He went out on to the steps of the building and there, below him, was a group of twenty junior officers. None of them was very drunk, but all were clearly quite merry. When they saw Lebed, they began to sing an old Russian folk song, 'Stenka Razin'. They were looking at him, perhaps expecting him to shake his fists at them and put them all on a charge. Instead, with as cheerful an expression as he could muster, he descended the steps and joined the crowd. 'You're not singing it very well, boys,' he said. 'Let's do it together.' He joined in and sang the last two verses on his own. The young officers fell silent and, when he had finished singing, Lebed said, 'Well, that's enough. It happens. Now go home and tomorrow let's start to serve.'

When the last of the officers had shuffled slowly away, Lebed returned to his office and put a telephone call through to the commander of the Airborne Forces, General Dmitry Sukhorukhov. 'Comrade commander,' he said, 'from my personal inspection, I am convinced that the 331st parachute regiment is a pitiable and shameful parody of an Airborne unit. In order to get it back into shape, I am asking you to let me have special authority for the transposition of personnel and additional finance.' General Sukhorukhov, who had taken over command of the Airborne Forces from their founder, General Margelov, seemed to appreciate the directness of the appeal and the fact that, on his first day of service as commanding officer of the regiment, by-passing all intermediaries, Lebed had come straight to him. He was given the authority he wanted and, a little while later, the money too.

Lebed was very fortunate. Conditions in other parts of the Soviet Army were similar, and often even worse. 'During my service in the Perm region, I lived for nearly a year in a tent in temperatures which, in winter, often fell below minus thirty,' one sergeant told me. 'And our food was so thin and inadequate that

I joined the queue in the officers' mess. When they stopped me I told them that not even dogs would touch our food.' In the remote outposts of the Soviet empire, ordinary conscript soldiers were often forgotten and left to their miserable, squalid fate. The fact that Lebed was so quickly able to create better conditions for his soldiers is not only a testament to his leadership skills but also, perhaps, another example of the political significance which was increasingly attached to the Airborne Forces.

In the new atmosphere of *glasnost* (openness), criticism of conditions in the armed forces soon began to appear in the press. In some of the more liberal newspapers it was not confined to the conditions of ordinary soldiers but appeared to Lebed to be a deliberate attempt to denigrate the army's traditions and undermine its role in Soviet society. The criticisms irritated him, not because *glasnost* was unnecessary but because the press used it to pour contempt on the army.

Yet *glasnost* was the real engine of change in the Soviet Union. Already, during Lebed's time at the Frunze Academy, people had seen how dangerous it was to live in a society which kept everything hidden from its citizens. In April 1986 it had taken the Soviet authorities three days to own up to the fact that there had been a major explosion inside the RBMK nuclear reactor at Chernobyl power station in Ukraine. Even then, the authorities were only forced to admit that the accident had taken place because the Studsvik nuclear plant in Sweden detected radioactivity thirty times the normal level and Swedish diplomats presented the Kremlin with the evidence of their scientists that radionuclides were escaping from a nuclear reactor.[14]

Chernobyl had been the catalyst which exposed the Soviet system to *glasnost*. Now, however, *glasnost* itself was to act as the catalyst for another explosion, the consequences of which were no less violent than those of Chernobyl and resulted, ultimately, in the destruction of the Soviet Union itself. In the next few years, the Kremlin was to turn more than once to Alexander Lebed, newly appointed to command the 106th Guards Airborne Division at Tula, and his fellow paratroop officers, in a desperate attempt to contain the storm.

5

THE CAUCASUS

*'Why talk of chains?' she retorted. 'We are both free
human beings. Yes,' she went on, looking thought-
fully at the floor and still smoothing his hair with
her hand, 'so much I've lived through these last
days, so much that I never had an idea of before!'*

IVAN TURGENEV, *On the Eve*[1]

Sumgait spreads like a cancer along the shores of the Caspian Sea
north of Baku, capital of Azerbaijan. From a distance, in the
summer, the steel pipes, stacks and chimneys of its vast petro-
chemical complex seem to shimmer and melt into a silver heat
haze. In winter, though, colder light reveals starkly the monstrous,
pollution-belching absurdity of this monument to Leonid
Brezhnev's Transcaucasian industrial fantasy.

Sumgait is a part of a grandiose network of installations
designed to harness and process the resources of the Caspian Sea
for Soviet industry. Offshore, just over the horizon, there is
even a city of grim apartment blocks which rise eerily from the
sea on a thin slither of rock, providing a depressing home to the
thousands of oil workers who toil on crumbling rigs nearby.
The town of Sumgait itself, though, is on the flat land which
stretches all the way along the shores of the Caspian, from the
mountains of Daghestan in the north to the Iranian border south
of Baku.

Rusting 'nodding donkeys' creaking in the fields by the coast
road testify to the millions of tonnes of kerosene, naphtha, *mazot*
and petroleum that have been produced from the rich oil deposits
in the area. For centuries, flaming tongues of natural gas have

seeped through fissures in the sandstone rocks nearby, causing the ancients to marvel at the power that lay beneath the earth and to worship the flames and their god, Zoroastra. The hideousness of modern Sumgait belies its magical past, though. It is overwhelmingly bleak, and even the train on the main line from Moscow to Baku avoids it.

In February 1988, however, when the full force of the region's history – long submerged beneath layers of Soviet denial – erupted in an orgy of ethnic violence, it was as if a burst of flame or a spark of combustible, subterranean energy had suddenly engulfed the town. For two days, Sumgait became the forum for a hysterical ethnic pogrom. It was as though a long psychological fault-line, filled with a heavy emotional charge and stretching through the region of Nagorny Karabakh* into Armenia, had suddenly ignited and poured out into Sumgait the centuries of suppressed fear and hatred between Azeris and their Armenian neighbours.

Demonstrations in Yerevan, the Armenian capital, had lit a charge which exploded at the other end of the fault-line in Sumgait several days later. The reason for the demonstrations was the treatment of Armenians by Azeris in the autonomous mountain enclave of Nagorny Karabakh, which lay inside Azerbaijan on its border with Armenia.

Mikhail Gorbachev's policy of *glasnost* had encouraged Soviet citizens to express themselves openly and without fear. On 13 February, Karabakh Armenians who claimed that the Azeri government was deliberately starving the region of investment in order to persuade them to leave, demonstrated in Stepanakert, the regional capital, where they demanded union with Armenia. Six days later, their demands found an echo in a large demonstration in Yerevan, in which thousands marched in support of Karabakh. When the regional Supreme Soviet in Karabakh, instead of awaiting orders from Moscow, voted by 110 to 17 for union with Armenia, the Kremlin appeared to hesitate, and Armenian demonstrators again took to the streets in a series of almost continuous demonstrations. On 22 February, over a hundred thousand people converged on Yerevan's Opera House Square.

* Also known, erroneously, as Nagorno-Karabakh.

The First Secretary of the Armenian Supreme Soviet, Karen Demirchyan, tried to calm the situation by announcing that an unpopular decision to allow the construction of an environmentally destructive synthetic rubber plant would be reviewed. The atmosphere in Karabakh and throughout Armenia, however, had already begun to turn ugly. Demirchyan's attempts to explain that the political status of Nagorny Karabakh was not open to discussion only served to provoke the crowds to greater frenzy. The Politburo tried to lend a hand by sending its representatives to help the local leadership in the two republics to reach a hasty compromise. Yegor Ligachev and Georgy Razumovsky flew to Baku, and Alexander Yakovlev and Vladimir Dolgikh went to Yerevan. They were too late, and, in any case, they had failed to understand the power of the rampant nationalism which had been kept well hidden for so long in the Soviet Union but was now being paraded aggressively by determined Armenian activists. It was not long before the Azeris responded in kind.

Gruesome stories began to circulate in Azerbaijan of the persecution of Armenia's Azeri minority. The blood-curdling tales of refugees from Kafan in southern Armenia caused a riot in Baku on 24 February. It was, nevertheless, contained and dealt with relatively quickly by the security forces. On 28 February, however, news reached Sumgait that two Azeris had been killed in the town of Agdam, which is just to the east of Nagorny Karabakh. The report provoked indignation among Azeris that the Armenians had gone so far as to attack civilians inside Azerbaijan and outside Nagorny Karabakh. The brutality of the Azeri response in Sumgait shocked the Soviet Union. Mobs surged through the streets and, for two days, Armenians in the town were hunted by their neighbours. The local police appeared to stand by and watch as Armenians were dragged from their apartments, hospital beds and seats on public transport. Tass, the official Soviet news agency, reported that '32 people were killed and 197 injured' in the riots, but the Armenians claimed that hundreds of their compatriots had been killed.

As news reached Moscow of the gangs of bloodthirsty Azeris stalking their Armenian prey through the streets of Sumgait, Gorbachev was haunted by the ghosts of history and the fear that there might be an even bloodier backlash in Armenia. 'Could they really erase from their memory the genocide of 1915, when the Turks slaughtered a million and a half Armenians and scattered two millions throughout the world?' he asked.[2]

Yet it was not simply the threat of an even bloodier Armenian retaliation that worried Gorbachev. What was now of greatest concern to him was the effect that the deteriorating situation might have on his policy of *perestroika* (reconstruction) and on the unity of the Soviet Union. He had no doubt who was to blame for the crisis: 'In both republics many highly placed officials had soiled themselves by corruption. But when *perestroika* began and they sensed that the ground was shaking under them, it was these elements who tried to provoke ethnic conflicts. The national feelings of people became the object of merciless exploitation. In their hands Karabakh was a mine laid underneath *perestroika*.'[3]

Yet, as Gorbachev read his intelligence reports from Yerevan and Baku about the unfolding drama in the Transcaucasus, he probably realised at last how unpredictable and uncontrollable was the genie that *perestroika* had released from its bottle. Throughout the Soviet Union, *glasnost* and 'new thinking' had begun to generate an attitude of impatient iconoclasm towards existing structures. In the non-Russian republics, campaigns by newly legalised, informal associations on cultural or environmental themes were quickly and inevitably underscored by an ethnic leitmotif. Often, as in the Baltic States, they drew on widespread public resentment of Russian domination, which fed the desire for independence, but sometimes they stoked up ancient inter-ethnic hatreds too.

At the same time, in his desperate attempt to use *perestroika* as a means of patching up the Soviet system, Gorbachev had realised that better relations with the West were of greater importance than the continued suppression of Eastern Europe. So he loosened the Kremlin's grip on its satellites and the tides of change began to sweep across Eastern Europe, stirring up demands for independence and the withdrawal of Soviet troops. The pressure for change which Gorbachev had released in Eastern Europe, however, could not be held back at the Soviet border. The captive nations inside the Soviet Union, among them Azerbaijan and Armenia, began to hope that they too might soon be free. In those countries, as so often in history, the national movements were given a boost by the presence of a traditional enemy, all too easily portrayed on both sides as being aided by Moscow.

The disturbances in Yerevan, Baku, Stepanakert and Sumgait gave a powerful impetus to the national independence movements in both countries. To the Armenian 'Karabakh Committee', which helped to co-ordinate the demonstrations, Karabakh was a symbol of Armenia's struggle for freedom. A beautiful mountain fortress region, it had been the traditional refuge of Armenians from persecution throughout history. In Karabakh, Armenian nationalism was more extreme than even the wildest *dashnak* (the old ruling party) sentiments in Yerevan. It was combined with a messianic view of Armenia's ancient Christian identity, a strong military tradition and a longing for revenge for the genocide of the Armenian nation. To any Armenian, Karabakh was the most Armenian of all places, a symbol of national resistance. Gorbachev knew that the passions stirred up by Karabakh on the streets of Yerevan and Baku could lead to the beginnings of the disintegration of the Soviet Union. Behind his expressions of concern at the bloodshed in Sumgait, Gorbachev's real worry was the threat to the Soviet Union itself:

> The massacre in Sumgait produced universal outrage, everyone was shaken. At the same time, sympathy was shown in the Muslim republics for the people of their faith. Events threatened to get out of control ... I demanded that those responsible should be swiftly brought to justice, and that steps must be taken so that chaos would not 'spill over' again. However, I also demanded that we avoid further attempts at a 'quick fix' in favour of working together patiently with our Armenian and Azerbaijani comrades.

Yet Gorbachev could not afford simply to work patiently. He was facing 'the most fundamental of Soviet dilemmas – how to democratise and modernise the largest country on the globe while maintaining the last multinational empire'.[5] The Sumgait pogrom had convinced him that there was potentially much more at stake than a few broken heads in an ugly race riot. What was happening in the Transcaucasus was a real threat to the continued existence of the Soviet Union. Gorbachev ordered troops into Sumgait to stop the pogrom.

As so often in moments of crisis, the Airborne troops were the Kremlin's preferred choice for the task. The 104th Guards

Airborne Division was already based at Kirovabad (now Gyandzha), but it had been ordered to Yerevan as a precautionary measure when the demonstrations started there. When rioting began in Sumgait, its commanders were told to return immediately to Azerbaijan to put down the anti-Armenian pogrom. They were joined by the 137th Ryazan Regiment from the division, which Alexander Lebed, who had just been promoted to full Colonel, was soon appointed to command – the 106th Guards Airborne.

The two units soon restored order, despite the fact that they were ordered to remain unarmed, and helped to mop up the blood from the streets of Sumgait. When Lebed later saw the damage done during the rioting, he was shocked. 'I was in Sumgait a little later and there I saw, for the first time after Afghanistan, in my own country (as I considered it then), burnt-out lorries and buses, fire-blackened homes but the bleached hair of people who had lived through terror and eyes, eyes. Then there was a scent of medieval sadism, bestial, inhuman cruelty, richly mixed with ignorance . . .'[6]

In the months after Sumgait, the atmosphere remained tense, threatening at any moment to flare up into violence again. All the time, under the tide of mutual loathing which Azeris and Armenians felt for each other, the current of national sentiment began to gain strength and feed the desire for independence.

Far away in Tula, in the divisional headquarters of the 106th Airborne, Colonel Lebed was trying to acquaint himself with his new command. His division was scattered over a large part of European Russia. There were two regiments with him in Tula, one airborne and one artillery, together with three service battalions and an air transport squadron, but the rest of the division was far away. The 331st Airborne Regiment was six hundred kilometres away in Kostroma. The 137th Regiment from Ryazan, 200 kilometres away, was in Azerbaijan, and the Efremov Regiment was 150 kilometres away. It made Lebed's task of getting to know his new division very difficult.

His predecessor as divisional commander, Major General Serdyechny, had not left the division in good shape. An abrupt, bad-tempered man, he was widely disliked and the failure of his leadership was evident wherever Lebed went. When he visited the Kostroma regiment, which he had commanded a year and a half earlier, he was horrified at its condition. Much of his good work had been undone and the slovenliness typical of much of the Soviet Army had now begun to creep back in. Much to the obvious discomfort of the senior officers of the 331st, Lebed insisted on a full tour of inspection of the regiment. He was the Colonel commanding a guards division, and he expected a guards regiment to be a cut above the rest. His description of his tour of inspection is a portrait of a guards officer's horror at an obvious lack of discipline:

There was a sullen watchfulness from the moment I arrived at the regiment. It jarred on me. In my time, I had introduced a number of improvements into the regiment, leaving it on the up-turn. I had left happy people, who had begun to respect themselves and know their own strength and, to be honest, I had expected a completely different reception. When two people are gloomy, there is a personal reason for it, but when everyone looks gloomy and cross, you have to look for a general explanation. And I soon found it. The officers who were with me were busying themselves with checking their own sections, but I went round the whole regiment, simultaneously inspecting everything thoroughly. One, two, three . . . seventeen soldiers without belts.

'Yevgeny Yuryevich,' I addressed my question to Lieutenant-Colonel Savilov, the commanding officer of the regiment, 'what about the main guard room, what are we to make of that?'

'Comrade Colonel, the political officer has really overstepped the mark here. Allow me to report later!'

Several soldiers had dirty pieces of cardboard sewn to their jackets on the right side of their chests. I stopped one of them. 'What is this?' He was nonplussed. On a piece of cardboard over a shabby rag, the word 'guards' was written in paste.

'Yevgeny Yuryevich, what are we to make of this? Why is there such a shocking mockery of a guards badge?'

'Comrade Colonel, there weren't enough badges . . . the political officer . . . please allow me to explain later.'[7]

Lebed's insistence on discipline was not mere authoritarianism but the professional pride of a career officer who knew that it was what made the army work. The army was different from the rest of society, and discipline was its central principle.

Of course, it is both possible and necessary to restructure relations in the army. We can and must bring officers and soldiers more closely together. We can and must regularise the working day. We can and must compensate any serviceman materially and morally for his extra efforts. There is a lot we could do and it would be humanitarian and just and reasonable, but no, there never has been and there never will be a democratic army anywhere in the world. If it happens, you can call it whatever you want but not an army. An army without leadership, without the force of command, without discipline, is nothing more than a rabble. In any military engagement, half of it would run away and the other half would be beaten.[8]

As Lebed toured his new division during the summer of 1988, gradually improving the state of the regiments under his command, the situation in Azerbaijan, where the 137th was still stationed, continued to deteriorate. After the demonstrations in Yerevan and the pogrom in Sumgait, the Kremlin had employed its usual tactics in the aftermath of unrest: economic windowdressing and a political crackdown.

A package of economic and cultural reforms, including a plan for the construction of new housing and the promise of more Armenian television programmes, had been followed by an order disbanding the Karabakh Committee, several of whose members were arrested. The arrests had prompted a huge 'stay at home' protest in Yerevan on 26 March. Gorbachev tried desperately to persuade the Azeri and Armenian leaderships to agree to impose an acceptable compromise. The Politburo instructed them to come to an understanding, but they could not, and simply referred the matter back to Moscow for a decision.

On 12 May, the regional soviet in Nagorny Karabakh repeated its demand to be transferred to Armenia. Demonstrators took to the streets again in Stepanakert and began a general strike. Under the pressure of public opinion, the Supreme Soviet of Armenia echoed the demand for the transfer of Nagorny Karabakh. The Supreme Soviet of Azerbaijan immediately declared its implacable opposition and announced measures to strengthen Azerbaijan's hold on the region.

Gorbachev was losing patience. He told the Politburo on 6 June that he suspected that people in the higher levels of power in the republics were deliberately fanning the flames and trying to start a fight. 'The one thing that we can never agree to is to support one people to the detriment of another,' he said. 'We must never be blackmailed into this. We will not permit, we must in no case allow the truth to be sought through blood!'[9] As attitudes hardened and the Party leadership in both republics began to support the demonstrators' demands with increasing openness, it was clear that the possibility of a mediated settlement, satisfactory to both parties, had all but disappeared.

On 6 July demonstrators blockaded the airport in Yerevan, and on the 12th the Nagorny Karabakh soviet repeated its demand for secession from Azerbaijan. Faced with this dangerously escalating crisis, the Politburo could not make up its mind what to do. Andrei Gromyko, the Chairman of the Presidium of the Supreme Soviet, wanted to send troops in immediately. Alexander Yakovlev, the Central Committee Secretary, suggested direct rule from Moscow. Foreign Minister Eduard Shevardnadze proposed giving Nagorny Karabakh the status of an autonomous republic. Gorbachev agreed with Shevardnadze, but dithered, still believing that the matter could best be resolved between the Azeris and the Armenians themselves.

When the Presidium of the Supreme Soviet met in a televised session on 18 July, Gorbachev spoke directly to the two peoples involved in the conflict:

> How do you wish to solve this problem? Victory at any price? Armenia wants to incorporate Nagorny Karabakh. Azerbaijan does not intend to allow this and will not yield even a millimetre. This is all unrealistic. We must find a compromise that will suit everyone. Only a common victory will be a real victory. You cannot resolve issues while you are fighting one another. This is a political blind alley. Sumgait and other events concerning Nagorny Karabakh made a deep imprint on the relations between the two peoples and it will take time for this to be smoothed over even a little. But even so, we must meet each other half-way and find a compromise.[10]

But the time for compromise was long gone. Moscow might perhaps have imposed a workable solution, such as full autonomy for Nagorny Karabakh, but Gorbachev failed to grasp the nettle.

Instead, he allowed events to career precipitously out of control, creating an unstoppable momentum towards independence in the Transcaucasian republics and adding to the centrifugal forces pulling the Soviet Union apart.

Gorbachev's failure to impose a solution quickly led to a rapid deterioration in the situation. Twenty-five people were killed in Nagorny Karabakh in armed clashes between rival ethnic groups on 18 September. After more killings on 21 September and the deployment of troops to guard government buildings, Moscow issued a 'special status' order, creating a virtual state of emergency in Nagorny Karabakh with a curfew in Stepanakert and the Agdam district. In mid-November, huge crowds took to the streets of Baku to protest at Armenian attempts to undermine Azerbaijan's sovereignty over Nagorny Karabakh, and the main democratic movement, the Azerbaijan Popular Front, which had been formed by leading intellectuals to call for a wide range of reforms, soon found itself pushed by popular opinion towards a hard line. At a series of mass rallies, a young worker, Neimat Panakhov, attacked both the republic's urban intelligentsia and its Communist Party leadership. The crisis had deepened yet further and, in an atmosphere that was rapidly growing more volatile and hysterical, it was clear that not even the most democratic of Azeri intellectuals could support the principle of self-determination in Karabakh. Moscow had missed its opportunity.

With a state of emergency in Karabakh, huge demonstrations in Baku and a growing refugee problem in both republics, there were increasing demands in Moscow that 'something should be done'. By the time Baku erupted in a new outbreak of violence, when the death sentence was passed on three Azeris convicted of offences during the Sumgait riots, the regiments of Alexander Lebed's 106th Guards Airborne Division had already been put on standby. They marched to their nearest airbases and took off for Baku.

Lebed was unhappy at having to undertake an internal security mission inside the Soviet Union, and blamed Gorbachev for the crisis:

After Sumgait, this was the second, significantly more power-ful, burst of popular emotion. These disturbances were very easy and logical to explain. Mikhail Sergeyevich [Gorbachev] had gone AWOL for a bit and, as usual, naughty little Vezirov and Demirchyan [Party First Secretaries of Azerbaijan and Armenia] exploited his absence and started fighting. Later it became clear that absence at the most imminent and decisive moment of a conflict situation was Gorbachev's style of work, but then we still didn't know it.[11]

As in most crises in which politicians send in troops in response to a demand to 'do something', the military objectives of the mission were unclear. Lebed was furious about the lack of a defined objective, sarcastically summarising the orders he had been given as, 'Fly there, dears – fly there. There's a bit of disorder. Someone's beating somebody else up – it's not clear who, but you investigate it on the spot and interfere; you've got big fists. But don't shoot, whatever you do. Talk to them, convince them – of course!'[12]

Lebed flew to Baku ahead of the rest of his division with the deputy commander of the Airborne Forces, Lieutenant-General Kostylev, and his operational group. When they left the Chkalovsky airfield in Moscow, the first snow had fallen and there was a wintry breeze. In Baku, though, they landed in the warmth of autumn. As they disembarked and were met by staff officers, they noticed how peaceful everything seemed around the airfield. The officers reported that for the third consecutive day thousands of people were demonstrating about Karabakh in Lenin Square in the city centre. They said that apart from occasional skirmishes between local gangs of Armenians and their Azeri neighbours, everything was remarkably calm.

Lebed and his colleagues were driven to the staff headquarters. On the way, there was no sign of any obvious disturbance. Indeed, the city seemed to be completely peaceful. The shops were open, the transport system was working, and people seemed quite happy. A small group of youths waved crescent flags and shouted, 'Ka-ra-bakh! Ka-ra-bakh!' At headquarters, an infantry staff group was in position and co-ordinating movements. Lebed was given the task of taking whichever regiment arrived first and moving in a westerly direction, along Neft-yanikov Avenue, towards Lenin Square, where he was to find the interior troops' command post and co-ordinate joint action with the senior director of the Ministry of the Interior, whose name and precise location, much to his irritation, no one was able to tell him.

He met the 51st Airborne Regiment as it arrived from Tula at Nasosnaya airfield, thirty kilometres from Baku, and set off towards Lenin Square in a jeep at the head of a column. In the centre of town, the crowds of people grew thicker and thicker. Four hundred metres from Lenin Square, it was impossible to move. Neftyanikov Avenue was packed from wall to wall with people heading for the demonstration and the column came to a complete standstill.

What was I supposed to do on the square? More particularly, what a parachute regiment was supposed to do in armoured personnel carriers with full battle kit and well-trained soldiers and sergeants, some of them excellent, but trained for war with an external enemy, I cannot imagine. I got out of the vehicle and people at once gathered round me. Their faces were not hostile. They were frightened: 'Why have you come here?' they asked. I told them straight: 'God knows! Apparently you've got some sort of disorder here.' They all tried desperately to explain that it wasn't like that. That the meeting was organised, political. There was no evidence of violence and, God willing, there wouldn't be. In general, they were nothing. I said to them that individually they were nothing and I too was nothing. The column would remain where it was and, if they had no objection, I would walk round the square. There were no objections. I took the commanding officer of the regiment, Lieutenant-Colonel Orlov, together with two automatic weapons and went on my way.

When Lebed and Orlov reached the square, they realised why there had been such a bottleneck on Neftyanikov Avenue. Armoured personnel carriers of the Dzerzhinsky Division of Interior Ministry troops were blocking the entrance to the square, and in front of them was a large group of soldiers with helmets, body armour and rifles. Lebed found a senior officer and explained who he was and where he was trying to go. He was allowed to pass through a narrow gap between the armoured personnel carriers and entered the square, astonished at the size of the crowd in it. He calculated that there must have been nearly four hundred thousand people there. 'It wasn't clear what the point of the barricades blocking the entrance to the square was. The Interior Ministry troops were practically surrounded. In front of them was a crowd and behind them was a crowd too. I got the impression that the main purpose of the barricades was to annoy people.'[13]

Lebed began to worry that the presence of troops without clear orders in the midst of a peaceful but emotional crowd could create problems. His anxiety was not diminished when he reached the command post, which was inside a converted bus. He introduced himself to the representative of the Interior Ministry troops, Major-General Safonov, who told him that there were no other Party or government representatives and that he was 'God, Tsar and military chief!' He claimed that he had no communications with anyone further up the chain of command. His task was to maintain social order and stop bloodshed, although he went on to point out that no one was destroying the social order. Lebed then asked why he had been sent and what actions he was supposed to co-ordinate with him.

'God knows,' said Safonov. 'Sit down and have a cup of tea.'[14]

Lebed left the command post none the wiser. He had been expressly ordered to maintain radio silence, so he decided to contact staff headquarters by telephone. With a couple of kopecks, he dialled a number he had been given from a call-box on the edge of the square. Another Major-General, this time with a nervous, high-pitched voice, answered the telephone. Lebed could not make out his surname. He outlined the situation in the square, said that he did not know what his precise orders were, and asked the General to confirm them. To his astonishment, the hysterical voice told him to attack at once and surround the House of Soviets.

Lebed was completely taken aback. He had just walked round the square, which was full of people, nearly all of whom were behaving themselves and even being friendly to the soldiers. So far, there had only been one report of trouble, and it had not been serious: a young Lieutenant had been punched on the lip by a man in the crowd who was suffering from schizophrenia. The incident had been quickly dealt with, however, and the man had been taken away by the crowd, who apologised to the Lieutenant. The officer, who was twice as tall and ten times as strong as his assailant, soon began to appreciate the comedy of the situation and joked about it with the crowd, who brought fruit for his men.

Lebed again tried to explain the situation in the square, but the high-pitched voice on the other end of the line simply became more and more hysterical. 'Colonel! I repeat! Attack immediately!' The General's insistence on an attack and his refusal to listen to reason confirmed Lebed's worst fears about the internal security tasks which the Kremlin now expected the army to fulfil. It was not clear in whose name the General claimed to issue the order for an attack, but he was sitting in staff headquarters and could indeed have had full authority from Moscow to order whatever was necessary to suppress any disturbances in the republic. Lebed, however, was not prepared to order his troops to shoot at civilians.

> If I had obeyed this order without thinking, I could have provoked colossal bloodshed because there was only one possible kind of attack in a situation where the crowd was so dense: everyone inside the armoured vehicles, automatic weapons through the loop-holes and machine-gun our way forward over the corpses. If such a large number of people had gathered in one place, it meant that they must have had a very good reason indeed. And these were peaceful people. I very concisely and, it seemed to me, fully explained exactly what I thought about his mental capacity and replaced the receiver.[15]

Lebed's refusal to obey the General's order was a typical act of insubordination. It may have been motivated, as he suggests, simply by his unwillingness to be a party to the slaughter of civilians – he would certainly have considered the order an affront to his concept of the dignity of an officer, and it would also have brought back his boyhood memories of the carnage he had witnessed in Novocherkassk, when MVD troops were ordered to suppress a peaceful demonstration. However, his refusal may also have been prompted, or at least strengthened, by a suspicion that the General did not have complete authority to give such an order. After all, an order to mow down civilians might have been possible under Brezhnev, but it seemed much less politically acceptable in the new climate of *glasnost*. Lebed probably knew that he was on comparatively safe ground in refusing the order. Nevertheless, it was a direct command and the thought must have crossed his mind that a refusal to obey it could have serious consequences.

In the event, when he returned to his column, his hunch that the General did not have proper authority to order the attack seemed to have been correct. The deputy commander of the Airborne Forces, Lieutenant-General Kostylev, was horrified by Lebed's account of his telephone conversation with the General. He told him that he was quite right to have refused to obey the order, and that under no circumstances was there to be an attack on the crowd. It was not, however, the last time that Lebed was to be told to fire at civilians and, in the future, it became clear that the Kremlin was quite prepared to order the army to attack peaceful demonstrators.

Mikhail Gorbachev, Boris Yeltsin, and the various political adventurists who tried to seize power from them, have all shown their willingness to use troops to suppress political opposition. In Gorbachev's case, as the possibility of the disintegration of the Soviet Union grew ever more real, he sought to balance his support for economic and political reform with concessions to appease hardliners, who wanted a tough crackdown on nationalist movements in the republics. Whenever Gorbachev turned to the military for support in a crisis, though, his style was always to try to distance himself from the consequences of his orders. As Lebed and other officers began to notice, Mikhail Sergeyevich tried to maintain the fiction of his own liberalism by means of a convenient illness or absence (a ruse Yeltsin later copied when he ordered the storming of Grozny). The events in Baku on the November afternoon, when a mysterious voice at staff headquarters ordered Lebed to attack a crowd of peaceful demonstrators, were a premonition of what was to come in 'hot spots' from Baku to the Baltic and, ultimately, even in Moscow itself, as political leaders tried to assert their authority through a chaotic chain of command, leaving local military officers with the responsibility of dealing with the increasing number of internal security problems.

The tense situation in the Caucasus, where inter-ethnic feuding continued in the big cities, together with the ever louder demands for independence which were being made in the Baltic States, began to convince Gorbachev that the future of *perestroika* was in jeopardy. On 3 December, he met Azeri and Armenian members of the USSR Supreme Soviet, together with the leaders of both republics and Nagorny Karabakh. He told them that they were 'on the brink of disaster'. Yet, instead of presenting them with a plan to deal with the situation, he told them that they, 'the respected representatives of the two peoples, must sit down and together find a way out of this mess'.[16]

It was a typical example of Gorbachev's ambiguous and inconsistent approach to crisis management, and in Baku, where Alexander Lebed had been given responsibility for one of the town's most potentially explosive regions, in which Azeris and Armenians lived together cheek by jowl and made no secret of their mutual loathing, it was clear that such a hesitant approach could offer no solution.

Already, Armenians had begun to leave Baku, convinced that they could no longer live amongst their Azeri neighbours. They were quickly replaced by Azeri refugees from Armenia. In the next few months, the numbers of refugees travelling both ways between Armenia and Azerbaijan continued to increase at an alarming rate. Full of fear and hatred for the neighbours whose prejudice had driven them from their homes, they were eager for revenge and their hunger for blood contributed to a further deterioration in relations and the rejection of the possibility of compromise.

As the fateful year of 1989 approached, Mikhail Gorbachev was faced with three overwhelming and interlocking problems: the continuing crisis in the Soviet economy, which made a radical and politically dangerous restructuring inevitable; the urgent need to take the heat off the economy by disengaging from both the arms race and expensive imperial commitments in Eastern Europe; and the danger presented by the rising tide of nationalism within the USSR's constituent republics, which was bound to be encouraged by the disengagement from Eastern Europe. At the same time, at the back of Gorbachev's mind was the fear that an attempt to deal with any of these problems would provoke a backlash from his own conservatives.

On 7 December 1988, almost as though it were a portent of what was to come in the year ahead, the Soviet Union was shaken by news of an enormous earthquake in Armenia. Measuring 7 on the Richter scale, the earthquake devastated thousands of buildings around its epicentre at Spitak in the west of the tiny republic. The towns of Kirovakan and Leninakan, together with numerous villages in the surrounding countryside, were almost completely destroyed. More than 25,000 people were killed, and harrowing television pictures broadcast all over the Soviet Union and the world showed the woefully inadequate emergency services struggling vainly to dig out hundreds of people who lay buried beneath the huge piles of rubble. The rescuers' work was made all the more difficult by the onset of winter and the closure of many of the road and rail links into the region.

Gorbachev, who was in the United States at the time, immediately broke off his visit and flew to Yerevan.

When I reached the earthquake region I was shaken by what I saw, but at the same time I felt a sense of admiration for what our people had done. I was told how on the first and most difficult night, when the city of Leninakan was cut off, the airport and roads destroyed and the railways unable to run, teams of physicians and construction workers, students and workers set out from Yerevan to provide aid . . . The entire country responded heart and soul to the tragedy suffered by their 'Armenian brothers. Against the background of incipient conflicts between the nationalities, we saw the extraordinary resource that our Union possessed. Again, I became convinced of how important it was to preserve the interaction and support that had become a part of our life, and to protect everything that was good in our tradition.[17]

When the dust settled, the republic's Communist leadership began to face up to the scale of the catastrophe, which had left over 400,000 people homeless. Offers of help poured in from other countries, including Azerbaijan. Yet, despite its desperate predicament, Armenia was not prepared to accept any assistance from its old enemy. Gorbachev missed the opportunity to use the tragedy at last to persuade the Party leadership in the two republics to work together, and his view of the response to the earthquake as a demonstration of the 'extraordinary resource' of the Union was absurdly optimistic. In Baku, Alexander Lebed witnessed the Azeri reaction to the news of the earthquake:

The only television was in the foyer of our improvised staff headquarters, and everyone was watching it: staff officers, soldiers from the operations group, workers from the local authority. When the announcer started speaking about something else, no one listened to him and, moreover, someone switched off the television. An oppressive silence hung over the foyer. Suddenly a sort of noise, or to be more precise a whole range of noises, burst into this silence, merging themselves into one general triumphant, cheerful howl, which grew stronger all the time. I was convinced that my ears were deceiving me, but judging by the way everyone turned their heads and started to listen, it wasn't that. There was a small balcony on the edge of the building. You could get out on to it from the corridor. Trying to investigate the nature of the sounds, I went out on to the balcony together with five or six officers. In a few seconds everything was clear.

On the opposite side of the street, diagonally across from the local authority building, there was a nine-storey block of flats. In all the windows, without exception, lights were burning and on all the balconies people were yelling, screeching, hallooing and laughing wildly. Empty bottles, burning paper and other objects were flying down. The nine-storey block of flats was not alone in its cannibal excitement. There were similar scenes in all the nearby buildings. The whole region was lit up and howling in ecstatic rapture. People who considered themselves civilised, to one extent or another well brought-up and educated; many of them, I suppose, believers who accepted the tenets of the Koran; these same people in a unanimous fit of passion were indecently, barbarously celebrating the colossal distress of other human beings. I really wanted to take my automatic rifle and cross that damned building with a long line of fire. Perhaps, in that way, I could have forced people who had reduced themselves to the level of baboons to think like human beings again. I had met so many kind, happy, clever, pleasant people in Azerbaijan. What passionate, convincing speeches many of them had made to me! Where had they gone, all these clever and kind people . . .?[18]

Far from showing the Soviet Union's 'extraordinary resource', the Armenian earthquake was an awful symbol of what lay beneath the surface of Soviet society, waiting to burst forth in the coming years. The glee with which ordinary Azeris in Baku greeted the news of their neighbours' misfortune gave Alexander Lebed and his fellow officers a vivid picture of the visceral, almost unquenchable ethnic hatred which was ready to ignite into numerous small wars on the fringes of the disintegrating empire. Taunted by the bestial triumphalism of the Azeris, many of them by now, in their turn, refugees from burned-out homes in Armenia and Karabakh, the Armenians of Baku packed up their belongings and prepared to leave. The tide of refugees heightened tensions in both Yerevan and Baku, creating demands for ever more extreme solutions and feeding the passions of the blood-thirsty mobs who roamed the streets.

Gorbachev's response was, as usual, confused and indistinct; hand-wringing, making pious noises, hoping the problem would go away before resorting to brutal half-measures which inflamed the situation unnecessarily. The rise of nationalism in the Soviet Union was not confined to Armenia and Azerbaijan; it merely had its most violent early expression there. *Glasnost* was encouraging demands for independence in other republics too. In the Baltic States, Ukraine and Georgia, the new 'popular fronts' which had grown rapidly out of recently legalised 'informal associations' began campaigning for more openness about environmental or historical issues (such as the crimes of Stalin or the Nazi–Soviet Pact), but soon moved on to demand secession. The more openness *glasnost* brought, particularly about the past, the more the crowds began to clamour for independence. When the 'popular fronts' of the three Baltic States held their founding congresses in October 1988, they became festivals of national renaissance, where anthems, which had not been sung in public for nearly fifty years, were heard again and the old national flags began to fly from buildings in the capital cities. In Vilnius, there was even a service of national rededication in the Roman Catholic cathedral, which had been restored after forty years as an art gallery.[19] On 16 November, Estonia declared itself a sovereign republic.

Gorbachev was trying to walk a tightrope between liberals and hardliners within the Communist Party while at the same time dragging the country towards democratic reform. In early 1989, he brought in his most significant political reform to date: multi-candidate elections to a new Congress of People's Deputies of the USSR Supreme Soviet. The precise responsibilities and functions of the new congress had not been defined, but it radicalised Soviet politics, fatally wounding the hegemony of the Communist Party and introducing the first scent of participatory democracy. It provided a forum for new anti-Communist campaigners, such as Andrei Sakharov, the dissident nuclear physicist who been exiled to Gorky. The election also gave Alexander Lebed, who had briefly returned to his divisional headquarters in Tula, his first taste of political campaigning. He did not enjoy the experience.

As commander of the garrison in Tula, Lebed was instructed to ensure the election to the Supreme Soviet of Colonel-General Nikolai Moiseyev, a member of the military council of the Soviet forces in Germany, as member for one of the Tula regions and some of the rural districts around it. The General's campaign visit to the Tula region was like a scene from Gogol's *Dead Souls*. Everything was prepared for his delectation, even though he had brought with him a large troupe of entertainers of his own, including singers, dancers, forty conscripts born in Tula, trinkets, souvenirs and 'vodka . . . vodka . . . vodka'.

At meetings with local dignitaries, Moiseyev would get so drunk that sometimes he was completely unable to speak. The sight of the drunken General convinced Lebed that politics was not for him. 'I said to myself there and then: God forbid, Alexander Ivanovich, that you ever become a Member of Parliament. You'll never be able to drink enough.'

His first impressions of the drunken General coloured his view of senior officers in the Group of Soviet Forces in Germany, whose activities he was later to criticise sharply. He described the connection between Tula and the army in Germany as being 'like connecting the sewage system to the water supply'.[20] Nevertheless, General Moiseyev won an easy victory at the polls and disappeared to a life of comfortable obscurity in the Supreme Soviet. The experience of managing voting in an army garrison, where the ballot is notoriously easy to falsify and difficult to monitor, no doubt stood Lebed in good stead for the future.

As the new Congress of People's Deputies prepared to meet for its first session, nationalism again threatened to disrupt the Soviet status quo. Popular fronts had emerged in many republics from the informal associations which *glasnost* had permitted and, in some areas, they had successfully contested the elections on a strong nationalist ticket. Gorbachev worried about how to respond to the new nationalist impulse:

> The Party's position was especially important under these conditions. However, it was simply unable to operate under conditions of democracy. The Party leaders, who were accustomed to dealing with economic affairs, became confused when they had to engage in democratic politics. From the very beginning the informal associations were declared to be opposition organisations. Instead of interacting with the opposition, valuable time was lost in the vain hope that the new organisations would just vanish, go away like a bad dream. If in the initial period there had been co-operation between the Party organisations and the informal associations, the elections of people's deputies in 1989 might have integrated the Party and the popular front into a common political process. But this did not happen.[21]

Events in the Caucasus were again spinning out of control. This time the Kremlin's problems were in Georgia. Like Armenia, Georgia was an ancient Christian kingdom which had been absorbed into the Russian empire early in the nineteenth century but had enjoyed a brief period of national independence after the Bolshevik revolution. Despite the fact that Stalin was a Georgian and many people still hero-worshipped him, national sentiment was extremely strong in the republic.

In October 1987, as soon as it became clear that *glasnost* would permit the formation of unofficial organisations, Georgian intellectuals had established the 'Ilia Chavchavadze Society', which began a cautious campaign for eventual independence under the slogan 'Fatherland, Language and Faith'. In 1988, two more radical groups appeared. The Society of Saint Ilia the Righteous, led by Zviad Gamsakhurdia, and the National Democratic Party, whose leader was Georgi Chanturia, both adopted strong separatist programmes. The National Democratic Party even called for 'Georgia for the Georgians' and threatened to mount a campaign of civil disobedience to win back Georgian independence. The Communists set up their own official group, the Rustaveli Society, which offered a half-hearted response to the demands of the nationalists.

The Georgians are sometimes called the Italians of the Caucasus, and the new political groups certainly espoused a variety of causes with a Latin excitability. Crowds came out on to the streets of Tbilisi to protest their grievances: the destruction of the Aragvi valley by the Caucasian Mountain Railway; pollution caused by the Baku oil refinery; damage to ancient monasteries; the lack of use of the Georgian language for official purposes.[22] When the Communist Party failed to respond to demands for action on these matters, the demonstrators quickly adopted a more stridently nationalist tone. In November 1988, more than 200,000 people joined a rally against proposed changes to the Soviet constitution, which might have threatened Georgia's sovereignty over the tiny autonomous region of Abkhazia. The Kremlin quickly withdrew the proposed changes when the local Party reported the strength of feeling in Tbilisi. However, the Kremlin's capitulation merely encouraged the nationalists, who returned to the streets in the spring of 1989, ostensibly to protest against the treatment of Georgian students who had been beaten up in Abkhazia after campaigning against the rector of Sukhumi University, an Abkhaz separatist.[23]

The demonstrations, which began on 25 March 1989, soon became the focus for nationalist demands for secession from the USSR. On 4 April, over a hundred Georgian nationalists demanding full independence, together with the full integration of Abkhazia, began a hunger-strike outside the Communist Party headquarters. When 100,000 people took to the streets two days later to support them, the local party leader, Dzhumbar Patiashvili, began to worry that he was losing control of the situation and cabled Moscow to ask for permission to arrest opposition leaders and impose martial law. The Kremlin was worried that the Georgian–Abkhaz tension underlying the rallies might be the start of a crisis similar to the Nagorny Karabakh conflict which had caused such hatred between Azeris and Armenians. The Politburo agreed to send troops to Tbilisi.

Lebed's old regiment, the 345th Parachute Regiment, which had been amongst the first Soviet troops into Afghanistan, had been one of the last units to leave after the signing of peace accords with the mujahideen. The regiment had only been withdrawn from Afghanistan two months earlier, in February 1989. Yet rather than the relatively comfortable posting it might have expected at a Russian base, it had been posted to Kirovabad (now Gyandzha) in Azerbaijan. The military base was in an appalling state, lacking the most basic facilities, and the regiment was not provided with the financial means to improve matters. As the officers and men struggled to make do, they were told to march 320 kilometres to Tbilisi. The march was not a problem for them, but they objected to being asked to undertake what Lebed described as 'a nice little police-gendarme task'. They arrived in Tbilisi to find a huge demonstration in support of independence and crowds who called them 'occupiers', 'mongrels' and 'scum'.

The crowds had begun to gather on the evening of 8 April under the equestrian statue of one of the great heroes of Georgian history, King Vakhtang. Eight thousand people observed an all-night vigil under the trees on either side of the elegant Rustaveli Prospekt. On the morning of the 9th, the order was given to disperse the demonstrators. Lebed's version of the events that followed is that the paratroops, who had been insulted and stoned by the crowd, only moved to escape the missiles which were being thrown at them and to capture vehicles which were blockading the government buildings. When they moved, the crowd panicked and scattered in different directions around the square. In the confusion, eighteen people, including sixteen women, lost their lives. Lebed's explanation is the one given by the authorities.

The truth, however, is different. The troops attacked with *cheremukha*, a toxic gas, and sharpened military shovels. They set about the crowd vigorously, and videotapes of them in action were soon broadcast around the world, causing severe embarrassment to the Soviet government.[24] Although Lebed's version of events is wrong, it is not clear to what extent the paratroopers of the 345th, rather than MVD troops, were responsible for the carnage. The army took the blame, in particular the future Russian Defence Minister General Igor Rodionov, who at the time was commander of the Transcaucasus military district, but MVD troops took the lead in the operation. They wore the same uniform as the paratroopers, making it difficult to identify who was responsible. Lebed claims that he only arrived in Tbilisi shortly after the operation, together with the rest of his division, which was one of three divisions sent to shore up the government of Patiashvili. Whatever the truth, Lebed's version is obviously at odds with Georgian accounts of what happened, and may be an attempt to exculpate his friend

Rodionov, who was widely blamed for the massacre and became known as 'the butcher of Tbilisi'. Lebed has resolutely defended his friend against claims that he was responsible for the atrocity, describing him as 'one of the cleverest and most educated generals of the Soviet, and now of the Russian, army. He is an intellectual and a man of honour.'[25]

Rodionov was not the only one who needed to escape blame. The massacre on Rustaveli Prospekt sent a shock-wave of alarm through the Kremlin. Gorbachev's attempt to deal with Georgian nationalism had begun characteristically hesitantly and ended in the use of force when it was already too late. Typically, Gorbachev had made himself scarce at the crucial moment when the decision to send in troops was taken, leaving others to interpret his wishes and do his dirty work for him. When he returned, he was able to deny all knowledge. Later he would write:

> When I arrived back in Moscow from London, I was informed immediately at the airport that troops had been dispatched to Georgia for the protection of 'important facilities'. It was difficult to get details 'on the move', but sensing that something was about to happen, I instructed Shevardnadze and Razumovsky to fly to Tbilisi. However, this trip was put off, because the next day the Georgian leadership informed us that the situation was stabilising. The storm broke on the night of 8–9 April.
>
> How many times I have had to withstand 'searching glances', or listen to direct reproaches that 'the General Secretary must have known everything that was undertaken by the Georgian leadership'. In March 1994, Gavril Popov [Mayor of Moscow] declared in an article: 'I will never believe that Gorbachev did not know.' And yet the truth is: the decision to use force was taken without consulting me.[26]

Despite Gorbachev's protestations, the truth is more likely to have been that he did not know because he did not want to know.

Lebed and his fellow paratroop commanders were again furious at being used to deal with an internal security problem which had been caused by the Party's incompetence. The fact that Rodionov and the army took all the blame, rather than the Party, and that graffiti soon appeared on the walls of Tbilisi with the message 'Death to the murderer Rodionov', annoyed Lebed intensely. 'There were demands to remove him from his post and put him on trial. I don't know, maybe I'm wrong, but it seems to me that General Rodionov could easily have cleared himself right then, while the tracks were still fresh, but he was too noble and disciplined for that.'[27]

Amidst the outrage in the aftermath of the massacre, Patiashvili was removed as First Secretary in Georgia and the Soviet Foreign Minister, Eduard Shevardnadze, returned to Tbilisi. Gorbachev slipped of the hook and escaped all public blame, but the armed forces remained resentful of the part they had been made to play. Ironically, the Tbilisi massacre was perhaps the worst act of violence perpetrated by the Soviet regime since the crushing of the demonstration which Lebed had witnessed in Novocherkassk in 1962. It was also a terrible political miscalculation, which strengthened the hand of nationalists in Georgia and the other republics, who refused to compromise with the Communist Party. Gorbachev later admitted that 'the echo of events in Tbilisi, painfully felt in all regions, had an adverse effect on all of our attempts to bring harmony to relations between nationalities in our country for a long time'.[28]

As Gorbachev struggled to turn back the rising tide of nationalism within the Soviet Union, events suddenly began to move with breathtaking speed in Moscow's East European empire. Poland had refused to submit to the Soviet imperial yoke and, since the early 1980s, the independent trade union 'Solidarity' had fought for free elections and an end to the one-party state. Despite martial law and the outlawing of Solidarity, a series of workers' strikes were organised in 1988, which finally forced General Wojciech Jaruzelski's government to come to terms with the opposition. Solidarity was legalised and semi-free elections for the Polish Parliament, the Sejm, were held in June 1989. The Communists were devastated at the polls and Tadeusz Mazowiecki, a Catholic newspaper editor, formed the first non-Communist government in the Soviet bloc since 1948.

It might have been possible for Moscow to isolate events in Poland and still maintain a grip on the rest of its empire. However, other countries, most notably Hungary, were ready to follow Poland's example. Imre Pozsgay's new reformist government in Budapest started to build better relations with Hungary's Western neighbours, and on 2 May 1989, as thousands of people from all over Eastern Europe took their annual holiday on the shores of Lake Balaton, the barbed-wire fences on the border with Austria were torn down.

Amidst these currents of change, Gorbachev himself sparked the unrest which removed the cornerstone of Moscow's empire and brought the whole edifice crashing down. In October 1989, he visited East Germany, where Erich Honecker's Socialist Unity government was unreconstructed and bitterly resistant to change. When Gorbachev arrived, crowds of adoring demonstrators took to the streets to demand that their government introduce *glasnost* and similar reforms in East Germany. With Poland and Hungary opening themselves up to the West, East Germany found that thousands of its citizens were disappearing over its borders. The gates of the prison camp had been flung open. With demonstrators on the streets and in the churches of Leipzig and Dresden, Honecker resigned and jubilant East Germans began to tear down the Berlin Wall.

The end of Honecker's regime and the removal of the Berlin Wall took away the cornerstone of the Soviet bloc. Within a year, East and West Germany were reunited, the Cold War was at an end and the Warsaw Pact was in ruins. Gorbachev had been seeking a gradual disengagement from Eastern Europe rather than a sudden collapse of the Empire. He had begun to introduce concepts of 'war prevention' and 'reasonable sufficiency' into his 'new thinking' as early as 1985, as a prelude to scaling down defence spending. In 1987 the Berlin Declaration of the Warsaw Treaty Organisation announced a new defensive military doctrine based on 'reasonable sufficiency'.[29] This was an open acceptance of the fact that the Soviet Union was losing the arms race and could no longer compete with the West. In a speech to the United Nations in 1988, Gorbachev had announced his intention of reducing the size of the Soviet armed forces by half a million.[30] He was hoping that a willingness to accept gradual change would attract the Western support so vital to transforming and demilitarising the Soviet economy. With this end in mind, after consultation with his Warsaw Pact allies, he had begun a cautious withdrawal of six tank divisions from East Germany, Czechoslovakia and Hungary. In total, his intention was to reduce Soviet forces in those countries by 50,000 men and 5,000 tanks.[31]

The United States Department of Defense recognised Gorbachev's predicament:

> Decades of investment priorities skewed to promoting the rapid build-up of military power in the Soviet Union have created a military giant that now overburdens a civilian economy crumbling from neglect. The accumulated problems which resulted from decades of centralized economic planning plus the burden of achieving superpower status have combined to threaten the foundations of Soviet military and political power . . . In trying to control all aspects of the economy from Moscow, the huge, over-centralized, self-perpetuating bureaucracy has mismanaged a resource-rich nation toward economic disaster.[32]

Dick Cheney, the US Secretary of Defense, was astonished at the scale of Soviet defence spending: 'The Intelligence Community has estimated that Soviet defense spending has increased steadily over the past twenty-five years, amounting to 15–17 per cent of estimated gross national product (GNP) in the 1980s . . . President Gorbachev himself has admitted to spending amounts equivalent to between 13 and 15 per cent of the country's GNP on defense, while some Soviet economists have speculated that the burden may be considerably higher, perhaps as much as 25 per cent of the Soviet GNP.'[33]

The Americans were, however, aware that Gorbachev was desperately hoping to draw them into helping him out of the mess. As Cheney wrote: 'While Gorbachev's announcements on cutting defense are largely in response to strong economic pressures, and represent his intention to redirect resources to economic needs, they also most certainly further Soviet efforts to constrain Western military modernization, give added impetus to the arms control process and enlist Western support to help salvage the USSR's economy.'[34] With the sudden round of revolutions in Eastern Europe, however, Gorbachev's bargaining power with the West had all but disappeared, and he found himself with the added problem of a huge, disgruntled, largely unpaid army returning home with almost no prospect of work or a decent home. The situation plunged the army and its senior officers into the centre of political debate.

The Generals began to feel themselves most severely under pressure when Georgy Arbatov, Director of the USA and Canada Institute of the USSR Academy of Sciences, and a senior adviser to the Soviet leadership on foreign policy, made a speech at the Second USSR Congress of People's Deputies in which he criticised the enormous military budget. Arbatov followed his speech with a series of acrimonious exchanges with Gorbachev's military adviser, Marshal Sergei Akhromeyev, in the pages of *Ogonyok* magazine. Arbatov demanded a dramatic reduction in the military budget and a transfer of resources to the civilian economy; an end to secrecy and the military's information monopoly so that the cost of weapons systems could be made public; and the restoration of civilian control of the armed forces. Akhromeyev responded with a hawkish line, insisting that there was still a threat from the West and that the state clearly appreciated this, since it set budget levels, not the military.

As the military struggled to fight off attacks from reformers in Moscow, the Soviet empire continued to break apart. In Eastern Europe, the last pieces were detaching themselves from the jigsaw. At the end of November a 'velvet revolution' in Prague ousted the Czechoslovak President, Gustáv Husák, bringing the dissident playwright Václav Havel to power. On 25 December, the Romanian President Nicolae Ceauşescu and his wife Elena were executed by firing squad after rioting in Timişoara in the west of the country triggered a full-scale revolution in Bucharest.

Gorbachev realised that these events gave a colossal impetus to the nationalist movements inside the Soviet Union. There was now a real danger of the country disintegrating, and he found himself trapped between reformers who wanted him to accommodate the nationalists and hardliners who wanted tough action to save the Soviet Union. The three Baltic States had already declared their sovereignty, and in December 1989 even the Communist Party in Lithuania announced its independence from the Soviet Party. As the clamour from hardliners in Moscow grew for Gorbachev to 'do something' about the Baltics, rioting broke out again in the Caucasus.

Gorbachev's half-hearted attempts to cajole the Armenian and Azeri Party leaders into finding their own solution to their differences, and his imposition of direct rule from Moscow on Nagorny Karabakh, had failed to bring about a settlement. By the end of 1989, the official Communist power structures in all the Transcaucasian republics had been effectively replaced by the nationalist movements. In November, the Communist Party of Azerbaijan had capitulated to the increasingly strident demands of the Azerbaijan Popular Front, which had launched a campaign of strikes and demonstrations to force the Azeri Supreme Soviet to declare the country a 'sovereign socialist state'.[35] The Front had also organised an economic blockade of Armenia, and protestors in Nakhichevan had torn down border markers and attacked guard posts on the Soviet–Iranian border in an apparent attempt to 'reunite southern Azerbaijan' (an idea promulgated by the Popular Front leader, Abulfaz Elchibey, which, not surprisingly, caused great irritation in Tehran). By the end of the year, the crowds were back on the streets of Baku, this time demanding secession from the USSR. And the large number of refugees from Armenia amongst them ensured that a frenzy of hatred was quickly whipped up against Baku's small remaining Armenian population.

By January 1990, there were probably as many as 30,000 Azeri refugees in Baku, many of them homeless and unemployed. They were furious that the Supreme Soviet of Azerbaijan had acqui-esced in the USSR's decision to retain responsibility for Nagorny Karabakh, despite its formal restoration to Azerbaijan in November 1989. There had been rowdy demonstrations in Baku for weeks, but on the evening of 13 January, after an acrimonious Popular Front meeting, gangs of thugs went on the rampage through the streets of Baku. High on nationalist rhetoric, they hunted down any Armenians they could find, breaking into their homes and dragging them into the streets where they were beaten to death. Houses in the Armenian quarter were burned down and people were thrown to their deaths from the roofs of buildings. If there was any motive in the orgy of violence, it was perhaps an attempt at 'ethnic cleansing' by homeless Azeri refugees who wanted to move into the homes of Baku's 200,000 Armenians. As the crowds stormed through the Armenian quarter, wild rumours, for example that an Armenian had attacked two Azeris with an axe, spread like flames through this city where fire had once been worshipped, spurring the rioters on to new extremes of hatred. The local security forces, almost powerless to help in the face of the mob, tried to hide some Armenians in their barracks and other government buildings. Eventually, they even took to ferrying terrified families across the Caspian Sea to Krasnovodsk in Turkmenistan. Soon, almost the entire Armenian population had disappeared from Baku.

Gorbachev noted that there were 'dozens of wounded and houses were destroyed. Emergency measures were needed.' Yet no emergency measures were taken. Gorbachev's response to events followed the usual pattern – hesitating until it was too late before ordering troops in to deal with the crisis and trying, as far as possible, to distance himself from the decision to use force. Alexander Lebed and his fellow officers in the Airborne Forces were astonished at the President's failure to act:

> The newspapers and television reported in a very dry, matter-of-fact, humdrum way that there was carnage again in Baku. They gave the number of casualties. People in the Soviet Union and the rest of the world had protested rather routinely and sluggishly. Our officers grew more and more astonished every day: 'How is it that there is carnage in Baku and we're still in Tula?' I don't know what efforts Gorbachev had made in the space of a week to stop the bloody internecine war but, apparently, having exhausted all his arguments, he remembered the old equation: Airborne Troops plus Air Transport equals Soviet power in the Transcaucasus, and on 18 January, our division was put on alert.[36]

Gorbachev had tried to avoid sending in the troops, fearing another massacre like the one in Tbilisi nine months previously. He may also have realised that his failure to act earlier had considerably exacerbated the problem, making the military task much harder. In addition, the Azeri Communist Party was virtually powerless and its leaders had begun to parrot the demands of the Popular Front. Two delegations from Moscow – one political, led by Yevgeny Primakov; the other military, consisting of General Varennikov, commander of the Land Forces, General Achalov of the Airborne Forces and the Interior Minister, Vadim Bakatin, who was responsible for the MVD troops – had sent back alarming reports about the crisis in Baku.

The situation awaiting the Soviet troops who landed in Azerbaijan was very different from the relatively calm and friendly reception Alexander Lebed had received in Baku in 1988. The political atmosphere in the republic changed as soon as Soviet military reinforcements began to arrive. Whereas previously hatred of Armenia had been the focus of the demonstrations, now the nationalists' blood was up and they turned their attention to the Soviet forces as representatives of Moscow, which had failed to guarantee the future of Nagorny Karabakh in Azerbaijan. The Popular Front and other opposition groups called for the with-drawal of all Soviet forces from the republic, and even began to attack military units in Baku. When troops landed at the military bases at Yevlak and Gyandzha, they were hemmed in by crowds of demonstrators and the road to Baku was blocked. They even-tually had to use armoured vehicles and helicopters to get over the roadblocks, only to find more barricades outside Baku itself.

By the time Lebed's division took off for Baku, the Soviet Interior Ministry was admitting that the death toll in Baku had reached 66, with 220 people injured and over 200 homes destroyed. The true figures were, no doubt, much higher. The 137th Ryazan regiment took off first for Baku, and Lebed fol-lowed with the Tula regiment. The situation at Kala airfield, thirty kilometres from Baku, where they landed at dusk, seemed to be worse than at other airfields further from the capital. There was gunfire near the airfield's perimeter fence, and Lebed was told when he landed that one of the transport aircraft had been badly hit in the fuselage. The divisional chief of staff told him that, although both the Ryazan and Kostroma regiments had mounted up and were ready to move out, all the exits from the airfield had been barred by lorries and concrete blocks. Lightly armed groups of between fifty and a hundred and fifty Azeri nationalists were manning the barricades, and there were also mobile groups which patrolled the perimeter fence, firing at aircraft as they landed. A group of paratroopers had already been sent to deal with them. The division's objective was as unclear as ever, although it had been bluntly outlined by the Defence Minister, Marshal Yazov himself, to the commander of the Ryazan regiment, Colonel Naumov. Lebed remembers Naumov's embarrassment as he told him of his conversation with the minister.

'The Minister of Defence raised his fist to my nose and said: "Just try *not* fucking well taking it! . . . Tell Lebed!"'

'That's all?'

'That's all!'

'Taking what?'

'Baku! There's nothing else to take.'

Lebed wryly observed that taking a town of two million people was not, perhaps, quite as easy as the Minister of Defence imagined. First, there was the problem of breaking out of the airport. Lebed started to talk to the nationalists on the barricades.

'I have to get through and I will get through. The army is not a cat which has been caught by its tail, squealing, scratching and unable to do anything. Peace be on your houses. You let me through and I guarantee that not a single hair will fall from your head.'[37]

The hysterical crowd was not prepared to listen, though, and swore that they would rather die than let Lebed's men pass. However, as the discussion continued, under cover of darkness, sappers cut through the perimeter fence three hundred metres on either side of the barricades and prepared an exit for the vehicles. When Lebed gave the command, the vehicles broke through and charged towards the barricades, the paratroopers firing into the air to create panic as they attacked from both sides. The nationalists at once took fright and fled. Not all of them managed to escape – ninety-two were arrested.

In Baku, demonstrators continued to gather in Lenin Square to demand the withdrawal of Soviet troops and the resignation of the Azerbaijan Supreme Soviet. Azeri militants seized control of the television station and broadcast appeals for help from neighbouring countries – it was not until Soviet troops blew up the station's power plant that they were silenced. The Popular Front was now co-ordinating attacks on government installations and raiding local armouries to seize weapons for its new militia. The few Azeris who tried to express remorse about the fate of the Armenian population were denied all access to the media by editors who insisted that any expressions of regret should be for the Azeris who had been killed by Armenian gunmen.

On 20 January 1990, Gorbachev at last declared a state of emergency. Typically, he blamed the delay in responding to the anarchy in Baku on everyone but himself. The local authorities in Baku 'were too divided and paralysed to control the situation'. The Supreme Soviet, 'in the face of increasing moral terror, proved incapable of making adequate decisions'.[38] After the declaration of the state of emergency, Soviet commanders no longer felt the need to show restraint. The objective now was to crush resistance and restore authority to the Azeri Communist Party – a forlorn hope, as it was thoroughly discredited and, in any event, its leaders had begun to call for the withdrawal of Soviet forces in a desperate attempt to curry favour with the mob.

Soviet forces advanced on Baku by land and from the sea, ruthlessly clearing the streets and sweeping aside resistance from the Popular Front's recently organised militias. The Soviet armoured columns crashed through manned barricades, killing hundreds of Azeris, and by the 21st they had regained control of most of central Baku. The Popular Front was still able to mobilise support on the streets, however. On the 22nd, tens of thousands of people defied the Soviet military authorities' ban on demonstrations and held a huge funeral procession for 60 Azeri victims of the violence. The Popular Front claimed that as many as 600 people had died in the most recent fighting, and ugly rumours spread that Soviet troops had been ordered to dispose of the bodies by night in the Caspian Sea, in order to conceal the true number of casualties.[39]

The challenge to Soviet authority grew even more serious when the Popular Front declared a general strike, which brought Baku to a standstill, and commandeered fifty ships, including oil tankers and barges, to blockade Baku harbour. They even threatened to destroy oil rigs and terminals, to sink ships and to stop navigation unless all Soviet troops were withdrawn. Despite the arrest of several important nationalist leaders on the 23rd, the strike continued and the port remained blockaded.

Hardliners in Moscow were horrified at the Azeri Popular Front's defiance of Soviet authority. They were determined that resistance should be crushed and an example made of Baku, if only to discourage nationalist elements in other republics. They prevailed on Gorbachev to order the use of yet more force. As dusk descended over Baku harbour on the evening of the 24th, Soviet tanks, field guns and ships began an artillery barrage of the blockading vessels. The 331st Kostroma Guards Airborne Regiment of Lebed's 106th Airborne Division were ordered to capture the Azeri nationalists' command post on one of the ships in Baku harbour. When they attacked, a small cutter, which had been commandeered by the nationalists, tried to intervene but four Soviet BMD armoured vehicles fired a salvo of 73mm high-explosive rounds at it. The cutter caught fire and eventually sank.[40]

The Soviet bombardment of Baku harbour lasted forty minutes and succeeded in lifting the blockade. The Azeri Supreme Soviet met again and tried to regain power under a new First Secretary, Ayaz Mutalibov.

Baku was still sullen and resentful of the Soviet presence. No one was prepared to return to work, and there was an atmosphere of tension and menace in the city. The homes of leading nationalists were raided and over a hundred arrests were made, after which the Popular Front went underground and the city settled into an uneasy peace. There was no rest for Lebed's men, though. One of his units, the Tula regiment, was ordered to fly to Dushanbe together with the 217th Guards Airborne Division when nationalist violence broke out there.

In Moscow, the intervention in Azerbaijan had created a split in the Politburo. Marshal Yazov, the Defence Minister, told a press conference on 26 January that the Kremlin's aim had been to pre-empt a meeting of the Popular Front on the 20th, at which its leaders would have announced that they had seized power. Eduard Shevardnadze's version of events was different, however. He insisted that the aim of the intervention had simply been to stop the slaughter in Baku, not to stamp out political opposition.[41]

Gorbachev claimed that the use of force was necessary in order to prevent violence, which is a little like a policeman saying that he had to hit the prisoner in order to stop him hitting himself:

> To this day, this action still receives mixed evaluations. Some feel that the state of emergency was declared too late, while others believe that it was not necessary at all. In answer to the former, I would say that the Union authorities could not go over the heads of the leaders of the republic to declare a state of emergency – the measure was introduced when the local authorities were paralysed. To others, I say that we had to stop the escalation of violence.
>
> The lesson I took from this tragic story is: authorities cannot avoid the use of force in extreme circumstances. Such action must be justified by absolute necessity and limited to a

considerable degree. However, a true resolution of the problem is possible only by political means.[42]

It was political means that Gorbachev now tried to use to bring an end to the threat from nationalism, not only in Azerbaijan but throughout the Soviet Union. He still hoped that democratisation could stop disintegration. At a plenary session of the Communist Party Central Committee on 7 February, he persuaded the Party to abandon its 'leading role', embrace the multi-party system and become a party of 'democratic socialism'. When the Congress of People's Deputies amended Article 6 of the Soviet Constitution in March, the Communist Party's monopoly of power formally came to an end.

There was still a chance that Gorbachev's strategy of democratisation, better international relations and economic restructuring might settle in and stabilise the situation in the Soviet Union. The Congress of People's Deputies, although a long way from being a proper democratic assembly with power to control the executive, nevertheless had begun to excite people's imagination. As a USSR institution, it had won considerable respect since the elections of spring 1989. Its sittings were broadcast live on television and they generated such interest that thousands of people skipped work to watch them. Debates in the Congress showed the public more clearly than ever before real *glasnost* in action: ministers, *apparatchiks* and even Generals were frequently criticised. And the sessions were good for Gorbachev too. He was able to preside over the deputies' vexatious disputes like Solomon, a final arbiter of the petty squabbles of lesser men. This was 'presidential democracy' in action. For a while, it appeared to be working, and it was the Congress that elected Gorbachev Soviet President.

Yet Gorbachev had missed the point. What he failed to understand until it was already too late was that the USSR was not, never had been and never could be a single society. There was no such thing as the *sovietsky narod*, the Soviet nation, and national identity was as strong as it ever had been amongst the nations of the Soviet Union. Ultimately, therefore, Soviet institutions were bound to run up against national institutions, which would inevitably have much greater popular legitimacy. Gorbachev may not have understood this, but his greatest and most dangerous rival, the former head of the Party in Sverdlovsk and, later, in Moscow, Boris Yeltsin, certainly did.

A very different character from Gorbachev, Yeltsin was stubborn, determined and ruthless. He loathed Gorbachev, whom he blamed for undermining his position as First Secretary of the Party in Moscow after he had attacked the privileges of the *nomenklatura*. He knew that the General Secretary's hesitant, ambiguous style of government was bound to make his attempt to keep the Soviet Union together more difficult. At heart, Yeltsin was a nationalist who realised that the future was with the nation state. In early 1990, Yeltsin, who had helped to create a powerful opposition group in the Congress, the Inter-regional Group of People's Deputies, came to the firm conclusion that power was shifting away from the Soviet centre to the republics. He decided to transfer his allegiance and stand for election to the People's Congress of the Russian Federation. His intention was to break the power of the Soviet state and make Russia master of its own destiny.

Yeltsin was at once supported by most of the liberal, non-Communist groups, who formed the 'Democratic Russia' alliance which campaigned for Russian sovereignty. The new programme of Russia's democrats was warmly welcomed in the Baltic States and other republics, which had been trying hard to 'jump-start' Russian nationalism. They knew that Russian sovereignty would secure their independence and break the Union.

Gorbachev too realised the danger. He bitterly castigated Democratic Russia (DemRossiya) and its new leader for their decision to

> set a course towards dismantling the Union state. DemRossiya managed to find a figure who agreed, for the sake of supreme power, to violate the will of his people. The Party *nomenklatura* of the Russian republic also shares responsibility for this sad outcome. Dissatisfied with the reformist wing and the policy of the CPSU leadership, unable to understand what they were being drawn into, Communist deputies in the Russian Supreme Soviet (with the exception of only three or four) voted for the Declaration of Sovereignty which drove the first nail in the coffin of the Union state.[43]

Yeltsin's victory in the Russian Congress elections and his subsequent declaration of sovereignty did indeed mark the triumph of his brand of Russian nationalism. However, it also signalled the beginning of a deep divide in Russian nationalism, with many Russians preferring to side with the Soviet Communist Party in support of the Soviet Union, which they saw as a modern Russian empire. This was the beginning of the 'red–brown' alliance which later posed such a threat to Yeltsin.

As an army officer, Alexander Lebed felt himself removed from all these political arguments. He merely objected to being asked to clean up the politicians' mess as pieces began to fall off the Soviet Union. And yet the army was now being drawn into politics more deeply than ever before. In the summer of 1990, Gorbachev agreed terms for the withdrawal of Soviet troops from the newly reunited Germany with Helmut Kohl, the German Chancellor. The return of the Western Group of Forces and the corrupt activities in which they soon began to engage was just one of the many military issues that continued to rumble through the Russian political system for years to come, eventually implicating Lebed's colleague Pavel Grachev and other senior officers. Yet in mid-1990, the fate of the troops returning from Eastern Europe was the least significant of the many issues which worried the military. The end of the Cold War and the looming break-up of the Soviet Union had called into question their very existence. Their future looked far from secure, and they began to fear what might happen to them in any 'divorce settlement' resulting from the break-up of the Soviet Union. In reality, by now they faced the choice of accepting the break-up of the Union and doing a deal with the nationalists; or trying, with Gorbachev, to preserve the best features of the Union and maintain some common institutions. Few would have accepted that the choice was already that stark, and many 'conservatives', such as the 'black Colonels' in the Congress of People's Deputies, preferred to campaign for old-style, hardline measures that were already out of date. Equally, however, the Russian nationalists and reformers who sought to break the power of the Soviet state did not yet appreciate the importance of reaching an accord with the armed forces.

In the summer of 1990, with Boris Yeltsin still riding high on a tide of reformist zeal, the reformers felt more bullish about the military. Just before the 28th Party Congress, forty-seven members of the Congress of People's Deputies and a number of civilian experts on the military, including Georgy Arbatov, signed a letter in the press claiming that the military was trying to stifle reform. They argued for Supreme Soviet control over the military budget, transferring resources from procurement of equipment to rehabilitation programmes for redundant servicemen, conversion of a substantial part of the military–industrial complex to civilian use, the creation of a new professional army, 'renewal' of the leadership of the Ministry of Defence, depoliticisation of the armed forces and an end to their use for internal security. These arguments were brusquely dismissed by senior figures in the Defence Ministry as 'unsupported hare-brained schemes'. They were particularly insulted by the reformers' clairvoyant insinuations that they would be prepared to turn against their own people if a 'complex situation' arose in society.

Lebed certainly agreed with many of the reformers' criticisms, which formed the basis of much of the discussion at the 28th Party Congress, to which, despite his subsequent denials that he was ever a serious Communist, he was elected as a delegate. 'I never considered myself a keen Party activist and never tried to attain the heights of power in the Party . . . Because of this, I never offered myself as a delegate to a Party Congress simply because it was not an area in which I could use my capabilities. But man supposes and God disposes.'

It is no doubt true that Lebed was not an enthusiastic, ideologically committed Communist, any more than Yeltsin or the hundreds of thousands of others who soon left the Party and became good democrats. Yet holding a Party card out of necessity is one thing, participating as a delegate in a Party Congress is quite another. Lebed was elected as a delegate by the Party cadres in the Tula regiment. His motivation seems to have been a growing interest in the developing political situation and an awareness that the congress was likely to be a decisive historical event. 'The 28th Congress of the CPSU was undoubtedly a turning-point in the life and activity of the modern Communist Party.'[44]

It was more than a turning-point: it marked the beginning of the end of the Soviet Communist Party and the emergence of an aggressively independent, and at once deeply divided, Russian Communist Party. Gorbachev had hoped that the 28th Congress would reinvigorate the Soviet Communist Party as a democratic socialist organisation, but it merely encouraged ambitious Russian Communist *apparatchiks* to play the nationalist card and establish their own republican party, leaving the arch-conservatives in control of the decaying Soviet Party. It also provided a forum for Boris Yeltsin's ostentatious departure from the Party and convinced Alexander Lebed, among many others, that the future no longer lay with the Communists.

Why had we, the Russian peoples, who had overcome the enemy in the greatest of all wars and paid for the victory with the blood, life and health of our people, been reduced to poverty? Why, with such colossal wealth (no other country on earth can compare with us) . . . are we rotting in poverty and destitution? Why is the horizon of a bright future not only not getting nearer but always drawing further away from us? Why are we not masters of our own country but some sort of shameful lackeys? Why couldn't we give a damn about nature? After all, it's not only ours but after us, there are our children, grandchildren, great grandchildren . . . And dozens, hundreds of no less bitter and unanswerable 'whys' . . .[45]

Gorbachev grew increasingly uneasy after the Russian declaration of sovereignty. He knew that Yeltsin was 'by nature a destroyer', and that his election as Chairman of the Russian Supreme Soviet 'would increase confrontation between Russia and the Union'. Russia's declaration of sovereignty was a direct threat to the Union. 'The supreme bodies of government of the Russian Federation were, in fact, declaring their intention to act on their own without consulting the Union. The act, which was aimed firstly against the centre, was essentially an ultimatum, a show of disrespect for the remaining republics.' Russia's declaration of sovereignty gave the green light to the nationalists in other republics too, encouraging them to pursue full independence and creating 'a chain reaction, during which analogous enactments were passed by all of the Union republics and later autonomous republics'. Despairingly, Gorbachev realised that a 'parade of sovereignties' had begun. The only way now of preserving the Union and holding together some power in the centre was by negotiating a new Union treaty with the republics.[46]

However, in this desperate situation, Gorbachev's own political position had changed. He became increasingly isolated, without the support of a powerful reformist wing ready to back his dream of a more democratic Soviet Union. The reformers had gone over with Yeltsin to 'Democratic Russia' or joined the new Russian Communist Party. Desperate to preserve the Union, Gorbachev could only turn to the hardliners for backing. He abandoned his only chance of keeping his remaining support from the reformers when he rejected a radical plan for the introduction of a programme of reforms designed to create the basis of a market economy within 500 days. The package of reforms, designed by Academician Stanislav Shatalin, proposed large-scale privatisation and huge cuts in public expenditure, particularly on military projects. Shatalin was enthusiastically backed by Yeltsin and the reformers, but Gorbachev knew that to accept his proposals would immediately put him at loggerheads with the 'forces of order' on whom he realised that he had to rely in his struggle to preserve the Union.

He therefore rejected the Shatalin plan and opted instead for a rival programme, sponsored by the Finance Minister, Valentin Pavlov, whom he now appointed to the post of Prime Minister in a reshuffle, which was full of 'conservative' appointments and marked a dramatic shift to the right. The most sinister change of personnel was the replacement of the comparatively liberal Interior Minister, Vadim Bakatin, who had been negotiating the transfer of police powers to the republics, with Boris Pugo, formerly chief of the Latvian KGB.[47] The appointments were greeted with horror both by reformers in Moscow and by many commentators in the West, who believed that Gorbachev had now shown his true colours as an authoritarian who had only been a reluctant reformer. One leading American historian of Russia told a group of senators that Gorbachev was 'a front for the KGB'.[48]

Surrounded by his new group of 'conservative' advisers, dominated by Marshal Dmitry Yazov, Pugo and the head of the KGB, Vladimir Kryuchkov, Gorbachev now set about trying to shock the reformers into supporting his new Union treaty. Amidst dark rumours in Moscow of an impending *coup d'état* and civil war, the 'forces of order' planned an unusual military exercise, designed to intimidate the opposition in Russia. The exercise was planned with Gorbachev's full authority although, typically, he distanced himself from obvious involvement in it by arranging a visit abroad. The plan was to bring a large number of troops into Moscow in a deliberate show of strength, sending a signal to Yeltsin and the Russian opposition that, if necessary, Gorbachev would use force to help him preserve the Union. The exercise would send an entirely different message to the West, however, where it might be portrayed as an attempted coup by hardliners in the Soviet government against the reformist Gorbachev, who was struggling so valiantly against them.

Gorbachev naturally turned to the Airborne Forces for help with the operation. Their commander, General Vladislav Achalov, had impressed him with his handling of the recent crisis in Azerbaijan. He was reliable, loyal and efficient, and Gorbachev trusted the Airborne Forces more than any other branch of the services. Achalov ensured that preparations for the exercise were made in complete secrecy and, contrary to the usual practice of giving unit commanders advance notice of a field exercise, the Airborne troops were given no prior warning. On 8 September 1990, without using the normal divisional command structure, Achalov telephoned his senior commanders and ordered them to place their regiments on a state of alert. Both Pavel Grachev's 103rd Guards Airborne Division in Vitebsk and Alexander Lebed's Tula Division, together with the 76th Guards Airborne in Pskov, prepared themselves for a mission without being given any specific details. They were told to equip themselves 'southern-style', which meant arming the troops to the standards used in Afghanistan, with flak jackets, live ammunition (which was never issued in advance for field exercises) and helmets (normally only worn in wartime).

The soldiers and junior officers were deeply suspicious about the issue of these items, which reminded them of preparations for actual combat deployments. As BMD-1 airborne assault vehicles were prepared for action and Il-76 transport aircraft were dispatched from Leningrad to airlift the 137th Ryazan and the 331st Kostroma regiments, Lebed was summoned to a meeting with General Achalov. He was told that he was to prepare his regiments for a parade. When he asked why he was being ordered to take such a large amount of heavy armour and live ammunition with him to a parade, he was told to stop asking stupid questions. The secrecy surrounding the operation was so great that the pilots who flew paratroopers to airfields outside Moscow informed the capital's military air traffic control that they were carrying food for children who had lost their homes because of the Chernobyl disaster. The troops were never deployed as fully as Achalov had planned, though. The commotion in Ryazan, the main depot for the mission, attracted the attention of the local council, whose chairman, a former paratroop officer, called General Achalov and asked why the troops were being armed and armoured vehicles loaded into transport aircraft. He was told that 'many paratroopers are helping with the potato harvest'.[49]

Soon other people were asking questions and, in the uproar that followed, forty-two reformist deputies even issued an appeal to the troops not to use their weapons against their own people. Clearly, amidst the coup hysteria in Moscow, Yeltsin had got the message. To reinforce the point, however, during the exercise, a car accident was arranged for the Russian leader, as a result of which he suffered concussion. The 'accident' was believed to have been staged by the KGB. By 18 September, the exercise had achieved its objective of firing a warning shot across the bows of the reformers and the last paratroop companies were withdrawn from their positions at airfields outside Moscow. It had been no ordinary exercise, and Lebed had no doubt that it had been autho-rised at the highest level:

> The commanding officer of a regiment could put a battalion on alert for training purposes. The commander of a division could put a regiment on alert. And the commander of the Airborne Forces, a division. That was an indisputable law. In the present case, two divisions were put on full alert and another three were standing by. It was clear to everyone that the commander could not do that on his own. That means the minister. Formally, only the minister could give a command like that. But the minister was Marshal of the Soviet Union, Dmitry Timofeyevich Yazov, who had seen the war and over four decades of service; he was a very disciplined and cautious man. That means – even higher. Who – one could only guess.[50]

After the success of the exercise, Gorbachev's 'conservative' friends were confident and aggressive. Pugo was behind the estab-lishment of Committees of National Salvation, which tried to launch coups, backed by MVD and OMON units, in Lithuania and Latvia in January. Regiments from the 76th Guards Airborne, supported by the KGB's Alpha Group, were also flown into Vilnius, where they seized key government installations. In their attack on the television tower at least fourteen civilians were killed. Gorbachev later pretended that he had wanted to solve the crisis by exclusively peaceful means but the KGB and the military had launched the operation without his knowledge. He claimed that he 'contacted Kryuchkov immediately after receiving news about the events in Vilnius and demanded an explanation'.[51]

No one, least of all Kryuchkov or Pugo, was forced to resign, and the truth is that Gorbachev went along with the crackdown in the Baltic because he believed that a show of force would strengthen his hand against the nationalists in Russia and the republics; it might also convince the 'conservatives' that he was prepared to make a stand to defend the Union. Gorbachev again threatened the reformers in March, when he banned a pro-Yeltsin rally in Moscow and ordered the deployment of troops on the streets during a debate on a motion of no confidence in Yeltsin as Chairman of the Russian Supreme Soviet.

Yet, despite these intimidatory gestures, Gorbachev could not rely wholly on the 'conservatives'. To an extent, he had shifted to the right in order to contain the right, but he needed an agreement with the reformers. He was pursuing a policy of brinkmanship, trying to drag the 'conservatives' towards reform; but a Soviet reform, not the reform demanded by Russian nationalists. In March, a referendum was held in nine of the fifteen Soviet republics (Armenia, Georgia, Moldavia and the Baltic republics refused to take part) on Gorbachev's plans for a new decentralised Union of Sovereign Republics. The result showed overwhelming support (76 per cent of those who voted) for the plan. Gorbachev was delighted. In Russia, however, voters had been asked an additional question: whether or not they supported the establishment of a directly elected Russian presidency. They did, overwhelmingly.

Buoyed by the result of the referendum on the Union, Gorbachev met Yeltsin and other republican leaders at his *dacha* at Novo-Ogarevo to discuss a new Union treaty governing relations between the republics and the centre. As the negotiations proceeded on the draft treaty, which was due to be signed on Tuesday 20 August 1991, Gorbachev began to grow increasingly wary of Yeltsin, who was elected President of the Russian Federation in a landslide victory on 12 June. By now, Gorbachev was becoming increasingly irritated by Yeltsin's disparaging public versions of their private conversations. He realised that Yeltsin was being encouraged to dictate terms rather than to reach an agreement: 'Not all the members of Yeltsin's entourage displayed a peace-loving mood. Some were simply unable to cool down after the "anti-centrist" excitement. They had worked themselves up to fever pitch and continued to condemn and castigate the President [Gorbachev] whenever the opportunity arose.'[52]

Gorbachev now began to suspect that 'the extremists in the "democratic" camp would continue to invite Yeltsin to revive the attack on the centre and the Union President'.[53] He knew that, with a democratic mandate as the first directly elected President of Russia, Yeltsin's real aim was now to destroy the centre and create a fully independent, sovereign Russia. The time for compromise had passed, and Gorbachev arranged another tactical absence, this time at his villa on a secluded bay outside the quiet little Crimean resort of Foros on the Black Sea.

6

MOSCOW – AUGUST 1991

'The sea is beautiful in the stormy gloom
And the sky is brilliant without blue;
But believe me: the maid on the cliff
Is more beautiful than the waves, the skies and the
*   storm.'*

A. S. PUSHKIN, 'The Storm'[1]

Strong winds were gusting across the airfield in Tula as General Colin Powell, Chief of the United States General Staff, arrived at the headquarters of the 106th Airborne Division in the summer of 1991. The General was making a goodwill visit to the Airborne Forces, whose political significance had recently been underlined by the appointment of their commander, General Vladislav Achalov, as Deputy Minister of Defence. Gorbachev clearly felt that Achalov was a man who could be trusted, and was rewarding him for his loyalty during the critical events in the Caucasus and the Baltic; but especially because of his steadfast support during the unusual sabre-rattling exercise in September 1990. Achalov knew that his appointment was also due to Gorbachev's recognition that support from the Airborne Forces would be crucial in the forthcoming year.[2]

General Powell's visit to Tula had been arranged by Achalov's replacement as commander of the Airborne Forces, his ambitious former deputy, General Pavel Grachev. Alexander Lebed, recently promoted to the rank of Major-General, now became Grachev's deputy. As he watched Grachev's frantic attempts to impress the laconic American General, Lebed realised that Grachev had been over-promoted.

The wind was blowing across the airfield at a speed of ten metres per second. Occasional gusts of wind even reached twelve metres per second. It was clearly not going to be possible to provide a parachute display for the American visitor. Lebed told Grachev that the wind was too strong too jump.

The commander agreed with me and then disagreed with me. He had his doubts but I insisted, commenting that Americans are Americans but the legs that would be broken were ours, Russian ones. Hospitality is hospitality, but not to that extent. I asked for permission to give the necessary orders. The commander wanted more specific information: 'Are there any planes in the air?'

'There are planes in the air but it doesn't matter, we'll bring them down.'

The commander immediately and sharply changed his decision. 'Jump! Stop whining! Let them see what Soviet paratroops can do. Get on with it!'[3]

As Colin Powell mounted the reviewing platform, accompanied by a large group of officers, the drone of aeroplane engines could be heard somewhere beyond the forest which surrounded the airfield. The winds were now so strong that the men had to make their jump far from the airfield. They were carried towards the dropping zone at a terrifying speed and, as they landed, they cut into the earth, turned head over heels and crashed into each other. General Grachev's callous and foolhardy decision resulted in the death of one paratrooper and several serious injuries.[4]

Lebed watched as Powell, horrified at the display, wandered around the reviewing platform asking his hosts, 'What are you doing?' Lebed recognised that General Powell was not some cold-blooded American imperialist who could calmly watch the Russians breaking their legs. 'He was a human being, a General, who knew the value of life and blood. He had a conscience and so he wandered around and kept repeating, "What are you doing?" And that was not only painful but also unbearably shameful.'[5]

Another important visitor came to Tula in the summer of 1991. Gorbachev's military exercise in September 1990 had convinced Boris Yeltsin to change his policy towards the armed forces. He could not allow the demands of his reformist supporters for cuts in the military budget to alienate him from the military. As he began to campaign in the Russian Presidential elections, he realised that he would be unable to win the battle against Gorbachev to build an independent, sovereign Russia without the support of the armed forces. The Soviet leader had shown that he was ready to use force if he did not get his way, and Yeltsin knew that to survive as President of Russia, even with a democratic mandate, he would need military support. Above all, he would need the support of the Airborne Forces.

Yeltsin assiduously courted the officers and men of the 106th Airborne. Lebed remembers him taking off his watch and presenting it to a young lieutenant before pulling another identical one out of his pocket to give to a sergeant.[6] When the officers sat down with Yeltsin at a large table groaning with vodka, however, the Russian leader turned to Grachev and quickly came to the point. He wanted to know how the commander of the Airborne Forces would react in the event of an emergency situation in the country, such as a coup. Yeltsin's bodyguard, General Alexander Korzhakov, remembers them having 'an eyeball-to-eyeball discussion' about how the Airborne Forces might behave in such a situation. Grachev was clearly impressed that this senior political figure was seeking his opinion. 'Yeltsin was the first high-ranking leader to have talked to Grachev so pleasantly and trustingly,' says Korzhakov.[7]

Yeltsin had not come to Tula simply to charm the paratroop commander, though; he wanted to make sure that he could trust him. In the warm afterglow of several glasses of vodka, he felt ready to ask the General a straight question. As Yeltsin recalled:

> I hesitated for a moment but then made up my mind to ask him a hard question.
>
> 'Pavel Sergeyevich,' I asked him, 'if our lawfully elected government in Russia were ever to be threatened – a terrorist act, a coup, efforts to arrest the leaders – could the military be relied upon? Could you be relied upon?'
>
> 'Yes, we could,' he replied.[8]

Whether or not Yeltsin was right to trust Grachev's assurances, he left Tula convinced that in the event of a serious attempt to threaten the elected government of Russia, he would be able to count on the support of the Airborne Forces.

Gorbachev also felt that he could trust the military. He had recently demonstrated his confidence in the loyalty of the Airborne Forces by bringing Achalov into government as Deputy Minister of Defence. In fact, he later appeared to be so confident of the military's support that despite a rapidly deteriorating economic situation in the country, growing opposition from Communist hardliners to his plans for a new Union treaty, and doubts about Yeltsin's commitment to them, he would feel able to leave Moscow and travel over a thousand miles to the Black Sea for a family holiday.

Although Gorbachev felt at this time that Yeltsin's 'political instincts would have warned him against wrecking the process of signing the treaty', he admits that he had serious doubts about the Russian leader's intentions. 'I could not get rid of the feeling that Yeltsin was holding something back. I did my utmost to warn him against wavering at this crucial and historic moment. As I was to learn later, Yeltsin was under pressure from his associates to attach some conditions to his signature of the treaty.' Gorbachev realised that 'reservations or attempts to thwart the coming into force of the treaty . . . could not be ruled out'.[9]

At the same time, Gorbachev professed to be concerned about the hardliners.

> It goes without saying that I did not rule out the possibility of a head-on clash between the forces of renewal and reaction. Moreover, since November–December 1990, the conservative forces had been making ample use of every opportunity to attack the President and the reformers at Supreme Soviet sessions, Congresses of People's Deputies of the USSR, Party plenums and all kinds of meetings and conferences, clamouring for the introduction of presidential rule or the declaration of a state of emergency.[10]

However, Gorbachev appeared to agree with many of the hardliners' arguments about the need for firm action to re-establish Soviet authority. He accepted the demands of members of his government for a clampdown. Gorbachev's Vice-President, Gennady Yanayev, remembers that

Gorbachev gave us the impression, after our detailed discussions with him, that he understood that something had to be done. Therefore, already in 1990 . . . he instructed the Chairman of the Government, the Minister of Defence, the Chairman of the KGB and the Minister of the Interior to draw up four versions of a plan which might possibly bring the situation under control.

The first was the introduction of a state of emergency in the various parts of the country where there was a difficult situation, for example Azerbaijan, Georgia, the Baltic States. The second was the introduction of a temporary state of emergency throughout the whole country, perhaps for three to six months. The third was the introduction of direct, presidential rule in the difficult areas, including those I've already mentioned. And the fourth was for the introduction of direct, presidential rule throughout the whole country, again for a certain period of time.

All these instructions were carried out in good faith by my colleagues. The draft documents were drawn up for the four versions. All these documents were presented to Gorbachev and he said, 'Yes, yes, boys, just wait a little bit and we'll put one of the versions into action.' He pigeon-holed them, shoved them to one side, as we say. Nothing was done. We saw that our discussions with him had had no effect. The situation in the country got worse.[11]

The hardliners had already started to lose patience with Gorbachev. Gennady Yanayev remembers that the most conservative members of the government were concerned that Gorbachev was conducting the Novo-Ogarevo negotiations without reference to the USSR Supreme Soviet:

A working group had been set up which had begun to write a draft Union treaty at Novo-Ogarevo. When the members of the Supreme Soviet found out, they demanded that the process should be transferred to the Supreme Soviet. Gorbachev was not in favour of this. Eventually Lukyanov [Chairman of the Supreme Soviet] was formally included in the process of drafting the treaty. In this 'guise', so to speak, Lukyanov got to know the draft and we found out that, surprise, surprise, under pressure from Russia and Ukraine, Gorbachev was surrendering one position after another. And the draft Union treaty already left no room for doubt that what was now being considered was not a federation. At the very best, it might be a confederation. But a federal structure and a confederal one are very different things.[12]

Yanayev and his colleagues realised that Yeltsin had persuaded Gorbachev to drop plans to preserve the Soviet Union as a new federation. Yeltsin's real aim, which was supported by Nazarbayev of Kazakhstan and Kravchuk of Ukraine, was the creation of a Commonwealth of Independent States. Yanayev's group asked for a meeting with Gorbachev.

We went to another meeting with Gorbachev, during the course of which he said, 'Just wait half a month more, and then we'll choose one of the four versions,' which I've already mentioned. Time moved on and no action was taken. But the work on the Union treaty continued. We told him that if he continued to give ground, we would have to turn to the members of the Supreme Soviet, to the people, to society. We couldn't continue to work with him as the senior leaders of the country. Under the constitution, we were obliged to fight for observance of the constitutional rules and laws, which operated in the country. We could not support this destructive, anti-centrist tendency.[13]

By June the conservative members of the government had become extremely anxious about the Novo-Ogarevo process and irritated by Gorbachev's failure to respond to their concerns. At a secret session of the Supreme Soviet of the USSR, they joined in attacks on Gorbachev. Yanayev remembers that

at the June session of the Supreme Soviet, Pavlov, Kryuchkov, Yazov and Pugo made speeches in a secret session, in which they called things by their real names. This is where the country's going. This is what's happening. Something must be done. Gorbachev was not at the session. He was sitting in his office. I was in Germany at the time and returned that evening. When I got to my car, I received a call from Lukyanov asking me to come to the following day's session . . . I went to the session. The members were very concerned that they were considering all these problems and Gorbachev wasn't there. I rang Gorbachev and told him, 'You should be here, President. There is a very serious discussion.'

'No, you sit there,' he said. 'Listen a bit. I've got a lot of work to do.'

The ministers made their speeches. Pavlov [the Prime Minister] spoke. Then there was a break for lunch and we were told then that Gorbachev was waiting for us – me, Lukyanov, the Minister of Defence Yazov, the Minister of the Interior and the Chairman of the KGB. So we had a conversation along the lines of: the members are criticising me and you are just sitting there and saying nothing. That's no good. What's going on? We are either in the same boat or we are not. We said to him, 'We *are* in the same boat but, sorry, we don't want to sink it. So, if the Supreme Soviet considers it possible to extend the sitting of the secret session and to take some decisions then, as the leaders of the USSR, we will support the members. We will go to the session and tell them what's really going on in the country.'[14]

Despite the threat from Yanayev's group, Gorbachev took no action against them and made no attempt to protect himself from them; he seemed just as content now to leave Kryuchkov, Pugo and Yazov, the most hardline members of the government, in place as he had been after the events in the Baltic, when he had certainly had a suitable excuse to remove them. The truth, however, was that Gorbachev continued to feel that he needed the hardliners to add muscle to his resistance to Yeltsin and the nationalists. So, when he left Moscow at the beginning of August, he was happy to leave the capital in the hands of Yazov, Kryuchkov, Pugo and Yanayev.

Gorbachev was a complex leader with a mind full of alternatives. His associates and subordinates found it difficult to deal with his rambling conversation and lack of clear guidance. He seemed unable or unwilling to explain his precise strategic objectives and, all too often, waited upon events before committing himself to a course of action. In a crisis, he had a tendency to disappear, leaving others to take difficult decisions for him, as had happened in the Caucasus and the Baltic. To many of those who worked closely with him, his style of leadership was confused, contradictory and ambiguous. Often the ambiguity was deliberate, a ploy to keep people guessing about his real intentions or sympathies. Boris Pankin, Soviet Ambassador to Czechoslovakia and later Gorbachev's last Foreign Minister, remembers how difficult it was to identify the Soviet leader's true intentions: 'He was like the train in Yevtushenko's poem that shuttles between the city of "yes" and the city of "no".'[15] Yanayev remembers that

> Gorbachev did not have a clear programme of action and all his steps, practical steps, were undertaken by means of 'trial and error'. He'd take a decision one day, which didn't work or was even harmful, so he'd suddenly dash off in the opposite direction. These political swings continued throughout virtually the whole period of Gorbachev's leadership of the Party and the state . . . He was never in his heart of hearts a Communist; he was always a social democrat. And the politics of Gorbachev at that time had begun to resemble the convulsive movements of a man suffering terribly from Parkinson's disease. He said one thing, thought another and did a third.[16]

When Mikhail and Raisa Gorbachev left Moscow on 4 August 1991, the underlying political situation in the Soviet Union was as volatile as it had been at any time since the October revolution. Even Gorbachev later admitted that 'events in the country were acquiring an increasingly alarming character'.[17] The economic reports which the Kremlin received were causing the government grave concern. 'The economic situation was getting worse every day,' says Yanayev. 'And by August 1991, I can tell you that the situation was simply critical. There was only three days' coal left at the metallurgical plants and the factories were "free-wheeling", as we say. A train load would arrive, they'd load up and use it straight away. There were no reserves. The strategic reserves were already being used.'[18] At the same time, work on the draft Union treaty had not been completed and Gorbachev 'urged all those involved in the preparation of the signing of the draft Union treaty to expedite their work'.[19]

The political effect of Gorbachev's decision to take a holiday at such a time is perhaps only comprehensible if one imagines John

Major deciding to take a villa in the north of Scotland shortly before a vote on the Maastricht Treaty. Gorbachev's decision to leave Moscow was, at the very least, reckless. Suspicions still persist that it was the first evidence of his complicity in, or tolerance of, the hardliners' attempt to seize power.

His absence irritated and confused his government. They felt that he was leaving them to deal with the chaos while he strolled along the seashore in the Crimea with Raisa. 'On 4 August 1991, in spite of the awful situation in the country, Gorbachev went off on holiday,' says Yanayev:

> He went off on holiday and I would add that blood was already being shed in the country – let's not forget events in Nagorny Karabakh, Azerbaijan and so on. Blood was already flowing and no effective measures had been taken. That is the first duty of the President, as guarantor of the constitution – to safeguard people's right to life. These were our people, after all. Things even got to the stage when forty-one Soviet servicemen were taken hostage in Nagorny Karabakh. Gorbachev telephoned me every day from the Crimea to say that they should only be freed without bloodshed, and I contacted Ter-Petrossian, the Armenian President, by telephone ten times every day and said, 'Come on, free these people.' He said, 'Yes, yes, sure we'll free them.'[20]

The Soviet servicemen had been taken prisoner by an Armenian paramilitary group, which wanted to use them as a lever to secure the release of nationalist fighters arrested by the Soviet armed forces in connection with the disturbances in Karabakh.[21] So, in addition to the economic difficulties now facing the country and the continuing arguments over the Union treaty, the Soviet government now faced a serious hostage crisis. Yanayev and the other ministers wanted to launch an immediate special forces operation to deal with it but, from his seaside villa, Gorbachev continued to insist that no blood should be spilled.

To the ministers in Moscow, it was as though Gorbachev had gone through the looking-glass and acquired a completely different perception of reality. He was adamant that the treaty would be signed on 20 August. Yet his ministers claimed that they were ignorant of its precise contents, worried about the rumours of what it contained, and concerned that they would have no opportunity to discuss it with Gorbachev before the signing. Yanayev remembers:

> The most senior members of the government did not know where the draft Union treaty had got to and what was in it. Work was still going on. We didn't know what was in it. We still don't know who was responsible for the leak but, on the 15th or 16th of August, the new version of the treaty appeared in the papers. When my colleagues and I read it – it was a horror. It wasn't a State but, as Mayakovsky said, 'a cloud in trousers'. You understand, it was nothing. And when the lawyers gave their opinion on this treaty, they said clearly that it wasn't any kind of federation but it wasn't a confederation either. It was something incomprehensible . . . And he was proposing to sign this treaty on 20 August.

Yanayev tried desperately to persuade Gorbachev to return to Moscow. 'I telephoned him and said, "Mikhail Sergeyevich, our opinion is that no way should you sign that treaty. We want you to come back and discuss it here."

"Oh, no. You know, I'm not feeling well. It's my back. I've got the doctors here. I can't fly. I'll fly back tomorrow evening, the nineteenth."'[22]

Yanayev was astonished by the President's lethargic reaction. Gorbachev was apparently intending to sign the Union treaty without discussing it with the members of his own government, and was now refusing to return to Moscow because he had backache. Yanayev remembers his sense of frustration after the conversation:

> If there's a fire in your house, your first duty is to put it out. Not just ignore it. But that is Gorbachev all over. Whenever there was a difficult problem like that, he would start trying to get away from it. So that he was clean. So that his democratic image wasn't spoilt anywhere. That's why he keeps saying that he didn't know anything about events in Tbilisi. He didn't know anything about Vilnius. He didn't know anything about Azerbaijan. He didn't know anything at all. Although not one single military unit could be transferred personally by the

Minister of Defence without the agreement of the commander-in-chief. And Gorbachev was the commander-in-chief.[23]

The position now was that all the senior members of Gorbachev's own government had serious reservations about the treaty. The loudest opposition to his plan to sign the treaty on 20 August was being expressed by the Vice-President, the Prime Minister, the Interior Minister, the Minister of Defence and the Chairman of the KGB. To all intents and purposes, in the absence of Gorbachev, they *were* the Soviet government. In addition, the Supreme Soviet was now expressing its grave reservations. Although only a pale shadow of a democratic institution, it was nonetheless the highest legislative authority under the Soviet constitution, and had declared its support for the principle of a treaty in July. Its Chairman, Anatoly Lukyanov, a former classmate of Gorbachev, was annoyed that the Supreme Soviet's demands for the new Union to include a single economic space, a single banking system and adequate tax provisions for the federal budget had not been adopted in the final draft.[24] The frustration and annoyance of all these senior figures at Gorbachev's attitude was underlined by their recollection of the referendum result earlier the same year, in which the Soviet people had shown their overwhelming support for the preservation of the Union. Now it looked as though Gorbachev was preparing to sell out the Union behind their backs. The KGB Chairman, Vladimir Kryuchkov, perhaps the hardest of the hardliners, had for some time been convinced that decisive action would have to be taken to save the Union.

On 16 August, after spending the morning signing state papers in the Kremlin, Gennady Yanayev went to visit a friend, the former editor of *Trud* newspaper, at his *dacha* outside Moscow. The editor had been ill for a long time, eventually becoming disabled, and Yanayev had brought him some medicine. The two friends sat on the *dacha*'s tiny verandah, enjoying the evening sunshine, drinking brandy and discussing the political situation. They were disturbed by a telephone call at eight o'clock from Kryuchkov. The KGB Chairman asked Yanayev to come to the Kremlin because 'a group of our comrades has flown to see Gorbachev. They're coming back now and we've got to discuss what we're going to do in the country.'[25]

Yanayev was at first irritated that Kryuchkov had sent a group of his agents to see Gorbachev without telling him, but he was reassured when he discovered that Pavlov, the Prime Minister, had been told. After a brief meeting with Kryuchkov in the Kremlin, Yanayev agreed to attend another meeting the following evening at a KGB residence near Lenin Prospekt.

The next meeting, on the 17th, was attended by Yanayev, Kryuchkov, Pavlov, Yazov and his deputies, Generals Varennikov and Achalov, the Central Committee secretary Oleg Shenin, and Oleg Baklanov, a Central Committee member with responsibility for the military–industrial complex. The group, which could hardly be described as anything other than the inner circle of the Soviet government, discussed sending a delegation to Gorbachev, which would inform him about the situation and say to him 'either you take measures yourself or let Yanayev do it'.[26]

General Achalov remembers the scene in the garden of the KGB *dacha*:

We all sat in the open air, drinking whisky and coffee. Pavlov was running the meeting. He made a report on the situation in the country. He spoke for about one hour, detailing the decrease in oil and coal production, and of industrial and agricultural output. I saw him for the first time and was quite impressed. He seemed to be firm and competent, and certainly compared favourably with Ryzhkov. He persuaded everybody of the need for urgent action. The Council of Ministers had met that day, and almost all of them were in favour of imposing a state of emergency in the country. Kryuchkov spoke by telephone to Gorbachev, who was calling from Foros, while we were there. When he hung up he said that Gorbachev sent his best wishes to us all. We all decided, immediately and unanimously, that the next day, the 18th, a delegation consisting of Baklanov, Shenin, Plekhanov and Varennikov would go to Foros.[27]

On the same day, Yazov stepped up military preparations for an emergency. General Achalov was ordered to put all divisions of the Airborne Forces on a state of alert. Most senior officers assumed that the divisions were being prepared for another deployment in the Caucasus, perhaps to deal with the Armenian hostage crisis. Alexander Lebed was on leave and, after a brief visit to his mother in Novocherkassk, he was planning to spend the next few days in his garden. He was disturbed, however, by a call from Pavel Grachev, telling him to take charge of an 'operational group' and to prepare the Tula division 'southern-style'. When Lebed asked why, Grachev promised that he would be given more information later.

The Soviet government delegation to Mikhail Gorbachev left Moscow on 18 August, arriving in Foros in the early evening. It consisted of Shenin, Baklanov, Varennikov, Valery Boldin, the head of the General Department of the Central Committee, and Yuri Plekhanov, the senior KGB officer who was head of presidential security. Gorbachev's version of what happened next is as follows:

At about five p.m. on 18 August, I was informed that a group composed of Baklanov, Shenin, Boldin, Varennikov and Plekhanov had arrived at the *dacha*. I was surprised, because I had not invited anyone. The head of my security guard was patently at a loss. It turned out that the guards had let the visitors enter because they were in the company of Plekhanov and Boldin. Nothing like that could have happened otherwise. For security reasons no one was allowed to enter my *dacha* without my consent.

I decided to find out what was going on. I tried to contact Moscow and talk first of all to Kryuchkov, only to discover that all five telephone lines, including the strategic communications line, were dead. Even the city telephone line did not work. I walked out on to the verandah, where Raisa Maksimovna was reading the newspapers, and told her that we had unexpected guests. Their intentions were unpredictable but we could expect the worst. She was shaken by the news but remained cool. We went to the nearby bedroom. My thoughts were racing: I shall not retreat, I shall not yield to any pressure, blackmail or threats . . .

. . . The guards told me that the visitors were edgy, wondering why they had not been received. When I left the bedroom I discovered that they had come up to the second floor without being asked. Their general behaviour was most uncivil, almost as if they were the hosts. I invited them into my study and asked them the purpose of their mission. Baklanov declared that an emergency committee had been created. The country was sliding into disaster, he declared – 'You must sign the decree on the declaration of a state of emergency.' In fact they had come with an ultimatum. Eventually I learned that they had brought with them different versions of documents prepared for my signature . . . I refused to sign any decree.[28]

Yanayev's version of the delegation's meeting with Gorbachev is completely different:

When the delegation flew to see Gorbachev, he listened to everything they had to say. Then he spoke, and his first question was, 'Has Yeltsin been arrested?' They said to him, 'No, we don't want to arrest anyone.' Yeltsin and Gorbachev, of course, hated each other, almost bestially. They hated each other so much that the one only had to hear the other's name before he'd start swearing. It was like folk lore.

Gorbachev listened to my colleagues' proposals and said, 'Well, you know, I'm ill. It'd be better if you took care of things.' His 'illness' was such that he could have quite easily flown. If you were interested in saving the country, you'd fly back dead . . . So there was a very polite discussion. Nobody said 'we're putting you under arrest'. It was agreed with him, and only because of that, that his communications would be temporarily cut off. But in our time, you didn't cut off communications. Gorbachev had several cars with special communications which could not be cut off anyway. They were satellite communications, which couldn't be broken off. Access to these was via machines which were in cases. The keys to these cases were with Gorbachev's bodyguards, who remained loyal to him to the last moment. In this way, Gorbachev chose a regime of apparent self-isolation, so that he looked clean. He was waiting to see if the Emergency Committee [GKChP] would work and there was no rebellion in the country. Then, in three days, he'd appear at a session of the Supreme Soviet, support all the actions of the GKChP and say 'now, as President, I'll do it myself'. And if not, then he was clean. And we understood this. We knew the games he liked to play . . . He was not against it. When they were all leaving, he shook each of them by the hand and said, 'All right, get to work. Good luck!' That's literally what he said.[29]

We shall perhaps never know for sure which of the two accounts is true. However, Yanayev's version certainly has some circumstantial plausibility. The very fact that those demanding emergency measures were not some extremist group on the fringes of the government but the government itself, all of whom had been appointed by Gorbachev and could easily have been removed at any moment by him, would suggest that they were acting with the tacit approval of the President or, at least, without his determined opposition.

Equally, his own record in earlier crises suggests that he may, indeed, have known what his Cabinet colleagues intended but hoped to avoid being implicated. The sequence of events in Baku, Tbilisi, Vilnius and the military exercise in Moscow, which was designed to frighten his political opponents, all seem to give the lie to his protestations of absolute innocence.

By the time the delegation returned to Moscow on 18 August, frustration with Gorbachev's continuing absence had spread across the political spectrum. Boris Yeltsin and the Kazakh leader Nursultan Nazarbayev had issued a humiliating rebuke to him over his handling of the Nagorny Karabakh dispute. They even offered to mediate between Azerbaijan and Armenia, 'if Gorbachev cannot find the strength to do so himself'.[30] The Soviet Cabinet had also made a public statement about the Union treaty. They demanded clarification and revision of several of its most crucial provisions. The public began to wonder how Gorbachev could possibly manage to sign the treaty in two days' time without the support of his own Cabinet. They did not know about the discussion which had just taken place in Foros. The Soviet government had no intention of signing on the 20th.

The KGB Chairman, Vladimir Kryuchkov, was sixty-seven years old and a veteran of the Soviet secret police with the military rank of General. A former lawyer, who had begun his career in a factory in Volgograd and worked his way up through the Young Communist League, he owed his rise to power in the KGB to Yuri Andropov, the same man who had also promoted Gorbachev. Kryuchkov became Andropov's deputy, responsible for the KGB's foreign intelligence operations. When Gorbachev became General Secretary, he made Kryuchkov KGB Chairman. As a former lawyer, Kryuchkov loyally supported Gorbachev's belief in the rule of law, even telling newspapers that law enforcement agencies, such as the KGB, should strictly abide by Soviet legislation, no matter how difficult the situation was.[31]

On 18 August, however, when the delegation had returned from Foros, Kryuchkov ordered the mobilisation of the KGB's own units of special forces, the Alpha and Beta Groups. The Alpha Group's officers were told to prepare two detachments, about 200 troops in total, for a mission to free the Soviet hostages in Nagorny Karabakh. This mission was a complete deception, though.[32] Their real mission, as it later became clear, was to deal with Boris Yeltsin and his advisers.

Yeltsin was in Kazakhstan on 18 August. He had formed an important alliance with Nursultan Nazarbayev, and the two leaders had worked together throughout the Novo-Ogarevo process to push for sovereignty and independence for their republics. Throughout the day, they had discussed tactics for the signing of the Union treaty and worked on a bilateral agreement between Russia and Kazakhstan. After their meetings, Nazarbayev took Yeltsin swimming in a mountain stream outside the capital, Alma-Ata. Yeltsin plunged into the cool water and then lay on the grassy bank sunbathing and staring up at the cloudless sky. His bodyguard, Alexander Korzhakov, politely reminded him that he should perhaps hurry as they had to leave. As they were about to depart, however, Nazarbayev announced that he had arranged a banquet and dancing. They were delayed for over three hours. Alexander Korzhakov recalls that 'later, informed sources told Yeltsin that a team had left Moscow to destroy our aircraft. And, in order to save us, it was necessary to delay take-off. It's difficult to believe all of this but nobody knows to this day whether the delay was specially arranged or not.'[33] Yeltsin later wrote:

> I don't think that our three-hour delay in departure from Alma-Ata was accidental . . . Alexander Tizyakov [one of the Committee of Emergency] . . . who had prepared a directive for his co-conspirators, said: 'It is necessary to recall . . . that in the conversation with Gorbachev an option was even envisioned whereby on the eve of the final decision to impose a state of

emergency, on 18 August, the plane on which the Russian government delegation, headed by Yeltsin, was travelling to Moscow from Kazakhstan should be destroyed in the air at night . . .[34]

Whatever the truth of the rumours about plans for an attack on Yeltsin's aeroplane, the Russian leader and his entourage arrived safely back at Moscow's Vnukovo airport in the early hours of the morning of the 19th. Despite his boss's fondness for elaborate conspiracy theories, Korzhakov later admitted that the real reason for the delay had probably just been the 'pleasant, extended relaxation', during which Kazakh girls had sung local songs and Yeltsin had played his favourite tunes with wooden spoons on the head of one of his officials.[35] When Yeltsin and Korzhakov arrived back at the Russian leader's *dacha* in Arkhangelskoye outside Moscow, however, they had stepped, without realising it, into the middle of a hornets' nest.

At 4 a.m., detachments of the KGB's Alpha Group, commanded by Viktor Karpukhin, made their way from the main road through the forest to Yeltsin's *dacha*. As dawn approached, the troops were hiding under camouflage cover on the edges of the forest, surrounding the house. They had still not been fully briefed on the purpose of the operation and were perplexed when orders came over their radios to stand by for a signal to arrest the Russian President, 'for the purpose of guaranteeing the security of negotiations with the Soviet leadership'.[36] A little later, Kryuchkov personally rescinded the order. He had decided to wait and see if Yeltsin could be trapped into breaking the new law on the state of emergency, which had just been announced.

As the KGB's special troops took up their positions, the Soviet news agency Tass announced that Gennady Yanayev had temporarily assumed the responsibilities of the President because of Gorbachev's ill-health, and a State Emergency Committee (GKChP) had been formed. In addition to Yanayev, Pavlov, Yazov, Pugo and Kryuchkov, its members were Baklanov, the first deputy Chairman of the Defence Council; Starodubtsev, the Chairman of the Farmers' Union; and Tizyakov, the President of the Association of State Enterprises and Industrial, Construction, Transport and Communications

Facilities. The Committee members were tacitly supported by other influential figures, such as Bessmertnykh, the Foreign Minister, and Lukyanov, the Chairman of the Supreme Soviet.

Yanayev argued with his colleagues for a long time before he agreed to sign the documents announcing the formation of an Emergency Committee. He was full of doubts about Gorbachev. 'I'll tell you quite honestly. I hesitated for a long time. I knew Gorbachev and how he'd always undermine us. I knew that, in any event, I was a *kamikadze*. Even if we were successful and he supported us, he'd get rid of me in a month under pressure from the democrats . . . I understood that if it didn't work, these people would try to take away my freedom and, possibly, my life. So, for me, this decision was exceptionally hard, very difficult. And my colleagues worked on me for several hours. But in the end, at seven o'clock in the evening, I signed the documents.'[37]

General Achalov remembers that, by the time Yanayev agreed to sign the documents declaring a state of emergency, he was drunk.

Dmitry Timofeyevich [Yazov] took me with him to a meeting in Pavlov's office in the Kremlin. About eighteen or twenty people were there. I saw Starodubtsev, Yanayev, very drunk, Pavlov, less drunk, Pugo, recalled from leave, Bessmertnykh, Grushkov, from the KGB, Lukyanov, also recalled from leave, and others. Varennikov had already gone to the Ukraine, but the others who had been to Foros were there. They told us that when they put the facts to Gorbachev he slithered, as usual. He was playing his games again, and let us down. They had come up with the idea that he was ill, but I truthfully don't know whether this was with his agreement or not. Then Yanayev took a paper that had been prepared, and said, in somewhat slurred speech, 'I'm now the President. All the powers of the Presidency are mine. I'll sign the document.' Then Yanayev turned to me and said, 'Well, Comrade General, order the troops into Moscow, to keep order.'[38]

It had been agreed that news of the declaration of a state of emergency would be broadcast at dawn on the morning of the 19th but, at midnight, the Generals were still arguing about using troops in Moscow. The plans which had been drawn up envisaged the use of troops in the event of serious civil disorder. Achalov argued against deploying troops in Moscow without an obvious threat to public order and without a clear plan:

> In any case, if we gave the order then, the working day would have started by the time the troops arrived, and there could be unpleasantness, since no tasks had been assigned. If necessary, I argued, we could bring the troops into the city on the following day. Yazov fetched Kryuchkov, and together we talked it through. We went to Lukyanov, who was sitting with Bessmertnykh, and together we agreed not to bring the troops into Moscow. Our conversation went on until 1 a.m. on 19 August. Yazov then told me to go to my working-place. He stayed with the others. I called Kalinin, the commander-in-chief of the Moscow Military District, and Samsonov, the commander-in-chief of the Leningrad Military District, at 0200 hours, saying that they should be aware of the conversation that had taken place. Thirty minutes later Kalinin telephoned me, saying that he had been ordered by Yazov to bring the troops into Moscow.[39]

The Emergency Committee's statement in the early hours of 19 August began with a sonorous incantation: 'Fellow countrymen! Citizens of the Soviet Union! In a dark and critical hour for the destiny of our country and of our peoples, we address you! A mortal danger hangs over our great homeland!' It announced that 'the country has in effect become ungovernable' and declared a six-month state of emergency.[40] According to Yanayev, it was one of the draft documents that had been prepared at Gorbachev's request as part of the package of four options for methods of re-establishing order in the country. 'It would have been impossible to produce these documents in one day. These were the drafts which had been presented to Gorbachev as one of the four options I have mentioned.'[41]

The statement announcing the formation of the Emergency Committee immediately set the wrong tone. It was hysterical and melodramatic, whereas the most sensible approach would have been to play down the significance of events and assume an air of normality. A separate statement, issued by Yanayev to the United Nations, was more restrained: 'The adopted measures are temporary . . . The major aim of the emergency situation is to ensure conditions guaranteeing personal and property security for every citizen . . . The entire complex of measures being undertaken is directed at the most rapid stabilisation of the situation in the USSR, normalisation of social and economic life, and realisation of the necessary transformations and creation of conditions for the country's all-round development.'[42]

The Emergency Committee was getting off to a bad start. The problem was not simply the hysterical tone of their initial statement. Before dawn on the 19th, they had already made two fatal blunders. The first was the decision to order hundreds of tanks and thousands of troops to begin moving on Moscow. 'The decision taken on the night of the 18th and 19th to put troops into Moscow was wrong,' Yanayev now admits. 'Particularly wrong was the decision to bring in armour. No way was it necessary. It immediately alarmed people, because using tanks is not the best way of solving problems. It was our mistake and a big mistake.'[43] An even bigger mistake, however, was the Emergency Committee's failure to arrest Boris Yeltsin.

Early on the morning of the 19th, the Russian leader was woken by his daughter, Tanya, who ran into his room shouting, 'Papa, get up! There's a coup!' As Yeltsin was dressing, Alexander Korzhakov arrived and confirmed the news. He had already telephoned other members of the Russian leadership and arranged for more security to come to Arkhangelskoye to protect Yeltsin. Soon Yeltsin's colleagues began to arrive at the *dacha*, which was still surrounded and under observation by the KGB. They began to write an appeal to the citizens of Russia, urging them to resist the decrees of the Emergency Committee.

'Literally an hour after my daughters typed our appeal to the people, it was being read in Moscow and other cities,' Yeltsin recalls. 'The Western wire services sent it out, professional and amateur computer networks transmitted it, and independent radio stations like "Echo of Moscow", stock market lines, and the correspondents' network of many national publications also passed it on. And many Xerox machines, previously banned, suddenly appeared out of nowhere!'[44]

The Emergency Committee clearly did not appreciate how many channels of communication now existed in modern Russia. The failure to isolate Yeltsin had given him the opportunity to gather together the Russian government and rally opposition to the coup.

Among the telephone calls that Yeltsin made as soon as he heard news of the coup was one to a recent acquaintance. When the Russian President found out that tanks and troops were advancing on Moscow, he called the commander of the Airborne Forces, Pavel Grachev. 'It was one of my first calls from Arkhangelskoye,' Yeltsin remembers.

Upon receiving news of the coup, I reminded him of our last conversation. Grachev was disturbed, there was a long pause, and I could hear his laboured breathing on the other end of the line. Finally, he said that for him, an officer, it was impossible to disobey an order. I said something to the effect that I didn't want to expose him to attack. He said something like, 'Wait a minute, Boris Nikolayevich. I'll send you a reconnaissance squad' (or security detachment, I don't recall). I thanked him and on that we said goodbye. Naina recalls that at that time, which was already early morning, I put down the receiver and said, 'Grachev's on our side.'[45]

Quite how much Grachev was ever on Yeltsin's side is still a matter of speculation. Korzhakov, who was present when Yeltsin telephoned the Airborne Forces' commander, is not so sure that he ever was. 'After August, rumours reached me about the double and even triple game that Grachev had allegedly been playing. But no one could confirm these rumours with written proof.'[46] It later became clear that Grachev had been involved in preparatory work for the imposition of a state of emergency, working with Kryuchkov and Yazov on the draft plans ordered by Gorbachev, since the beginning of the month.

'They began work on 5 August,' says Yanayev, 'drafting the documents, helping with one of the four options. Pavel Grachev took part in this business of drafting documents – the Chairman of the KGB and Grachev. They got Grachev along even though he couldn't write more than two words.'[47] Whatever the truth may have been later, on the morning of 19 August, it seemed to Yeltsin that Grachev was ready to help him in his hour of need.

As armoured vehicles of the 2nd Guards 'Taman' Motor-Rifle Division and the 4th Guards 'Kantemirov' Tank Division, together with paratroopers from the 106th Guards Airborne, began to move into Moscow, Pavel Grachev assured Yeltsin that a company of paratroopers was on its way to guard the Russian Supreme Soviet building, the 'White House'. He told his Chief of Staff, Yevgeny Podkolzin, that the greatest care should be taken to ensure that there were no civilian casualties. At the same time, however, he confirmed to Marshal Yazov that he would send a battalion, rather than a company, to the White House. Yeltsin might feel that the paratroops were going to protect the Russian Parliament, but Yazov knew that they would stand by for his order to take it, if necessary. The orders to 'guard' the White House and other buildings were sufficiently ambiguous to allow Grachev to play a double game, as he waited to see whether the Emergency Committee would succeed.

After his conversation with General Grachev, Yeltsin left Arkhangelskoye. There were already tanks in the centre of Moscow and on the Kaluga highway, which led from Yeltsin's *dacha* to the capital. Yeltsin's bodyguard, Alexander Korzhakov, knew that, if the KGB special forces in the compound around the *dacha* decided to stop the Russian leader leaving, resistance would be virtually impossible. 'We wouldn't have survived for long, maybe until we'd exhausted the last round of our pistols and a few automatic rifles.'[48]

Yeltsin and Korzhakov decided to leave the compound openly in a large cortege of official vehicles. Yeltsin, who refused to wear a flak jacket, sat in the back of the presidential limousine as it left the *dacha*, with the Russian flag flying proudly on its bonnet. On the Kaluga highway, the tank crews heading for Moscow stared with curiosity at the black Chaika as it sped past them. When Karpukhin, the Alpha commander at Arkhangelskoye, realised that the Russian leader had gone, he screamed over the radio at his men, 'Why didn't you arrest Yeltsin?'[49]

When Yeltsin reached Moscow, he set about making the White House a centre of resistance to the Emergency Committee. He also began to realise that everything might not be quite as it seemed, and that Gorbachev might be more deeply involved than anyone suspected. As he read through the various documents announcing the state of emergency, he was surprised to find Anatoly Lukyanov's statement expressing concern that there were serious errors in the final draft of the Union treaty and calling for its signing to be delayed. It was unlikely that such a close friend of Gorbachev would have turned against him. Yeltsin recalled:

> As I read Lukyanov's statement about the treaty, I tried to understand what was behind it. The first possibility was that Lukyanov had betrayed his friend and boss, Gorbachev. The second possibility was more complicated, but had to be taken into account: Gorbachev knew about the whole situation, and the coup was being orchestrated according to a scenario he had prepared. The idea was to have other people do the dirty work to clear Gorbachev's path, then he could return from vacation to a new country under a state of emergency . . . Gorbachev would then appear on the scene, having used Yanayev and Lukyanov to torpedo the Union treaty.[50]

As he read through Lukyanov's statement, Yeltsin realised that the ambiguous nature of Gorbachev's position gave him the opportunity to turn the tables on the Soviet leader. The next few hours would be a test of will.

He had once described Gorbachev as his 'potential opponent, the lover of half-measures and half-steps'.[51] Now, he knew that his old enemy would be waiting on events, unsure which way to turn without a clear view of the path ahead. Equally, without Gorbachev's unequivocal backing, the Emergency Committee would be reluctant to impose its will as ruthlessly as might be necessary in the face of growing public opposition. Already, Muscovites were responding in their tens of thousands to Yeltsin's call to oppose the declaration of a state of emergency. Huge crowds had begun to converge on the White House, encircling it in a protective human chain. As Yeltsin discussed the situation with senior members of his administration – Rutskoi, Burbulis, Silayev, Shakhrai, Khasbulatov and others – he noticed a tank approaching the building.

> As I watched, the armoured vehicle was surrounded by a crowd of people. The driver stuck his head out of the hatch. People were not afraid to approach the tanks; in fact, they were even throwing themselves under them. They weren't afraid – although they were Soviet people, raised in the Soviet system. People were even lining up; they weren't afraid of the tank

treads. They weren't afraid of being arrested, although they were being threatened with a crackdown every hour over the radio and television. Suddenly, I felt a jolt inside. I had to be out there right away, standing with those people.[52]

He made his way through the crowds and climbed up on to a tank, where he made an emotional speech, urging the crowds to defend the White House and man barricades to prevent an assault.

Yeltsin had understood the situation perfectly. The White House had become the symbol of resistance to the Emergency Committee and a rival authority to the Kremlin. Every moment that the Emergency Committee allowed the Russian government to continue to incite people to defy its orders, its position became weaker. Sooner or later, if they were serious, Yanayev and his colleagues would have to try to take control of the building and arrest the Russian leadership. To do that, they would need to use the troops outside, many of whom were already beginning to fraternise with the crowds. The future of the Russian government and the fate of what remained of the Soviet Union now lay in the hands of the paratroops who had been assigned to 'guard' the White House. If they were prepared to storm the building and shoot anyone who got in the way, Yeltsin's fate would be sealed. If not, they would have to disobey a direct order. The man who would take the decision was their commander, Pavel Grachev's deputy, Major-General Alexander Lebed.

When Yeltsin began his speech to the crowds outside the White House, Lebed was still on the outskirts of Moscow, together with the bulk of the 106th Airborne Division. At 1 p.m., however, Grachev told him to join the 2nd Battalion of the 137th Ryazan regiment at the White House. When he arrived outside the building, the crowds were so dense that he could not find the 2nd Battalion. Cars and trolley-buses had been overturned to form barricades, and people were edgy and emotional. When they saw his Major-General's uniform, they became hostile and abusive, many of them assuming that he had come to give orders to attack them. It was not until 5 p.m., after several furious telephone calls to Grachev, that Lebed finally made contact with the 2nd Battalion in the forecourt of the Comecon building on the corner of Kalinin Prospekt. The soldiers were relieved to see him, assuming that he would be able to explain the situation to them, but, as

Grachev still had not briefed him, he was almost as confused as his men.

He made a short speech to the crowd, reminding them that his soldiers were 'sons of the people' and would not fire at them. Then he asked them to find Yeltsin's bodyguard, Alexander Korzhakov, whom he had met during exercises in the Tula division. After a short while, Korzhakov arrived together with a delegation from the Russian President's office. Lebed explained that he had been sent by Grachev, who was responding to Yeltsin's request for a company of paratroopers to guard the building. Lebed then asked Korzhakov for a special favour: 'He asked me for one thing – to arrange a personal meeting for him with Boris Nikolayevich [Yeltsin]. I took him into my office and offered him some tea. Then I went to Yeltsin and told him about Lebed, who had arrived on Grachev's orders and was now asking for a private conversation. After taking advice, we decided to arrange the meeting in the back room of Yeltsin's office. This place had been thoroughly checked – it wasn't bugged.'[53]

The meeting lasted for twenty minutes. Lebed explained that his objective was to stop disturbances around the White House and to prevent damage to it. Yeltsin questioned him on his orders, unsure whether or not Lebed had come in good faith.

'What was your purpose in coming here?' Yeltsin asked.

'To organise the guarding and defence of the Supreme Soviet building with a paratroop battalion.'

'On whose orders?'

'On the orders of the commander of the Airborne Forces, Lieutenant-General Grachev.'

'From whom will you guard us and against whom will you protect us?' Yeltsin persisted. Lebed recalled:

As this question was not clear to me either, I gave an evasive explanation: 'From whom does a guard post guard? From anyone who threatens the integrity of the post or the life of the guard.' The President seemed pleased with this answer. He expressed some concern about the fate of Gorbachev. Then he started to question me about the reaction of the armed forces to the coup. I answered that they hadn't reacted at all because they didn't know about it. Yeltsin didn't say anything although he was obviously surprised and even a little annoyed by this.[54]

However, Yeltsin was pleased at the meeting with Lebed and, as they parted, he told him that he trusted him. He agreed to allow Lebed to move a company of paratroopers into the White House and ordered Korzhakov to arrange for them to be escorted through the barricades. The President and the General agreed to maintain regular contact and to meet again soon. Whilst Yeltsin was encouraged by the meeting, Lebed was becoming convinced that his oath of loyalty to Gorbachev, as President of the Soviet Union, was being severely tested. Although he had told Yeltsin that he would not allow his battalion to be used against other forces in the event of an attack on the building, Lebed was furious that his men were once again being exploited by the Kremlin to confront crowds of civilians, and he began looking for a way to avoid obeying any order that might come from the Defence Ministry to storm the White House. His next meeting with the Russian President was to be one of the turning-points in Yeltsin's struggle against the Emergency Committee.

Whilst Yeltsin had set about the organisation of resistance to the coup with determination and confidence, the Emergency Committee soon ran into trouble. A disastrous press conference by Yanayev had the opposite effect to the one intended; far from reassuring the public, it heightened tension and led one correspondent to describe the members of the Committee as 'forbiddingly dim and so far inefficient even in tyranny'.[55] Attempts to clamp down on the media were only partially successful. The independent 'Echo of Moscow' started to broadcast from the White House, and many of the newspapers that had been banned began to appear as broadsheet posters on walls all over the capital. Strains soon appeared between the members of the Committee as it became clear that the initial display of force had not cowed the opposition into submission. The Deputy Prime Minister, Vladimir Shcherbakov, made it plain that he was refusing to serve the Emergency Committee. By the morning of the 20th, the Prime Minister, Valentin Pavlov, had begun to panic, and resigned from the government on the grounds of ill-health and high blood pressure. Rumours had begun to circulate ever since Lebed led his men into the White House that the army was deeply split and that many units were ready to side with Yeltsin.

Marshal Yazov feared that Lebed had already had gone over to the Russian President. He telephoned Grachev and asked, 'Has

Lebed betrayed us? He has been seen going into the White House and talking to Yeltsin's people.'[56] Grachev assured him that Lebed had betrayed no one. Yazov was not convinced, however. His deputy, General Achalov, remembers his concern about the reliability of the troops. 'I saw that he was in a very bad state, extremely worried about what was going on. He knew that I understood, and told me that my job was just to control the units that were being used, nothing more.'[57] The Defence Minister demanded to know who had told Lebed to move his troops into the White House and Grachev, who was still hedging his bets and trying to stay close to Yazov, pinned the blame on Lebed. Shortly after dawn, Lebed received an angry telephone call from Grachev.

> He began brusquely: 'What have you done? Where have you taken the battalion?'
> 'What do you mean where? To the RSFSR Supreme Soviet building, on your orders.'
> 'You didn't understand me correctly.'
> I became angry. 'Comrade Commander, my office writes everything down. All arrangements, instructions and orders are noted by three clerks in the record of military engagements.'
> My experience with lawyers and investigators in numerous enquiries had taught me long ago to keep a record of everything. The commander calmed down a little.
> 'Well, don't get upset. But you did make a stupid mistake. The boss is not happy.'
> 'Which boss?'
> 'What do you mean, which one? The minister. Remember: you made a stupid mistake. Come here and bring the battalion out, just like you brought it in.'
> I hung up and thought about the call. Like any normal person with character and self-respect, I don't like to feel like a puppet.[58]

Yazov and Kryuchkov were beginning to panic. The tank and motor-rifle regiments in the city centre were openly fraternising with the demonstrators. Soldiers assured people in the crowds around the White House that they had no intention of firing on them. Every minute that Yeltsin remained in the White House, the chances of the coup succeeding became more and more remote. The Emergency Committee was approaching the point where it would have to decide between storming the White House or capitulating. Yazov had realised that if he decided to order the storming of the White House, he would first have to ensure the removal of all Airborne troops in the area. This was the reason for Grachev's call to Lebed, ordering him to withdraw his battalion. Later, Grachev tried to make out that the reason for the order was his concern about the safety of civilians in an area so full of troops; it was clear to the defenders of the White House, however, that the real reason was to prepare for an attack on the building by the KGB's Alpha forces.

Before Lebed withdrew his battalion from the White House, he requested another meeting with Boris Yeltsin. By now Lebed was furious with the Ministry of Defence and the Emergency Committee for putting him in a situation where his men were expected to confront their own people. The idea that what was happening was a coup against the legitimate government seemed absurd. 'It wasn't a coup, it was a piece of theatre,' he said.[59] It was clear to him that what had begun as an attempt to re-establish the Kremlin's authority had gone badly wrong and now, with Gorbachev once again conveniently absent and chaos on the streets, events seemed to be giving legitimacy to Yeltsin's claim. Lebed makes no mention of this second meeting with Yeltsin in his memoir of the coup, merely giving a brief description of his encounter with Yuri Skokov in the White House, who 'expressed his disappointment that the battalion had been there such a short time'.[60] However, Alexander Korzhakov remembers a much more significant meeting with Yeltsin himself. It was as a result of this meeting that Yeltsin finally resolved to make his fundamental challenge to Soviet power.

Korzhakov says that Lebed told him that he had been ordered to withdraw his battalion.

He was supposed to carry out the order at two o'clock. I asked: 'Who can change the order?'

'Only the Commander-in-Chief of Russia,' replied Lebed.

I reported this to Boris Nikolayevich and we again met in the back room of the President's office. Lebed repeated: 'I have received an order and I feel obliged to report it to you. In as much as they sent me to protect you, I can't withdraw my soldiers without warning.'

We considered the order which Lebed had received as a signal for an attack. If they were withdrawing the paratroops, it meant that Alpha was ready to take the White House. Boris Nikolayevich said to Lebed: 'I will order you to leave the paratroops.'

'I cannot refuse to carry out an order, because I swore an oath,' the General answered. 'But I swore the oath to Gorbachev. Now there is no Gorbachev. It's not even clear where he is. But there is a way out. If you, Boris Nikolayevich, as President of Russia, issue a proclamation appointing yourself Commander-in-Chief, I will place myself under your command.'[61]

Yeltsin declined Lebed's offer and the meeting ended without agreement. As they parted, Lebed reminded the President that he did not have the right to break his oath and that nothing was dearer to him than his honour as an officer. At eleven o'clock, he began to withdraw his battalion from the White House. The soldiers were sorry to go, as they had struck up a good relationship with the crowds around the White House. As they withdrew towards Leningradsky Prospekt, many people threw cakes, sweets and coins through the windows and hatches of their vehicles; others worried that the troops' withdrawal meant that something awful was about to happen.

In the meantime, Yeltsin was having second thoughts about Lebed's suggestion. He gathered his most senior advisers and asked their opinion. 'Boris Nikolayevich considered Lebed's proposal with Shakhrai and Burbulis,' says Korzhakov, 'after which, towards 1700 [hours], a proclamation was issued, which legally appointed Yeltsin Commander-in-Chief. What stopped the document being issued before two o'clock? We are always late. Alpha probably wouldn't have stormed military units, which had guns and armour. Maybe there wouldn't have been any bloodshed at all.'[62]

Lebed was summoned to the Defence Ministry for a meeting with senior army and KGB personnel, including Yazov, Achalov, Grachev, the land forces' commander General Varennikov and Major-General Karpukhin, commander of the KGB's Alpha Group. They were discussing a plan, codenamed 'Operation Grom', for the storming of the White House at four o'clock the following morning. When Lebed arrived, the Defence Minister said with heavy sarcasm that he had heard reports that he had already shot himself. Lebed replied that he could not see any reason why he should have done so.[63]

According to Yanayev, the Defence Minister also wanted to know if it was true that Lebed had gone over to Yeltsin. 'At that time, there were widespread rumours that Lebed had defected to Yeltsin and Yazov said, "Have you defected, Lebed?" "No, not at all, Comrade Marshal of the Soviet Union. I am ready to carry out any order of yours as Minister of Defence." That was all. It was a double game. That was Lebed's first betrayal.'[64]

Grachev asked Lebed to report on the situation outside the White House, and he gave a deliberately pessimistic appraisal.

I reported that there were about 100,000 people outside the Supreme Soviet building. The approaches to the building were blocked with numerous barricades. In the building itself, there was a well-armed security detachment. Any force would lead to colossal bloodshed. Lastly, I gave my view, based on my own experience, of where it would all end up. They didn't allow me to continue. Valentin Ivanovich [Varennikov] interrupted me. Staring intently at me through his spectacles, he said curtly: 'General, your duty is to be an optimist. Instead of which, you are spreading pessimism and insecurity here.'[65]

Lebed's pessimistic report may not have been what the Generals wanted to hear, but it was entirely accurate. It was becoming increasingly clear to other senior officers that Yeltsin's resistance could not be crushed without a massacre of civilians; for many of them, it was a price they were not prepared to pay. They began to look for ways to frustrate Yazov's orders and to do what they could to ensure that an order was not given to attack the White House. The air force commander, Air Marshal Shaposhnikov, one of the first senior officers to rebel against the Emergency Committee, made sure that orders to airlift extra troops into Moscow were frustrated. Even the KGB's Alpha commanders had their doubts. Two Lieutenant-Colonels, Goncharov and Golovatov, carried out a poll of their men about the order to prepare for 'Operation Grom'; they unanimously decided that the order was illegal and against the constitution.[66]

Planning continued for 'Operation Grom', despite the fact that many of the executive officers involved were now trying to ensure that an attack did not take place. The Emergency Committee was still convinced, however, that Yeltsin's position was weaker than it appeared. 'Although Yeltsin describes his conduct at this time very heroically, he was demoralised,' says Yanayev. 'Moreover, when rumours began to circulate that the White House would be stormed on the night of the 20th and 21st, Yeltsin went down into the basement. He had an armoured Zil and it had already been agreed earlier with the American Embassy that he could escape there, as it was only a few metres away. It was only at the last moment that he refused.'[67]

When General Achalov visited the White House at one in the morning, however, he realised that any grounds for optimism were misplaced. 'The city was deserted but there were huge crowds, more than 70,000 people, I'd say, at the Parliament building. Taxi drivers were still ferrying youths from the railway stations, many of them drunk. People were also taking food and drink to the demonstrators. It was raining, and the crowds were completely out of control. I went back to the Ministry and reported to Yazov that it was impossible to do anything. "Comrade Minister, there would be terrible bloodshed and we might not succeed," I told him.'[68]

In the meantime, General Karpukhin, commander of the KGB's Alpha Group, reported that some of his units were refusing to attack the White House. Air force helicopter pilots declared that they would not land assault troops on the roof of the building. General Grachev had seen which way the wind was blowing and told his commanders that, if orders came to attack the White House, they would be illegal. By 1 a.m., therefore, as Achalov inspected the chaos outside the RSFSR Supreme Soviet, the commanders of both the KGB's special forces and the Airborne Forces had made clear their opposition to an attack. The Emergency Committee was beginning to realise that it had lost control of events. General Achalov reported on the situation at a meeting of senior government figures in Kryuchkov's office:

Most of the GKChP was there, by now sober but grey. I reported that nothing could be done that day. Then Varennikov went home and I returned to Yazov. It was 0500 by this time.

'Look, it's getting light,' Yazov said, standing by the window. I left him, then went to see what was happening in town. At 0700 I returned to Yazov, who said, 'That's enough. I'm not taking part in any more of this. Call a meeting of the Collegium [the main Military Council of the Ministry of Defence].'[69]

At the meeting, General Shaposhnikov told Yazov bluntly that the state of emergency had failed and he would have to step down. 'I said that for the sake of the authority of the armed forces he had to resign as Minister, and we had to announce that the Committee was illegal . . . Yazov agreed, but said that he would not resign from the GKChP. "I don't want to deceive anybody," he said. "I got involved in this thing."'[70] Depressed and exhausted, Yazov resigned as Defence Minister and ordered the withdrawal of all troops from Moscow. After a brief discussion with the other members of the Emergency Committee, Yazov and his colleagues decided to fly to Foros to speak to Gorbachev. They left the hapless Yanayev in the Kremlin, meditating over his bottle on the reasons why it had all gone wrong.

'We didn't want any bloodshed,' says Yanayev. 'They wanted to drown us in blood. They needed blood.'[71] In the event there *was* bloodshed, but not at the White House. Crowds throwing stones and Molotov cocktails trapped three military vehicles on the 'Garden Ring' road. In the ensuing fracas, three people died and at least ten were injured, crushed by the vehicles or shot by small-arms fire.[72] 'It was the blood with which Yeltsin wanted finally to drown us. It wasn't our fault. We didn't send them to go berserk and the soldiers didn't have orders to open fire. We didn't want bloodshed. We weren't political cynics. We were not governing with the logic of a *putsch*.'[73]

It is probably true that Yanayev and the Emergency Committee did not want bloodshed. After all, if they had been prepared to accept civilian casualties and behave as the Chinese leadership had done in Tiananmen Square, it would have been relatively easy to take the White House. Yanayev claims that no order was ever given to storm the building. 'If a decision had been taken to storm the White House, I assure you that the army, the KGB and the MVD would have carried out the order . . . If Yazov or Kryuchkov had ordered the storming of the White House, it would have been taken in twenty minutes.'[74]

It is also true that the Emergency Committee did not see itself as leading a *coup d'état* or a seizure of power. Indeed, it could not logically seize power, since all its members already occupied the most senior positions in the state. In the early hours of the morning of 21 August, it also became clear that they did not have the ruthlessness necessary to prosecute a *putsch*, perhaps because that had never been their intention. 'We simply wanted to draw the attention of the country, of deputies, of society, to what was happening, and to make Gorbachev take some emergency measures for the introduction of basic order in the country; not repression, but order.'[75]

As the crisis at last reached its *dénouement* and the Committee realised that there was no way forward without violence, Yanayev and his colleagues confronted their dilemma: 'When my comrades said to me, "Well, what are we going to do?", I said, "We are going to do nothing. We can't. I won't have any blood. I can't take responsibility for any bloodshed because we planned all these measures as a demonstration of our readiness and our determination to save the country and not to kill its citizens. That is too high a price."'[76]

Yanayev dismisses the claims of Grachev and other senior officers to have thwarted plans for the storming of the White House. He has no doubt that if an order had been given to take the White House, they would have obeyed it. 'We had no doubt that all the appropriate forces in the army would carry out an order. If we had been political cynics like Yeltsin, we would have given it. Grachev said to Yazov, "Comrade Marshal, you've got to take some measures. The crowd is going crazy."'[77]

Lebed had no doubt that the White House could easily have been stormed if the Emergency Committee had had no regard for civilian casualties. He told a Parliamentary commission that the building could have been taken by firing 'two or three dozen anti-tank rockets into the building, without any special concern for the crowd standing outside'. The troops outside would simply have to wait for flames and smoke to drive the defenders out of the building. 'Those who were lucky would jump from the first floor, those who weren't would jump from the thirteenth.'[78]

Fortunately, Yanayev and his colleagues balked at such ruthless measures. Ironically, however, they were exactly the tactics Yeltsin was to use to storm the same building only two years later.

When the members of the Emergency Committee were arrested and Gorbachev returned sheepishly to Moscow, it soon became clear that Yeltsin was a very different character to the General Secretary. Charismatic, ruthless and, above all, capable of turning events quickly to his advantage, Yeltsin set about consolidating the hold on power which the collapse of the Emergency Committee had given him. He was in a position of supreme strength because, as Gorbachev noted, 'the leaders of the coup had dislodged the stone that started a landslide'.[79] He publicly humiliated Gorbachev in front of the Supreme Soviet and then, together with the leaders of Ukraine and Belarus, began to plan the end of the Soviet Union.

General Lebed's suggestion that he should become commander-in-chief of all forces on Russian territory had convinced him that the army would subordinate itself to him. There was no reason for the Union to control the armed forces and no point now in the Union continuing to exist. The Emergency Committee may not, as Yanayev claimed, have 'thought with the logic of a *putsch*' but, as Yeltsin's supporters began to dismantle their barricades and the Russian President turned his gaze from the White House to the Kremlin, he certainly did.

What had happened had indeed been, as Lebed said, 'not a *putsch* but a piece of theatre'. The real military coup took place after the collapse of the Emergency Committee. Air Marshal Yevgeny Shaposhnikov, who had done more than almost any other officer to ensure that there was no attack on the White House, was appointed Soviet Minister of Defence. In accepting the appointment, he swore an oath of loyalty to Mikhail Gorbachev as President of the Soviet Union, despite the fact that Yeltsin had already laid claim to all the forces on Russian territory. On 8 December, however, Yeltsin signed a joint statement with President Kravchuk of Ukraine and President Shushkevich of Belarus, which declared that 'the USSR, as a subject of international law and geopolitical reality, ceases to exist'. Yeltsin had simply written the USSR out of existence, without consulting Gorbachev as Head of State of the USSR and in direct opposition to the will of the people as expressed in the referendum in March.

The statement could have plunged the Soviet Union into civil war, particularly if the armed forces had remained loyal to the

Soviet President. Yeltsin had prepared his coup thoroughly, however. Air Marshal Shaposhnikov countersigned the statement and the Soviet armed forces ceased to exist along with the Soviet Union. Boris Pankin, who had been made Soviet Foreign Minister after his public opposition to the state of emergency, was astonished that Shaposhnikov turned against Gorbachev:

> Shaposhnikov supported Yeltsin. Nobody noticed but it was real treachery, because he had a legal President who had appointed him as Minister of Defence. I was the Minister of Foreign Affairs, Bakatin was the Chairman of the KGB, and Barannikov was the Minister of the Interior. The entire government consisted of the President and four close colleagues. And one of these four trusted people just turned. And when Gorbachev found out that the army had betrayed him, that was it. He no longer bothered to oppose it.[80]

Lebed soon realised that Yeltsin was little different from the other leaders who had occupied the Kremlin.

> Power became a different colour, but its essence was preserved. For example, if you took two opposite figures – the secretary of a regional Party committee and a democrat – and mixed them together, it would be ridiculous. But in Russia, it's normal. Yeltsin was the First Secretary of the Sverdlovsk regional Party committee, the First Secretary of the Moscow city Party committee, a candidate member of the Politburo and a member of the Central Committee of the CPSU, but at the age of sixty-five he decided that he was a democrat and the whole world decided that it believed him. It's ridiculous. Power remained the same, it just changed its colour.[81]

As Lebed was soon to discover, however, what motivated Yeltsin was power itself, not its colour. The new master of the Kremlin was as ruthless as any of his recent predecessors, driven by a sense of his own destiny and determined, whatever the cost, to keep hold of the power he had won. It would not be long before Alexander Lebed once again found himself playing the Kremlin's power games.

7

THE RIVER DNIESTER

'The Russian driver has an excellent scent that serves him better than his eyes; that is how it sometimes happens that, speeding along with his eyes shut, he always gets somewhere in the end.'

N. V. GOGOL, *Dead Souls*[1]

On his return to Moscow from Foros in August 1991, Gorbachev had told reporters that he felt as if he was coming back to 'another country'.[2] By the end of the year, however, the Soviet Union was not simply 'another country'; it had ceased to exist altogether. The scale of the apparent change brought about by Yeltsin's coup was vast. Not only was the country of which Gorbachev had been President abolished, but the Party of which he had been the General Secretary was proscribed. Many of the symbols of Communist power were removed; the Leninist slogans on top of factory buildings and apartment blocks were soon replaced with Western advertising. Cheering crowds had watched as a statue of Felix Dzerzhinsky, founder of the Cheka secret police, was toppled from its perch outside the Lubyanka, headquarters of the KGB; it was soon removed to an obscure corner of Gorky Park where it lay, upended, alongside other Soviet heroes who were suddenly no longer fashionable.

Yet, despite the removal of these hated symbols and the enormity of the change that seemed to be taking place, there was a sense that this was an unfinished revolution. Some things had changed, but much had remained the same. Most importantly, the levers of power were still in virtually the same hands. This was not Poland or the Czech Republic, where the collapse of communism had brought power to dissidents who dreamed of democracy and human rights. In the Soviet Union, whilst the ideology changed with the failure of Gorbachev's *putsch* and the success of Yeltsin's coup, the *apparatchiks* stayed in control. Men such as Nazarbayev of Kazakhstan, Shushkevich of Belarus, Kravchuk of Ukraine and Yeltsin himself were Party bosses who had only recently decided they were democrats. They might, like Yeltsin, have had the convenience of public support in an election, but their instincts remained autocratic and, like Yeltsin too, they were quite ready to ignore a democratic expression of the popular will – such as the referendum on the future of the Soviet Union – when it did not suit them. Unlike the new leaders of post-Communist central Europe, their dream was not democracy but power, and their waking thoughts were all about how to keep it.

The problems facing the Kremlin had also remained, despite Gorbachev's departure. The Kremlin's new master faced an enormous economic crisis, which was unlikely to be made any better by arguments over the apportionment of the Soviet Union's debts and assets. Like Gorbachev, Yeltsin soon found himself beset by numerous problems with the nationalities of the empire. Trouble came from those non-Russian peoples who suddenly found that, against their will and without their consent, they had become subjects of the new, sovereign Russian Federation rather than the Soviet Union; conversely, it also came from those Russians outside the Russian Federation who equally suddenly found that, by virtue of Yeltsin's abolition of the Soviet Union, they were now living in a foreign country. Like Gorbachev too, Yeltsin soon found himself confronted by a chaotic domestic political situation, in which his position looked increasingly precarious as he tried to pursue his predecessor's policy of dragging the extremes with him towards economic reform. But Yeltsin dealt considerably more effectively and ruthlessly with his political opposition than Gorbachev. A natural autocrat, he set about designing a new constitution, which was heavily weighted in favour of the presidency. Yet amidst the turmoil following the end of the Soviet Union, Yeltsin's greatest worry was not his political opposition but the military.

The main problems facing Yeltsin all involved the military. The economic crisis was largely the result of decades of preferential investment in the military–industrial complex and the vast proportion of the federal budget devoted to military expenditure. Domestic political turmoil had been fuelled by the various military problems associated with the end of empire, such as the withdrawal of Soviet troops from Eastern Europe and the argument over ownership of Soviet military assets by the successor states. At the same time, nationalist pride was hurt by the West's triumphalism at the end of the Soviet Union and by the rush of the newly liberated countries of Eastern Europe to join NATO. Yeltsin's main concern, however, was to ensure that the army remained loyal to him and could not be used by his political opponents. Lebed's suggestion that he appoint himself commander-in-chief had enabled him to consolidate his power and complete the coup but always, at the back of his mind, was the fear that he might not be able to rely on the army.

Air Marshal Shaposhnikov, the last USSR Defence Minister, whose betrayal of Gorbachev had finally sealed Yeltsin's victory, was made commander-in-chief of the armed forces of the new Commonwealth of Independent States. His job was to ensure that Russia retained control of those forces currently stationed in other republics which it considered to be of strategic importance.

In May 1992, Pavel Grachev was appointed Defence Minister of the Russian Federation. Distinguished only by his ambition, Grachev had certainly been over-promoted long ago. Yet Yeltsin felt that he could rely on him. He almost certainly knew of the double game Grachev had played during the August *putsch*, but such knowledge perhaps gave him even more leverage over his Defence Minister. Equally, Grachev was a good courtier. Fawningly loyal and subservient, he knew exactly how to play Yeltsin. Both Alexander Lebed and Alexander Korzhakov are convinced that Yeltsin knew that Grachev had played a double role during the *putsch*.

'He knew, of course,' says Lebed. 'He had balanced himself between Yeltsin and Yazov, but after the *putsch* he leaned towards Yeltsin's side.'[3] Grachev employed the usual *modus operandi* of flatterers and courtiers, telling his master only what he wanted to hear and not troubling him with bad news. In the short term, Yeltsin's objective was not to build a strong Russian Army but to destroy the former Soviet Army as a semi-autonomous centre of power capable of challenging his authority. He wanted armed forces which were capable of defending certain key strategic interests without creating such a large strain on the Russian economy. For the first time since the Bolshevik revolution, military spending would have to be reduced to a level that the country could actually afford. In the past, objectives, procurement and expenditure had all been firmly rooted in Soviet military doctrine. Now there was no doctrine. The old Soviet military thinking had died with the Soviet Union, and it was not until the end of 1993 that the Defence Ministry of the Russian Federation adopted a new one. In the interim, the chaos and drift in the armed forces suited Yeltsin.

In the intervening period, however, he wanted a stable core on which he could rely in the event of domestic difficulties. Ever since his visit to the 106th Guards Airborne Division at their base in Tula in the summer of 1991, Yeltsin had recognised the crucial importance of the Airborne Forces. During the *putsch*, their role had been decisive. Now, Yeltsin wanted to ensure that Russia kept control of key Airborne units. His military planners had suggested that they might form the basis of a Mobile Force, which would be the core of a new model Russian Army, but they would also be the ultimate guarantor of his political survival.

It was not only the Russian President who was impressed by the Airborne Forces; the leaders of other republics too wanted to take charge of those units stationed on their territory. The Russians insisted, however, that whereas some Soviet Army units outside Russia would be allowed to transfer their allegiance to the government of their local republic, the Airborne Forces were of strategic significance and should remain under the control of the CIS commander-in-chief, Air Marshal Shaposhnikov. In discussions on the apportionment of military assets between the Soviet Union's successor states, Russia therefore made it clear from the outset that it regarded the Airborne Forces as a special case. Alexander Lebed was appointed to represent the Airborne Forces in the negotiations.

Casual observers were surprised that Lebed did not follow Grachev into a senior command. His role in the August *putsch* had attracted the attention of the media, and he had been hailed as the 'defender of the White House' and the 'saviour of democracy'. Bouquets of flowers and presents had arrived at his offices

in Tula, but he soon showed his irritation at the public outpour-
ing of gratitude. When a television reporter told him that his eyes
had been filled with tears of joy when he heard the news that
Lebed's troops had 'gone over' to the President, and asked how he
felt about his role as 'defender of the White House', he replied
sarcastically: 'As is well known from history, over 3,000 people
helped Vladimir Ilyich Lenin to carry a log on a "volunteer day".
We already have over 3 million defenders of the White House
and, as I'm frightened of getting lost in this enormous, heroic
crowd, I hereby officially refuse the title of "defender of the
White House".'[4]

Such remarks did not endear him to Russia's new rulers, but
Lebed insisted that he did not consider himself a democrat and
that until recently he had been a loyal Party member; his only
concern, he said, had been to prevent bloodshed. Yet he was
being more than a little disingenuous. He had undoubtedly
played a crucial role in ensuring Yeltsin's victory; the presence of
his paratroops at the White House had encouraged resistance
and his proposal that Yeltsin should declare himself commander-
in-chief had led to the real coup in December. Whatever the
reason for his gruff refusal to acknowledge the applause, many
people suspected that Lebed remained much closer to Yeltsin
than his public comments led them to suppose. Indeed, despite
the assessment of his friend, Valery Vostrotin, that 'if Lebed had
only kept his mouth shut then he would be a Colonel-General by
now', his role as representative of the Airborne Forces in negotiations with the other republics was of great importance to the
President.[5]

Yeltsin had only been able to destroy Soviet power with the
assistance of the other republics. He had encouraged them to seize
power for themselves, but now he found that there was a problem. Lebed remembers: 'Boris Nikolayevich had said: "Take as
much sovereignty as you want!" They weren't shy, they took it.
And, as an integral part of its sovereignty, every Union republic
counted the little piece of the Soviet Army that happened to find
itself on its territory. They took everything without exception,
whether they needed it or not; they could decide that later.'[6] As
the Airborne Forces' representative, Lebed was part of a
group representing all the services which conducted negotiations
with the defence ministries of the new republics, under the

Chairmanship of Colonel-General B. Y. Pyankov. Lebed took part in a series of difficult negotiations in Kiev, Minsk, Vilnius and Kishinev.

'The negotiations had a tense atmosphere. They were different in the various republics. The Belorussians were the most civilised. It was the only republic where logic, evidence, common sense and good advice carried any weight. Those negotiations were conducted in absolutely the right atmosphere.' In Vilnius too, negotiations were constructive, despite the Kremlin's violent attempt to crush Lithuanian independence only a year earlier. The Lithuanians were 'close to the Belorussians, but with nuances'. The Ukrainians were more of a problem, however. Although they were friendly during the breaks between sessions, laughing, joking and sharing cigarettes, 'as soon as they sat down at the negotiating table again, under the watchful eye of their democratic political commissars, it was all over and the lines were strictly drawn'.

Lebed's greatest problem, however, was with the bombastic, ultra-nationalist, Moldovan Defence Minister, General Kostash, who looked like 'a suckling pig' and made absolutely no attempt at civility. 'It stops being a negotiation when seven out of every ten words are swear-words. Then it has to be called something else.' The problem at issue was the 300th Airborne Regiment, which was stationed in Kishinev and happened to be commanded at the time by Lebed's brother Alexei. General Lebed was not about to deliver his younger brother, together with his regiment, to General Kostash.

'I'll take the regiment,' Kostash fumed.

'How will you take it when 96 per cent of the regiment do not wish to be taken?' replied Lebed.

'It's on our territory, so it belongs to us! We'll put concrete blocks in front of all the gates.'

'Just because you barricade it won't make it yours.'

'Then we'll take it by force.'

'But it's a regiment. Try to understand. A regiment. It would be like the old Russian joke: "I've caught a bear." – "Then bring it here." – "It won't come." – "Then come here yourself." – "It won't let me."'7

Lebed refused to allow the transfer of the regiment, but it remained at its base in Kishinev throughout the spring and summer, as the situation in Moldova deteriorated. Later it became clear that it was not just the 300th Airborne Regiment that refused to transfer its allegiance, but that a large part of the population of the east of the republic, east of the river Dniester, had no wish to belong to Moldova.

Lebed left Moldova as the first distant rumblings of the storm began to be heard over the Dniester. He had been instructed to find bases in Russia for Airborne units from the 'near abroad'. His units were a small part of the huge quantity of men and equipment which was now supposed to return to Russia from the ruined outposts of the Soviet empire. Gorbachev had agreed that all Soviet troops would be withdrawn from Czechoslovakia and Hungary by mid-1991, and they had returned to bases which were wholly unprepared to receive them. Soldiers and their families were now living in tents and warehouses at the height of the Russian winter. This chaotic situation was getting worse all the time. The Soviet government had agreed to a phased withdrawal of its Western Group of Forces from Germany, with 30 per cent leaving in the first three years and the final 10 per cent in 1994. There were plans too to complete the withdrawal of Soviet forces from Poland by the end of 1993.

Yet the conditions facing soldiers returning home to Russia were only a tiny part of the problem. Military discipline in many of the units in Moscow's former empire had now all but disappeared. Often unpaid and facing the prospect of a bleak future without a roof over their heads, many officers and men began to look for other ways to provide for themselves and their families. Soldiers serving in Germany had the best opportunities to feather their nests. With German unification, Soviet soldiers were suddenly exposed to Western capitalism, and those officers and NCOs whose salaries were paid in Deutschmarks were soon able to enjoy its fruits. Some units became little more than trading houses, buying up Western goods in eastern Germany and selling them on in Russia. One analyst calculated that 'a shrewd Soviet officer can be a wealthy man in less than a year by trading, making up to 30 roubles from each DM 1 officially earned'.[8] The conscript soldiers did not hesitate to take a lead from their officers. With little more than pocket-money for pay, they began to sell off their equipment. Hats, belts, uniforms, binoculars and fuel were all sold to the local population.

Finding themselves in this new eldorado, it was hardly surprising that many of them did not want to return to Russia. Throughout 1991, there were hundreds of desertions from the Western Group of Forces, including a regimental commander, Colonel M. Kolesnikov. Hardly surprising either was the fact that it was not long before more than hats and belts were offered to the Soviet forces' business partners. Already in 1990, Soviet soldiers had tried selling two RPG-7 rocket launchers to passers-by in Budapest. The soldiers had also tried to interest their customers in four other launchers, three warheads and seven stabilisers.[9] Yet this was small beer; it took the Western Group of Forces to realise the army's full commercial potential.

Within months of German reunification, the Western Group of Forces had become the centre of a huge network of corruption. Arms and military technology were being sold off at an astonishing rate. On one occasion, officers of the Western Group offered a range of Russian-made equipment, including armoured vehicles, Kalashnikov rifles and a MiG-29 fighter plane, to German policemen posing as businessmen in an undercover operation.[10]

When the Chief Military Prosecutor, Grigory Nosov, investigated the Western Group of Forces, he presented General Grachev with a report which showed that the army was now riddled with corruption. At the lower end of the scale, Nosov named numerous individual officers who were running currency-exchange operations and selling tobacco or alcohol from their homes on bases in Germany. At the higher end, however, billions of roubles were flowing out of the military budget and into bank accounts and businesses run by serving officers. It soon became clear that officers at the very highest level were involved in corrupt commercial activities of one sort or another. It was as though, with the death of the old ideology, they had decided not to bother pretending to be an army any longer; the only thing that mattered now was to make as much money as quickly as possible by whatever means necessary.

Many of the illegal and corrupt activities of the Western Group of Forces were undertaken with the collusion of highly placed officials in the Russian government. They arranged contracts for the supply of goods at inflated prices, which allowed senior officers and suppliers to make substantial profits. General Matvey Burlakov, the commander of the Western Group, was personally involved in many of the business dealings of his subordinates. His commercial activities also brought him into regular contact with executives of an Austrian firm which won contracts to supply the Russian forces with foodstuffs, despite the fact that the army received lower tenders from other firms. The food provided by the Austrian firm was of a very poor quality. Sometimes it made the soldiers ill, often it was returned as inedible.[11] Yet the Austrian firm continued to supply the Western Group of Forces for more than three years.

General Burlakov's involvement with the firm's executives was the very least of his commercial activities, however. Soon he began to help the Western Group of Forces to sell off large amounts of the military equipment that should have returned to Russia. It was not long before he drew Pavel 'Pasha' Grachev into his network of corrupt business deals. As the deadline drew closer for the last remnants of the Western Group to return to Russia, and when the Generals had sold off as much of its equipment as they dared, Burlakov presented Grachev's son with a brand new Mercedes as a 'thank you' present on the occasion of the boy's marriage to the daughter of General Kharchenko. The press eventually nick-named the Defence Minister 'Pasha Mercedes', and a whispering campaign began about his involvement in the 'Generals' busi-ness'. Corruption in the military was no longer confined to the Western Group of Forces, if it ever had been. It had now clearly reached the very heart of the defence establishment.

Before long, the full extent of the 'Generals' business' and its bloody consequences became apparent, as large parts of the former Soviet Union's arsenal found their way into the hands of tyrants, terrorists and the belligerent factions in civil wars or regional conflicts around the world. The Russian Procurator General's Office later found the deputy director of Rosvoor-uzhenie, the state arms company, trying to sell $50 million worth of 'special materials' to Libya, in contravention of a United Nations embargo. Russian arms began to pour into the former Yugoslavia too, despite an embargo there. In one deal, at the height of sanctions, ninety-two T-72 tanks arrived in Serbia; they were followed a few months later by eighty-three 122mm Howitzers, which were shipped via Ukraine. At the same time, the military's export company, Voentekh, also delivered T-72 tanks to the Serbs' Croatian enemies. For a long time, the Russian government turned a blind eye to the Generals' trade in Soviet arms and the activities of Rosvooruzhenie and Voentekh. Senior ministers even appeared, on occasion, not only to condone some of the more irresponsible arms deals but actively to encourage them; Foreign Minister Andrei Kozyrev reportedly signed an agreement with Iraq's deputy Prime Minister Tariq Aziz to replace tanks, defence systems and radar installations destroyed during the Gulf War.[12]

Initially corruption in the armed forces seemed little different from corruption anywhere else. Typically, it involved the theft of state assets or their use to finance private commercial activities. In the last days of the Soviet Union, as huge quantities of finance and other valuable assets disappeared to banks in the West, Russian-run companies were established which co-ordinated reinvestment, ensuring that important Soviet industrial assets remained in the hands of the same *nomenklatura* which had controlled them under the Communists. Connections in Moscow often ensured that contracts were awarded to firms which were 'in-house'. A contract to supply the army with food, however, was nothing compared to the major 'deals' which effectively transferred control of industrial assets, enterprises and resources from the *nomenklatura* in the public sector to the same *nomenklatura*, now in the private sector. The ambitious programme of privatisation designed by Anatoly Chubais, which was supposed to make the transition to a market economy irreversible, merely provided the *nomenklatura* with the opportunity for an investment bonanza in which they could snap up many of the prizes of Soviet industry. In the first five months of 1993 alone, more than 2,500 unlawful privatisations were detected.[13]

The Russian government's privatisation programme was a gift to the *nomenklatura*, which is hardly surprising when one remembers the background from which Yeltsin and his team came. One study on the subject by a leading Russian academic institution estimated that 75 per cent of the government, 60 per cent of parliamentarians, 83 per cent of regional governors and 41 per cent of top business people had links to the *nomenklatura*. In the economy, as in so many other spheres of Russian life, amidst the dramatic change, much remained the same.

In the summer of 1992, as Pavel Grachev settled into the Ministry of Defence and contemplated the array of opportunities for personal gain which now seemed to present themselves to him on a daily basis, he began to feel uneasy about the presence of his former deputy. General Lebed knew the real nature of the double role Grachev had played during the August *putsch* and could easily confirm Yeltsin's suspicions. Equally worrying was Lebed's irritatingly sanctimonious insistence on his 'officer's honour', and his view that soldiers should not involve themselves in commercial activities. Grachev wanted to get Lebed out of Moscow and away from the Airborne Forces, which were of such political importance. General Achalov, the Airborne Forces' former commander, who was now in disgrace because of his role in the August *putsch*, knew that Grachev saw Lebed as a threat:

> At that point Grachev was trying to free himself of Lebed in any way possible . . . First of all, he envied his deputy's decisiveness and professional courage. Second, he was aware that Lebed was spotless, and had full knowledge of several of his boss's confidential affairs in Afghanistan. How he became a Hero of the Soviet Union, for example. Or to which highly placed bureaucrats he gave trophies from his conquests of Afghan caravans, and in gratitude for what. Third, Grachev was in a panic that Lebed would tell Yeltsin how he had bustled about between Yanayev and Yeltsin, giving his loyalty to Yeltsin only when it became clear that the Emergency Committee's plans had failed. Fourth, Grachev had already become alarmed by Lebed's increasing popularity in the military's general command.[14]

When General Podkolzin became the Airborne Forces' commander, a job Lebed might have expected, Grachev redoubled his efforts to rid himself of his troublesome former deputy, trying to persuade him to enter the General Staff Academy, ostensibly on the grounds that it would prepare him for the highest levels of command in two or three years. Lebed declined the offer, as he also did an attempt to interest him in a command far away in Siberia. He wanted to stay in the mainstream and was determined to resist the attempts to sideline him. Grachev's opportunity came, however, when events in Moldova took a turn for the worse.

*

Long the subject of contentious international border disputes, most of the newly independent republic of Moldova had been known, until the end of the Second World War, as Bessarabia, a province of the Kingdom of Romania. Annexed by Stalin in 1944, it became Moldavia, one of the fifteen republics of the Soviet Union. Stalin diluted the Romanian population with Russians and Ukrainians, forcing the inhabitants of the new republic with typical brutality to forget their old identities and become loyal citizens of the Soviet Union. Soviet Moldavia, which gave Stalin an important strategic access to the Danube and central Europe, was one of the richest republics in the Union and its citizens enjoyed a comparatively prosperous lifestyle. Despite its tiny size, it accounted for over 2 per cent of Soviet agricultural production. It was the Soviet Union's major producer of grain and tobacco, and it also supplied sunflower oil, sugar beet and other agricultural products to the big cities of Russia and Ukraine. Amidst such an abundance of produce, including the finest wines and brandies, life for the average citizen was better in Moldavia than almost anywhere else in the Soviet Union, with the possible exception of Georgia.

Yet, beneath the surface, nationalism continued to boil. In the 1960s the temperature increased with Ceauşescu's independent foreign policy and Romania's growing challenge to the legitimacy of Moscow's annexation of the territory. In the 1970s and early 1980s, industrialisation, urbanisation and the suppression of the republic's Romanian heritage began to cause the first sparks of ethnic conflict. The Party bosses, Simion Grossul and Ivan Bodiul, whose beautiful young wife reputedly had the highly dubious pleasure of being regularly seduced by Leonid Brezhnev, responded to the growing public unrest with the usual Marxist slogans and secret police methods. With Gorbachev and *glasnost*, events in Moldavia followed the same pattern as those in other republics, where public discontent initially focused on issues of universal importance, such as the destruction of the local environment, before assuming its ultimate, divisive ethnic character. One prominent Soviet writer of Romanian origin, Ion Druta, had published an article in 1987 complaining that the Dniester had become one of the most polluted rivers in the country. When he added that the Moldavian lands were 'hostages in the hands of totally irresponsible people' and that 'national traditions and moral principles were sacrificed in Moldavia', it was clear that nationalism would soon replace environmentalism as the main concern of demonstrators in Kishinev, as in so many other Soviet cities.[15]

The demands of Romanian nationalists, which initially focused on cultural and linguistic issues, such as the use of the Latin alphabet rather than Cyrillic script, soon became more overtly and aggressively political. As in other republics where the tide of nationalism was beginning to roll, opposition groups and informal organisations quickly formed themselves into a Popular Front which soon built up a membership of almost 1 million people. Demonstrators dared to wave the Romanian flag openly on the streets of the republic for the first time in decades, and denounced the Soviet annexation of Bessarabia and northern Bukovina. At one rally in August 1989, over 750,000 people marched through the streets of Kishinev and sang the Romanian national anthem, 'Wake Up, Romanians'. When interior ministry and KGB troops brutally broke up another demonstration in October, the crowds turned on the authorities. The KGB headquarters was set on fire and the Communist leadership fled in panic. The Party First Secretary, the Brezhnevite Simion Grossul, was replaced by Petru Lucinski, a protégé of Mikhail Gorbachev.

Moscow hoped that with the removal of the Brezhnevite old guard in Kishinev, support for the nationalists would decline. After all, with Ceauşescu still in power in Bucharest, the nationalists' dream of union with Romania was not as popular as they would have wished. Gorbachev knew that Moldavia's Romanians had nowhere to go. When Ceauşescu was overthrown in December 1989, however, the situation changed completely. The Moldavians eagerly supported their Romanian brothers' revolution. Petru Lucinski's attempts to deal with the Popular Front were pushed aside by the new current of radical change. Local elections in March 1990 gave the Popular Front a huge majority in the Moldavian Parliament, which soon appointed the nationalist Mircea Snegur as President of the Republic. Pan-Romanian nationalism was now at its height, both in Moldavia and in Romania itself. On 6 June, nationalists on both sides of the river Prut, separating Soviet Moldavia from Romania, staged an unofficial demonstration in which Romanians on opposite banks of the river made a 'bridge of flowers' and crossed over for emotional reunions with relations whom they had not seen for four decades.

Amidst the emotional scenes on the banks of the Prut, the 'bridge of flowers' marked the symbolic reunification of the Romanian lands. When the Moldavian Parliament, later the same month, adopted the Romanian tricolour as the national flag, changed the republic's name to the more Romanian-sounding 'Moldova' and declared its sovereignty, the Russian minority in the east of the country began to feel nervous. Their growing sense of alienation was increased by a decision of the Moldovan Parliament on the official language of the republic. It was to be Romanian, and non-Romanian citizens were given five years to learn it. The decision provoked a wave of strikes in Tiraspol and other industrial cities on the left bank of the Dniester. Moldova's other minorities, particularly the Turkic Gagauz and the Ukrainians, joined the Russians and, amidst claims by some Russians that the Romanians were returning to their fascist past, the atmosphere became very tense. Backed by Gorbachev, who wanted to put pressure on the Moldovan leadership to draw back from the brink and accept the new Union treaty, Russian leaders in the republic made plain their intention to resist Moldovan independence. In August, the Russian and Gagauz leaders declared their regions independent from Moldova and organised referenda to demonstrate public support for their decisions. President Snegur responded by declaring that the referenda were illegal. He called for the formation of volunteer detachments to defend the republic. Throughout 1991, there was sporadic fighting in the region. After the August coup and the break-up of the Soviet Union, the conflict intensified as the Russian community feared that, with Moldova's declaration of independence on 27 August, it was about to be abandoned to the Romanian nationalists.

To General Grachev, the conflict seemed to have all the potential combustibility of another Yugoslavia, where the local Russian community might soon become the victims of a similar explosion of inter-ethnic hatred. By December 1991, the situation had become so serious that the Russian 14th Army, commanded by Lieutenant-General Yuri Netkachev, together with Russian Cossack volunteers, had been drawn into the conflict on the side of the so-called Dniester Moldavian Republic (a breakaway republic on the east bank of the Dniester, with the Russian acronym PMR, formed by Russians who refused to accept the legitimacy of the new Moldovan republic) and become involved in serious clashes with Moldovan government forces. By the early summer of 1992, there had already been hundreds of civilian casualties.

Grachev's intelligence reports showed that the 14th Army was on the verge of a humiliating defeat, in which its considerable stockpiles of arms would be overrun and the television news would be full of pictures of Russian refugees leaving their homes. Defeat could only be averted by a brutal Russian response which would be bound to shock the international community. Yeltsin would approve Lebed's appointment to command the 14th Army, hoping that his tough, loyal, incorruptible General would save civilian lives and rescue the army's massive stockpile of arms. The army's defeat, or its involvement in a barbarous counter-attack, however, would be bound to destroy Lebed's credibility in the eyes of the President and the public.

Military insiders had little doubt that Lebed's appointment was part of a calculated attempt to derail his career. One retired Colonel in military counter-intelligence, Viktor Paramoshin, remembers that

> the decision on Lebed's further assignment was made very carefully. On the one hand, he had to serve outside Russia. On the other, in a place where he would get 'burned' fast. According to our intelligence reports, we expected the situation between Moldova and Transdniestria to break out into armed conflict. It's likely that Grachev thought Lebed would actually be a catalyst, instigating an international scandal, which would be his undoing. This was a great mistake on Grachev's part. He gravely underestimated the capabilities of his primary future rival.[16]

Lebed arrived in Tiraspol with strict orders from Grachev to ensure that the 14th Army kept out of the fighting between the Moldovan volunteers and the separatists. He had no intention of waiting for the two sides to tear each other apart, or of allowing them to continue to massacre civilians. He soon realised that Grachev wanted him to be an 'Aunt Sally' and the convenient scapegoat in an inconvenient conflict which the Minister of Defence was not interested in winning. The politically dangerous situation in which he now found himself was an opportunity at last to seize the initiative and use his new command to protect innocent Russian lives.

An expert in psychological warfare, Lebed had travelled to Tiraspol under an assumed name, Colonel Gusev – *gus*, the Russian for 'goose', being the closest relation of the swan, *lebed*.[17] He wanted to keep his arrival in the region quiet until the right moment. When he reached his headquarters with a company of heavily armed, well-trained paratroopers, he set about strengthening the position of the 14th Army, which had become demoralised and combat-shy. The situation was so bad that he ordered the immediate mobilisation of the 14th Army's reserve unit, the 59th Guards Motor-Rifle Division. As he waited for the Moldovans to renew their attacks on Bendery and the Transdniester, he received intelligence reports of preparations for an imminent assault. He tried to contact Grachev to clarify his role, but the Defence Minister had absented himself and could not even be contacted on his special communication channels. Grachev's deliberate absence played into Lebed's hands, however, giving him the opportunity to issue orders that otherwise would almost certainly not have been approved.

The 14th Army was in such a poor state that it probably would have been unable to resist the Moldovan attack, so Lebed launched three powerful artillery barrages. The first one rained down on an attempted river crossing, burning up most of the Moldovans' equipment. The second fell simultaneously nearby, and the third was laid in the night over the same area. The sheer weight and brutality of the three barrages destroyed the Moldovans' will to continue with their push. Asked later whether he had given any thought to the Moldovan victims of the barrage, Lebed replied: 'Yes, I thought about them. But I also thought about how there would have been 10 or 100 times as many victims on both sides, had widespread fighting broken out. There were so many munitions in the 14th Army's supply depots that had these fallen into opposition hands, the fire fights would have continued for dozens of years. Armenia and Azerbaijan, Georgia and Abkhazia are proof of that.'[18]

Lebed's sledgehammer tactics brought the fighting in the

region to an end and created the climate for negotiation. He quickly reinforced his position with some astute political and psychological manoeuvring. He ensured that local newspapers reported his arrival in the region, spread rumours of his brutal service record, including atrocities in Afghanistan, and claimed that he was on the point of ordering a full-scale attack on Moldovan territory. When he judged that the Moldovan Defence Minister, the same Kostash with whom he had discussed the fate of the 300th Guards Airborne Regiment a few months earlier, had been suitably intimidated, he held an extraordinary press conference at which he appealed to the people of the region, over the heads of politicians in Kishinev and Moscow. None of his remarks were cleared beforehand with the Defence Ministry in Moscow, and it was another typical example of his gross insubordination. Yet it worked, and gave him the opportunity to impose an uneasy cease-fire in the region. He reported to Grachev that he had told the journalists that 'there is no international conflict on the border between the Transdniester Moldavian Republic and the Republic of Moldavia [sic]. Thirty-nine per cent of the population of Transdniester are Moldavian, 29 per cent are Ukrainian, 24 per cent are Russian. These nationalities have always lived with each other in peace. The people were born here and grew up here. The graves of their forefathers are here. Genocide against our own people is taking place here.'[19]

Lebed described the devastation which the conflict had created. He claimed that 650 people had already been killed and 4,000 wounded on the Transdniestrian side alone. The number of refugees was between 120,000 and 150,000. Factories, including an oil refinery, a bio-chemical plant and a brewery, had been set on fire in Bendery, where over 50 per cent of the housing had been destroyed. In the same town, almost all the schools, kindergartens and medical facilities had been severely damaged and were no longer in use.

'I can confirm officially,' said Lebed, 'that here on the territory of Transdniester, there is no post-Communist, pro-Communist, neo-Communist nor any other kind of regime. There are simply people living here, who are being systematically, thoroughly and brutally annihilated. Moreover, they are being annihilated in such a way that the SS of fifty years ago look like schoolboys in comparison.'

After an apocalyptic description of some of the dangers facing the Transdniester region if the conflict continued, from widespread flooding because of the possible destruction of a reservoir dam to the explosion of poisonous gas tanks, Lebed made it clear that he did not intend to allow Moscow to ignore the situation. 'The shadow of fascism hangs over this land of plenty. I think that our formerly great country should know about that. And it should remember how much it cost to break the back of fascism forty-seven years ago. It should stir its historical memory and remember what concessions to fascism can turn into.'[20]

This emotional rhetoric was the background against which Lebed declared that he intended to impose a solution – if necessary, without reference to Moscow. He may have been sent to the Transdniester as part of Grachev's ploy to destroy his career but, now that he was here, he intended to be the master of events. This most 'Bonapartist' of Russian Generals suddenly found himself in the position of Napoleon in command of the Army of Italy. He told his officers that he was assuming full responsibility. 'I, and no other, will personally answer for my actions,' he said, and his words were warmly applauded throughout the armed forces, which had grown tired of being betrayed by politicians.[21]

He told Grachev that he had 'spoken as a Russian officer who has a conscience. At least I know that for sure. I have spoken in order that everyone should think. I say again: I have spoken – and you, Comrade Politicians, and you, Dear People, think about it.' His remarks at the press conference had been addressed over Grachev's head – 'above all to you, Boris Nikolayevich Yeltsin, the first President of a free Russia' – and Grachev was furious.[22] On 4 July, he sent a curt telegram ordering Lebed to stay away from the media:

I categorically forbid you to appear on radio, television or in the press, giving your evaluation of current events. It is the prerogative of the government and the Supreme Soviet of Russia to evaluate the actions and decisions of the government of Moldova. Your task consists of the successful leadership of the 14th Army, the prevention of attacks on military targets, and the preservation of the lives of your servicemen. Contact Snegur, the President of Moldova, by telephone and exchange opinions with him about the current situation.[23]

The bitter exchange of telegrams between the two Generals continued for several days. Lebed refused to contact the Moldovan President, saying that both his hands and his conscience were stained with the blood of his own people. Grachev again ordered Lebed to contact Snegur, 'regardless of your subjective opinion'. He added, 'I would not want to think that the President and I had made a mistake in appointing you to command the 14th Army.' By now, Lebed had nothing but contempt for Grachev and his reply to the Defence Minister's latest telegram was not simply insubordinate but downright mutinous. 'With all respect to you,' he said, 'I will not enter into discussions with Snegur. I am a General of the Russian Army and I do not intend to betray it.'[24]

Grachev's attempt to undermine his rival had failed, and now Lebed had the upper hand. The Defence Minister could do little about his mutinous subordinate because his resolute action and readiness to accept responsibility for his decisions had made him, in a matter of weeks, the most popular General in the Russian Army. When a ceasefire agreement was signed at the end of July, Yeltsin too seemed pleased with the forceful 'non-intervention', which had put a stop to an embarrassing local conflict and prevented the disappearance of yet more supplies of Soviet arms. He soon realised that it had also given him a useful political asset with which to court nationalist opinion in Russia: Lebed's strong-arm tactics showed that the President was prepared to act tough to defend Russian citizens in the 'near abroad'. For the moment, Grachev had been outflanked, and he tried to shore up his position by pretending he had played a leading role in Lebed's success. He had no doubt now, however, that Lebed was an enemy whose destruction was essential for his peace of mind.

Increasingly unpopular throughout the army, Grachev was floundering in a sea of problems with which he was ill-equipped to deal. The massive upheaval in the army caused by the relocation of troops was aggravated by cuts in the defence budget. Beset by scandals, his chaotic attempts to develop a new Russian military doctrine made him look impotent in the face of NATO expansion. Worse still, however, was the fact that whilst the army was losing its respect for him, his rival had become its new hero. General Lebed was now the toast of the officer corps, and people spoke of him as a future Minister of Defence or even President. In the Transdniester, he was treated as a national hero. To many of the 600,000 Russian-speaking population he seemed almost like a god who had delivered them from the hands of their enemies. Some reports describe grateful women and pensioners gathering in crowds outside his hotel and falling to their knees to kiss his boots whenever he appeared.[25]

Lebed's popularity and his repeated displays of disobedience were becoming so irritating to Grachev that he began to plan the withdrawal of the 14th Army. When rumours reached Lebed that he might be ordered to pull his men out of the Transdniester, he was furious, and another angry exchange of telegrams began with Grachev. In 'an appeal from the officer corps of the 14th Russian Guards Army', Lebed pointed out that although negotiations had begun between Moldova and Transdniestria, the situation remained volatile. He complained that the 300th Guards Airborne Regiment was about to be transferred to Moldova and that funding had been stopped for the construction of housing for the 14th Army. He went on:

At the same time, the local population (to which 45 per cent of our officers belong), the people of Transdniestria, see the 14th Army as the only guarantee for peace and security in the region and understand the fact that they are stationed here as support from Russia. We admit that at some time the army must be withdrawn. But believe us, who are actually here, that at the present such an attempt would be seen by people as a tragedy, a betrayal by us and by Russia. It would lead to nothing other than a new and more serious wave of war, and to the stealing of weapons and equipment from the army. It is quite possible that the arms would then be turned against Russian servicemen and their families by both sides in the conflict.

As we have good reason to expect new political games over the 14th Army, the Officer Corps requests that you clarify absolutely the fate and prospects of the army, together with all related questions, which we consider that we have a right to ask. Above all: who will defend our families in the event of the army's withdrawal and a new outbreak of war in Transdniestria; and who will put a roof over our heads in our new posting?[26]

Grachev's reply was redolent with the malice that he now obviously felt towards his bumptious, impertinent subordinate. He told him that he had no right to discuss the matters he had raised at meetings with the officers of the 14th Army because military regulations permitted 'councils of officers' only at brigade or regimental level and in certain specific units. Furthermore, as a combat General, he should pay no attention to rumours which simply undermined morale. Grachev continued:

What you describe as the transfer of the 300th Airborne Regiment is absolutely no concern of yours. It is not part of your responsibilities, so do not interfere in affairs which are not part of your official duties. I repeat once again, politics is the business of the political leadership and, to a certain extent, of the Minister of Defence and that is all. Remember that once and for all.

The fate of the 14th Army will be decided after the fate of Transdniestria has been fully resolved by political means . . . The army will only be withdrawn after the full agreement of the people of Transdniestria and Moldova. I have received a communiqué from the Defence Minister of Moldova in which he once again protests about your insulting statements about the Republic of Moldova and the Russian Federation; about the state flag of the republic, which you describe as fascist; and the fact that you will not blindly subordinate yourself to the Minister of Defence of Russia. Please confirm this so that I may make a final decision. At the moment, I reckon: 1) I am being deceived; 2) This is a game by you to get cheap capital with the public; 3) You've gone out of control and are directly disobedient.

Lebed's reply was insultingly brief. '*You* are being deceived,' he said.[27] Despite his astonishing insubordination, however, Lebed's popularity was now so great that Grachev could neither dismiss him nor even order his transfer to another posting.

In the autumn of 1993, Lebed was prevailed upon to stand as a candidate in elections to the Supreme Soviet of Transdniestria. Already convinced that he was being propelled towards a political career, he probably felt that the elections in Transdniestria provided a useful opportunity to get a foot on the ladder and to

1. Alexander Lebed's mother, Yekaterina Grigoryevna. A former post-office telegrapher during the Second World War, she still lives in Novocherkassk. Here she inspects one of her son's election posters.

2. Babrak Karmal, who came to power in Afghanistan after Soviet paratroops and KGB Special Forces launched 'Operation Shtorm' in December 1979, assassinating his rivals and capturing Kabul. In its desperate attempts to support Karmal's government during the following decade, Moscow deployed hundreds of thousands of soldiers in Afghanistan but was unable to crush Afghan resistance.

3. Afghan mujahideen resistance fighters show off their weapons and prepare for an operation against Soviet troops. In the early stages of the war, Soviet armoured columns were especially vulnerable to attack by small, flexible detachments of Afghan guerrillas.

4. Ahmad Shah Massoud, the main Afghan resistance leader, who inflicted heavy casualties on the Soviets during their offensives in the Panjshir Valley.

5. The end of the 'era of stagnation'. Leonid Brezhnev's coffin is carried at a funeral parade on Red Square by the Soviet Prime Minister Nikolai Tikhonov (left); the new General Secretary, Yuri Andropov; Konstantin Chernenko, who soon succeeded him; and the Foreign Minister, Andrei Gromyko.

6. The earth moves: Mikhail Gorbachev kisses the East German leader Erich Honecker in Berlin in October 1989. Gorbachev's visit stirred up 'Gorbi-mania' as East German demonstrators demanded *glasnost* and other political freedoms from their leaders. Within months the Berlin Wall was breached and Moscow's East European empire had crumbled.

7. Soviet soldiers leaving East Germany: with the collapse of communism in Eastern Europe and the reunification of Germany, Gorbachev agreed to phased withdrawals of Soviet troops. As they waited to withdraw, Soviet officers and their men often went into business, trading military goods for Western currency.

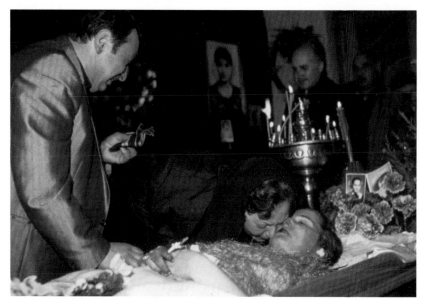

8. Funeral in Tbilisi: the family of a woman killed during demonstrations by Georgian nationalists on 9 April 1989. Eye-witnesses claimed that Soviet paratroops used military shovels and gas to attack the crowds. Gorbachev denied all responsibility for the decision to send in troops.

9. Bodies on the streets of Baku. Lebed and his division were ordered to the Azeri capital after anti-Armenian rioting in 1990.

10 & 11. Moscow 1991: The *putsch* that never was. Almost all of Gorbachev's Cabinet were members of the Emergency Committee (GKChP), including (above) Vladimir Kryuchkov, the KGB Chairman, and Dmitry Yazov, the Defence Minister; and (below), at a disastrous press conference, the Interior Minster, Boris Pugo; the Vice-President, Gennady Yanayev; and the Party Central Committee Secretary, Oleg Baklanov.

12. The Russian President Boris Yeltsin addresses crowds outside the White House from the top of a tank. The failure to arrest Yeltsin before he could organise resistance was a fatal error. Although the Emergency Committee sent KGB troops to his *dacha*, Yeltsin and his bodyguard Alexander Korzhakov (on Yeltsin's left) escaped and made straight for Moscow.

13. Gorbachev returns from holiday on 22 August 1991. The Soviet leader had apparently been incarcerated in his villa at Foros on the Crimean coast on the orders of the Emergency Committee.

14. Hail and farewell: Yeltsin welcomes Gorbachev to the Russian Supreme Soviet on 23 August. Gorbachev soon realised that he had returned to 'a different country' and that Yeltsin was its master.

15. The real *putsch*: Boris Yeltsin with Air Marshal Yevgeny Shaposhnikov, Yazov's replacement as Soviet Defence Minister. Without informing Gorbachev, Shaposhnikov gave his consent to the declaration by Yeltsin and the Presidents of Ukraine and Belarus that the Soviet Union would cease to exist.

16. Russian volunteers from the Dniester Republic shoot at a Moldovan sniper near the village of Koshnitsa on 30 March 1992. The fighting in the former Soviet Republic of Moldavia was only brought to an end when Alexander Lebed was appointed to command the Russian 14th Army.

17. The White House after it was shelled and stormed by Russian Army units in October 1993. Unlike the *putsch*-ists of August 1991, Yeltsin did not hesitate to use the army against his political opponents.

18. The President's man: Defence Minister General Pavel Grachev under a portrait of President Boris Yeltsin. Grachev ensured that Yeltsin got the military support he needed to storm the White House.

19. Russian tanks heading for Grozny, capital of the rebellious republic of Chechnya. Yeltsin was determined to crush the Chechens but Grachev ordered a disastrous armoured assault on Grozny, resulting in thousands of casualties and the loss of hundreds of armoured vehicles.

20. Russian troops among the ruins of Grozny. After the failure of Grachev's initial assault, Grozny was subjected to a sustained artillery barrage which reduced the city to rubble.

21. The Chechen President, Dzhokhar Dudayev, a former Soviet Air Force General.

22. The Chechen Chief of Staff, Aslan Maskhadov, a former Soviet Army Colonel.

23. Chechens demonstrate their loyalty to General Dudayev in front of the ruined Presidential Palace in Grozny.

24. A Russian soldier plays a piano abandoned in a park in central Grozny.

25. Two key members of the 'party of war': Interior Minister Viktor Yerin (left), and Defence Minister Pavel Grachev.

26. Lieutenant-General Alexander Lebed with Grigory Yavlinsky, leader of the liberal 'Yabloko' bloc, at a protest march against the Chechen war in April 1995. Lebed was by now openly critical of General Grachev and was preparing to leave the army for a career in politics.

27. 'Hero' to the Chechens, 'terrorist' to the Russians: Chechen field commander Shamil Basayev, who led a raid on Budyonnovsk, 100 miles inside Russia.

28. President Yeltsin with Prime Minister Viktor Chernomyrdin (centre), who negotiated with Basayev in Budyonnovsk, and General Grachev.

29. 'OUR TIME HAS COME – RUSSIA IS WITH US': a campaign poster for the Congress of Russian Communities, the political movement led by Yuri Skokov which Lebed joined for the Duma election campaign. Lebed's relations with Skokov were not good, and he ended the partnership after the elections.

30. The Tsar-maker: businessman Boris Berezovsky, who helped to finance an advertising campaign for Alexander Lebed in the first round of the presidential elections in order to weaken the communists and allow Yeltsin's re-election.

31. Anatoly Chubais, who ran Yeltsin's re-election campaign and became Kremlin Chief of Staff. Shortly after the first round of the elections, Chubais called a press conference to announce that he was the victim of a conspiracy by Yeltsin's bodyguard Alexander Korzhakov, who was promptly dismissed.

32. The new deal: Yeltsin congratulates Lebed after his appointment as Secretary of the Security Council. The appointment was Lebed's reward for agreeing to endorse Yeltsin in the second round of the presidential elections.

33. Lebed and his bodyguards arrive in Chechnya for negotiations to bring the war to an end.

34. Lebed negotiating the details of a peace agreement with Aslan Maskhadov in the village of Novy Ataghi.

35. Lebed with the NATO General Secretary Javier Solana, at NATO headquarters in Brussels in October 1996. By now Lebed had adopted a 'relaxed' attitude towards NATO expansion. Shortly after his visit to Brussels, he was dismissed from his post as Security Council Secretary.

36. Whispering the Kremlin's secrets: General Alexander Lebed listens to General Alexander Korzhakov. Both sacked by Yeltsin, Lebed and Korzhakov formed an alliance and Lebed campaigned for Korzhakov's election to the Duma.

37. Lebed and his wife Inna in Paris, February 1997. Increasingly denied access to the Russian media after his dismissal, Lebed tried to maintain a high profile abroad, with visits to France, Germany and the United States.

38 & 39. Possible rivals in the next race for the presidency. The enthusiastic free-marketeer Boris Nemtsov (left), Deputy Prime Minister and former governor of the Nizhny Novgorod region, and Yuri Luzhkov (right), whose dynamic management style has transformed Moscow.

establish a useful base of political support. During the last few months in Tiraspol, he had begun an intensive programme of political and cultural self-education. Along with his study of Plato and the Russian literary classics, however, he was beginning to think about a political manifesto. When he stood for election in Transdniestria, it was still crudely and aggressively nationalist. In his election address, he called for the eventual fusion of Transdniestria with 'the reborn state', by which he meant Russia. His uncompromising stand won him 87 per cent of the votes. His involvement in the politics of Transdniestria soon convinced him, however, that his faith in the region's leadership had been misplaced. It was not long before he realised that the President of the Dniester Republic and his acolytes were a lot less tolerant than the Moldovans, whom he had repeatedly called 'fascists', and that the administration in Tiraspol was as corrupt as any in Russia.

Lebed's disillusionment with the politicians of the Dniester Republic came as Russia entered its first major political crisis since the August *putsch*. A plethora of new political parties, some serious, others extreme or absurd, had burst on to the scene since the fall of the Soviet Union. Yet the clash of political parties on the streets did not reflect the real nature of the battle for power, which was being fought out between Yeltsin and some of those who had been his closest supporters at the time of the August *putsch* – men such as Ruslan Khasbulatov and Alexander Rutskoi. The battle was partly about economic issues, as the Russian public began to buck at the furious pace of the drive towards a market economy and the ravaging effects of monthly inflation of 30 per cent, but the essence of the crisis was constitutional. Ever since the final collapse of Soviet power, relations between the presidential administration and the Congress of People's Deputies, the Russian Parliament, had begun to deteriorate. In the past, the Parliament had been Yeltsin's power-base. Now, however, he wanted the maximum power to continue running the country without the constraints that Parliament kept seeking to impose. Ruslan Khasbulatov, the Speaker of the Parliament, on the other hand, was not interested in simply creating a system of parliamentary democracy in which his legislature might act as a mere check on the executive. He was trying to use the Parliament as a base from which to challenge Yeltsin's authority and establish a rival centre of power.

Ruslan Khasbulatov was a distinguished academic, a pipe-smoking professor who had used his position at the influential Plekhanov Institute in Moscow to criticise orthodox Marxist–Leninist economics and develop his own theories. He had become a close supporter of Boris Yeltsin and was at his side in the White House throughout the August *putsch*. As Chairman of the Congress of People's Deputies, he was now at the top of a pyramid of national, regional, district and local soviets, a vast network stretching from Moscow to the smallest villages deep in the provinces. Yeltsin's advisers realised that Khasbulatov wanted to use this network to rival and eventually destroy the President's authority. 'Attempts are being made to concentrate all power in the soviets, to restore the levers of power to the Communist *nomenklatura* and destroy the achievements of August 1991,' Yeltsin's spokesman, Vyacheslav Kostikov, said.[28]

In contrast to the power structure Khasbulatov was building in the regions, Yeltsin's own network was much less extensive. Although the mayors of Moscow and St Petersburg were strong supporters, the presidential apparatus was not strong in the provinces. Despite the appointment by Yeltsin of regional governors, many regions felt a stronger allegiance to Khasbulatov's Congress of People's Deputies, which was the highest authority in the land under the existing constitution. That constitution was outdated and rooted in the era of Communist Party hegemony, when the Congress simply rubber-stamped decisions of the Central Committee. It had the power to veto any decision by the President or his government and, as one Western observer noted, 'there was no obligation on the legislature to do anything at all that was constructive or beneficial to the national interest'.[29] The Congress was also the only body that could change the constitution and, although there was widespread agreement that such a relic from the Communist past – it had been drawn up in 1977 – was no longer appropriate, the Congress itself would never agree to changes that diluted its power.

For most of 1992, Yeltsin had operated under an agreement with the Congress, which gave him 'special powers' to appoint ministers and run the economy for twelve months. When it came to an end, however, the Congress began to flex its muscles, trying to impeach the President and rejecting his choice of ministers. Yeltsin's position looked dire indeed when Valery Zorkin, the

Chairman of the Constitutional Court, accused him of attempting a coup and the Vice-President, Alexander Rutskoi, openly sided with the Congress, telling Yeltsin, 'I warned you and have tried to act, as far as it was possible, to bring these irresponsible figures who have reduced Russia to a state of humiliation to justice.'[30] The government produced a half-hearted statement in support of Yeltsin, which was read out to the Congress by Viktor Chernomyrdin, the new Prime Minister; it provoked shouts of 'Resign!'.[31] Amid rumours of an imminent coup or even a civil war, General Grachev also spoke to the Congress, reminding its members that 'the armed forces will abide by the constitution, which prohibits the use of the armed forces for political aims . . . The army has maintained stability so far but the situation is heated. A split in the army would end in bloodshed.'[32]

Yeltsin tried to steer his way out of difficulty by ordering a referendum, which was held on 25 April 1993. Although the results showed that 59 per cent of the population supported Yeltsin, there was no outright majority in favour of early parliamentary elections. Forced to think again, Yeltsin tried to outflank the Congress in the summer by announcing the creation of a Federation Council, composed of all Russia's regional governors. He hoped that it would champion his plans for constitutional reform. Unfortunately, however, the governors proved to have an annoyingly independent spirit. Yeltsin then realised that a confrontation with the Congress was inevitable. He knew, though, that in the event of such a confrontation, he would have substantial public support as the referendum had shown that despite eighteen months of painful economic 'shock therapy', he was still popular. He would also enjoy the unreserved, indeed desperate, backing of the West, which had already invested so much political and economic capital in him that it dared not contemplate the possibility that he was less than a perfect democrat.

The means by which Yeltsin now chose to settle his quarrel with the Congress were far from democratic. They showed his willingness, however, to act with the ruthless decisiveness that Gorbachev had lacked; and whereas Gorbachev had sought to convey his wishes by dark hints and ambiguous suggestions, before disappearing to avoid any blame, Yeltsin was open about his intention to confront the Congress. He claimed to have a strategy to hold new legislative elections, in defiance of the Congress, by the end of the year. 'It will cover about two and a half months,' he said. 'Part of August – I call it the artillery preparation – then September, the crucial month, then October and probably part of November.'[33]

On Tuesday, 21 September 1993, Yeltsin made a special television broadcast in which he declared that the Russian Parliament had been suspended and that elections for a new legislature would be held in December. Despite disagreements within the government and a furious argument between General Barsukov, the head of Kremlin security, who urged caution because of the possibility of armed resistance for which the security forces were ill-prepared, and General Grachev, who insisted that all would be well, decree number 1400 suspending the Congress went into effect at 8.00 p.m. 'Russia was entering a new epoch,' Yeltsin remembers. 'We were shrugging off and cleansing the remains of the filth, lies and falsity accumulated for seventy-odd years. Just a few more shakes and we would all start to breathe more easily and purely. If I hadn't firmly believed this, it would not have been worth starting any of my efforts in the first place.'[34]

Khasbulatov responded to the President's decree by convening an emergency session of the Congress in the White House, at which deputies voted to impeach Yeltsin and declared Rutskoi President in his stead. A new government was formed, in which the former commander of the Airborne Forces, General Achalov, was the Defence Minister. The armed forces were told to take their instructions from him. As the Congress continued in permanent session and Yeltsin's advisers waited on events, the deputies appealed for help from regional bosses and military commands around the country. Whatever sympathies they may have had, army officers in the provinces were not prepared to commit themselves, despite the enthusiasm of politicians in the regions. In the Dniester Republic, Lebed's popularity made him an attractive potential ally for the Congress. He was approached by an envoy of Alexander Rutskoi, who ordered him to attend a conference with him. Lebed treated the order with contempt, saying, 'With human beings, I conduct myself in a human way. With swine, like a swine.'[35] His long-standing dislike of Rutskoi accounted for his immediate dismissal of his overture, but he later turned down a request from Yeltsin too. He was asked by the President to make a televised address to the people, but he had no wish, as an army officer, to involve himself in domestic political squabbles. 'I am a commander of the army and my ceiling is the one that I have been given – my army, and it should only be used in extraordinary situations. Therefore, I refused.'[36]

Instead, he agreed to make an appeal to all servicemen not to let a civil war be launched in Russia. Soon, however, the White House began to attract a rag-bag collection of mercenaries and volunteers from the extremist 'red–brown' fringe, who were eager to seize the opportunity to destroy Yeltsin. When Lebed discovered that the fighters included volunteers from the Dniester Republic, who were sent by the separatist government in Tiraspol against his express orders, he was furious and later called for the prosecution of the republic's defence and security ministers.

Yeltsin was careful to prepare the ground before attacking his opponents. With such a motley crew of misfits and desperadoes manning the barricades at the White House, it would not be long before public sympathy for the Congress evaporated. Indeed, Khasbulatov's tone soon became more hysterical and, when Yuri Luzhkov, the Mayor of Moscow and an important Yeltsin ally, cut electricity and hot water supplies to the White House, the deputies began to sound increasingly desperate. Yeltsin was confident that, when the time was right, he would be able to count on the security forces. He had visited the 2nd Taman Guards Motor-Rifle Division and the 4th Kantemirovets Tank Division a month earlier. He had also brought the MVD's OMON troops under firm control and supported the modernisation of the 19th Dzerzhinsky Special Operations Motor-Rifle Division, which had begun to hire professional soldiers and train as an elite police unit under its commander Lieutenant-General Anatoly Kulikov.[37]

Even so, the loyalty of the military could not be taken for granted. The circumstances would have to be right before the military could be persuaded to act with the force necessary to crush the revolt. In this regard, the appearance of large numbers of extremists among the rebel volunteers was helpful, and the cordon around the White House was kept loose enough to allow neo-Nazi and Stalinist volunteers to enter. Even more crucially important, however, was the need to encourage the rebels to overestimate their strength and imagine that military units were ready to support them in the event of an uprising. To this end, Grachev ensured that his deputies, Kolesnikov, Gromov and Deinekin, kept channels open to Rutskoi.[38] At the same time, Yeltsin's aides used the Federal Agency for Government Communications and Information (Fapsi) to feed a stream of disinformation to the rebels.[39]

On Sunday, 3 October, frustrated by two weeks of waiting as Yeltsin gradually tightened the noose around the White House, and convinced by the disinformation with which he had been fed that the public would soon turn against Yeltsin, Rutskoi made a provocative speech calling for an uprising. A Communist demonstration by the supporters of Viktor Anpilov, the hardline Communist leader, arrived at the White House to support the rebels. When news was relayed to the crowd, ostensibly 'from Soviet Leningrad . . . that sailors at Kronstadt base are rallying to our side', Rutskoi began to believe that the tide was turning. His faith grew stronger when he saw several hundred soldiers of the Dzerzhinsky Division line up and hand over their helmets and riot shields to the rebels. Yet the Interior Minister, Viktor Yerin, had ensured that the Dzerzhinsky Division would remain loyal to Yeltsin, and later admitted that 'not a single one of our forces broke his oath'.[40]

The apparent defection was a deception designed to make the rebels overestimate support for them. Yeltsin's aides now hoped that they could be incited to break out and cause a real threat to the safety of ordinary citizens, which would provide the perfect excuse to finish them once and for all. As the rebels continued with their jubilant demonstration outside the White House, snipers in the nearby Mir Hotel and the Mayor's office fired at them. The combination of euphoria at the news they were receiving of support for them and anger at the sniping goaded Rutskoi and Khasbulatov into urging their supporters, in front of the world's television cameras, to break through the cordon surrounding the White House and try to seize control of government buildings in central Moscow, including the Kremlin. The crowds managed, or were allowed, to pass through the cordon and, as they stormed the Mayor's office, the Congress became convinced that an authentic popular uprising was at last under way. Filled with revolutionary fervour, Rutskoi and Khasbulatov issued an emotional appeal:

Dear friends! The victory is not yet final, armed units of the commanders who have sold out may still be flung at you. They are supported by Yeltsin's underlings and stooges. Be vigilant and stand firm. We appeal to all collectives, to all citizens of our motherland: do not obey the criminal decrees and orders of the Yeltsinites. Unite around the lawfully elected government bodies – the soviets of people's deputies. We call on soldiers of the Russian Army and Navy: display civic courage, preserve your military honour in loyalty to the Constitution, support the concrete deeds of popular power and the law. Russia will be grateful to you and will give genuine patriots their deserved appreciation.[41]

Later in the day, as the rebels' supporters rampaged around the centre of Moscow, a chaotic army of neo-Nazis, Stalinists, drunken Cossacks and old women were led by the retired General Albert Makashov in an assault on the television tower at Ostankino, in the Moscow suburbs. Programmes from the Ostankino tower were broadcast throughout the country and, when the Ostankino news service was suddenly cut at the start of the attack, it seemed as though this key installation was about to fall to the rebels. There was a desperate 'race' to save it, but all was not as it seemed.

The Ostankino television centre was full of special forces marksmen from the 'Vityaz' unit of the Dzerzhinsky Division, whose fellow soldiers had supposedly just defected to the rebels. Makashov's ragtag army had been drawn into an elaborate trap, and they soon came under heavy fire from the Vityaz men, only one of whom was killed in the ensuing fighting. Broadcasting at Ostankino was cut off completely during the fighting on the orders of the station's director, Vyacheslav Bragin, who was a supporter of Yeltsin, and no one saw the hail of fire which poured down, killing sixty people, including passers-by and foreign journalists. Yeltsin later lavished praise on Viktor Yerin, the Interior Minister, who controlled the Dzerzhinsky Division.

The stage had now been set for the bloody final act. The massacre at Ostankino, cleverly re-dramatised as a desperate battle to save the airwaves for democracy, was enough to convince most Russian citizens and ever-eager Western embassies that there was now no alternative but to use force against the rebels. Yet even now, the military had its doubts about the need for an operation to storm the White House. When Yeltsin visited the Alpha special forces unit, there was silence when he asked directly if they would fulfil an order from the President. Even Grachev himself, according to Alexander Korzhakov, Yeltsin's bodyguard, had his doubts:

> 'Boris Nikolayevich, I will only agree to take part in an operation to seize the White House if I have your written authorisation.'
> There was a tense silence again. The boss had an evil gleam in his eyes. He stood up silently and moved towards the door. He stopped near the threshold and looked at 'the best defence minister of all time' extremely coldly. Then he said quietly:
> 'I will send you a hand-written order.'[42]

Grachev's attempt to cover his back was soon forgotten by Yeltsin, despite the fact that those present at the meeting felt that it would probably cost him his job. Yet as Korzhakov says, Yeltsin 'forgave him and later forgave him even more'.[43] The reason, no doubt, was the eventual success of the operation that Grachev now began to plan with his deputy Konstantin Kobets and Interior Minister Yerin. The irony of Yeltsin's storming of the White House, as mentioned earlier, is that it involved the actual use of the brutal tactics that, in August 1991, Lebed had described to General Achalov as the minimum amount of force necessary to take the building. Then, Achalov and the other putsch-ists had balked at such a display of force in the heart of Moscow. Now they were on the receiving end, and Yeltsin would not hesitate.

Grachev put together a force of 2,000 soldiers, which included members of the 106th Guards Airborne Division, the 2nd Taman Motor-Rifle Division, the 4th Kantemirov Guards Tank Division and units of Alpha and Vympel special forces. Just as Lebed had suggested, tanks shelled the White House before an assault by paratroopers and the special forces. The assault, which resulted in hundreds of casualties, was successful; Khasbulatov and Rutskoi were marched out of the building by their captors and taken to Lefortovo prison. CNN provided live coverage of the events and the world rejoiced at the triumph over evil of Boris Yeltsin, the Russian 'democrat'.

The events of October 1993 left Yeltsin stronger than ever, able at last to call direct elections to a new legislature and to ensure, with a new constitution, that it had few of the powers of its predecessor. From his position in the Dniester Republic, Alexander Lebed had watched events in Moscow with disgust. The army had once again been drawn into domestic political squabbling, and he felt little sympathy for either the President or the Congress. Yet the events had opened his eyes about the nature of the regime in the Dniester Republic, which had been so ready to send mercenaries to join the gangs of extremists at the White House. When, as a member of the republic's Supreme Soviet, he heard senior officials deny any involvement in the October events in Moscow, he resigned his seat in Parliament and announced that he had 'no moral right to continue being a deputy'.[44]

Lebed's concern about the regime in Tiraspol was not confined, however, to his disapproval of the support that had been given to Rutskoi and Khasbulatov. The Dniester Republic was an international pariah, recognised only by the similar breakaway republics of Abkhazia and Serbian Krajina. Its half-hearted attempts, together with its Gagauz counterpart, to form a loose tripartite confederation with Moldova, were blocked by Moscow, which was wary of encouraging separatism on its own territory and refused to recognise the region's independence. Lebed worried that President Igor Smirnov's administration in Tiraspol was turning the Dniester Republic into a centre of international terrorism and illegal gun-running. In 1994, his aide Colonel Mikhail Bergmann announced that his men had intercepted a shipment of automatic weapons bound for Simpferopol in the Crimea for the use of Crimean secessionists.

When Lebed was asked whether he would describe anyone in Smirnov's entourage as corrupt, he replied: 'The question has to be phrased differently – who may I describe as uncorrupted in the local government?'[45] He criticised the President for building a *dacha* for himself in Yalta, driving a Lincoln limousine, and distributing a total of 908 pistols to his friends and acquaintances. Whilst Smirnov lived a life of comparative luxury, his economic policies and, specifically, the introduction of a local currency had created widespread poverty. The enormous bureaucracy that

Smirnov maintained also created a huge strain on the region's economy, with the republic's seventeen ministries and numerous committees and commissions costing 18 billion roubles in 1993.[46]

After such devastating political criticism, it was not surprising that Smirnov and his allies tried to persuade Moscow to remove Lebed from the republic. Some reports even suggested that they had tried to pay off officials in the Russian Defence Ministry to make Lebed redundant. In 1994, the acting security minister of the Dniester Republic, Oleg Godyma, complained to Sergei Stepashin, chief of Russia's Federal Counter-Intelligence Service, of Lebed's 'destabilising role in the Dniester situation'.[47] Godyma's complaints found a sympathetic audience in General Grachev's Ministry of Defence. The success of the military operation to crush Yeltsin's political opponents had sent Grachev's star soaring high into the Kremlin firmament. Flushed with success and jubilant at the victory over his enemies, the President had forgotten the slights and suspicions of the past. Grachev was again unreservedly 'the best defence minister of all time'. So it was not long before Grachev turned, from his position of strength, towards his old rival.

Lebed had skilfully resisted attempts in the past to withdraw the 14th Army, arguing that its continued presence in the region was necessary both as a stabilising force against the increasingly undemocratic Tiraspol administration and as the only reliable safeguard of the stocks of armaments. In August 1994, however, Grachev changed tack. This time, he tried a more subtle approach, by issuing a directive on reforming the 14th Army demoting it to divisional status, which meant that it would be commanded by an officer of a lower rank than Lebed. The directive was issued whilst Lebed was still on leave, but he quickly realised its importance and cut short his holiday. He did not return to Tiraspol, however, but instead went to visit Cossack detachments in Rostov. The Cossacks treated him as a hero and fêted him as one of their own. It did not take long for news of his visit to reach the Defence Ministry, which quickly understood the message it was intended to receive: that Lebed not only enjoyed the support of a large part of the regular army, but also of the Cossacks.[48]

Clearly, it would not be as easy to remove Lebed as Grachev

had imagined. On his eventual return to Tiraspol, Lebed held a press conference at which he announced the possibility of an imminent resumption of hostilities in the region. In such circumstances, it would be irresponsible to withdraw the 14th Army. He was daring Grachev to go through with his directive, but the Defence Minister blinked and accused his officials of misleading him. When Lebed later refused an offer to command Russian troops in Tajikistan, Grachev issued a statement saying that he would remain in command of the 14th Army and that there was no plan to oust him.

Grachev blinked again in another, much more public, row a few months later. Lebed's condemnation of the Tiraspol administration's open corruption had struck a popular chord with the army and the public. They knew that Lebed really wanted to attack corruption in Russia itself, and it was not long before he started. The catalyst was press coverage about the corrupt business dealings of the Western Group of Forces. The idea of Russian officers using their positions to advance their careers as businessmen revolted him, but it did not surprise him that Pavel 'Pasha Mercedes' Grachev had become involved in the affair. What did surprise him, however, was that Grachev had now brought the commander of the Western Group of Forces, which was riddled with corruption, into the Ministry of Defence as his deputy minister. Lebed commented sarcastically that the President had obviously not read about the sale of army goods in Germany. In a televised statement, he said that Burlakov had 'demoralised the army's strongest group to the last man, and all of Russia's public prosecutors are on his trail'.[49] He added that he would not allow Burlakov to visit the troops under his command in the Dniester Republic. 'I don't welcome thieves here,' he said.

Grachev sprang to Burlakov's defence, saying that, if he turned out to be innocent of corruption charges, Lebed would be dismissed and sent to the reserves. Lebed intensified his attacks, however, and when Burlakov was eventually dismissed after a long press campaign, he described his firing as a 'triumph for justice'. He added, with staggering insolence, that Grachev himself should resign, 'for the very good reason that everybody is now criticising the Defence Ministry . . . Grachev must go, if only to safeguard the honour of the army and its morale.'[50]

Corruption in the armed forces was now the big issue in the Russian press and it threatened to overwhelm the Ministry of Defence. A young journalist, Dmitry Kholodov, had been investigating corruption in the Western Group of Forces for months, and his articles had been published in the newspaper *Moskovsky Komsomolets*. At first, they had been confined to stories of embezzlement but, before long, Kholodov began to turn up details of arms deals and the theft of nuclear materials. The stories brought him to the attention of some of the most powerful people in Russia's defence establishment.

On the morning of Monday, 17 October, Kholodov received a telephone call from someone he apparently knew, possibly a regular 'source'. He was told that an important package of documents was waiting for him in Moscow's Kazan railway station. He picked up the documents from the station's cloakroom and returned to his office to read them. The package was booby-trapped, however, and it exploded.

'I was only 1.5 metres away from the door leading to the politics and law department at 1.15 p.m.,' another journalist, Sergei Bychkov, remembers. 'All of a sudden, as I was walking toward the door, the corridor shook before my eyes and everything was enveloped in a cloud of yellow smoke ... Flames blazed inside the room ... When the flames were put out we saw a charred body in the corner. It was Dmitry Kholodov.'[51] Over 10,000 people attended a rally in memory of Kholodov, and there was a widespread public belief that his killers would be found within the Ministry of Defence.

'Who profited from the killing?' asked the *Moscow News*. 'It is an open secret that a struggle among several factions has long been under way in the Ministry of Defence. Until recently, it had been quiet but cruel. The fight has been waged not for the principles of military reform or military development – today no one cares about this – but for the right to have undivided sway over material resources and control of secret arms and equipment sales.'[52]

Dmitry Kholodov had begun to uncover the corruption at the heart of Russia's defence establishment, and he had paid for his efforts with his life. Not even he, however, could have imagined that the 'power structures' would be capable of the corruption, brutality and cynicism which they showed towards the end of

1994. As winter fell over the plains of southern Russia, General Pavel Grachev pushed his country into a war which eventually cost tens of thousands of lives before the Kremlin was forced to turn to General Lebed to negotiate an honourable peace.

8

CHECHNYA

*'The wicked Chechen leaps ashore
And sharpens his dagger.'*

M. Y. LERMONTOV,
'A Cossack Lullaby'[1]

Alexander Lebed was still serving in Moldova, in command of the
14th Army, when the Kremlin began to turn its attention to a
tiny republic on Russia's southern periphery. Lebed's swift, determined action to defend the Russian population on the banks of
the Dniester had prevented a bloodbath in Moldova. In
Chechnya, a breakaway republic inside the Russian Federation,
however, there were greater historical ethnic tensions and an even
worse problem with the arms trade. Chechnya was destined to
become the most intensely bloody and costly battlefield the
Russian Army had seen since the Second World War. In the alleys
and amongst the rubble of its capital, Grozny, the quality of
Defence Minister Grachev's new Russian Army was tested, and
tens of thousands of young conscript soldiers were slaughtered.

The war marked the final parting of the ways between Lebed
and Grachev. It quickly strengthened Lebed's doubts about
Grachev's ability as a senior officer, and confirmed his suspicions
that the Minister of Defence was personally corrupt. It showed
that, under Grachev, the Russian Army had become a pathetic
rabble of unpaid, unmotivated, ill-disciplined conscripts whose
lives could be carelessly thrown away as part of the President's
election strategy or to suit the private interests of the leaders of

the military–industrial complex and the 'power structures'. It made clear that none of the lessons of recent conflicts, particularly Afghanistan, had been learned, and that the poverty of strategic thinking in government circles meant that the automatic response to a crisis was simply to escalate the level of violence in an attempt to escape it. It was a testimony to the hollow reality of Russia's sham democracy and its bogus new constitution. It showed President Yeltsin in his true light as a tyrant, prepared to condone the bombing of civilian targets as part of a cynical campaign to present a new 'tough' image to the electorate. It exposed the hypocrisy and short-sightedness of Western governments, which were prepared to introduce sanctions, 'no-fly zones' and even military intervention in an attempt to stop the bloodshed in the Yugoslav Federation, but turned a blind eye and carried on writing out cheques to prop up Boris Yeltsin in the Russian Federation. It was the greatest and most humiliating blunder of Yeltsin's presidency, costing him the support of many of his closest friends. It was ultimately, though, one of the major causes of Lebed's rise to prominence and the downfall of some of his bitterest enemies.

It is for these reasons that it is important to understand the causes of the war and its murderous course. For although Lebed did not become directly involved in the Chechen war until long after crisis had become slaughter, it was he who finally brought it to an end and stopped the devastating humiliation of the Russian Army. The Chechen war and the peace agreement, which he concluded, show more clearly than anything else the stark contrast between his values and the cynicism of the Kremlin *apparat*.

Chechnya has been a thorn in Russia's side or, more precisely, its southern underbelly, for over two hundred years. Its inhabitants, who call themselves *Nokhchi* and their homeland *Ichkeria*, are a fearsome, warlike people whose clans have inhabited the mountains of the northern Caucasus and the plains that stretch beneath them towards the fertile grain-belt of southern Russia for thousands of years. A strong military tradition and a fierce determination to defend their beautiful land are the most prominent features of their ancient culture. In the past, the Chechens buried their dead in full battle-dress, built elaborate watchtowers to warn of the encroachment of invaders into their mountain fastnesses, and composed love poems to the most prized of their possessions, the two-foot *kinzhal* dagger. Their tradition speaks of the lineage of their clans, stretching into the mists of early history, beyond Islam or Christianity, whispering of mysterious links with the Pharaohs of Egypt and of unknown secrets and treasures lying hidden in the undiscovered snowfields of the higher Caucasus. The romantic glory of their history and the wild splendour of the Caucasus were reason enough to assume that any Russian attempt to subdue them would be a dangerous and costly undertaking. 'Who would not fight for this land?' one Chechen rebel said to me. 'Who could possibly give up this beauty?'[2]

Not just the Chechen military tradition and love of their land, but three centuries of bitter fighting against the Russian and Soviet empires should have been enough to demonstrate the foolishness of General Grachev's boast in December 1994 that Russian troops would capture Grozny in a matter of hours. Those Generals, security service chiefs and shadowy figures from the military–industrial complex who made up the 'Party of War' and persuaded Boris Yeltsin that his problems with the Chechens could be solved by military means had clearly forgotten their history. And history has the same sort of contemporary significance in the Caucasus that it has in Ireland or the Balkans.

For centuries, the Muslims of the northern Caucasus had helped to frustrate Russia's expansionist designs on the decaying remains of the Ottoman and Qajar empires to the south. Three centuries of subjugation under the Tartar–Mongol yoke had left a scar of almost atavistic hatred for neighbouring Muslims on the Russian soul, and this deeply-rooted psychological characteristic, together with a fervent imperial ambition to obtain access to the warm water ports of the south, led to numerous expeditions to subdue the Caucasus.

In 1785, after the Russians had extinguished the independence of the Crimean Tartars in 1783 and brought Georgia under Russian protection the following year, a Chechen shepherd, Sheikh Mansur Ushurma, declared a *jihad* against them and set about organising a united resistance by the Muslim tribes of the northern Caucasus. Sheikh Mansur, who preached an ascetic form of Islam and urged the strict application of Shari'a law, inspired his followers with religious zeal and turned them into a formidable guerrilla army, which soon inflicted severe damage on the Russian Army. When a Colonel Pieri was returning with an infantry regiment and cavalry support from Sheikh Mansur's native village of Aldy, which he had razed to the ground, he was surrounded in a dense forest and his men were cut to pieces by Mansur's partisans.

Sheikh Mansur was captured six years later, and eventually died in a Russian prison, but his example had shown the vulnerability of Russian troops to swift, surprise attacks by determined guerrilla bands on well-chosen terrain where there was no opportunity to engage in an open, pitched battle. Sheikh Mansur's example was followed with even greater success for much of the nineteenth century by Shamil and other Naqshbandi Imams.

In 1816, General Alexei Petrovich Yermolov was appointed Governor of Georgia and the Caucasus. A distinguished soldier, who had been decorated on the field by Suvorov in his teens and had already become a Colonel by the age of twenty, he commanded both the Russian and Prussian guards at the fall of Paris in 1814. After the deaths of Kutuzov and Bagration, he became the most prominent soldier in the Russian empire. He was, however, exceptionally ruthless, with a streak of cruelty and arrogance which soon fanned the flames of resistance in the Caucasus. 'I desire that the terror of my name should guard our frontiers more potently than chains of fortresses, that my word should be for the natives a law more inevitable than death,' he said.[3] Even the Tsar, Alexander I, was embarrassed by his excesses. When called to account, though, Yermolov insolently replied that 'condescension in the eyes of Asiatics is a sign of weakness and, out of pure humanity, I am inexorably severe. One execution saves hundreds of Russians from destruction and thousands of Muslims from treason.'[4]

In the ruthless execution of his policy, putting the innocent to death together with the guilty, surrounding villages and slaughtering all the inhabitants, and selling captured women as slaves or distributing them to Russian officers, including himself, as 'native wives', Yermolov outraged the Caucasus. His barbarous actions, however, set a pattern in the future both for Russian methods and for determined resistance to them.

Yermolov and his successors built a series of fortresses along parallel lines and advanced gradually from village to village, provoking the bitter hatred of the Chechens as they went. When Imam Shamil, a Dagestani Avar, eventually unified the tribes of the northern Caucasus in opposition to imperial rule, Russia sank into a long and costly guerrilla war with an increasingly daring and successful enemy. The Chechen and Dagestani rebels under Shamil's command were distinguished not only by natural military prowess but also by a religious fervour which seemed to make them almost completely fearless. To nineteenth-century Russian soldiers, they appeared able to continue fighting fiercely even with the gravest of wounds, just as, a century later, defiant cries of '*Allahu akbar!*' would ring out even after the densest and most deafening of Russian rocket attacks.

The Chechen warrior's apparent ability to defy death has long been a subject of grim fascination for Russian soldiers, colouring the descriptions of the many great writers who served in the Caucasus. One of Lermontov's characters, for example, exclaimed: 'I've seen a man beaten to pulp with the end of our muskets and having been pierced with a bayonet, and riddled like a colander, still waving his *shashka* [sabre] around his shameless head . . . They don't seem to know when they ought to die – indeed, these villains can hardly ever be killed. They are a people without the slightest idea of propriety.'[5] Shamil himself was said to have been seen pulling a bayonet out of his chest before killing the soldier who had put it there and leaping over a high wall to make his escape.[6] Similar stories abound today about the likes of Shamil Basayev and Salman Raduyev, the most popular of the Chechen field commanders, so it is easy to imagine the terrified bewilderment of modern Russian conscript soldiers in the face of such an implacable enemy.

Despite repeated Russian expeditions against him, by the end of 1841, Imam Shamil controlled the whole of Chechnya and most of Daghestan, which he ruled with a state structure based on the principles of Sufism and the Shari'a law. His guerrilla army was now well established, highly disciplined and capable of inflicting severe damage on the Russians. He harried his enemy continually along its over-extended lines of communications, making the most of surprise attacks by highly mobile mounted troops, unencumbered by heavy equipment and able quickly to disperse themselves among the local population. 'Resorting to the usual solution of mediocre Generals, the Russians sought to gain success by increasing the size of their expeditions, but achieved adverse results,' noted one historian.[7] In June 1842, Baron

Grabbe, the commander of the Caucasian Line, led an expedition comprising 10,000 men and 24 guns. It was an unmitigated disaster. Grabbe was forced to retreat after three days of heavy fighting in the forests, where he lost 66 officers and 1,700 men.

The Tsar was so furious at Shamil's continuing success that, despite occasional, half-hearted attempts to pursue political solutions in tandem with military action, he decided to send another, larger expedition. Count Vorontsov was appointed Viceroy of the Caucasus and charged to lead an expedition on Dargo, with 21,000 men and 42 pieces of artillery. When he occupied Dargo, he was surrounded, losing 3,916 men (including three generals), three guns and all his supplies.[8]

It was not until 1859, after thirty years of war, that the Russians were able finally to subdue Shamil. He was captured in his last stronghold, Gunib, which Prince Bariatinsky had surrounded with 40,000 men. The Russian victory over Shamil was achieved by a scorched-earth policy in the Chechen lowlands and 'the system of the axe' in the forests. Russia was helped too by the fact that foreign powers allowed her a free hand. Not even the Crimean War persuaded Britain and France to open up the Caucasian front. Despite the enthusiastic support of adventurers like David Urquhart, the first Englishman to visit Circassia, and James Longworth of *The Times*, a newspaper which frequently criticised British policy towards the Caucasus, Britain and her allies failed to use the opportunity provided by resistance in the Caucasus to stop Russian expansionism. The idea that the Caucasus was Russia's 'back yard', and that it could do as it pleased there, was not, unfortunately, confined to the nineteenth century, but appears to be the depressingly pusillanimous attitude of the British Foreign Office at the end of the twentieth century too.

After the final conquest of Shamil, Chechnya was kept under tight military control. The regular uprisings which nevertheless continued to erupt were brutally suppressed. In the 1860s, many leading Chechens were arrested and deported, without trial, to Siberia. Mass emigration to the Ottoman Empire began, encouraged by the Russians, with 5,000 families leaving in 1865.

When Russia was convulsed by revolution in 1917, the Chechens and other north Caucasian peoples saw a new opportunity to seize independence. The Bolsheviks at first appeared ready to accommodate them. A decree of 2 November 1917, entitled 'The Declaration of the Rights of the Toiling and Exploited People', recognised the equality and sovereignty of all peoples and established the right to self-determination 'up to and including secession and the formation of an independent state'.[9] Another declaration, of 20 November 1917, addressed 'To All Toiling Muslims of Russia and the East', announced that 'henceforth your beliefs and customs, your national and cultural institutions are declared to be free and inviolate . . . Know that your rights, like the rights of all the peoples of Russia, are protected by the whole might of the revolution and its organs, the Soviets of Workers', Soldiers' and Peasants' Deputies.'[10]

The Chechens and their Muslim neighbours in the north Caucasus (the Ingush, Dagestanis, Ossetes, Kabardines, Balkars and Karachays) seized the initiative and quickly responded to the opportunity Lenin appeared to have offered them, by creating the Republic of the North Caucasus Mountains and declaring their independence from Russia in 1918. Turkey, Austria–Hungary, Germany and even Great Britain (by now sufficiently worried about its oil interests in the Caspian Sea to register an interest in the Caucasus) all recognised the new republic. Independence was short-lived, however. Soon it was caught up in the Russian civil war, torn between the unforgiving Tsarist General Denikin and Lenin's new People's Commissar for Nationalities, Comrade Joseph Stalin. Eventually the new Soviet authorities broke up the remnants of the mountain republic into more manageable 'autonomous *oblasts* [regions]'.

Stalin's rise to power, and his brutal treatment of troublesome nationalities who got in the way of his grand strategic designs, led to a rebirth of Chechen separatism. There were peasant revolts in the mountains of Chechnya almost every spring, and major uprisings in 1924, 1928, 1936, 1940 and 1942. Often the revolts were the result of deliberate provocation by NKVD 'chekists', such as the occasion when the Regional Party Committee tried to establish a pig-breeding farm in Dargo. In view of the strict Muslim faith which had sustained the Chechens through decades of revolt, this was clearly an act of insufferable provocation. The Party boss, a Muscovite named Yegorov, was told as much by his Chechen and Ingush colleagues, but he replied, 'If Chechens do not eat pork, so much the better for the pigs. No one will steal them.' The pig farm lasted twenty-four hours. The pigs were brought into the village during the day by the NKVD and at night the Chechens killed them. To the Chechens, bringing pigs into a Muslim village where no one had seen them before was an act of gross blasphemy. To the NKVD, opposing the will of the local Party boss was an act of gross insubordination. Thirty Chechen 'bandits' were arrested and deported to Siberia. 'There are,' according to one account, 'thousands of examples of such pointless provocation.'[11]

The NKVD responded to unrest with systematic purges, executions, arrests and deportations. Fourteen thousand people were arrested as a result of the 'General Operation for the Removal of Anti-Soviet Elements', which was carried out throughout the Chechen–Ingush Autonomous Republic on the night of 31 July 1937. One order for the arrest of all the accused had been signed by the prosecutor, and they were all condemned after one and the same trial by an 'extraordinary troika' of the regional Party chairman, the prosecutor and the NKVD chief, appropriately named Dementiev. All of them were sentenced either to death or to the concentration camps. The thousands who were executed were shot in the hall of an NKVD building facing the Sunja river in Grozny. Their bodies were taken, under cover of darkness, to a forest near the Goriachevodskaia mountain.

Stalin's persecution of the Chechens reached its hysterical climax on 23 February 1944. Previously, the NKVD had tried to isolate and arrest suspected trouble-makers. Now they decided to arrest and deport the entire nation. The Chechen–Ingush Autonomous Republic ceased to exist, and its people vanished from the land that had been their home for six thousand years. Four hundred and fifty thousand Chechens were rounded up and deported to Kazakhstan and Siberia. Half of them died en route, as the NKVD used an outbreak of typhus to get rid of them in a 'natural' way.[12] An eye-witness description of the deportation shows the hideous efficiency of the NKVD:

In the second half of January and the first half of February 1944, special detachments of the NKVD began to arrive in American Studebaker lorries. The newspapers published an appeal to the population: 'Let us make an example of our roads and bridges', and 'Let us help our dear and beloved Red Army in its manoeuvres in the mountains!' Thus the army occupied the mountains and each *aul* [village] was supplied with its own garrison.

Then came the day of the Red Army: 23 February 1944. In the evening the Red soldiers built blazing fires in the village squares and there was singing and dancing. The unsuspecting villagers came to see the festivities. When they were assembled in the squares all the men were arrested. Some of the Chechens had weapons and there was some shooting. But resistance was rapidly eliminated. The men were locked up in barns and then a hunt began for those who had not gone out. The whole operation was effected in two or three hours.[13]

Many Chechen men were simply shot on the spot before they could offer resistance, and in the village of Khaibakh, where the local population tried to resist arrest, 700 people were herded into an ancient watchtower and burned alive.[14] The Soviet government subsequently made a weak attempt to justify the deportation on the grounds of national security, claiming that the Chechens had collaborated with the Germans and, therefore, had to be relocated in a less sensitive area. The excuse was absurd, as the Germans never reached the Chechen–Ingush republic during the war; nor could the Chechen–Ingush have deserted from the Red Army and joined General Vlassov's corps since they were prohibited from serving in the Red Army.

The real reason for the deportation was summed up by a Chechen historian:

It was for their secular and just pursuit of freedom and independence that the Chechens and Ingush were destroyed and their republic was liquidated. On a small stretch of land in the Caucasus two worlds came face to face: a colossal police despotism and an enclave of true human aspiration. The struggle between good and evil, between democracy and totalitarianism, was being enacted in the Caucasian mountains for decades while the outside world remained largely ignorant and indifferent. Furthermore, the strategic position of the Caucasus made it imperative for the Bolsheviks to finish the task which the Tsarist conquerors had left unfinished: to create in the Caucasus a new colonising force combining military and police functions and incorporating subjugated natives who would be obedient in defending Soviet imperialist interests.[15]

Evidence that the Chechens had ever existed in their homeland was eradicated during the course of the decade following deportation. The very word 'Chechen' was banned in schools and newspapers and removed from monuments and signposts. History was rewritten, and government records blotted out any mention of the republic and its people. Suddenly, it was as though they had never existed. In the camps of Siberia and Kazakhstan though, the Chechens kept alive their spirit of independence and the hope of returning to the Caucasus. Alexander Solzhenitsyn described them in *The Gulag Archipelago* as the one nation that 'refused to accept the psychology of submission'. In captivity and exile, they were as rebellious as ever. Solzhenitsyn remembers that 'no Chechen ever tried to be of service or to please the authorities. Their attitude towards them was proud and even hostile.'[16]

In Chechnya itself, some of the few who had managed to escape took to the mountains and forests, living as *abreki*, bandits of honour, who emerged from hiding only to terrorise Soviet officials. The last of these, an old man named Khazaki Magomedov, who was prepared to continue fighting as long as his homeland was subject to Soviet rule, was finally killed in action by a detachment of KGB troops in 1979. The old man had been fighting since the deportation, and died with his rifle in his hand. His last shot, according to local tradition, hit a KGB Major between the eyes.[17]

In 1957, Nikita Khrushchev officially rehabilitated the Chechen nation and they were allowed to return to their homeland. Their experience in exile had strengthened them, however, and made them more determined to resist attempts at Sovietisation. They waited patiently for the chance to begin the struggle for independence once again and, when the Soviet Union finally began to break apart, their opportunity came.

As stated, it is impossible to understand the course of recent events in Chechnya without a knowledge of the history of Russian and Soviet attempts to subdue the Caucasus. History explains the Chechens' yearning for independence and their readiness to fight for it. In many ways, it legitimises their claim to it.

And it shows that today's Chechens have more reason than any preceding generation to relish the opportunity to strike back at their oppressors. Among the many criticisms which Alexander Lebed made of General Grachev's decision to invade Chechnya was the assertion that he was totally ignorant of history. He said sarcastically that he supposed Grachev must have been asleep during the lectures at the Frunze Academy on military history because, otherwise, he would have known how successful small nations can be against much stronger invaders when they are motivated and the invaders are not. The Red Army's experience in Finland in 1939, he said, should have ensured that Soviet soldiers had learned that lesson.[18] He might have added that Grachev had clearly learned little from his experience in Afghanistan.

Chechnya's chance to bid for freedom was greatly facilitated by the rise to power of Dzhokhar Dudayev, a former Soviet Air Force General and uncompromising nationalist who knew that Gennady Yanayev's drunken *putsch* against Gorbachev had sounded not only the death-knell of the Soviet empire but also the chance to break free from the Russian Federation. Since 1989, the Chechen–Ingush Autonomous Republic had been ruled by Doku Zavgayev, a Communist Party hack and chairman of the old-style local Supreme Soviet. With the August *putsch*, however, he blundered badly, backing the wrong horse and irritating Yeltsin's supporters in Moscow, who considered him a traitor. Dudayev seized his opportunity with lightning speed. His Chechen National Congress issued appeals for an indefinite general strike and a campaign of civil disobedience. Chechens serving in the Soviet armed forces were instructed to disobey the orders of the *junta*. Dudayev, cleverly, also explicitly commanded that 'in the present situation the *ukaz* [decree] of the President of the RSFSR be followed'. Dudayev, along with Askar Akayev of Kirghizstan, was one of the few leaders of national republics who, immediately on hearing of the coup, declared his support for Boris Yeltsin. As a result, he earned Yeltsin's gratitude and bought himself some time. His intention, however, was not to maintain the status quo but to change Chechnya's situation radically and permanently.

Dudayev's supporters demanded the dissolution of the local Supreme Soviet; the removal of Zavgayev; presidential and legislative elections; a new constitution and a referendum to determine the republic's relationship with the USSR and the

Russian Federation. Such demands were hardly radical and could be heard all over the Soviet Union at the time. In the context of *perestroika*, it is possible that Gorbachev himself might have supported some of them – Dudayev certainly respected Gorbachev's honourable intentions.[19] Yeltsin too might have been expected to be sympathetic, given his support for independence or decentralisation in other regions. He should perhaps have paid more attention to the wise words of Nursultan Nazarbayev, the President of Kazakhstan, who outlined a radical plan for restructuring relations between the republics of the Soviet Union in a speech on 26 August to the first session of the USSR Supreme Soviet after the failed coup:

> For me it is obvious that the union can no longer be a federation. We have spent too long chasing after the past . . . How do I envisage that future union? Having entered into contractual economic agreements among ourselves, we republics have in mind broad economic relations with everyone who agrees to that. It will not benefit any of the fifteen republics in economic terms to go their separate ways at present. Common union bodies retain certain functions. In my opinion these should be the protection of common borders, a supreme council for control over nuclear arms under a ministry of defence in which all members of the union would take part, controlling those who have their finger on the missile launch button . . . As for the army in each republic . . . we would send the requisite number of servicemen to the union ministry of defence. If an external threat arises, the ministry would combine all our armed forces to defend the union . . . International relations should be shared only in working out general trends, including the problems of disarmament.

Thus far, Nazarbayev's speech had much to commend it to Yeltsin and his supporters. It appeared to be a way of preserving some of the strengths of the Soviet Union whilst guaranteeing the independence of its constituent republics. However, as Nazarbayev's speech continued, his real plan turned out to be much more controversial. He proposed that the new freedoms of the fifteen Union republics should also be given to those autonomous republics which wanted them: 'By republics I have in mind *all* republics, including the autonomous ones which have declared themselves sovereign, and those which will want to do so . . . In other words, we are proposing that a confederative treaty be concluded. I am convinced that only then shall we attain genuine equality for the republics.'[20]

Nazarbayev's plan did not meet with Yeltsin's approval. He might have succeeded in breaking up the Soviet Union but he had no intention of letting Russia fall apart. Ten of the sixteen autonomous republics in the Russian Federation were quickly cajoled into declaring their support for the status quo and demanding that the RSFSR should sign the new Union treaty on behalf of a united Federation. Even if Yeltsin had wanted to help the autonomous republics struggling for independence, there is little that he could have done in the circumstances. After the August *putsch*, his hands were tied. His victory was the result not just of the support of democrats but of his successful use of Russian nationalism. In his hour of greatest need, he had declared himself commander-in-chief of all the armed forces on Russian soil and appealed to the patriotic instincts of Russian officers. To have supported Nazarbayev and allowed the disintegration of the Russian Federation, within a month of the *putsch*, would have been unthinkable.

While Yeltsin was busy in Moscow planning the new Union treaty, events in Chechnya were moving quickly, driven by Dudayev's relentless struggle to consolidate his power and push for full independence. By 1 September, Grozny was full of demonstrators who had taken control of the television station and the telephone exchange. Armed units of Dudayev's Chechen National Congress seized the offices of the Council of Ministers and, on 6 September, they stormed the Supreme Soviet, which was immediately disbanded. Doku Zavgayev, the Party First Secretary, fled to Moscow and presidential elections were called for 27 October.

Moscow had now woken up to what was happening in Chechnya and, after a brief visit to Grozny, the Russian Vice-President, Alexander Rutskoi, declared that Dudayev's supporters were a 'gang terrorising the population'.[21] He urged Yeltsin to get tough with the Chechen National Congress and order the confiscation of all illegally-held arms. On his advice, the Presidium of the RSFSR Supreme Soviet ordered that all weapons were to be handed over to the federal authorities by midnight on 10 October. Dudayev immediately responded by claiming that this was 'virtually a declaration of war on the Chechen–Ingush republic' and ordering a general mobilisation of the Chechen male population.[22] Fifty thousand people demonstrated in Grozny in support of Dudayev's stand and, on 27 October, he was elected President of the Chechen Republic, which he declared to be an independent and sovereign state on 2 November.

By 9 November, Yeltsin had finally lost patience with the situation in Chechnya. He declared a state of emergency, ostensibly to protect 'constitutional order'. Dudayev responded by cancelling the decree and imposing martial law in the republic. As he appealed to all Chechens and Caucasian Muslims to begin a jihad against Russia, his 'national guard' surrounded a large force of Interior Ministry (MVD) troops, which had landed at Khankala airport outside Grozny. Yeltsin's state of emergency decree showed that he had clearly underestimated Dudayev. It was one of his many blunders, resulting in the opposite effect to the one he intended. The decree allowed Dudayev to stir up nationalist feeling against a crude Russian threat. It also undermined the opposition to him, allowing him to portray anyone who criticised his policy as traitorous and willing to support the Russian crackdown. 'We are grateful to Yeltsin for this decree,' said one of Dudayev's advisers, 'as it has solved all our inner contradictions.'[23]

Yeltsin's next blunder was his failure to develop and support an effective opposition to Dudayev. Whilst his regime became progressively more authoritarian, Dudayev was able to use both threats of direct intervention and attempts to overthrow him, such as a half-hearted *coup d'état* in March 1992, as a means of bolstering his position and enhancing his legitimacy. After the failed coup, he declared that 'the Russian empire is trying to keep its grip on the colonial people in its dying agony . . . There is no going back to the stable of Russian serfdom.'[24] Instead of trying to develop policies that would assist the emerging parliamentary opposition to Dudayev, Russia imposed an economic blockade and tried to disrupt transport and communication links, which merely caused even more resentment towards Moscow among ordinary people. As a result, Russian policy helped to precipitate the slide into lawlessness in 1994 and made a sensible negotiated settlement less likely.

Moderate opinion in the Russian government towards Chechnya was not in the ascendant in 1994. The Deputy Prime Minister, Sergei Shakhrai, recommended that Russia should sign a treaty with Chechnya, similar to one it had just agreed with Tatarstan, another separatist former autonomous republic. He proposed new elections in Chechnya and talks between Moscow and all the Chechen political parties, whether in power or in opposition. Shakhrai persuaded the new Russian legislature, the State Duma, to back him and the Prime Minister, Viktor Chernomyrdin, appointed him as head of the Russian delegation for talks in Grozny. The 'Tatarstan solution' began to look a distinct possibility and, although it was clear that Dudayev would hold out for full independence, many ordinary people in Chechnya would have been satisfied with the sort of economic freedom the Tatars now enjoyed.

However, Shakhrai was not given the chance to pursue his initiative. The Chairman of the Federation Council, Vladimir Shumeiko, and Sergei Filatov, the head of the presidential administration, rejected the notion of a treaty and called instead for the unconditional classification of Chechnya as part of the Russian Federation. Shumeiko began whispering in the President's ear, accusing Shakhrai of 'pursuing an anti-Yeltsin policy'.[25] As a result, Yeltsin dismissed Shakhrai as Nationalities Minister in May 1994, and the possibility of a 'Tatarstan solution' went with him. The 'Party of War' was now beginning to circle round Yeltsin, and when offers of talks on the status of Chechnya were received from Dudayev in August and September, they were unreservedly rejected. The Kremlin was now set on a different course and, as Defence Minister Pavel Grachev – of all people – should have realised from his experience in Afghanistan, it was likely to result in Russia being dragged deeper and deeper into a military conflict from which it could not extricate itself easily or cheaply.

There was no single reason for Russia's military involvement in Chechnya. Rather, there were a number of different factors which combined with an unrealistic assessment of the risks involved to make covert military operations and then open war seem a necessary and, ultimately, even attractive political option. Some of Russia's apparent concerns were realistic or, at least, had a loose connection with reality. It is undoubtedly true that, with the break-up of the Soviet Union, there was a genuine concern about the fate of Russian minorities in the far-flung reaches of the former empire. The fate of the large Russian populations 'left behind' in the Baltic States, Kazakhstan and Ukraine was a subject of intense interest to politicians in Moscow, particularly to members of the 'red–brown' nationalist block, which had recently become so powerful and appeared to have an increasingly tight hold on the President.

The popularity among the general public of a tough policy to protect the interests of Russians in the 'near abroad' was demonstrated in Moldova, where General Lebed had used the 14th Army to defend the Russian population on the eastern bank of the Dniester against attacks by Romanian nationalists. The Kremlin must have assumed that any action to defend Russians in Grozny against the 'lawless' Chechens would be equally popular.

Although an International Alert fact-finding mission in 1992 had reported that there was no evidence of any discrimination against Russians, by the end of 1993, Russians living in Grozny had certainly begun to feel the pressure.[26] A small group of Russians to whom I spoke in November 1993, during a visit to Chechnya, told me of the regular harassment to which Russians were subjected, saying that Russian homes had been burgled, people had been beaten up in the streets and there had even been shootings.[27] There is little doubt that, in the turbulent days of late 1993 and 1994, such things did happen. In part, however, they may have been a result of the Russian economic blockade and the frustration which many Chechens felt because of it. If the reason for the Chechen war was to protect the Russian population from such attacks and ensure that their civil rights were respected, it had precisely the opposite effect. As the bulk of the Russian population was concentrated in Grozny, it bore the brunt of the civilian casualties when the war began. The Russian government showed no concern for Russian civilians in Chechnya during the war, so there is little reason to suppose that, in reality, they had cared much for them before the war either.

The Chechen conflict has often been portrayed, particularly in the Western media, as an 'oil war', although Chechnya itself has no oil deposits which could possibly be of any strategic interest to Russia. Its total extractable oil reserves amount to barely 50 million tonnes and, in 1993, less than 1.25 million tonnes were extracted, not even 1 per cent of the total Russian extraction figure.[28] However, although Chechnya's own oil deposits are of no great significance, those of several of its near neighbours most certainly are. Soon after the break-up of the Soviet Union, the international oil industry began to show an interest in the Caspian Sea, which it recognised as a potential source of oil and natural gas for well into the next century. The size of oil and gas deposits meant that the region could soon rival the Middle East as a producer, and end the traditional reliance of many countries, including much of Western Europe, on the Gulf states for their supplies. Grozny was an important refining and processing centre, sitting astride pipeline routes from Kazakhstan and from Baku in Azerbaijan. Western oil and gas companies were soon active in Kazakhstan and, in 1994, the Azerbaijan International Oil Consortium, headed by British Petroleum, signed a contract with the Azeri government of Heydar Aliyev to develop offshore reserves in the Caspian Sea. Despite protests from Moscow that international maritime law did not recognise Azerbaijan's right to the reserves, the Caspian oil boom was about to begin in Russia's 'back yard'.

Whilst Lukoil, the Russian oil exploration company, headed by the Azeri Vagit Alekperov, sought and eventually obtained a share of the Azerbaijan International Oil Consortium, the Russian oil distribution company Transneft, with refining capacity in Grozny and links to the military–industrial complex, was considering how oil from the Caspian would reach the affluent markets of Western Europe. There were three possibilities: the first was through Iran and Turkey to Ceyhan on the Mediterranean; the second was through Georgia to the Black Sea; and the third was through the northern Caucasus to Grozny and then west to the Russian port of Novorossiysk on the Black Sea. The last option would enable the Russian government to accrue significant revenue from the transportation of the oil through its territory; it was also of great interest to those parts of the oil and gas lobby, the so-called 'fuel–energy complex' (TEK), such as Transneft, which had controlled much of the refining and distribution capacity in the area.

With assets in the region capable of bringing huge profits when the oil started to flow, Transneft was naturally keen that something should be done about Chechnya. Thus the fuel–energy complex began to exert pressure on the government for a solution.

It found a sympathetic listener in the Prime Minister, Viktor Chernomyrdin, the former head of Gazprom, Russia's largest oil and gas company, who was ready to ensure that the industry's concerns were heard in the Kremlin.

Although the Russian oil industry's interests were by no means significant enough to have been the sole cause of military intervention, they were undoubtedly a factor and they fed a much larger anxiety in the Kremlin about the trouble in Chechnya spreading to the rest of the northern Caucasus, undermining Russia's ability to influence events further south in the Transcaucasus. Moscow had every reason to fear the spread of Chechnya's struggle for independence to other republics because it was certainly Dudayev's intention to create a pan-Caucasian front, which would break Russia's hold on the Caucasus. His views had been published as early as June 1991 in an article he wrote for the Grozny newspaper *Bart*: 'We must not forget that we bear a responsibility for the fate of our sister-nations in the Caucasus. The union of all the Caucasian nations on an equal basis is the only possible way for the future. As we hold a central, geographic, strategic and economic position in the Caucasus, and have the necessary human potential, we must be the initiators of this future union.'

He proposed the re-establishment of the 'Mountain Republic', which had been 'one of the most important efforts to create a common Caucasian home'.[29] He emphasised that this was his central objective during an interview with me in 1993, when he said that his intention was to create an Islamic Federation in the northern Caucasus, which 'would enjoy good relations with its neighbours in the Transcaucasus but bring to an end outside control of the region and allow the wealth of the Caucasus to be developed for the benefit of its own people'.[30]

Despite his professed desire for good relations with his neighbours in the Transcaucasus, however, Dudayev was quite ready to interfere in their internal affairs. He sent volunteers to fight on the Azeri side against the Christian Armenians in Nagorny Karabakh and, with Eduard Shevardnadze in power in Georgia, rather than his friend Zviad Gamsakhurdia, he intervened in Georgia's dispute with its Muslim Abkhaz minority.

I was shown evidence of the lengths to which he was prepared to go when I was in Georgia in 1993. In Sukhumi, Dzhaba

Ioseliani, one of the Georgian commanders in the civil war, showed me documents taken from captured Chechen volunteers, fighting on the side of the Abkhaz separatists, which appeared to be the identification cards of members of 'the security service of the North Caucasian Mountain Republic'.[31]

He was ready to tackle his Muslim neighbours, too, if they got in the way of his plans for a Mountain Republic. Shamseddin Yusuf, the Chechen Foreign Minister, told me in 1993 that the Chechen government was ready to 'remove' President Aliyev of Azerbaijan on the grounds that he was a Russian stooge.[32] It was not just Chechnya's relations with its Caucasian neighbours, however, that must have alarmed Moscow. The company he kept elsewhere was enough to raise eyebrows in the Kremlin and beyond – he visited both Libya and Iraq in 1993 and told me of his admiration and sympathy for Saddam Hussein.[33]

Despite these legitimate concerns about Dudayev's activities and intentions, official attempts to provide a justification for Russia's military intervention were often mere propaganda. Chechnya under Dudayev was portrayed as a centre of corruption and Mafia activity. The Chechens were alleged to have spread their criminal networks beyond Grozny, becoming responsible for all the crime and extortion rackets in Moscow (indeed, presumably on the basis of this, the Moscow police soon obtained the right to arrest and detain any Chechen for thirty days without trial). Their activities were also supposed to constitute an international threat, a notion assiduously promoted to organisations such as Interpol by the Russian Interior Ministry (MVD) and the security service (FSK).

The myth of the Chechens as a 'bandit nation' of gangsters and Mafiosi certainly helped to demonise them. One otherwise intelligent Russian woman told me that often she could not sleep at night for fear of 'the Chechens' breaking into her flat in Moscow and murdering her. Despite such fears, however, which were the result of ancient prejudices, there was relatively little truth in these assumptions. And whatever truth there was in Russian allegations that the Chechens were involved in illegal and corrupt activity was partly the result of Russia's economic blockade, which meant that a degree of corruption was inevitable as the normal methods of ensuring the movement of capital and goods were closed. Furthermore, there is no evidence that Dudayev himself was primarily interested in personal enrichment, although he was certainly not a pauper. His commitment to the principle of national self-determination was well established. As one commentator noted: 'That he remained nonetheless unconverted to the Soviet system was proven in his brave stance during the Baltic secessionist crisis: he found himself, at the height of his career, in command of the north-western strategic bomber squadrons in Estonia, when he publicly declared that he would not fire on the Estonian demonstrators, and furthermore, even arranged for the Estonian national flag to be flown during a display at his base.'[34]

However, Dudayev was certainly involved in commercial activities, mainly oil and arms trading, which were of great concern to members of the Russian government. Their concern though was not the nature of his activities but the fact that he was able to threaten to release details of their own involvement in them. Grozny was a significant arms entrepôt and, under Dudayev, it was an irresistible attraction for the Russian military–industrial complex, offering *de facto* independence but *de jure* membership of the Russian Federation. This meant that arms were both easily exportable and deniable; they could be transferred to Grozny, still ostensibly within the Russian Federation, and then sold to difficult customers or 'pariahs' with whom it was impossible to admit any open connection. If necessary, arms could be registered in Moscow as having been lost or captured in an action against Dudayev.

For example, heavy arms left behind in Chechnya by Russian troops withdrawing in 1991 were bought by Dudayev for 8 billion roubles in 1991 prices.[35] In this way, arms shipments were made both to Yugoslavia, contrary to the arms embargo, and to Armenia for use in Nagorny Karabakh. Indeed, President Aliyev of Azerbaijan complained to Yeltsin, during a recent state visit, about the arms shipments to Armenia.[36] A member of Dudayev's circle told me that, whilst Dudayev no doubt profited from these transactions, he was hoping they would help him tie senior Russian military figures into a commercial relationship with him and thus reduce the likelihood of an attack. In view of his connections as a former Soviet Air Force General, and his knowledge of the arms-trading activities of General Grachev's most intimate associates, it is not entirely unlikely that he might have sought to develop a relationship with people whom he perceived to be not only easily corruptible but also the greatest threat to his nation's independence.

The bizarre arms trade even continued after the outbreak of open hostilities. When I asked Dudayev about the source of arms for his guerrilla fighters, and whether he had received any assistance from Arab countries, he answered, 'Why do I need help from Saudi Arabia? I don't need their tanks. I am fighting a guerrilla war and I get all the help I need from the Russians.'[37] A few months later, a source close to the FSK confirmed to me that senior Russian officers, including a member of the General Staff, were involved in supplying arms to the Chechens.[38] Dudayev's supporters also claimed that the subject of arms transactions had been discussed during Dudayev's meeting with General Grachev at Mozdok on 6 December 1994, a week before the outbreak of hostilities.[39]

The former Soviet Foreign Minister, Boris Pankin, a member of an international tribunal investigating the Chechen war, believes that the arms trading business, in which senior Russian officers had become involved with Dudayev, may have been one of the major causes of the war. 'It could have been useful to the military to cover up all these affairs with the arms which they'd left in Chechnya and maybe sold there. And so that it didn't come out, they bombed everything and wiped it out.'[40]

Some factors clearly weighed heavily in Moscow's decision to attack Chechnya; others were little more than a convenient background against which to camouflage less noble motives. Perhaps the least noble but, ultimately, most decisive motive of all was expediency. Both Boris Yeltsin and the military–industrial complex had good reason to believe that a short, dramatic intervention to remove the Chechen secessionists would be in their interests.

Elections to the Russian Duma in December 1993 had resulted in a surprisingly strong result for the Communist, nationalist and agrarian parties. Yeltsin's political planners began to panic about a possible landslide against reformist candidates at the next Duma elections, scheduled for 1995, and defeat for Yeltsin in the 1996 presidential elections. The President decided to play the 'red–brown' card by abandoning all but the least controversial reforms, dismissing unpopular ministers and flirting with nationalist opinion. Without a party of his own, and deprived of the advice of reformist ministers, Yeltsin came increasingly to rely on the 'power structures', chiefly the FSK security service and the General Staff. Against this background, the idea of a brief military adventure in Chechnya seemed politically attractive. It would divert public attention away from the growing division in government circles about economic issues, and show Yeltsin as a tough, 'no-nonsense' leader, determined to deal resolutely with the Chechen 'bandits'.

'Chechnya was an internal affair, a struggle of political forces,' says Boris Pankin. 'It was the battle of Yeltsin and his group for survival, to hang on to power. Further, in order to increase his authority, he had to show a strong hand. People would respect him for getting tough and not tolerating opposition. It was a pre-election strategy.'[41] Like Mrs Thatcher in the Falkland Islands, Boris Yeltsin would defend his nation's sovereignty and reap his reward from a grateful public in a better performance in the polls.

The army's motives in persuading Yeltsin to allow them to tackle the Chechen crisis were not concern for the President's political position. They were worried about plans to cut back on military spending as part of an economic stabilisation package. The military, however, no longer had the influence it had enjoyed during the Soviet era. What was needed was an 'emergency' to re-establish the army's claim on the public finances. Vladimir Mau, a professor at Moscow University and adviser to the reformist former Prime Minister Yegor Gaidar, explains:

> The budget debate in the Duma of April–May had revealed that the military lobby had far less clout than the agrarian lobby. Slimming down the armed forces and improving their efficiency was a vital necessity. But this went against the interests of the majority of the Generals, and what better way of avoiding cuts than by a short, small-scale war. A war would be given priority over all other considerations, creating a situation in which it would be very difficult to object to military spending. It was of no consequence to the Generals that the outcome of such wars is usually very different from that envisaged by their instigators.

Mau also points out that, as Dudayev's popularity began to wane during 1994, 'the regime of the Chechen separatists could have been brought to an end by skilful manoeuvring. But this would not have suited the purpose of the military lobby.'[42]

However, the head of Yeltsin's administration, Sergei Filatov, announced on 12 August 1994 that the government had rejected the use of force in Chechnya. For a moment, it appeared that the government was genuinely committed to settling its dispute with the Chechens peacefully. Certainly, at the time, there was a good chance of finding an acceptable compromise. In the face of an economic breakdown, Dudayev's regime was losing its popularity and wanted a deal with Moscow. Yet on 25 August, at a meeting chaired by Filatov, representatives of the presidential administration and the 'power structures' of the army, the interior ministry and the FSK decided to remove Dudayev by force. There was to be no attempt to reach a compromise.[43]

The 'Party of War', composed of such men as General Grachev; the security service chief Sergei Stepashin; Interior Minister Yerin; the President's increasingly powerful bodyguard General Korzhakov; Security Council Secretary Lobov and the Deputy Prime Ministers Soskovets and Yegorov, decided that previous attempts to encourage the opposition to Dudayev by supplying arms and financial support to forces hostile to the Chechen President had been a failure. They had been too little, too late, and entirely counterproductive, serving only to hand Dudayev a significant propaganda advantage. Stepashin's security service had begun to push for a much larger commitment to the Chechen opposition and, at the meeting chaired by Filatov on 25 August, it was decided that the FSK would co-ordinate a major effort to provide a force capable of removing Dudayev.

Public opinion had already been assaulted with a barrage of propaganda against Dudayev's 'criminal' regime, and the Kremlin had recently issued a statement on the situation in the Chechen Republic, which claimed that

> hundreds of people have been physically annihilated . . . The actions of the ruling group of the Chechen Republic has strengthened opposition attitudes towards the course [it has undertaken]. In the republic healthy forces are multiplying that struggle for the restoration of constitutional order, for the most basic law and order, for the creation of good relations with Russia . . . We believe that healthy forces of the Chechen people

itself will put an end to this lawlessness, to this orgy of crime, fear and violence on the long suffering Chechen land.[44]

The scale of covert operations against Dudayev began to increase immediately after Filatov's meeting with representatives of the 'power structures'. An FSK Lieutenant-Colonel, Stanislav Krylov, was captured in Grozny conducting a reconnaissance mission and, in late September, opposition forces began to launch attacks with sophisticated Mi-8 and Mi-24 helicopters, which could only have been crewed by the Russians.[45] In November, the 'Party of War' decided to help the opposition to launch a full-scale assault on Grozny. They gambled that the introduction of Russian troops and armour into the opposition forces would be enough to topple Dudayev and ensure a more pliant regime; if not, if something went wrong and Russian servicemen were killed or captured, it would be a sufficient reason to sanction a much larger response by the federal authorities. The FSK began a recruitment campaign within the Russian armed forces to persuade soldiers to 'volunteer' for action in Chechnya. Three young Russian officers – Captain Andrei Rusakov, Captain Alexander Shikhalev and Lieutenant Alexei Rastopka – described how they were recruited:

Everything started with a talk in early November 1994 with the regimental intelligence officer [an officer of the FSK military branch], Major Gordeyev, who described the opportunity of an interesting posting. He promised to give detailed information at a meeting in the Mess on 5 November . . .

Candidates for the mission, over fifty officers and men from all over the division, were there. We were addressed by the senior intelligence officer of the division, a Lieutenant-Colonel, who didn't give his name. He introduced two FSK officers who, owing to the secrecy of the operation, neither showed their identity papers nor gave their names. Later, one of them who accompanied the party to the artillery depot near Mozdok suggested they call him Denis Ivanych. But the officers were convinced this was a pseudonym because each of them was advised to use a pseudonym too. The FSK officers proposed to the meeting that everyone should sign a contract (a separate one for each person) in which they agreed to take part in combat operations in return for an attractive reward. The task was to enter Grozny and support the opposition.

Fees ranged from five million roubles for servicing equipment to six million for taking part in combat operations. The contract covered compensation of five million roubles in the event of injury and, in the event of death, seventy-five million for the family. The possibility of capture was not covered. There was only one copy of the contract, which was kept by the FSK officer. They said this was for secrecy.

After the contract had been signed, an advance payment of one million roubles was made. All officers were promised either leave of absence to visit their families or a training course at the Gorokhovets education centre in Nizhny Novgorod. Enlisted soldiers were promised an early discharge. Preparations for the mission were secret. The regimental intelligence officer insisted that no one should know about the mission, not even the commanding officer. But it was clear that the divisional commanders knew. When the contractors were brought to Chkalovsky air base on 9 November, the chief of staff of the division, Colonel Orlov, arrived and took away his twenty-two subordinates, saying that the permission of neither the Defence Minister nor the President had been given for their dispatch. Then only contractors from other divisions went to Mozdok. However, the delay was a short one. Ten days later the group was told to be ready to leave in three hours.[46]

On arrival in Mozdok, the men were transferred to an artillery depot, where they were given tanks which had recently arrived from Maikop and Volgograd. Thirty-four tanks were prepared at the Mozdok base and had their markings painted over. Some of the tanks were crewed by Chechen opposition forces, others by Russians. At dawn on 26 November, under the overall command of Chechen opposition field commanders, three armoured columns followed by infantry units advanced on Grozny. The attack was a disastrous failure. Twenty tanks were captured by Dudayev's forces and several others were destroyed. Seventy 'Slavic mercenaries' were taken prisoner and Dudayev threatened to have them shot unless the Kremlin acknowledged that they were Russian servicemen.

Russia could no longer keep its covert operations in Chechnya secret. The captured Russian soldiers were shown on television and it soon became clear that they were regular army soldiers who had been recruited for the mission by the FSK. Stepashin and the Defence Minister, Grachev, were caught red-handed, and Grachev tried to wriggle out of accepting the blame by telling one of his many lies about the conflict. Denying any Russian involvement in the attack on Grozny, he said that, 'If the army had operated in Chechnya, firstly I would never have allowed tanks to enter the city. It's wild ignorance. And second, if the army *had* fought . . . one Airborne regiment within two hours would have been able to decide the whole thing.'[47] In just over a month, his boastful remarks were to return to haunt him.

The attempt to overthrow Dudayev in a brutal assault on Grozny had been exposed for all the world as a Russian covert operation. Nevertheless, the Kremlin's embarrassment only served to strengthen the hand of those who now demanded the open commitment of Russian forces to a campaign to recapture Chechnya and protect civilians there. Alexander Kinichkin, a former KGB Lieutenant-Colonel, compares the November attack on Grozny to the actions of German *agents provocateurs* on the Polish border in 1939: 'History shows that a war begins with enemy aggression or a provocation by the side which is supposed to be defending itself. It seems that hostilities in Chechnya began with a provocation too, after which the federal authorities brought in troops "for the protection of civil rights and the ser-vicemen of the Russian army".'[48]

A full military intervention was not long in coming. Grachev was now desperate to cover his tracks. For the past few weeks, the Russian press had been full of allegations about his involvement in the corrupt commercial activities of senior Soviet Army officers in the Western Group of Forces during the final days before the withdrawal from Germany. At the beginning of November, his deputy in the Defence Ministry, General Burlakov, had been sacked after repeated accusations of corruption. Recently, the newspaper *Moskovsky Komsomolets* had called him a criminal and accused him of being behind the death of Dmitry Kholodov, the young journalist with a file on corruption in the armed forces. A week before the attack on Grozny, he had had to defend him-self before the State Duma against accusations of corruption and incompetence. Sergei Yushenkov, Chairman of the Duma Defence

Committee, had urged Yeltsin to set up a commission to report on the 'unsatisfactory moral climate in the army'. He had also called on Grachev to step down and save the President further embarrassment. 'If Grachev resigned it would be best for all concerned,' he said.[49] He was even attacked at a meeting of the Security Council. Russia's Human Rights Commissioner, Sergei Kovalev, quoting the Foreign Minister Andrei Kozyrev as his source, says that Grachev was accused of cowardice for pretending that the first he knew about the attack on Grozny was when he heard about it on television.[50]

Now that Grachev's covert war in Chechnya was public knowledge, he certainly could not afford to allow Dudayev to remain in power much longer. Apart from anything else, after the November attack, the Chechen leader was threatening to release details of arms deals and other embarrassing transactions.[51] Grachev agreed to meet Dudayev at Ordzhonikidzevskaya, a village in southern Russia, and the two Generals emerged from the meeting smiling and calling for champagne to toast their success in avoiding war. It was 'peace in our time', though. The meeting was a total sham, and whilst Grachev talked 'peace' with Dudayev, his colleagues prepared for war.

Soon after the meeting at Ordzhonikidzevskaya, Russian aircraft bombed the two airports outside Grozny, Khankala and Severny, destroying civilian aircraft and some Czech light trainer aeroplanes. They also attacked a housing estate and Dudayev's residence. Troops moved in large numbers towards the Chechen border. Nikolai Yegorov was named as the new Nationalities Minister to co-ordinate 'the restoration of legality' in Chechnya, which was widely interpreted as meaning that the Kremlin had ruled out compromise. And two other leading members of the 'Party of War', Viktor Yerin, the Interior Minister, and Sergei Stepashin, director of the FSK, joined General Grachev on the Chechen frontier in Mozdok, which was rapidly becoming a base for a possible armed assault on the rebel republic. The 'Party of War' had decided that the best way of ending the Chechen crisis was by escalating it.

On 11 December 1994, 40,000 troops from a variety of Russian armed forces entered the Chechen Republic from the east, west and north. It quickly became clear that Russia had dispensed with constitutional niceties and was ready to bludgeon the Chechens into submission. 'Of course, if anyone considered the legislation existing in this country,' said Sergei Kovalev, 'he would have concluded that the army couldn't be used in conflicts of this type. Only internal forces could be used and Yerin [the Interior Minister] had quite powerful forces at his disposal. But internal forces do not have aeroplanes or tanks – they are not necessary for the escort of prisoners or the dispersal of demonstrations and you can secure camps without heavy armaments and artillery.'[52]

In an attack on Nizhny Naur in northern Chechnya, T-80 and T-82 tanks, Mi-8 helicopters and Su fighter-bombers were used. Clearly, in their attempt to 're-establish legality', the 'Party of War' was prepared to ignore Russian law; and in its determination to make Chechnya remain part of the Russian Federation, subject to the Russian Constitution, it was prepared to deprive the Chechens of the most basic rights afforded to them under that constitution. In signing an *ukaz* ordering military action and aligning himself firmly with the 'Party of War', President Yeltsin had shown the shallowness of his commitment to uphold the constitution, maintain the rule of law and defend human rights.

The invasion quickly encountered widespread opposition both within Chechnya and among the Russian public. Political opinion across a broad spectrum was hostile. Alexander Lebed, still serving in Moldova but becoming increasingly outspoken, was horrified both at the constitutional implications of the invasion and at the way Grachev was prepared to throw the army into another political mess. He announced that none of his men would go to Chechnya, and said that it was 'absolutely unclear why we are killing people'.[53]

Lebed's immediate opposition to the war was shared by many of the democratic politicians who had been Yeltsin's closest supporters. In Moscow, Yegor Gaidar, the former Prime Minister, organised anti-war demonstrations on Pushkin Square. Like Lebed, he had no doubt that the war was a military and political disaster:

If I had not worked in government, did not know Pavel Grachev, did not understand the far from brilliant state of our armed forces and how weak the FSK was, I might have had the illusion that the war would be quick, effective and almost bloodless. But I understand that this is nonsense, that it won't just take two hours and a parachute regiment; it will actually be a hard, bloody, drawn-out war. I am coming to the firm conviction that we have no alternative other than clearly and resolutely to speak out against a military solution to the Chechen problem.[54]

Whilst Lebed might never have had much confidence in the President, Gaidar and his supporters felt genuinely betrayed by Yeltsin's decision to support Grachev and the 'Party of War': 'However much we speak out today against the beginning of this adventure, the very fact that responsibility for it lies with Yeltsin is an inescapably powerful blow to all democrats.'[55]

Sergei Kovalev, who had been appointed to his position as Human Rights Commissioner by Yeltsin himself, had no doubt about the President's responsibility: 'Without doubt, the first person guilty for these criminal actions is President Boris Nikolayevich Yeltsin. Only he could sanction this military operation.'[56] In the storm of protest that followed the Russian invasion, Yeltsin was nowhere to be seen. He had begun to adopt his predecessor Mikhail Gorbachev's tactic of disappearing at times of crisis to avoid facing criticism. After signing the decree ordering the invasion, he made one of his frequent tactical disappearances and left Grachev to take the flak. This time, the reason for his absence was not another of his prolonged drinking bouts but, ostensibly, an operation on his nose.

As Russian troops began to encounter opposition both from Chechen forces and from peaceful demonstrators, it became clear that senior army officers were unhappy at the prospect of doing the Kremlin's dirty work in Chechnya. General Eduard Vorobyov, Deputy Commander of Russia's Land Forces, refused to take command of the operation and resigned his commission. Sergei Yushenkov, Chairman of the Duma Defence Committee, commented that 'General Vorobyov did not want to stain his honour'. Eleven Generals wrote to the Duma questioning whether they could accomplish their mission. And when the senior paratroop commander, Major-General Ivan Babichev, at the head of an armoured column made up of paratroopers, elements of the 19th Motor-Rifle Division and some Interior Ministry troops, was confronted by a large crowd of unarmed civilians in the village of Davydenko near Grozny, he refused to advance any further, saying, 'It is not our fault that we are here. We did not want this. They [the Russian leaders] can condemn us but we are not going to shoot. We are not going to use tanks against the people . . . This contradicted the constitution. It is forbidden to use the army against civilians.'[57]

Babichev's refusal to advance was born of the same frustration that Alexander Lebed had felt in the Caucasus and during the Moscow *putsch*. Lebed later said that if he were given command over Russian forces in Chechnya, he would retreat. He added that he would only order his men to attack Grozny 'provided I was given a regiment entirely composed of the sons of those politicians who, from their lofty positions in the Kremlin, decided to go to war as if it were a fishing trip'.[58]

Grachev's answer to the growing opposition to the invasion was, predictably, escalation of the conflict still further. Furious at the Generals who refused to attack their fellow citizens, he took over personal command of the conflict and ordered massive air strikes on Grozny. Three Generals from the North Caucasus Military District – Alexei Mityukhin, Vladimir Chirindin and Vladimir Potapov – were sacked for 'indecisiveness and inaction'. As the bombs fell on Grozny and Russian government spokesmen insisted that the Chechens were blowing up their own buildings to prove that the Russian leadership was 'waging war against the Chechen people',[59] Dzhokhar Dudayev offered to join in unconditional peace talks. No one in the Kremlin was listening, though, and, despite Grachev's assurances on 29 December that Grozny would not be stormed 'in the classical sense',[60] on 31 December he gave the order for an armoured assault on the Chechen capital.

The operation was as badly organised and chaotic as might have been expected. Columns of barely trained conscript soldiers in tanks and BTR armoured personnel carriers stormed Grozny and, although some of them reached the centre, they were quickly surrounded by highly mobile groups of Chechen guerrillas, armed with anti-tank rockets and grenade launchers. The Russians appeared to be completely unprepared, and even senior commanders seemed not to have been briefed about the operation. Sergei Kovalev, who was in Grozny at the time with a small delegation from the Duma, is sure that even officers at brigade level had received no written orders or briefing about the attack.

Normal practice for an operation of the size of the attack on Grozny was for every soldier to be briefed.[61]

Gleb Yakunin, an orthodox priest and member of the Duma, who had arrived in Grozny on 30 December, remembers watching the scenes of chaos and carnage from his vantage point in Dudayev's presidential palace:

> A heavy bombardment began and it was difficult to leave the palace, but we could see how the rebel fighters went out, carrying grenade launchers, into the neighbouring streets and destroyed the armoured vehicles. Immediately, prisoners appeared – young lads. They were in a terrible state. Dirty and dishevelled, they said that they had been badly fed and, most importantly, that they had been deceived: they hadn't been told that they were going to storm Grozny, they were told that they were going to accompany a medical aid convoy.
>
> Dudayev's soldiers said that their tactics, when they came under heavy fire, were to take cover in their trenches, let the armour pass and attack from the rear. Apart from the air strikes and artillery which demolished the peaceful city, the narrow streets of Grozny were flooded with BTRs and tanks. Our soldiers, who didn't even have maps, were an easy target for the grenade launchers. And, under the extreme stress of the situation, those who were not hit or taken prisoner, were firing like madmen at the buildings in front of them. Many of them were blocks of flats and so they shot peaceful civilians. Apart from that, some of the tanks which had not been hit tried to use the flats as cover, smashing down walls, doors and windows as they drove in.[62]

In the chaos, Russian casualties were enormous. One of the units most closely involved in the attack, the 81st Regiment of the 131st Motor-Rifle Brigade from Samara, was almost entirely destroyed: in one battalion, only one officer and ten men survived.[63] Sergei Kovalev describes the experience of one officer who was taken prisoner:

> They spent the whole night at the station, where they took huge losses – very few of them were left alive and there were only two or three BTRs left (at the beginning, if I'm not mistaken,

there were no less than fifteen vehicles). They loaded up the
BTRs with wounded, put in as many bodies as would fit. The
remainder of the survivors sat on the armour and tried to break
out of the town. They remembered how they had come into
the town. But they came to a crossroads – right or left? Let's
go right! And almost all were killed, only a few were taken
prisoner. If they'd gone left, maybe they'd have stayed alive.[64]

Things were rapidly going from bad to worse for the hapless
General Grachev. His covert war had failed. The initial invasion
had not remotely cowed the Chechens into submission, and now
it was clear that resistance was not going to collapse at the first
sight of Russian tanks entering Grozny either. He had ordered his
troops into an action which, only a month ago, he had insisted he
would never sanction because it was so unprofessional: sending a
column of armour to attack an urban target without infantry support. Now he had brought about the pitiable consequences which
he had so accurately predicted. Despite the praise which Yeltsin
had recently heaped upon him, in an attempt to shore up his position after so many hostile charges against him, 'the best defence
minister of all time' was proving to be a liability to his master.
Indeed, every action he had taken so far had merely served to
strengthen Dudayev and entrench his position.

As the world woke up on New Year's Day 1995, gun battles
were raging in Grozny, where the bombed-out hulks of Russian
armour and the corpses of conscript soldiers littered the streets.
Western commentators, shocked at television pictures of Russian
tanks in action during the festive season, compared Yeltsin's attack
on Chechnya to Brezhnev's invasion of Afghanistan. At the
beginning of another crucial year for the President, with Duma
elections in the autumn, Grachev had managed to drag the
President into a winter war and the biggest crisis of his career.
'Only an idiot', said Alexander Lebed, would start such a war in
the winter.[65]

Yet, as Lebed was later to realise, there was a desperate, twisted
logic to Grachev's plan. As he had long suspected, it was explained
by the corrupt business dealings of the Defence Minister's closest
colleagues. For months after the storming of Grozny, Lebed
could not understand why Grachev would have ordered a frontal
assault by a column of tanks, unsupported by infantry, when only

a month earlier he had insisted that such an order would be 'wild ignorance'. There had to be another reason. Lebed believes that the Chechen war itself, and Grachev's decision to send tanks into Grozny in particular, were the direct result of the minister's involvement in illegal arms trading:

> ... because at the time of the liquidation of the Western Group of Forces, [Grachev] and Burlakov [Grachev's deputy] had stolen 1,600 tanks and sold them in Riga ... The procurator was investigating it. The late journalist Kholodov got close to the truth. He was blown up. After that the investigation stopped. One thousand six hundred tanks disappeared and that's not an insignificant number. It had to be explained some-how. Therefore, a military conflict was necessary. In Russia there is a saying – war writes off everything. Another one is: a wise man laughs, a cunning man believes and a fool goes to war. In the entire history of the Great Patriotic War, there were three cities which tank columns entered: Stalingrad, Nuremberg, Berlin. That's all. Even there they didn't take tanks into a city, because they understood that in a city a tank is vul-nerable. Any small boy can throw a cigarette end from a balcony and there's no tank left. But in Grozny, they took them in.[66]

Lebed is convinced that 'in the overall picture of this war, there are still many details which are worth investigating. Because, as I looked into the source and conduct of the war, those who started it ultimately gained more than they lost. Because teaching a lesson to the people with whom they'd previously done business and who'd stopped satisfying their growing appetites, was only one task of those who started the war.'[67]

> The other task was to hide the traces of the sale by General Burlakov of any number of tanks. This story begins at the moment when the late journalist, Dmitry Kholodov, raised the question of the misappropriation of 1,600 tanks from the Western Group of Forces ... Kholodov was close to the truth. The tanks were actually stolen. In as much as a tank is not a box of matches, generally the number of them in the country is relatively easy to calculate. And here – one thousand six

hundred tanks were missing. Therefore, the need arose to create circumstances where a large amount of armour could be destroyed.

Lebed is in no doubt that Burlakov sold the tanks, 'probably to the former Yugoslavia'. His theory is based on investigations in Chechnya at the end of the war and an examination of confidential papers and sources to which he would have had access during his brief period as the Kremlin's security chief in 1996.

This hidden scenario begins to make much clearer the apparent contradiction when the Minister of Defence says, 'Sending tanks into a town – how stupid', and the following day tanks drive into the town in columns and are burnt there. This is my personal opinion, arising from my investigations of the situation on the spot. There are many details in the overall picture of reasons for the war which merit a thorough, professional investigation, which should be carried out by the General Procurator.

Burlakov has long ago gone quiet. Grachev has gone quiet. They've got a lot to be quiet about. For them, the saddest possible situation has come about: the war has come to an end. As is well known, a war can write off everything. And now it's gone and ended. And when peace comes, and people try to organise some sort of state based on the rule of law, then questions arise: why? What for? Who? Such questions simply cannot but arise. Tens of thousands of people were killed, hundreds of thousands were wounded, there are hundreds of thousands of refugees and colossal damage to property. Why, the question arises, was all this done? If it was for a military victory – well, it wasn't going to be achieved like that. For me, for example, the first question is always: what did they hope to achieve? And just now, unfortunately, the answer is: they wanted simply to make sure no one was any the wiser. They needed any kind of trouble where they could burn hundreds of tanks. Because there, where there were hundreds, they could write off thousands. So, a tank blew up, its turret flew off, we'll take the turret and write down one tank; we take the body – another tank; the left track – a third tank, and so on . . .[68]

To the Western mind, unaccustomed to such cynicism and, perhaps, seduced by the notion that such a state of affairs could not possibly exist in Boris Yeltsin's new Russia, Lebed's description of Grachev's motivation may seem improbable. However, to anyone who knew the depths to which senior military officers had already sunk in their commercial activities, it is not unreasonable. It certainly offers an explanation for the extraordinary series of contradictory orders which Grachev issued and the desperate haste with which he pushed unprepared troops into ill-conceived operations. It might also explain his tendency to respond to one disaster by leaping into an even bigger one.

Indeed, his predictable response to the deepening crisis was to order a further escalation of the violence. Over a hundred heavy artillery pieces pounded Grozny from positions in the uplands on the edge of the city. As many as nine hundred shells an hour rained down indiscriminately, devastating residential areas. As the city was still full of civilians, many of them Russians who had been unable to take refuge with relations in the countryside, it was a hideous, unpardonable atrocity. Western foreign ministers, who had been so vocal about the Serb shelling of Sarajevo, now found it convenient to avert their gaze as Grachev's bombardment flattened Grozny, burying many of its citizens in the rubble. Whether or not Grachev was trying to bury the evidence of his crimes too, his 'big war' tactics were disastrously counterproductive.

Television pictures of the ruins of Grozny, with streets of public buildings and apartment blocks now bombed-out and looking for all the world like Dresden or Berlin in 1945, horrified people in the West and in Russia. As it became clear that at least two thousand soldiers had died on New Year's Eve alone, and as ghoulish rumours began to circulate of unburied bodies in the streets of Grozny being torn apart and eaten by starving dogs,[69] Russian public opinion turned violently against the war. The Chechens themselves, far from being cowed by Grachev's barbarous assault on their capital, were immeasurably strengthened by it. There was a 'blitz spirit' among the population. The attack had confirmed Dudayev's legitimacy, too, and he acquired a new lease of life as a warrior, bravely leading the defence of the capital for over two weeks until his presidential palace, the symbol of resistance, finally fell, on 19 January. Grachev marked his Pyrrhic victory with a typical distortion of the truth, describing it as 'unique in military history, in that the Chechen defenders – estimated at 15,000 – outnumbered the attackers by three to one'.[70]

The fall of Grozny did not, however, mean the end of Chechen resistance. Dudayev escaped into the mountains of southern Chechnya, from where he and his commanders planned a highly effective guerrilla campaign, which made the maximum use of a force of no more than 5,000 active fighters. Their tactics owed much both to the nineteenth-century tradition of Shamil and to the experience of Afghanistan. They were well trained, and it soon became clear that Dudayev had long been expecting that he would have to fight a guerrilla war to secure Chechen independence. Indeed, Shamil Basayev and a group of over seventy fighters had travelled abroad for a training programme during the year preceding the Russian invasion. A close colleague of Basayev told me that he had spent six months in Pakistan and Afghanistan being trained in guerrilla tactics.[71] Typically, the Chechens operated in small, mobile groups, often no more than three men, with one man carrying a grenade launcher and his two colleagues supporting him with automatic weapons. Their discipline was compounded by a strong motivation based on an adherence to the principles of Islam. All the fighters with whom I spoke were very genuine in their religious faith, strictly observing principles such as the ban on alcohol, and believing that if they were killed in battle they would die a martyr's death and attain *azot* or eternal paradise.

The commander of the Russian Airborne Forces, Colonel-General Yevgeny Podkolzin, who lost 244 men in the storming of Grozny, was astonished by how well organised the Chechens were. His briefings from the FSK director, Sergei Stepashin, had led him to expect that his troops would be engaged in a police operation against Chechen 'bandits'.

'The director told us that we'd be up against criminals and bandits who had been released from jail,' he told a news conference, 'but in fact we encountered a well-trained army.'[72]

The Chechens' discipline was in sharp contrast to the behaviour of Russian troops. Although officially the Chechen campaign was conducted by Interior Ministry (MVD) troops, soldiers from virtually every division of the Russian Army, including elite special forces, eventually took part in the conflict. Hundreds of thousands of troops were committed to the North Caucasus military region for the campaign, in direct and flagrant breach of the Conventional Forces in Europe (CFE) Treaty, which placed strict limits on the numbers of troops and the amount of armour that could be deployed on Russia's southern flank. The majority of Russian soldiers serving in Chechnya were conscripts. Two young infantrymen whom I met after they had deserted to the Chechens were fresh-faced, guileless boys of eighteen, who had been told that they were going on an exercise to St Petersburg only to find themselves starving under canvas in Chechnya. They were never paid and hardly ever fed. After they had traded their weapons with the Chechens for food, they deserted and fled to a Chechen village.[73]

The pitiable condition of Russian troops was one of the most shocking features of the war. It was certainly one of the things that most angered Alexander Lebed. 'It is a disgrace that senior officers treated our own soldiers like that,' he admitted. 'They turned the Russian Army into a rabble.'[74] Only half of the Interior Ministry troops had received proper combat training, and the armour which the Russian forces used in the early stages of the war was antiquated – old T-72 tanks, for example, instead of new T-90s, a fact which perhaps lends credence to Lebed's theory about Grachev's decision to 'write off' large amounts of armour.

For the ordinary Russian soldier, Chechnya was perhaps worse than any conflict since the Second World War. Budapest, Prague and Kabul had all been captured relatively easily. In one night of fighting in Grozny, however, the Russians had taken more casualties than in a whole year in Afghanistan. One veteran of Afghanistan, who was now fighting with the Chechen rebels, told me, 'Afghanistan was an anecdote. Chechnya is a real war.' The difference between the Soviet Army in Afghanistan and the Russian Army in Chechnya was also immediately apparent to him. 'Soviet forces in Afghanistan were under much stronger discipline than Russian troops in Chechnya. There were fewer attacks on civilians in Afghanistan. In Chechnya, though, they're just told to do what they want. If they fancy a girl, they just take her and she'll disappear.'[75]

After the barbarism of the storming of Grozny, Russian operations continued to be characterised by their clumsy brutality. As Russian troops became increasingly vulnerable to attack from guerrilla units, air strikes and heavy artillery were used to terrorise villages suspected of harbouring *boyeviki* (rebel fighters). Targets were attacked with artillery shells, Grad missiles and helicopter gunships, which dropped fragmentation bombs and even, on occasion, nail bombs. Chechens suspected of being connected with the rebels were arrested and sent to so-called 'filtration camps', where torture was widespread. Even if they were not *boyeviki* at the time of their arrest, the experience of one of the FSK's filtration camps made most Chechens who survived them determined to join the rebel fighters.

A young Chechen to whom I spoke near the village of Urus Martan told me of the horrific tortures to which he had been subjected. They included the insertion of needles under his finger-nails and the use of a special metal 'crown', which could be tightened by screws, placed over the temples. As the 'crown' contracted, the skull was gradually broken, and the pressure was enough to force a prisoner's eyeballs out of their sockets. The pain was intense. The young man who spoke to me was lucky: his skull was only lightly fractured and, although he was beaten every day for a month and badly burned, he was eventually released. He was determined to dedicate what remained of his life to helping the *boyeviki*.[76] In February 1995, Sergei Kovalev gave evidence to a Duma committee investigating the background to the Chechen conflict, in which he said that over 1,000 Chechen civilians had died as a result of the repeated beatings of prisoners in filtration camps and summary executions by the security forces.[77]

The widespread use of mercenaries by the Russians also led to many atrocities which further antagonised the civilian population and increased support for the rebels. These mercenaries, known as *nayomniki*, had been recruited by the FSK, and the worst of them had come from prisons and penal institutions after volunteering for service in Chechnya in return for a reduction in their sentence. They were utterly ruthless and had no compunction about looting, raping or murdering civilians. Russian commanders may have thought that the use of *nayomniki* would frighten the civilian population into submission, but it had the opposite effect, stirring up more hatred and contempt. The rebels despised them and, whereas they were prepared to take conscript soldiers prisoner, captured *nayomniki* were simply shot.

In April 1995, one of the most shocking atrocities of the war took place in the village of Samashki in western Chechnya. After the village elders were told to surrender to the authorities more weapons than the population could possibly have possessed, the village was surrounded and at least 200 civilians were butchered by Russian troops. Anatoly Shabad, a member of the Duma, visited the village shortly after the massacre. Despite his identity card, clearly showing him to be a member of the Duma, the soldiers who were still surrounding the village refused to let him in, but he was disguised and smuggled in with a group of local women. He saw evidence of 'the mass murder of peaceful inhabitants' of the village:

> At the time, they still hadn't buried the bodies and everything was still fresh . . . Houses had been burnt out where there was no trace of any gunfire . . . They had burnt peaceful citizens in their cellars and then moved on down the road, burning all the houses on their way and exterminating all the male population. Judging from witnesses' accounts and from the corpses which I saw on 12 April, the task was to kill any male who fell into their hands, any male older than a certain age, say fifteen or sixteen.[78]

The Russian tactics backfired badly. There was no attempt to 'win hearts and minds' and, to an even greater extent than in Afghanistan, the civilian population became radicalised and militarised. General Lebed recognised that Grachev's tactics were turning the civilian population into loyal supporters of Dudayev's fighters. 'It is not just Dudayev's forces but the entire Chechen nation which is now fighting Russia,' he said. 'Men . . . are ready to fight for the rest of their lives.'[79] He was characteristically uncompromising and insubordinate in his assessment of the Defence Minister's conduct of the war. With coruscating sarcasm, he attacked Yeltsin's rosy view of Grachev, telling a Western reporter that he was 'undoubtedly a wise man, perhaps even the best defence minister of all time. He has succeeded by barbaric bombing raids in turning indifferent civilians into fanatical soldiers.'[80]

Although the Russians managed to achieve some measure of success in the spring of 1995 by using more special forces to establish a presence in lowland towns, such as Shali and Urus Martan, and even in Shatoi and Vedeno in the highlands, their success was limited and often illusory. Even in the lowland areas outside Grozny, at nightfall Russian troops would abandon positions which they had occupied by day and retreat to their heavily fortified base. In the highlands and along the main highways, Russian columns became an easy target for Chechen guerrilla units and losses of men and equipment were high. The burnt-out shells of armoured vehicles pushed off mountain roads soon littered the banks of the river Argun, which flows from the highlands down to Grozny.

As the war continued, Dudayev became ever more confident. When I met him before the war, he seemed somehow both sinister and faintly ridiculous. A strange man in an ill-fitting suit and a Homburg hat, with more than a passing resemblance to Peter Mandelson, he was given to issuing blood-curdling threats whilst cracking his knuckles as he clenched his fists. When I met him again in 1995, however, in a village well within the area supposedly controlled by the Russians, he was wearing neatly pressed combat fatigues and highly polished boots. He paced the room energetically as he outlined the future direction of the war. This was no longer a pantomime villain but the military and political leader of a national liberation movement, who was convinced that 'Russia's attack on Chechnya will end not in the destruction of Chechnya but in the break-up of the Russian Federation'.[81]

He spoke with contempt, rather than fear, of his enemy. 'The greatest threat which mankind faces now,' he said, 'is not fascism or communism but "Russism", which is a combination of Russian chauvinism and the Russian slave mentality. They want to conquer so that they can destroy. They want to degrade everything and bring it down to their level. But they will never conquer us. We can go on fighting for decades, for centuries.'[82] With his well organised, highly disciplined guerrilla troops, equipped and re-supplied by the Russians themselves, Dudayev was almost certainly right. His ability to inflict damaging and highly embarrassing humiliation on his enemy was becoming more and more evident.

By June 1995, after the Russian military had fought its way out of its disastrous start to the war and even secured some modest gains, rumours began to circulate in Moscow that Boris Yeltsin was about to elevate his beloved Defence Minister, General

Grachev, to the rank of Marshal, the first such appointment in post-Soviet Russia. The plan was soon dropped, however, when one of Dudayev's leading commanders, Shamil Basayev, led a hundred fighters in a daring raid on the southern Russian town of Budyonnovsk, an important supply base for the Russian army in Chechnya. The raid caused a humiliating reversal for the 'Party of War'.

After cutting off all communications with the town and destroying military and administrative targets, Basayev took his wounded to the local hospital, together with large numbers of hostages. The response of the Russian authorities to this new crisis, which soon received worldwide television coverage, was typically heavy-handed and inept. An astonishingly incompetent assault was launched by troops who shelled a wing of the hospital which contained women and children. As a result, at least thirty hostages were killed. Despite Basayev's decision to release all the women and children and, as far as possible, to shield the hostages, a second assault was launched, in which more civilians were killed by Russian troops. The Russians could not, however, capture the hospital and Basayev issued a string of tough demands for the release of the hostages, including free passage back to the border, an immediate ceasefire in Chechnya and the start of peace negotiations.

The fate of the hostages provoked a serious crisis in Moscow. Events in Budyonnovsk were once again making Chechnya front-page news and ensuring that the world could not ignore the ugly little war in Russia's back yard. They had also begun finally to try the patience of Viktor Chernomyrdin, the Russian Prime Minister, who was growing increasingly irritated with the incompetence of the security services and the Russian hawks' obsession with prosecuting the Chechen war. He announced that he would take over management of the hostage crisis and travelled to Budyonnovsk, where he quickly agreed to Basayev's demands in person.

Although one does not approve of the use of hostages, it is undoubtedly true that the raid on Budyonnovsk constituted a major success for the Chechens, which significantly weakened the position of the 'Party of War' and led to the beginnings of attempts to reach a negotiated settlement. The end of the hostage crisis brought profound repercussions in Moscow, where the

Duma passed a vote of no confidence in the government and thousands of paratroops were ordered on to the streets, ostensibly to prevent terrorist outrages. The anger of the Duma, many of whose members had strongly criticised the war, was directed mainly at Yeltsin and the 'Party of War', rather than at Prime Minister Chernomyrdin, whose swift acceptance of Basayev's terms was seen to have prevented a bloodbath in Budyonnovsk.

'If we could impeach the President, we would,' said Grigory Yavlinsky, the leader of the liberal Yabloko bloc in the Duma. 'We can do only one thing to show we are against the civil war in Chechnya and that is a vote of no confidence in the government.'[83] Political commentators in Moscow realised that if the Duma repeated its no-confidence motion within three months, it would become binding and Yeltsin would be forced to form a new government.

The Duma's uncompromising position strengthened Chernomyrdin's hand and allowed him to demand the resignation of leading members of the 'Party of War'. Just before a debate on a no-confidence motion a week later, the Kremlin announced the dismissal of Sergei Stepashin, the director of the FSK; Nikolai Yegorov, the Deputy Prime Minister responsible for co-ordinating policy towards Chechnya; and Viktor Yerin, the Interior Minister (although, as an old friend of Yeltsin, he was appointed to a new post as deputy director of foreign intelligence within a week).

Despite the Duma's onslaught on the government's Chechen policy, the war was far from over. General Grachev remained in office, still determined to crush the Chechens and silence Dudayev for ever. Grachev's time was running out, though. The health of his patron, President Yeltsin, was becoming increasingly precarious and, a week after narrowly avoiding defeat in the Duma, he suffered a heart attack, which his aide Viktor Ilyushin described as being 'linked to intellectual, moral and physical stress'.[84] With Duma elections scheduled for December and presidential elections the following spring, Russia was heading into a period of turbulence when Chechnya would still be at the top of the political agenda. As General Grachev considered what might lie ahead in the summer of 1995, he must have looked nervously over his shoulder at the activities of his troublesome rival, Alexander Lebed, who had grown frustrated at not being given a senior command and was now turning his attention to politics. When Lebed announced his retirement from the army and joined forces with Yuri Skokov's political party, the Congress of Russian Communities, it was clear that he was going to continue campaigning for an end to the war and gunning for Grachev. And to the Defence Minister's consternation, the Russian public quickly began to talk excitedly about Lebed as a possible presidential candidate.

9
THE STATE DUMA

'"That's not certain," said Prince Andrei. "M. le Vicomte is quite right in supposing that things have gone too far by now. I imagine it would not be easy to return to the old regime."

"As far as I could hear," Pierre, blushing, again interposed in the conversation, "almost all the nobility have gone over to Bonaparte."'

COUNT TOLSTOY, *War and Peace*[1]

Lebed had decided back in 1994 that he would leave the army and enter politics. The war in Chechnya had further convinced him that his duty now was to march on to the political battlefield where, unrestrained by any military code, he could confront Grachev and all those who had brought Russia to ruin. He had no comprehensive political programme, and much of what he did have was centred on the army and its role. Yet his few political principles were based on a rejection of communism as a result of his own experience; a deep cynicism about the new 'democratic' system, caused by the knowledge that it was still run by the same *nomenklatura*; concern about the social effects of market reforms, which were nonetheless necessary; and a rejection of the arbitrary, dictatorial methods which had been so widely used in the recent past.

'I never thought about it,' he said, when I asked him why he had decided to enter politics.

I was born a soldier. Then I got into the army. Fought in Afghanistan. When I was in Afghanistan, the first discrepancies began. I was never out of battles but, whenever I switched on the television, they showed how the Russian Army was building roads and how everybody there loved us. Then, from 1988, starting with Karabakh, the international conflicts began, where I was a direct participant. And again, it was a lie. In 1990, I was elected as the representative of the Airborne Forces to the 28th Party Congress, at which I arrived a doubting Communist and left as a non-Communist. I saw the ignorance, the mediocrity and the pettiness which for some reason was governing us. The strangest thing was that all of us clever and strong-willed people were like a sort of herd, which just followed behind them. That way, we were going nowhere. And soon we got to 1991. The system collapsed in three days. It's not clear what happened to the 18-million-member Party, nor why the secretary of a regional committee of the CPSU didn't feel inclined to defend his regional committee with an automatic rifle in his hands. Everyone just went off to commercial positions, which they'd prepared earlier. The system dissolved. In 1991, there was some sort of hope that everything would change – the power that had plagued everyone had collapsed. But it soon became clear that nothing would change, and nothing could change, because power had simply changed its colours . . . Power remained the same but just changed its colour in order to conform. Yes, of course, the economic reforms in the country were necessary, and now they're even more necessary than six years ago. But reforms are for the people, and power should be well connected with the society it governs. It should feel its areas of pain and not view the people as some kind of impotent material which could be moulded into something or just thrown away. I was sick of all that. I decided that it had to be changed, but not by dictatorial methods. And that's no longer possible in such a large territory – everybody would just run away. Now only legal, constitutional authority is possible.[2]

Lebed's entry into politics had been widely forecast by both friends and foes. Throughout late 1994 and the early part of 1995, his attacks on Grachev and the authorities in Moscow had become more strident and political in their tone. He appeared ever more keen to court the media and develop a political profile. The media, in their turn, seemed ready to push him as a colourful alternative to the other grey *apparatchiks*. As early as September 1994, surveys showed that there was widespread support in the armed forces for the 'Bonapartist solution', with Lebed running for President. Lebed had responded to the growing excitement about his possible entry into politics like a true politician, by deliberately inciting more interest whilst appearing to try to damp it down; he said that he would continue his military career, but did not rule out political involvement 'if the circumstances require it'.[3]

Yet despite the enthusiasm for Lebed, there was also a serious campaign to discredit him and break his wings before he could take off. Encouraged by his enemies and by his own frequently less than diplomatic tone, some of his unguarded remarks were seized upon to create the impression of a dictatorial nationalist waiting in the wings for the chance to seize power and turn back the clock. In an outspoken interview with *Izvestiya*, he appeared to suggest that the Chilean dictator, General Augusto Pinochet, was one of his role models. In words that returned to haunt him, he said:

> I do not in principle praise General Pinochet. But what did he do? He led the state from total collapse and put the army in first place. With its help he made everybody go back to minding their own business . . . Now Chile is a prospering country, despite its ridiculous location . . . This supports the theory that when one hits the fist once on the table, a hundred men – on the altar of the fatherland – the issue is closed. Or is it better with a situation where five men die every day, seemingly loose change, but in time it adds up to a million?[4]

Later he seemed almost to revel in the scandal his remarks created, and even pretended to favour the idea of a military dictatorship. 'What's wrong with a military dictator? In all its history, Russia has prospered under the strictest control. Consider Ivan the Terrible, Peter the Great, Catherine the Great or Stalin.'[5] Yet despite his comments, Pinochet is not a role model for Lebed, whose only serious view about him is that 'Chile's gross domestic product is now 7 per cent. That means that on the whole his work might be judged quite positively.'[6] In any case, if any Russian politician could be said to have modelled himself on the ageing Chilean dictator, it would surely be Boris Yeltsin rather than Alexander Lebed. After all, Yeltsin's use of the armed forces against his own citizens, and his creation of an economic system based on monopoly capitalism, are but two of the most obvious features of his government which bear comparison with the regime of General Pinochet.

However, Lebed has always meant his reservations about democracy to be taken seriously. He is not opposed to the *principle* of democracy, but is against it in its current, twisted form in Russia; it is not democracy itself that he dislikes, but Russia's new 'democrats'. 'I do not believe and never have believed in our pseudo-democracy,' he said early in 1994.[7] His view was that real democracy had not arrived in Russia with Gorbachev and *glasnost*, still less with the August *putsch* and certainly not with Yeltsin's bombardment of the Congress of People's Deputies. Russia had never had real democracy at any time in its history and, perhaps, the very concept was alien to the country. If real democracy is to be built in Russia, the foundations will have to be properly laid.

'I am convinced,' he said, 'that I will not live to see the day when we have real democracy. It has to be built brick by brick, without hurry. It is a colossal task to build up a system of laws that will defend the weak. We Russians have never had a horse on that field.' For democracy to work in Russia would require 'a colossal transformation in the people's consciousness and in educating them to observe the laws'. For that to happen, however, people would have to have confidence that the law had begun to operate in the interests of the majority, and Lebed was pessimistic about the prospects: 'Personally, I am convinced that I will not live to see this day.'[8]

Lebed's hesitation about democracy is a matter of priorities rather than principles; it implies, above all, the need to create a law-based society which respects and trusts its own institutions. It implies too the need for institutions to work for the benefit of individual citizens. As one Western observer commented: 'In the simplicity of his thinking, one can see in Lebed an underlying sense of the common good and of the obligations of a sheltering society, an implicit grasp of the difference between right and wrong, and an avowed respect for the natural rights of the individual. In this, Lebed is anything but a throwback to Leninism.'[9] As he entered politics, Lebed was, perhaps, as he himself admitted, 'a semi-democrat', but more like General de Gaulle than General Pinochet.[10]

General Lebed had long resisted attempts to remove him from command of the 14th Army, despite the fact that he recognised that his military career had been effectively blocked. 'I am fed up with serving in Grachev's army, controlled as it is by God knows what,' he said in May 1995. 'But I cannot leave Tiraspol just like that, for I bear responsibility for the situation in the region and I will not permit various types of criminals fraudulently to sell Russian weapons. The point is not even in who will pocket the millions of dollars. I have such an amount of arms and ammunition that there will be enough of them for three Chechnyas. To keep them intact, I am prepared to endure any fight.'[11]

At the beginning of September, however, President Yeltsin signed a decree discharging Lebed from the armed forces, and he left command of the 14th Army to an unpopular Grachev appointee, General Yevnevich, whose aircraft was prevented from landing in Tiraspol by a group of angry women who feared that Lebed's removal would mean a resumption of hostilities. On his retirement from the army, Lebed immediately entered the race for the Duma and took up a position he had earlier accepted as Vice-Chairman of the Congress of Russian Communities (CRC), a new political organisation that had recently been established by Yuri Skokov and Dmitry Rogozin.

Skokov was a technocrat who had close links to the military–industrial complex and had been director-general of a scientific production association. However, he was also a former member of the Moscow City Committee of the Communist Party, where he had worked closely with Boris Yeltsin. For a long time, he was regarded as one of Yeltsin's greatest supporters, and the President had made him Secretary of the Security Council in April 1992. Despite his subsequent resignation, Skokov's strong links to Yeltsin are one of the many reasons why some observers suspect that Lebed may have had a much closer political understanding with the President than he has admitted. The Congress of Russian Communities, however, also contained Sergei Glazyev, who was seen as one of the most irreconcilable opponents of the government.

At first glance, the Congress of Russian Communities seemed an appropriate vehicle for Lebed's political ambitions. Comparatively well organised and with the active involvement of some senior and experienced political figures, it offered Lebed a comfortable seat, and second place on the party list, on the campaign wagon for the Duma elections. In so far as either Lebed or the CRC had a coherent philosophy, there seemed to be a broad ideological fit too. The CRC emphasised the need to build a strong state and defend the interests of Russians. However, despite the superficial similarities in their political outlook, the relationship between Lebed and Skokov was not easy. Both were ambitious and Lebed, insubordinate as ever, disliked sharing power in the party. In the run-up to the Duma elections, however, he was careful to show the press that he was a loyal team player, loftily dismissing rumours of a rift with Skokov.

'There are people who are very eager to do some wishful thinking,' he said. 'We maintain equal partnership relations and I am not going to comment on that which does not exist . . . Skokov has both experience and professionalism to his credit. He knows the whole of the political kitchen . . . It is the team, I repeat, that plays. And there can be no doubts on this score.'[12] Skokov, who realised that Lebed was a huge electoral advantage, was equally careful, going out of his way to stress that Lebed was not the junior partner in their relationship:

In politics, the notions of first and second are conditional. If a team is playing on the political field, the most important thing is to use each player's strong points. For instance, when I worked in Boris Yeltsin's team and saw how the people worshipped him at that time, my task was to help the President and I was not bothered by whether I was the first or the second.

My relations with Alexander Lebed are somewhat different. We are partners who work together on the creation of a team capable of tackling the tasks that I mentioned above. If we are able to do this, this will be our common victory, and it is absolutely unimportant which of us is the first or the second. In this respect there are no contradictions between us. I appreciate Alexander Ivanovich for his decency, natural wit, ability to assume responsibility and capability to learn on the move, so to speak. I believe that his political perspectives are very good. True, attempts are constantly being made to organise a quarrel between us, but they do not succeed and, I think, will not succeed thanks to Alexander Ivanovich's balanced nature, among other things.[13]

Despite the soothing phrases for the benefit of the media, however, Skokov was clearly the sort of newly converted 'democrat' whom Lebed purported to despise. The CRC was a flag of convenience rather than the perfect vehicle for Lebed's ultimate ambitions. Opinion polls showed that Lebed was much more popular than either Skokov or the CRC, and one of his assistants confessed that Lebed did not like being 'spoon-bait' in the hands of the 'fisherman' Skokov, and would soon 'fish on his own' instead.[14]

Not long after he had joined the CRC, he set up his own movement, 'Chest I Rodina' (Honour and the Motherland), which ostensibly aimed at reforming the Russian Army and 'rallying society in the name of strong, peaceful and rapidly developing Russia'.[15] In reality, however, it was designed to give him the leeway to develop his wider political ambitions without Skokov, if necessary. The organisation's board included Lebed's ally, General Igor Rodionov, who had been blamed for the massacre in Tbilisi; Sergei Goncharov, the leader of the veterans association of the Alpha special detachment; and Mikhail Kolchin, chairman of the independent trade union of military men. Lebed ensured that all of them were put on the CRC federal list for the Duma elections.

Russia was scheduled to go to the polls on 17 December 1995, at a time of profound political disillusionment. Capitalism had indeed come to Russia, and many of its blessings were already evident on the streets of Moscow, where there was a new entrepreneurial energy. The economy seemed to have survived its bumpy introduction to world markets, and the rouble even appeared to have become a reasonably secure currency. 'The economy is at last stabilising,' chirruped a typically up-beat Western leader columnist. 'Monthly inflation is at its lowest for three years, industrial production has stopped falling and although corruption and fraud are rife, private markets for goods and capital are flourishing.'[16]

Yet, for many Russians, the brief period of optimism after the August *putsch* and the end of the Soviet Union in 1991 had been quickly followed by a depressing feeling that nothing ever really changes in Russia. Changes appear to take place at breathtaking speed on the surface, but underneath, in the great depths below, nothing moves. Beyond Moscow and St Petersburg, in the vastness of the Russian provinces, life seemed the same as before, if not worse. There, people were grumbling that they had not been paid for months or that their pensions and other social benefits had simply disappeared. They did not share the optimism of entrepreneurial 'new Russians', such as businessman Andrei Zaborsky, who believed that 'the economy is set to take off . . . Wealth will spread out to wider and wider circles.'[17] They saw only factories closing down, jobs disappearing, investment drying up and crime increasing. They were deeply dissatisfied and frightened of the future. In the countryside, workers on collective farms feared the possibility of land privatisation, which would somehow deprive them of their livelihood. In the regions, people felt that Moscow was ignoring them. Old people believed they had been forgotten. Anyone who travelled beyond Moscow during the last quarter of 1995 could sense the mood of disenchantment. Millions of people, such as pensioner Mikhail Matveyev, were ready to use the Duma elections as a protest vote, 'to make the powers-that-be in Moscow wake up to the dissatisfaction of ordinary people'.[18]

The beneficiaries of this mood of public disenchantment were unlikely to be democratic politicians, such as Yegor Gaidar or Grigory Yavlinsky, who were widely seen as the architects of the country's current misfortunes. Gaidar, the former Prime Minister and leader of 'Russia's Choice' Party, had designed the economic reform programme. Yavlinsky, leader of the liberal 'Yabloko' – the Russian word for 'apple' and an acronym for the 'Yavlinsky bloc' – was an economics graduate of the Plekhanov Institute who had designed a plan for radical economic reform, rejected by Gorbachev, in the last days of the Soviet Union.

They were even more unpopular than the Prime Minister, Viktor Chernomyrdin, who had founded his own new political party, 'Our Home is Russia', which was full of *apparatchiks* like himself. The former boss of Gazprom, the Soviet oil and gas conglomerate, had overcome his initial reservations about the market economy, which he had described as a 'bazaar'. His new enthusiasm was, no doubt, due in part to the fact that he was rumoured to have kept a significant stake in Gazprom which, with privatisation, was set to become one of the largest oil and gas companies in the world. Despite widespread rumours about his wealth, this classic Soviet manager was nevertheless seen as a good Russian *muzhik* (bloke) and a reasonably safe pair of hands. He had the advantage of massive funding behind him and easy access to the media. It was clear that Chernomyrdin's 'Our Home is Russia' was way out in front of other 'centrist' or liberal parties.

The problem for Chernomyrdin and his friends in government, whose overwhelming priority was to continue with the economic reforms that had done them so much good, came not from the liberal wing but from the 'red–brown' fringe. In the atmosphere of disenchantment in the country, many bewildered voters were turning back to the Communist Party, now recasting itself in a less aggressively Marxist–Leninist mould as a market-friendly social democratic party; while others had decided to support the Agrarians, a faceless and badly-led party which claimed to represent the interests of collective farmers but was, in fact, closely allied to the Communists; and a surprisingly large amount still appeared ready to support the Liberal Democratic Party of Russia.

Gennady Zyuganov, the Communist Party leader, served in the propaganda department of the Central Committee of the Soviet Communist Party before becoming a founding member of the Russian Party. Keen, throughout the campaign, to reassure Westerners and liberals that he was not an old-fashioned Soviet die-hard but the moderate leader of a progressive party with a social conscience, his message was, at least, consistent: there should be a return to a centrally-run economy and private-property ownership should not be abolished, but the state should control the military–industrial complex, transport and energy. The welfare state must be rebuilt and corruption crushed.[19] In front of less sophisticated audiences, however, he soon switched back to the old rhetoric, telling crowds of Communist loyalists in Moscow that the country was living in a 'pre-revolutionary situation'[20] and praising Lenin and Stalin in front of old people in Kursk, for building the state 'which threw back the fascist military'.[21]

Consistency was not Vladimir Zhirinovsky's strong point. The leader of the Liberal Democratic Party mixed a bizarre political cocktail of blood-curdling, apocalyptic extremism with an anarchic populism, delivered in the style of a theatre of the absurd. He was the Sid Vicious of Russian politics, who mocked the democratic freak show. Whilst his 1993 election campaign had shocked outsiders into believing that he was another Hitler in the making, by 1995 he had become a parody of himself, revelling in the absurdity and tastelessness of his own propaganda. Anxious always to

shock rather than to impress his audience, he took a bizarre pleasure in weaving sexual imagery and revelations into his political
campaigning. In an article in his newspaper, *Zhirinovsky's Falcon*,
he once described the Lenin period as 'rape', Stalin's era as 'homo-
sexuality', Khrushchev's as 'masturbation', Brezhnev's as 'group
sex' and the current period as 'impotence'.

Standing by a ballot-box a year before the Duma elections, he
announced that the period of 'impotence' was over, though.
'Today is the beginning of the orgasm,' he said. 'I promise that
you will all feel the orgasm next year.' His political manifesto-
cum-autobiography, *The Last Thrust South*, a sort of surrealist
Mein Kampf, contains similar extraordinary revelations. He
dwells at great length, for example, on his failure to persuade a girl
at a sanatorium on the Black Sea to take off her knickers, and
then says that, perhaps, if he had had a happier childhood and a
sweetheart, he might have had no interest in politics. 'God, why
didn't she take those knickers off?', the newspaper *Moskovsky
Komsomolets* exclaimed.[22]

His behaviour inside the Duma itself was no less bizarre. In
one famous incident, he became involved in a fight with a priest,
who was also a liberal deputy. As his henchmen attacked the
priest, Zhirinovsky screamed, 'Beat him! Strangle him! Rip off his
cassock!' When a female member of the Duma attempted to come
to the priest's rescue, Zhirinovsky pulled her hair. Later he told
reporters that 'such women always get into men's fights just to be
close to men's bodies'. As if to prove his point, he confessed that
he had spent the previous evening in a night-club with the porno-
graphic film star La Cicciolina, a member of the Italian Parliament.[23] Despite his ludicrous tomfoolery, however, Zhirinovsky
was a fanatic whose dangerous dreams chimed with the popular
subconscious. Intolerant of Jews, Kazakhs and other minorities,
Zhirinovsky liked to proclaim that soon Russian soldiers would
be wearing summer uniforms and washing their boots in the
warm waters of the Indian Ocean.

Unlike Zhirinovsky and the Liberal Democrats, Lebed did not
see himself as part of the extreme nationalist fringe. Indeed, he
was careful, at a very early stage in his career, to distance himself
from Zhirinovsky, whom he dismissed as 'a dangerous clown'
and insisted that he would 'never join forces with a madman like
him, even if power should be the reward'.[24] His attitude towards

the Communists was more ambiguous and less immediately dis-
missive. In truth, however, Lebed and the Congress of Russian
Communities had a broad popular appeal, and hoped to pick up
votes from both the Communists and Zhirinovsky's supporters.
The key to the Communist vote was mainly social welfare and the
promise of a crackdown on crime, but it might also be attracted
by the appeal to nationalists of military reform, a tough line on
NATO expansion and support for Russian communities in the
'near abroad'. However, during the Duma election campaign,
Lebed was still finding his ideological feet and beginning to
develop a political programme. Many of the ideas he initially
championed were subsequently dropped, and he appeared much
more flexible than his grim exterior or many of his pronounce-
ments might have suggested.

His views on NATO expansion, at the beginning of the Duma
election campaign, were apocalyptic. He believed that if Eastern
European countries were allowed to join, 'there will be a Third
World War that will bury everyone under its rubble'. NATO only
existed to counter a threat from a potential enemy, just as 'every
military bloc is aimed in some direction, against someone'. Who
was NATO's enemy, he asked. 'If it is China, then the bloc should
be in another part of the world. If the enemy is in Europe, then
who can be NATO's enemy – the Czechs, Bulgarians or Poles?
That is ridiculous . . . There is only one obvious enemy, and that
is Russia.'[25] More recently, however, Lebed's position has
changed, and his outright hostility to NATO expansion has
become dismissiveness of an option that he believes the West will
soon find impractical. 'If you want to expand and take in Poland
and pay for it, feel free. It's your money.'[26]

Lebed was soon to change some of his other early assessments,
too; most notably, his outspoken criticism of President Boris
Yeltsin. In 1995, he claimed that 'Yeltsin is now living entirely on
his instinct for survival, correctly fearing that he will be held
responsible for (1) the collapse of the nation; (2) the attack on the
White House in 1993; (3) economic chaos and savage privatisation; and (4) arming the Chechens in the early 1990s.'[27] As soon as
the political situation changed, however, in the aftermath of the
Duma elections, he stopped his attacks on the President.

Yeltsin's advisers had recognised the seductive appeal of the
red–brown fringe long ago. Their greatest fear was an alliance of

the extremes, with old Communists joining forces with new nationalists to defeat the government. This fear had led to attempts to court nationalist opinion by denouncing NATO expansion, trying to pursue an independent policy in the Balkans, threatening to sack the apparently liberal Foreign Minister Kozyrev, and even attacking Chechnya. There was no danger of a red–brown alliance in the elections on 17 December, although Communist and nationalist parties would almost certainly co-operate afterwards in the Duma. The real danger was of a red–brown alliance in the presidential elections the following year, when Yeltsin would be vulnerable in the second round. The Duma elections were, therefore, a dress rehearsal for the main event, which was to follow six months later.

There was another reason why the Duma elections were not, in themselves, of great significance: Yeltsin's new constitution, which he had introduced after he had shelled the Congress in 1993, ensured that real power was concentrated in the hands of the presidential administration. The Duma could easily be manipulated or sidelined, as it had been during the course of the Chechen war, despite its repeated criticism of the government. The elections were, however, an opportunity for Yeltsin's administration to assess the disposition of forces and plan their strategy for the following year. They were a chance to examine how far an election could be managed and controlled. Above all, they were an opportunity to create a powerful extremist enemy, a new 'bogeyman' to frighten the voters back to the protective embrace of the President.

The elections came at a very difficult time for Boris Yeltsin. Economic conditions and people's perception of their own individual circumstances were, in many ways, the least of Yeltsin's problems. Far more serious, from the point of view of the longer term and the chance of successfully running in the presidential elections, were his own health and the continuing war in Chechnya. Towards the end of October, Yeltsin suffered his second 'mild' heart attack of the year, which his aides said was simply due to exhaustion after a visit to the United States and a recurrence of the heart ailment, ischaemia. Reports in Moscow suggested that it was brought on by a drinking binge on the flight home.[28]

It soon became clear, however, that the President's medical

condition was worse than his aides had originally admitted. He pulled out of an important conference in Moscow on Yugoslavia with the Presidents of Serbia, Croatia and Bosnia, which had been designed to appeal to nationalist sentiment by boosting his image as a Balkan deal-maker, and his press secretary, Sergei Medvedyev, announced that he would be kept under close medical supervision for more than five weeks.[29] In fact, Yeltsin only returned to work in the Kremlin at the end of December, ten days after the Duma elections.

In his absence, there was a mixture of panic and an unseemly attempt to grab the levers of power. Some reports spoke of attempts to transfer control of Russia's nuclear arsenal to Prime Minister Chernomyrdin. These were, apparently, resisted by General Alexander Korzhakov, the President's bodyguard, who ensured that the briefcase containing the nuclear 'button' stayed by the President's bed in his sanatorium. Korzhakov realised that 'whoever has the button, has power'.[30] He led the campaign by members of Yeltsin's entourage, who were terrified of losing their positions, to ensure that power stayed with the President. 'They'll defend Yeltsin's powers tooth and nail,' said one government insider. 'Because they know that when he dies, they go.'[31] The terrifying prospect that faced them now was that, even if Yeltsin did not die, it seemed highly unlikely that he would be able to run in the presidential elections.

With only just over a month before the Duma elections, there was a mood of deep unease in Moscow. Many people doubted that the government would allow the elections to take place, and the Central Electoral Commission had refused to register Grigory Yavlinsky's 'Yabloko' party, the main liberal rival to Prime Minister Chernomyrdin's 'Our Home is Russia'. Some members of the administration seemed distinctly nervous. Pavel Grachev, who perhaps had more to lose than most of Yeltsin's entourage, had managed to hold on to his job as Defence Minister, despite accusations of complicity in the murder of the young investigative journalist Dmitry Kholodov and the recent humiliation of being fired on by his own troops after a drunken fishing expedition in the Sea of Japan.[32] Ridiculed in the armed forces and despised by the public, he was not prepared to take any chances on a change of power without his consent, and ordered troop reinforcements to Moscow. As the Taman and Kantemirov divisions were brought up to full strength, Muscovites feared Yeltsin's imminent death, the declaration of a state of emergency and the cancellation of the Duma elections.

Against this background of high political tension in Moscow, the war in Chechnya threatened to erupt again. After the failure of a brief ceasefire at the end of July 1995, Yeltsin had announced another offensive to 'disarm the rebels by force'. It too had failed, however, and after returning to their fortified bases around Grozny, the Russians had again resorted to the aerial bombardment of Chechen villages. Russian policy now seemed to be based on wishful thinking, and the Kremlin's stooge in Grozny, Doku Zavgayev, announced that presidential elections would take place in Chechnya on 17 December to coincide with the Russian parliamentary elections. General Dudayev, the Chechen leader, described Zavgayev and his rival in the bogus elections, Ruslan Khasbulatov, former speaker of the Russian Congress of People's Deputies, as 'traitors' and 'scum'. One of his guerrilla commanders, Shamil Basayev, promised to wreck the elections and called them a Russian plot to start a civil war in Chechnya.

On 5 December, a car bomb exploded at the headquarters of Moscow's puppet government in Grozny, killing eleven people. Dudayev defiantly proclaimed that his forces would go on fighting for independence, even if the 'whole world goes up in flames'. He was unwilling to accept anything less than full independence. 'We Chechens are unique,' he said. 'No Tatar or Bashkir variant will do for us. Our genetic code dictates that we should live only according to our own will, not as part of any other state.'[33] At almost the same time as the bomb exploded in Grozny, Basayev's men planted a radioactive container in a Moscow park. Its whereabouts were only revealed after an extensive search and widespread public anxiety. The effect of the Chechens' terror campaign was to torpedo the Russian government's attempts to 'normalise' the situation before the Duma elections. Now, once again, Chechnya was at the forefront of everyone's minds.

It was extraordinary, however, that the Yeltsin administration had ever managed to stop public attention focusing on the Chechen war, and had even begun to change public opinion. It happened because of the heaviest type of media manipulation, the effects of which – on both the Duma and the presidential elections – cannot be underestimated. After all, in normal circumstances, with adequate coverage of the appalling treatment both of civilians and of Russian servicemen in Chechnya, with hundreds of tearful Russian mothers wandering the ruins of Grozny in search of their conscript sons, those who had campaigned most ardently against the war, such as the liberals Gaidar and Yavlinsky, might have expected to benefit at the polls.

When the Kremlin's secret war in Chechnya began in 1994, and throughout the early part of the campaign, one newspaper, *Sevodnya*, and a television station, NTV, had carried particularly accurate and courageous reports of events in the northern Caucasus. They were both owned by the businessman Vladimir Gusinsky, who controlled one of Russia's most powerful new commercial organisations, the banking, property and media group 'Most'. The federal security services and the 'Party of War' in the Kremlin did not take kindly to the honest reporting by Gusinsky's organisation. The corporate headquarters of Most were surrounded by armed soldiers from Yeltsin's presidential security service, who beat up the security guards in the building, raided Gusinsky's offices and warned him to be more careful in future. The raid was almost certainly carried out with the authorisation of Yeltsin's security chiefs, Alexander Korzhakov and Mikhail Barsukov. Gusinsky was forced, as a result, to go into exile in England. Not even his powerful friend Yuri Luzhkov, the Mayor of Moscow, could help him. In due course, the 'Party of War' got what it wanted and Gusinsky was able to return to Russia. By then, however, his television station had stopped broadcasting its damaging reports from Chechnya.

Despite the appalling circumstances in which they were being held, the Duma elections went ahead on 17 December 1995. Yavlinsky's 'Yabloko' was exhausted by the campaign to stop it registering. The Congress of Russian Communities' lacklustre campaign had failed to make an impression, possibly because Lebed had been tightly reined in by Skokov. Zhirinovsky looked unlikely to match his success in the 1993 elections. The battle was between Zyuganov and Chernomyrdin. The Communists were fuelled by popular discontent, whilst 'Our Home is Russia' had a massive funding advantage and much more exposure to the media. Chernomyrdin's campaign was professional and slick – so slick, in fact, that even Glenn Hughes, the former bass guitarist of Deep Purple, found himself giving a concert in aid of 'Our Home is

Russia', whilst under the impression that he was performing for 'the Russian people'.[34]

The election results were exactly what Yeltsin needed. The Communist Party was back as a major force in Russian politics, with 21.9 per cent of the vote. Yet its performance was a long way short of an overwhelming victory. Zhirinovsky's Liberal Democrats had not collapsed, as many of Yeltsin's entourage had feared. With 11.1 per cent, their share of the vote had been halved since 1993. They had done exactly what Yeltsin had hoped, though; they had shown that a radical nationalist candidate could still deflect votes from the Communists. Support for the democratic parties individually might have been weak, but collectively it was greater than the Communists' share of the vote. In the face of a Communist 'bogeyman', this was the base on which Yeltsin would be able to build. Although Alexander Lebed had won a seat as the member for Tula, he had been hampered by having to fight in Skokov's shadow and had not managed to establish an adequate basis on which to mount a credible challenge to Yeltsin himself. He could clearly be useful, however, in drawing support from Zyuganov in the forthcoming battle. Given that the spectre of a Communist revival would also help Yeltsin's plaintive cries for support from the West, it was little wonder that the President's first reaction to the results was: 'We have no reason for concern or to regard the election as a tragedy.'[35] Indeed, the results seemed to have made up his mind about the presidential elections, and he summoned Alexander Korzhakov to his hospital bedside.

Korzhakov remembers that Yeltsin lifted his head up from the pillow with difficulty and quietly announced: 'Alexander Vasilyevich, I have decided to stand in the elections.'

Korzhakov replied: 'Boris Nikolayevich, we never doubted that you would. There is no other possible candidate. Of course, if you had a successor, you could retire in peace and know that he would continue your work. And we would campaign for your successor. But it's not your fault that there isn't one. Maybe the presidency is your cross? You have to carry it further.'[36] The President listened to Korzhakov's reply with a blissful expression on his face.

Yeltsin's decision to stand was greeted with dismay in some quarters of the government. Viktor Chernomyrdin, who had loyally supported the President despite his reservations about the conduct of the Chechen war, began to prepare his own campaign. Russian electoral law required presidential candidates to collect a million signatures of people who supported their campaign and, by the middle of February, Chernomyrdin had already secretly collected one and a half million. But he seemed unsure about whether to launch a campaign if Yeltsin insisted on standing. He hoped that pressure might still be put on Yeltsin and he tried to arrange a meeting with Korzhakov, who might have persuaded the President to withdraw. Korzhakov, however, recognising the doubt in Chernomyrdin's mind, avoided meeting him until it was already too late for registration. 'In the end, the date passed, and the name "Chernomyrdin" did not appear on the list of presidential candidates. What stopped one of the most promising candidates? Possibly he understood that, if Yeltsin won, he would never forgive the betrayal. And Viktor Stepanovich [Chernomyrdin] did not really believe in his own victory.'[37]

Whilst still in hospital, Yeltsin had decided that he wanted Oleg Soskovets, the First Deputy Prime Minister and a key member of the 'Party of War', to manage his election campaign. When Korzhakov pointed out that he was an important and conscientious member of the government, Yeltsin replied, 'I don't care about the government. The main thing for me is winning the election.'[38] According to Korzhakov, Soskovets' appointment was resented by other members of Yeltsin's entourage, who began undermining his position. Much of the opposition came from Viktor Ilyushin, head of the President's private office, who may have feared that Soskovets' appointment as campaign chief would give him the opportunity to become Yeltsin's successor. Soskovets was gradually sidelined, however, and the key figures in campaign planning soon became Anatoly Chubais, the architect of Russia's privatisation programme, who was ostensibly 'removed' from his job as Deputy Prime Minister in January 1996, and Yeltsin's daughter Tatyana Dyachenko, who fancied that, like Claude Chirac in France, she could become her father's image-maker.

Despite the bizarre in-fighting amongst Yeltsin's supporters, the analytical groups working for Chubais and Soskovets appreciated that the essential dynamic of the presidential campaign had been supplied by the Duma elections: with the 'democrat' Yeltsin facing the Communist Zyuganov, the election could be fought and won with a 'red' scare. However, at the beginning of 1996, the situation did not look promising for Yeltsin. Opinion polls had recently shown that his personal popularity rating was not even in double figures, and there was widespread public concern that his health was so bad that, even if he did become President, he would soon die in office. Yeltsin's team needed help to remake his image and establish the Communist threat. Above all, they needed campaign finance and media support. Anatoly Chubais, whose privatisation of state assets had turned a small band of state managers and *apparatchiks* into multi-millionaires almost overnight, helped to galvanise the support of Russia's 'new rich' for the President. Together with Tatyana, he helped to create a remarkable deal in which the leaders of the two largest financial and media conglomerates joined forces to back Yeltsin, despite their intense rivalry.

Boris Abramovich Berezovsky was a talented Jewish entrepreneur who had made a fortune dealing in cars through his company, Logovaz. Before long, he moved into automobile manufacturing, banking, oil and the media. His media interests included *Nezavisimaya Gazeta* and an important stake in Russia's biggest television channel, ORT. Early in 1996 he 'rallied a dozen or so bankers and businessmen to back Boris Yeltsin's campaign to stay President'.[39] Berezovsky realised that his commercial empire gave him political influence, and he was keen to use it to the full. The businessman and former member of the Duma, Artyom Tarasov, who visited Berezovsky at his Logovaz headquarters in the middle of January to ask for his support in the elections – he intended to run as a 'pro-business' candidate and had almost collected the million signatures he needed to register – was told: 'Oh, excuse me, Mr Tarasov, but you're too late. We already decided to support Yeltsin in these elections a week ago. And we hired the man, a key man, who promised to guarantee us an election win for our money. This is a Mr Chubais. We gave him open credits, not only me but other people from the height of business, and that's why Mr Chubais guaranteed to us that Yeltsin would win.'[40]

At a meeting of the World Economic Forum in Davos, Berezovsky discussed the election campaign with his rival, Vladimir Gusinsky, the former theatre director who hoped to make his Most Group 'a media empire to rival Rupert Murdoch's'.[41] It was only a year since the offices of Most had been raided by soldiers from the presidential security service, forcing Gusinsky to leave the country and change his television station's reporting of the war in Chechnya. Now he was being politely asked to help the campaign to re-elect the President. Perhaps he felt he was being made another offer he couldn't refuse; more likely, he realised that, with more privatisations to come if Yeltsin won, he was staring a gift horse in the mouth. Despite their differences in the past, he agreed to back Yeltsin and ensure that his media empire, including the NTV television station, supported the re-election campaign. He seconded Igor Malashenko, the director of NTV, to join the Yeltsin campaign team, and he himself attended several planning meetings. A Western advertising executive, whose agency had run several high-profile political campaigns in the West, was astonished when she saw him, together with Berezovsky, Chubais, Tatyana Dyachenko and Igor Malashenko, at a meeting about election advertising strategy. At the meeting, someone even asked in jest how much it would cost to bribe every regional election official to submit false returns. When a figure of $600 million was mentioned, it was decided that if they spent that much on advertising, they would win anyway.

Korzhakov alleges that Chubais and his team profited personally from the huge amounts of money that were being raised by the campaign. In April he complained to the Prime Minister, Viktor Chernomyrdin, and told him about the amounts that were apparently being spent. The Prime Minister, who was increasingly concerned that Yeltsin's popularity did not seem to be improving, said: 'They're big sums of money. You can do a lot for two hundred million. This is hard currency.'

'It's a lot to steal,' replied Korzhakov.

'They'll steal in any event. How much is a different matter. What's the result of all these deals? What will we get out of it? They'll steal all the same.'[42]

The Yeltsin campaign's strategy was to minimise the potential split in the President's vote and maximise the potential split in Zyuganov's. The campaign team was determined to ensure that democratic, liberal or 'business' candidates did not draw voters away from Yeltsin. Yavlinsky could, almost certainly, not be stopped from standing as a candidate. The attempt to prevent his party from registering at the Duma elections had failed, but

he had won only 8 per cent of the vote and could easily be portrayed as an irrelevance in the big battle between 'democracy' and
communism.

More worrying, however, were the many unpredictable candidates, such as Artyom Tarasov. When he told Berezovsky that he
intended to run without his support, the Logovaz boss replied:
'No way. We unfortunately won't allow you to participate at all in
this election because we don't want people playing on the same
ground as Yeltsin.' Tarasov says that 'then there was another
surprise for me. I asked him, "How will you do this, Mr
Berezovsky? I have collected a million signatures and I will provide, if necessary, two million or three million. I have a group of
people who'll start working." He said, "No way. Your signatures
will not be registered. So don't spend your time and money." I
asked how this was possible, and he replied, "We will check all the
signatures." He said "we" and he meant the real Yeltsin team. I
understood that it was very serious because he said "we": "*We*
will not allow you to participate. *We* will check your signatures."'

Tarasov soon found that what Berezovsky had said was true.
His candidature was not registered, despite the fact that he had
collected 1,347,000 signatures.

> They checked my million signatures in two days, two people,
> and they said 492,000 signatures belonged to other persons, so
> they weren't real. And I couldn't argue . . . And I understood
> later that they had a very clever campaign. They, of course, reg-
> istered everybody who played on Zyuganov's ground. If I had
> been from the Communist Party, they would have helped me to
> collect signatures and they would have been very happy to reg-
> ister me. That's why they registered Lebed and they were very
> happy with Gorbachev, with everybody who would take some
> votes from Zyuganov.[43]

Lebed was not just 'playing on Zyuganov's ground', however.
He appealed to voters across the political spectrum, including
some liberals – indeed, he discussed the possibility of co-operation
with Yavlinsky – but many of his supporters were the disaffected,
who would otherwise have supported Zyuganov. Early in 1996,
Korzhakov tried to persuade him not to stand: 'I spoke to him
for four hours,' he recalled. 'The basic idea was: you help the

President, give him a shoulder to lean on. I offered him command of the Airborne Forces. I said: "That's your limit, why do you need politics? You and I are the same age, we've had the same upbringing, we even became Generals at the same time. You don't understand economics. Why do you want to be President?" I explained it simply. But he insisted: "I know my worth."'[44]

Korzhakov's view was not shared, however, by analysts working for Chubais and the campaign team. They realised that whilst Lebed would take some votes from Yeltsin, he would take many more from Zyuganov, and his real use would come in the second round of the election. As a Trojan horse on Zyuganov's ground, he could potentially deliver part of the Communist leader's vote to Yeltsin. It was this analysis that convinced the campaign team and its financial supporters to help Lebed in the last weeks of the campaign. According to *Obshchaya Gazeta*, Lebed and Yeltsin had reached a tentative agreement in late April, and financial support was made available to Lebed in the closing weeks of the campaign by Boris Berezovsky.[45]

Suddenly, Lebed's campaign changed. He was no longer dependent on the Congress of Russian Communities or his own 'Honour and the Motherland' movement. Now he had really powerful supporters, and his advertisements appeared frequently on the main television channels. It was clear that his image had been spruced up by consultants. He appeared in smart suits, smiling beside his attractive wife, Inna. His deep voice rolled over the airwaves, repeating his campaign messages, which had been sharply honed by the slick new team of advisers that had suddenly been made available to him. With experienced image-makers and speechwriters such as Alexei Golovkov, who had worked for the 'Russia's Choice' campaign in 1993, and Vitaly Naishul, the libertarian economist, who encouraged him to adopt a progressive, tax-cutting agenda, he was starting to look like a serious contender. The price of all this support before the first round was the 'shoulder to lean on' which Korzhakov had requested for the President. His attitude towards the President suddenly became much more respectful.

Neither Lebed nor Yeltsin has ever admitted that there was a deal before the first round, but as one banker said, 'It was evident that Lebed and Yeltsin had something going on. Quite aside from the money Lebed was receiving and the airtime he was allowed, he was the only presidential candidate who did not attack Yeltsin.'⁴⁶ Konstantin Borovoi, a businessman and independent member of the Duma, had no doubt that there had been a deal. 'The agreement between Lebed and the presidential team was made before the first round of elections. A lot of money was invested in Lebed, which explains why he had the second-largest advertising campaign after Yeltsin.'⁴⁷

The tacit understanding with Yeltsin even persuaded Lebed to change his tone about the war in Chechnya. Instead of outright condemnation and a demand for an immediate withdrawal of Russian troops, Lebed began to take a more hawkish line, arguing that Russia could not allow itself to be humiliated. In a long article in *Nezavisimaya Gazeta*, the influential newspaper owned by Berezovsky, he asked:

> Why is little Chechnya in a condition to dictate to Russia? Why is the bandit and terrorist Dudayev dictating to Russia? Because the people, thanks to the 'wisdom' of our politicians, didn't understand what the war is about and didn't understand why our soldiers are shedding their blood. And the war is not just about territory. What is important to us is both the integrity of our territory and the integrity of the Russian soul. Once and for all, Russia must explain to the world and to itself: we will no longer retreat anywhere. There have been enough shameful defeats. There will be no more. The Russian people are going to restore their pride, their dignity. Only this, this dignity, this inner strength will force the world to respect us.⁴⁸

Lebed's article in *Nezavisimaya Gazeta* was virtually the polar opposite of the position he had adopted the previous year. Then he had refused to allow troops from his 14th Army to fight in Chechnya under any circumstances, and had even declared that Moscow should 'declare the Chechens the victors and pack our bags. And move on.'⁴⁹

If Lebed's new line on the Chechen war was the result of a tacit agreement with Yeltsin's campaign team, it was also, no doubt, a response to a shift in public opinion which had been affected by the dramatic change in media coverage of the fighting. It was also perhaps indicative of the Russian public's exasperation with Chechen 'terrorism'. As the Russian aerial bombardment of

Chechen villages continued throughout 1995 and early 1996, Chechen rebel commanders resorted to a strategy of attrition, which involved lightning raids on Russian towns by lightly armed guerrilla groups.

In January, Salman Raduyev's 'Lone Wolf' group took 3,000 Russian civilians hostage in the village of Kizlyar in Dagestan. 'Lone Wolf' released most of the hostages after killing a policeman and two families who refused to co-operate with them, but they kept some civilians and thirty-seven MVD policemen as 'human shields' for their journey back to Chechnya. When they reached the village of Pervomaiskoye, they were stopped by helicopter gunships. Raduyev offered to release thirty women and children in return for a safe passage to Chechnya. The Russians, however, rejected the offer and, on 15 January, stormed the village with a barrage of heavy weaponry, including tanks, Mi-24 HIND helicopter gunships, BMP-1 armoured vehicles, 160mm mortars and 122mm light field guns. The weapons involved were completely inappropriate and showed Moscow's disregard for the lives of the hostages. The brutality of the Russian operation undermined the kudos that Yeltsin hoped to accrue as a result of his 'tough' action.

The Chechens continued with their campaign, however, and although the frequent acts of 'terror', combined with media coverage that was overwhelmingly sympathetic to the government, helped to soften public condemnation of Yeltsin's war, there was still an ever-present threat that the war would spill over into the election campaign. Yeltsin could not afford to look indecisive and weak as well as brutal, which was why he had launched his assault on Pervomaiskoye, regardless of the fate of the many civilians and hostages, including women and children.

Despite the media's slanted reporting of events in Chechnya, some politicians, such as Grigory Yavlinsky, continued to speak out against the 'genocide' in Chechnya. Lebed did not, however. Continued attacks by him in the last months before the election might have severely damaged the President but, with an agreement with Berezovsky in his pocket to provide extra airtime, he knew that his best chance of ending the Chechen war was by waiting until he could do something about it in government.

By the last fortnight of the election, Chubais and the campaign team were firmly in control of events, but few people suspected the extent to which they had been able successfully to manipulate public opinion. One young journalist was astonished after an interview with Igor Malashenko to see Berezovsky arrive and embrace Gusinsky, supposedly his bitter enemy. When, moments later, Yevgeny Kiselev, NTV's political commentator, who had been deeply hostile to the President in the past, arrived too, she knew at once that a deal had been done about coverage of the election campaign. Suddenly, the election result seemed to be a foregone conclusion.[50] When Yeltsin addressed his final campaign rally a few days before polling day, he announced that he was confident of victory and was wondering who his successor might be in the year 2000. '*Yest takoi chelovek*,' he told his cheering supporters. They knew exactly what he meant: '*Yest takoi chelovek*' ('There is such a man') was Alexander Lebed's campaign slogan, and Yeltsin could not have given a clearer public indication of the fact that he had done a deal with him.[51]

Polling was on the same day as the Russia–Germany match in the Euro 96 football tournament, and Yeltsin's campaign team suddenly appeared to panic that, despite all their warnings of a new 'red' threat, they might fall victim to a disastrously low turnout. The Prime Minister, Viktor Chernomyrdin, publicly implored voters to get down to the polling station, 'so as not to trade your future for an extra hour in front of the television set or at your *dachas* and vegetable plots'.[52] In Moscow, however, there were long queues outside polling stations, and the first exit polls showed Yeltsin slightly ahead of Zyuganov, with a substantial level of support building up for Alexander Lebed. Twenty-four hours later, when 98 per cent of the votes had been counted, it was clear that Lebed would be the Kremlin's king-maker. Yeltsin, with 34.82 per cent of the vote, and Zyuganov, with 32.13 per cent, were neck and neck. Lebed astonished commentators with the size of his vote. With 14.71 per cent, he had easily out-distanced the liberal Grigory Yavlinsky, who had 7.41 per cent, and Vladimir Zhirinovsky, whose vote had collapsed to 5.84 per cent.

The second round would be a straight fight between Yeltsin and Zyuganov, but Lebed was now the key to victory. Zyuganov announced that he wanted him to join his coalition, but most observers realised that Lebed was about to announce his support for Yeltsin. 'He won't depart from democratic positions,' his press secretary, Vladimir Klimov, said. 'I think if he does not just call on his supporters to vote for Yeltsin but receives guarantees that the administration will accept precise points of his programme, his voters will understand.'[53] When he eventually announced his deal with Yeltsin, however, many of his supporters were angry and disappointed. For Lebed, though, the deal was just what he wanted. Not only did it seem to offer a springboard to the presidency itself in due course, but also the chance to bring to an end the war in Chechnya. It also, finally, offered the opportunity to settle some scores with Grachev.

On 18 June 1996, details of the deal Lebed had done suddenly and dramatically emerged with an announcement from the Kremlin that President Yeltsin had appointed him to the post of National Security Adviser and head of the presidential Security Council. The new job gave Lebed the responsibility for overseeing the armed forces, the police and the security services. He announced that he also intended to use his position to fight crime, reform the army and crack down on official corruption. Yeltsin was full of praise for his new security supremo. 'This is the union of two politicians, two different programmes,' he announced. 'Lebed's programme will enrich mine.'[54] As he grinned at the television cameras, Yeltsin knew that he had just bought himself a ticket to victory in the second round of the elections. The price of the ticket, however, was the scalp Lebed had wanted for a long time – Yeltsin's longest-serving minister, 'the best defence minister of all time', Pavel Grachev.

Grachev did not go quietly; he tried to put troops on alert and his secretary, Yelena Agapova, tried to organise a campaign of telegrams to the President from military units urging him to keep him.[55] It was to no avail, however, and with Grachev's departure, Lebed had finally destroyed the man who had first been his friend and then his bitter enemy for so long. Now he had the opportunity to try to seek an honourable end to the chaos and carnage that Grachev had created in Chechnya.

As Russia gasped at the speed with which Lebed had secured Grachev's dismissal, Anatoly Chubais moved equally quickly to bring about the removal of a group of *his* most powerful enemies. Throughout the election campaign, Chubais and Tatyana Dyachenko had been trying to undermine Alexander Korzhakov and the other shadowy security figures around the President. On the Wednesday evening after polling day, late-night television viewers were startled by an announcement that two senior aides on Yeltsin's campaign team had been arrested and interrogated at gunpoint for eleven hours. The announcement was made on Gusinsky's NTV channel by Yevgeny Kiselev, who claimed that another *putsch* was about to take place and that its first victims were the two aides, Yevstafyev and Lisovsky. It subsequently transpired that they had been interrogated on the orders of General Korzhakov about an attempt to remove $500,000 from the Yeltsin campaign headquarters. Korzhakov claimed that he had been asked by the President to keep a watchful eye on his campaign finance.

Whatever the truth, the incident was used by Chubais, probably with the support of Tatyana Dyachenko, to secure the removal of his rivals Korzhakov, Barsukov and Soskovets. It was claimed that Korzhakov and Barsukov wanted to force the President to cancel the elections and declare a 'government of national unity'.[56] Chubais declared that they were part of 'forces which did not see any future for themselves in the conditions of the normal democratic conduct of elections'.[57] He moved quickly, calling a press conference on the morning after the arrests and announcing that the affair had been an attempt to engineer compromising material about him. 'They directly threatened Yevstafyev,' he said, 'and demanded from him the evidence about Chubais and Chernomyrdin. In the best traditions of the Soviet KGB, they told him that Lisovsky had already given evidence about me, and they threatened that criminal proceedings would be brought against him and he would be sent to prison.'[58]

The affair was probably the result of a classic but rather clumsily implemented attempt by Korzhakov to pin *kompromat*, compromising material, on his enemies, but it had backfired. Chubais and his allies had reacted quickly and created the spectre of yet another coup, drawing Lebed, who was woken in the early hours and told of news reports of an attempted coup, into the general hysteria. Although he subsequently came to believe Korzhakov's version of events, he over-reacted in a television interview at 4 a.m., declaring that 'any mutiny will be crushed, and crushed with extreme severity. Those who would plunge the country into the depths of bloody chaos do not deserve pity,' thus lending credence to the rumours of a coup.[59]

Later the same day, Yeltsin appeared before the television cameras, looking tired and drawn, to announce the sacking of

Korzhakov, Barsukov and Soskovets. 'They have taken too much and given too little,' he growled.[60] The 'liberals' in the President's entourage had won, and Chubais gloatingly announced that 'if any one of the dismissed heads of the power structures gets into his head the crazy idea of using force, it will be suppressed by a single movement of General Lebed's little finger'.[61] However, despite the assurances of Chubais and the earlier paeans of praise by Yeltsin, Lebed was soon to discover that his new job did not make him as powerful as either he or the country had imagined.

10

THE KREMLIN

'In a department . . . but best not say in which department.'

N. V. GOGOL, 'The Overcoat'[1]

'I have absolutely nothing to hide; I am absolutely, in the fullest meaning of the word, a well-intentioned man. I am humble, I am ready to adapt myself to circumstances; I want little; I want to do the good that lies nearest, to be even a little use. But no! I never succeed. What does it mean? What hinders me from living and working like others? I am only dreaming of it now. But no sooner do I get into any definite position when fate throws the dice from me. I have come to dread it – my destiny . . . Why is it so? Explain this enigma to me!'

I. S. TURGENEV, *Rudin*[2]

The Russian news agency Itar-Tass reported on 23 April 1996 that General Dzhokhar Dudayev, the Chechen rebel leader, had been killed in a rocket attack on the village of Gekhi-Chu, south of Grozny.[3] Hours later, however, in a statement published by another Russian agency, Interfax, his personal secretary, Saipudi Khasanov, claimed that he was 'alive and working a normal regime'.[4] It was not until twenty-four hours later that the Chechens began to mourn the loss of their rebel President, when Shamil Basayev, one of the senior Chechen field commanders, confirmed that he was indeed dead and announced that the military council had appointed a nationalist poet, Zelimkhan Yandarbiyev, as his successor.

Dzhokhar Dudayev, the ex-Soviet Air Force General who had kept Europe's largest army at bay for sixteen months, had apparently been killed in a rocket attack as he stood in a mountain pasture, talking on a mobile phone to King Hassan of Morocco, whom the Russians had accepted as a peace mediator. Initial reports suggested that a Russian fighter, which had locked on to his satellite signal, had fired rockets killing him and destroying his jeep. 'This is the Soviet way,' said a villager who lived nearby the scene of the assassination. 'To hit a man when he is trying to arrange peace talks with you.'[5]

Despite the evidence of Dudayev's death, however, reports persisted that he had survived the attack. A Chechen spokesman in Istanbul claimed to have spoken to him thirty-six hours after he had supposedly been killed.[6] His body was never shown, and nor was his grave. Witness accounts of his condition after the attack differed about the extent of his injuries, and there were even rumours that, only a few days earlier, he had told friends that 'soon in Chechnya the dead will rise from their graves'.[7] There was widespread scepticism about the ability of the Russian air force to mount such an efficient attack, which involved the use of the sort of technologically advanced 'smart' systems perfected by the Americans, and it assumed, in any case, that Dudayev had spent such a long time on his telephone, with an uncharacteristic disregard for his own security, that it had been possible to bring a fighter aircraft into position to target him.

Russian intelligence fed the conspiracy theories. Sergei Stepashin, head of the FSK, discounted the idea that his top men could have killed Dudayev in a secret operation, and his colleagues told Western reporters that 'Dudayev was not stupid. He never, ever spoke for too long on the satellite phone. The longest we ever tracked him was for 1 minute 45 seconds. Then he would hang up and move.' Colonel-General Deinekin, head of the air force, who had known Dudayev well, denied that his pilots had killed him and General Tikhomirov, the Russian commander in Chechnya, insisted that 'federal forces had nothing to do with the death of Dudayev'.[8]

The heavy-handed denials by Russian commanders of their forces' involvement were designed to stir up mutual suspicion among the Chechens themselves, splitting the 'die-hards' away from the 'moderates', with whom a ceasefire might be negotiated. Yeltsin had desperately wanted a ceasefire before the presidential elections but he refused, despite Dudayev's repeated overtures, to negotiate with the rebel leader. With Dudayev dead, however,

Yeltsin was now prepared to negotiate face-to-face with the new Chechen leadership. His overriding aim was to reach an agreement that would create an appearance of 'normalisation' before the presidential elections. As a symbol of the return to normality, his aides even suggested that it might be possible, if all went well, to arrange for him to visit Grozny before polling day. The Chechens, on the other hand, realised that Yeltsin was particularly vulnerable during the approach to the elections and might be more than usually ready to make concessions. Equally, they knew that they had nothing to lose; face-to-face negotiations with the Russian President would help to increase their legitimacy and authority.

So it was that on 27 May, the bearded figure of Zelimkhan Yandarbiyev, still clad in battle fatigues and an Astrakhan fur hat, arrived at the Kremlin for talks with Boris Yeltsin. At the end of a day of negotiations, Yandarbiyev and Viktor Chernomyrdin signed an agreement that there would be a ceasefire at midnight on 31 May and an exchange of prisoners two weeks later.[9] To the outside world, it looked as though Yeltsin had 'pulled off something of a coup'.[10] Yet the conditions for peace did not exist; Yeltsin still hoped that he could square the circle and reach a peace with the Chechens which would, nevertheless, guarantee Russia's territorial integrity. The problem was that the Chechens would accept nothing less than full independence, whilst hardline nationalists in Russia, whom Yeltsin was still trying to court ahead of the elections, would resist the break-up of the Russian Federation.

When the 'peace agreement' was signed, Yeltsin declared triumphantly that 'we have resolved the key problem of peace in Chechnya. This is a historic day, a historic moment.'[11] Whilst Chernomyrdin kept Yandarbiyev a virtual hostage in the Kremlin, as they worked on the final details of the agreement, Yeltsin made a brief publicity-seeking visit to Grozny. The photographs of the Russian President with pliable supporters of the puppet government were meant to show that life had returned to normal, as Yeltsin campaigned in what was just another part of the Russian Federation. The Kremlin emphasised that Chechnya would soon have more powers than any other part of Russia. Yet, within a week, it was clear that the agreement had broken down.

On 2 June, four Russian soldiers were killed and five others were injured when a tank was destroyed by a Chechen land-mine in Grozny. Both sides were quick to accuse each other of breaking the truce. Many Chechen field commanders were openly hostile to the ceasefire, doubting Yeltsin's motives and believing that it was wrong to give him such an obvious electoral advantage. 'If I speak the truth, I do not believe that Yeltsin will keep his word,' said Doku Makhaiev, the rebel commander in southwest Chechnya, who claimed that he had been against the Kremlin meeting from the outset. 'It is Yeltsin who began the war, and I did not think we should give him points ahead of the elections,' he said.[12] For Makhaiev, who had already lost three brothers and was soon to die in action himself, there could be no compromise; it was a fight to the death for full independence.[13] 'We have suffered too much to stop now. Of course, we do not want to fight, but there can be no road back, we will fight to the last Chechen.'[14]

With only six days until polling day in the first round of the elections, faced with the rapidly deteriorating situation in Chechnya, which threatened to erupt into open war once again, and under pressure from his financial backers, some of whom now wanted a deal with the rebels for their own commercial reasons, Yeltsin panicked and signed a military agreement to withdraw Russian troops by the end of August, starting with the 245th Motor-Rifle Division in Shatoi, in the south of the republic. The agreement was a clear betrayal of Moscow's puppet Chechen regime, and an open admission by the man who had begun the war, President Yeltsin, that it had never been necessary. After eighteen months of bloodshed, the loss of thousands of fighting men and the destruction of the Russian Army's reputation, Yeltsin finally appeared ready to accept the legitimacy of the rebels' claims. The problem now was to negotiate an honourable withdrawal. This was to be the most important task facing the Secretary-elect of the President's Security Council, Alexander Lebed.

As Yeltsin's health again deteriorated during the final stages of his successful election campaign against the Communists, Lebed might have expected a free hand to bring peace to Chechnya. He had purged Grachev and most of the 'Party of War' within twenty-four hours of his appointment as security Secretary. Yet there was still severe resistance in some influential quarters to his desire to secure a negotiated settlement. Lebed knew from experience that the Chechen war could ultimately offer the Russian Army no better prospects than the Soviet intervention in Afghanistan; the conflict had to be stopped, and the only way to do it was by negotiating directly with the rebel leaders. He demanded authorisation to conduct peace talks and to control military operations in the area. Although he was supported by his old colleague, General Igor Rodionov, whose appointment as Defence Minister he had managed to secure, the Interior Minister, Anatoly Kulikov, and other hardliners took advantage of Yeltsin's return to his sick-bed to try to frustrate his ambitions. Kulikov bitterly resented what he called Lebed's 'maniacal lust for power', and argued that Russia should strengthen its military presence in Chechnya in order to choke off the armed opposition and provide support for Doku Zavgayev's puppet government. Peace talks only helped the rebels. 'The separatists are resorting to ever more wily moves to achieve their goals at these negotiations, using the ceasefire to upgrade their own fighting potential,' he said.[15]

Whilst Kulikov resisted Lebed's peace initiatives in the Kremlin, on the ground in Chechnya there were also powerful figures determined to carry on the fight. Mentally unbalanced by the loss of his son in the war, the Russian commander in Grozny, General Konstantin Pulikovsky, was determined to prevent a peace settlement which involved any concessions to the Chechens. Another Russian commander, General Tikhomirov, issued an aggressive ultimatum to the Chechens to release 1,000 prisoners or face tough counter-measures. When the Chechens refused, a major offensive was launched against the villages of Gekhi and Mekheti. Air strikes and artillery were used in the attack on Mekheti, which was suspected of being Yandarbiyev's headquarters. Infantry and armour assaulted Gekhi, another rebel stronghold where Doku Makhaiev lived with what remained of his family after eighteen months of war.

Lechi Makhaiev, Doku's father, who was wounded in the attack, told me that on 9 July a large detachment of regular soldiers and *nayomniki* mercenaries had arrived in the village, together with armoured support. 'The soldiers, particularly the *nayomniki*, did not expect to meet any resistance. They were surprised by the scale of the response because the *boyeviki* were very well armed.'[16] Doku Makhaiev's fighters held out until a sustained aerial bombardment of the village began. Doku, who was severely wounded, was taken in a jeep by a Russian deserter to look for medical attention. The deserter had been looked after by the Chechens for several months and claimed to have gone over to them. He was one of several young conscripts who had been housed and fed by Doku's family after they fled from their regiments. Instead of seeking medical help, however, the deserter drove Doku straight to a Russian checkpoint, where he was shot on the spot. Later he helped the Russian security services to identify rebel fighters as they tried to withdraw from the village during the aerial bombardment. Despite Doku's death and Russian boasts that the rebels had 'lost their command structure and capability for organised resistance', the Chechens held out in both Gekhi and Mekheti for several days, destroying sophisticated armour and killing one of the most senior Russian officers in Chechnya, Major-General Nikolai Skripnik, the deputy commander of the North Caucasus military district.

By the end of July, with both sides now desperate for revenge, Lebed's prospects of achieving a negotiated settlement looked bleak. Senior Russian commanders were determined to 'finish off' the Chechen rebels, no matter what the cost in civilian lives. On 5 August, however, a brilliant Chechen counter-offensive left the rebels in control of Grozny. Over a thousand Chechen fighters, under the command of Shamil Basayev, had managed to infiltrate the city centre, seize Russian strongpoints and shoot down helicopter gunships. By the time that Boris Yeltsin was inaugurated as President of Russia on 9 August, in a gloomy ceremony which again drew the world's attention to his poor health, it was clear that Russian forces had been defeated in Grozny. With thousands of Chechen fighters now well dug in amidst the city's ruins, easily able to resist the repeated Russian attempts to flush them out, and with huge crowds of civilian refugees streaming from the capital clutching white flags, the Kremlin was facing another humanitarian catastrophe.

Russian commanders such as General Pulikovsky were screaming for vengeance, but any attempt to retake Grozny would have created another massive, and very public, bloodbath. The Russians now had no realistic alternative but to sue for peace and try to reach an agreement that allowed them to withdraw their troops with some honour. The situation in Grozny was a military disaster, but it had created the conditions for the negotiated settlement that Lebed wanted. In fact, as there was nothing for the Russians to negotiate but total withdrawal, there were persistent rumours that the Chechen infiltration of Grozny might not have been wholly unaided.[17]

At the height of the fighting in Grozny, Lebed flew to Chechnya on 11 August for a meeting in the south of the republic with the senior Chechen field commander, a mild-mannered former Soviet Army Colonel, Aslan Maskhadov. The meeting marked the start of Lebed's programme of intensive shuttle diplomacy, which was designed to bring the war to an end and extricate Russian troops as quickly as possible.

The first meeting between Lebed and Maskhadov was remarkable because it took place whilst Russian troops were still engaged in heavy fighting in Grozny and senior commanders were trying to persuade the Kremlin to sanction another major offensive. Despite the action in Grozny, Lebed did not hide his view that there was no military solution to the conflict. 'We have to read our own history,' he said. 'In the last century, Russia could not defeat the Chechens. Diplomacy won. That's how we should act today.'[18]

When Lebed sat down to discuss terms with Maskhadov, he was not only concerned about the cost of the war in civilian lives; he was so horrified at the condition of Russian troops in the region that he was willing to accept almost any agreement that allowed him to withdraw them. On his way to the meeting, his car had been fired at by his own side and the soldiers he had met at checkpoints had been poorly dressed, ill-equipped and under-fed. One Chechen commander remembers that Lebed seemed desperate for an agreement: 'He begged us to allow them to withdraw – he simply wanted any agreement that allowed Russia to save face.'[19] The reason for Lebed's apparent desperation was his realisation that the main problem was not the Chechens themselves but those hardliners inside the Kremlin and the armed forces who wanted to continue fighting. He knew that the removal of Grachev had not ended the demand in the Kremlin for a military solution in Chechnya; it had merely created a small window of opportunity for him, through which he might begin to look for peace.

The fundamental problem remained, however. As *Izvestiya* commented:

Alexander Lebed has made one discovery for himself: the reasons for the Chechen war lie in a completely different place from the one where people usually seek them. For a long time, popular opinion has linked the Chechen adventure to the activities of an unseen 'Party of War', to which Pavel Grachev, Viktor Yerin, Oleg Soskovets, Alexander Korzhakov, Mikhail Barsukov and Nikolai Yegorov belonged. Now they have all been dismissed. But the war continues. From this one can draw only one conclusion: the reason for the war is the policy of President Yeltsin and not the intrigues of his favourites. Consequently, stopping the war means stopping Yeltsin.[20]

Lebed had demanded a range of powers from Yeltsin to enable him to bring the war to an end. At a press conference after his first meeting with Colonel Maskhadov, at which he announced a new ceasefire, he declared that the President was about to sign a decree giving him the extra powers he wanted; in effect, he was apparently to become a Tsarist-style 'Governor-General' for the republic.[21] But his seizure of extra powers did not endear him to other senior figures in the Kremlin. He had already earned an icy rebuke from Viktor Chernomyrdin for trying to persuade Yeltsin to appoint him Vice-President in July, and his attempts to take a direct hand in economic policy had irritated Anatoly Chubais, who had returned to the Kremlin as Chief of Staff. Now, his demands for more power were accompanied by sharp criticism of government policy towards the Caucasus in the past. He was particularly critical of the failure of a commission headed by Chernomyrdin to do more to bring peace. The criticism was tactless and ill-advised; Chernomyrdin was supportive of Lebed's peace initiative and had backed his talks with Maskhadov. 'Lebed is a military man, he is used to tackling these sorts of problems. I am sure that he will cope with the task. He simply must do this,' he had said recently. Now, however, the Prime Minister, among others, had marked his card, and it was not long before Yeltsin himself began to undermine his efforts.

Lebed realised that his attempts to negotiate a peace agreement were being sabotaged; the initial flimsy truce which he had agreed with Aslan Maskhadov had been broken within hours, after Russian helicopter pilots fired rockets at a column of refugees.[22] There were clearly powerful forces that wanted to prevent the signing of a peace agreement. Yet there was no realistic alternative to a negotiated settlement. Every day brought further humiliation for the beleaguered Russian troops in Grozny, where Shamil Basayev's men had surrounded thousands of soldiers in their command posts. 'The Russians can take the city back,' Basayev admitted. 'It would take half a year and they would have to destroy the town. They can take it even in a month, but it would cost them 10,000 to 15,000 men.' Lebed knew that there were senior people close to the President, particularly the Interior Minister, Anatoly Kulikov, who were quite prepared to pay that price. So, before his next visit to Chechnya, he launched a public attack on Kulikov, denouncing him as 'one of the main culprits in the war' and demanding his dismissal.[23]

The attack was designed to destroy Kulikov's influence over the President and drag Yeltsin behind the peace plan which Lebed was almost ready to present; Lebed also hoped that it would at last bring him undisputed control over the Interior Ministry, which not only had its own troops stationed in Chechnya but was also responsible for fighting crime and corruption in Russia.

Despite his outspoken assault on Kulikov, however, together with an invitation to the President to 'take a choice: it's him or me',[24] Lebed had not prepared his ground carefully enough, and more seasoned Kremlin politicians realised that the removal of the Interior Minister would leave the security Secretary too powerful. Kulikov issued a defiant statement: 'In connection with the false accusations and insults against me by [Lebed], I am sending a report to the President asking him to resolve the issue of my tenure of office. If these accusations are not formally withdrawn I will offer my resignation to the President. Maybe I will write it today.'[25] Kulikov was in no danger, however; the President was under pressure to clip his outspoken security Secretary's wings.

Lebed was suddenly confronted with an order from the President to restore the situation in Grozny as of 5 August 1996, before Shamil Basayev's attack. The order conflicted with Yeltsin's election campaign pledge to withdraw Russian troops from Chechnya by the beginning of September; given Yeltsin's state of health and his disappearance from public view, there was widespread speculation that it had been issued by members of his staff with a facsimile signature.[26] Lebed quickly denounced it as a forgery, but General Pulikovsky used it as an excuse to order renewed military action against the rebels. Determined to avenge the death of his son, he issued an ultimatum to the Chechens to leave Grozny or face an aerial and artillery bombardment. As Lebed shuttled between Moscow and the Chechen village of Novye Atagi, where he was negotiating the final details of an agreement with Colonel Maskhadov, refugees began to leave Grozny in their thousands. *Izvestiya*'s correspondent, Besik Urigashvili, described the situation as Grozny waited for Pulikovsky's ultimatum to pass its deadline:

> Right now, according to various estimates, there are between 120,000 and 150,000 peaceful inhabitants of Grozny. They are being asked to leave the city by the humanitarian corridor which runs from Staraya Sunzha to Petropavlovsk and Argun by eight o'clock on 22 August. General Konstantin Pulikovsky has asked the media to convey his request to the peaceful inhabitants of Grozny to leave the city. True, it's not clear how the commander's wishes can be conveyed to people who are sitting in dark cellars without electricity and without the most basic comforts.[27]

Lebed was determined not to let Pulikovsky wreck the chance of a peace agreement. With the support of the Defence Minister, Rodionov, he ordered Pulikovsky's removal from his post and cancelled the ultimatum. 'There will be no more ultimatums,' he told the Chechens. Rebel commanders began to realise that he was serious about peace. 'He is a military man,' said one. 'He has seen it all, he has fought in wars and seen blood being spilled. I think he is a serious man and keeps his word. But if they break this agreement we will give them a lesson they will never forget.'[28]

The Interior Minister, Kulikov, later claimed that Pulikovsky's ultimatum was in fact Lebed's idea, part of a scheme to give him some negotiating leverage with the Chechens. 'That ultimatum was agreed with Lebed,' he claimed. 'We had a meeting of government ministers and Lebed said, "I have discussed this. [The plan] is I leave [Chechnya], Pulikovsky gives his ultimatum and shakes them up a bit, and then I go down and cancel the ultimatum."'[29] However, in view of Kulikov's intense personal dislike of Lebed, this version can probably be discounted.

With the removal of Pulikovsky, the immediate military threat to the peace negotiations was lifted. Now Lebed could concentrate on hammering out an interim deal with Maskhadov which would allow the Russians to withdraw from Grozny, separate the two fighting forces and prevent further clashes by creating joint command posts. Both Lebed and Maskhadov were keen to focus on the military realities of the situation rather than the political dispute between Moscow and the Chechen rebels. 'When two neighbours fight over where the boundary between their property lies, it's no use urging them to compromise. First you have to pull them apart and stop the fight, then calm them down, and only then can you ask them to use their common sense, and not act under the influence of adrenalin.'[30]

As they worked in shirt-sleeves at a table covered with a large military map of Chechnya, Maskhadov seemed positive and even generous towards Lebed. 'The Chechen military leader's actions held no hint of arrogance or the posture of a victor dictating terms,' Alexander Zhilin of *Moscow News* reported. 'More than that, about an hour after the talks started between Lebed and Maskhadov on Thursday, the Chechen leader ordered that the Chechen siege of the Russian units be partially lifted and that they be given the chance to remove their wounded from the area, get foodstuffs, etc.'[31]

The meeting was 'highly productive' and allowed the two leaders to 'come up with lightning-fast solutions to the problems at hand'.[32] Although the negotiations were frequently disturbed by reports that one side or the other had violated the moratorium on combat operations, obliging them to contact local commanders directly and order them to cease fire, by four o'clock in the afternoon it was clear that 'Lebed and Maskhadov had managed to lay the groundwork for stopping active and large-scale combat operations, and for the first time had also hit on some substantial solutions to a number of problems on the military agenda'.[33]

The outline settlement reached by Lebed and Maskhadov was based on a five-year postponement of a decision about the final status of the territory. The two sides in the conflict assented to end all military operations and withdraw their forces to agreed points outside Grozny. The Russians also undertook to pull their remaining forces out of the mountainous southern districts of Nozhai Yurt, Vedeno and Shatoi. Lebed was careful to refer the agreement to legal experts in the Ministry of Foreign Affairs to ensure that it did not appear to imply an acceptance of Chechen sovereignty in international law. The Russians were allowed to save some face; by agreeing to disagree over the question of Chechen independence, they could maintain the fiction that Chechnya remained a part of the Russian Federation.

The settlement marked the end of the most intensely bloody war Russia had fought since 1945. Lebed calculated that it had resulted in 80,000 dead and 240,000 wounded.[34] His agreement was a triumph for common sense and reason over the brutal expressions of self-interest and corruption that had kept the war going for so long. It was hardly surprising that Yeltsin, whose totalitarian instincts had been largely responsible for the war, did not seem to approve of the peace agreement. When journalists and political observers in Novye Atagi heard the news that the President was 'not entirely satisfied'[35] with Lebed's progress in Chechnya, they were astonished. Their first reaction was 'deathly silence, followed by utter bewilderment. By making this rash statement, obviously the handiwork of Yeltsin's entourage, the President damaged his own reputation more than that of the Security Council Secretary.'[36]

The ceasefire entered into force on 27 August 1996; Lebed and Maskhadov signed the final draft of the peace agreement at Khasavyurt in Dagestan on 30 August in the presence of Tim Guldimann, the representative of the Organisation for Security and Co-operation in Europe. The final text reaffirmed Yeltsin's decree of 25 June 1996, ordering a complete withdrawal of Russian Ministry of Defence forces from Chechnya and establishing a joint commission to supervise transitional administrative and economic arrangements.[37] Lebed was adamant that the agreement allowed Russian soldiers an honourable departure from Chechnya. 'The troops are leaving at my command because the war could not be won. They did not win because it was not possible. Therefore, they did not lose either.'[38]

The agreement ought to have guaranteed Lebed a hero's welcome on his return to Moscow, but the official reaction was grudging and ambivalent. Yeltsin had managed to soften his tone before the signing ceremony, and his spokesmen told reporters that he had telephoned Lebed to say that he 'generally approved'.[39] Yet there was no rejoicing that the slaughter was over; there was instead a feeling, carefully nourished in official circles, that Russia had suffered a bitter defeat and that Lebed had signed not a peace agreement but a shameful document of surrender. 'They won,' said the headline in *Moskovsky Komsomolets*. Lebed had now done what Yeltsin expected of him; he had delivered victory in the second round of the elections and forged a way out of the Chechen imbroglio without causing the President to lose face. According to Yeltsin, if the peace agreement was in any way a humiliation, then Lebed was to blame, and not the President.

With peace in Chechnya, Lebed had achieved *his* main aim; now he hoped to be able to concentrate on his other priorities: fighting crime, stamping out corruption and introducing military reform, all of which, he hoped, would strengthen his authority and boost his campaign for the presidency. His attack on crime and corruption would be hindered by the fact that his attempt to persuade Yeltsin to remove Kulikov as Interior Minister had failed; with his ally General Rodionov at the Ministry of Defence, though, he might be able to begin the much-needed reform of the armed forces.

The essence of Lebed's plan for military reform was the creation of a smaller, more efficient organisation. Whilst he believed that Yeltsin's election promise to end the draft and create a fully professional army by the year 2000 was wholly unrealistic, he wanted to reduce the size of the Russian armed forces by a third, creating a smaller number of fully manned, combat-ready divisions. He imagined that the 'small mobile fists' which he had in mind would be able to 'solve all problems'.[40] Despite Rodionov's presence in the Ministry of Defence, however, his room to manoeuvre was severely restricted. Almost immediately after his appointment as Secretary of the Security Council, Yeltsin had established a parallel 'defence council', which competed for influence and undermined his authority.

His initiatives to combat crime and corruption ran headlong into difficulties, as he, no doubt, knew they would. Lebed's belief in the importance of the rule of law was at the heart of his political philosophy, and he was determined to use his Security Council position to tackle Russia's growing crime wave and the corruption at the centre of the system. He negotiated an anti-crime agreement with Moscow's popular Mayor, Yuri Luzhkov, as a field test for a nationwide strategy: 'Then we will see who is stronger – the Moscow Internal Affairs department or the local rogues.'[41] His attempts to make further moves in the battle against crime were hamstrung by the continuing presence in the Interior Ministry of his enemy Anatoly Kulikov, whom Yeltsin had refused to sack. Kulikov was not interested in the anti-crime agreement in Moscow; he was waiting for his moment to strike back at Lebed.

Throughout September Lebed's resentment of the criticism of his Chechen peace deal and the lack of co-operation for his other initiatives grew, making him increasingly outspoken both about the shortcomings of his government colleagues and his own presidential ambitions. When Yeltsin's health again deteriorated significantly, and the Kremlin revealed that he would shortly undergo a heart by-pass operation, Lebed said publicly that he should hand over his executive powers. His comments undermined the carefully crafted image of Yeltsin still firmly in control of the government. According to Lebed, Russia was now being run by a restricted circle of advisers with access to the President. 'I think it would be proper to do the following – if you fall ill, you transfer authority,' he said. 'Otherwise, a dangerous situation is set whereby it is possible to rule the country in the name of the President. This does not suit me at all.'[42] It might not have suited Lebed, but others were ready to make the most of the situation.

Anatoly Chubais, the head of the presidential administration and Yeltsin's Chief of Staff, had been irritated by Lebed's demand for more power, referring to it as 'a serious mistake for a novice state leader'.[43] At the end of September, however, he persuaded Yeltsin to transfer responsibility for the 'power ministries', which Lebed expected to be part of his preserve, to the Prime Minister, Viktor Chernomyrdin. At the same, Chernomyrdin was relieved of responsibility for the Federal Tax Service and the Federal Securities Commission, which were now to be overseen by Chubais and the presidential administration.[44] As Yeltsin prepared to submit to the surgeon's knife, the power of the Secretary of the Security Council had become largely illusory. Even his responsibility for overseeing top military appointments was taken away and given to Yuri Baturin, Yeltsin's former security adviser. When Lebed threatened to resign, Yeltsin made a surprisingly cheerful broadcast from his hospital bedside, in which he urged people not to 'rush to change the portraits' and heavily criticised

Lebed. 'He needs to get down to business now, carry out the tasks he already has and make more effort to work with the Prime Minister and with the other services. You can't quarrel with everyone all the time. You can't settle issues that way. Our state apparatus must live in peace.'[45]

As Lebed left Moscow on a visit to NATO's headquarters in Brussels, he must have realised that the ground had been prepared for his dismissal. In his public remarks, he was tactful and conciliatory, claiming that he had been misrepresented in reports that he had threatened the West with a new deployment of 'rusty' Russian missiles if NATO went ahead with its planned eastern expansion. Calling for 'a complicated but civilised dialogue' with NATO on European security, he said that 'some commentators of ill-will have been saying that [I am] threatening NATO with nuclear weapons . . . These are the worst fairy tales of the Cold War.'[46] At a meeting with the NATO Secretary-General, Javier Solana, he said that he was opposed to expansion, but 'Russia is not going to go into hysterics'.[47] The visit boosted Lebed's reputation in the West and Solana told reporters that he had enjoyed 'a very civilised and very rational discussion' with him.[48]

In Moscow, however, whilst Lebed was speaking at NATO headquarters, Anatoly Kulikov began openly to campaign for his dismissal, calling a press conference to announce that Lebed had capitulated to the Chechens and exaggerated the number of casualties in the war for his own political ends. In a typical attempt to produce *kompromat* on Lebed, Kulikov revealed that the Security Council Secretary had used a man accused of bank fraud in collusion with Chechen criminals as one of his envoys to the separatist leadership. The reason for Kulikov's sudden attack, which was clearly sanctioned by other senior figures in the Kremlin, was widely suspected to be the fact that Lebed had committed the unforgivable sin of lending his personal support to the campaign by Chubais's bitter enemy, Alexander Korzhakov, to win a by-election in Tula for the seat in the State Duma, which Lebed had vacated on his appointment to the Security Council. Lebed's appeal to the voters in Tula to 'make the right choice' had surprised political analysts, but he clearly felt that Korzhakov's experience would be useful as the battle to succeed Yeltsin intensified with every new bulletin on the President's health. Korzhakov might also have been able to offer Lebed a network of regional contacts and some financial support. 'I have seen a lot and know a lot,' Korzhakov said to the obvious consternation of the Kremlin. 'I know how people climbed up the ladders of their careers; I know about the intrigues that existed, about secret meetings, lots of things.'[49]

It was hardly surprising that a campaign to discredit Korzhakov soon started. He was accused of running a 'state racket' together with the sports minister, Shamil Tarpishev, Yeltsin's former tennis coach, through the National Sports Fund, which had made millions of dollars from its right to import duty-free alcohol and cigarettes. As this bizarre piece of *kompromat* began to appear in the media, it was clear that Lebed's alliance with Korzhakov had cost him the support of the independent television channels and the national newspapers. Chubais's friends in the media, who had been prevailed upon to support Lebed during the election campaign and had more recently backed his search for peace in Chechnya, now turned their backs on him. They knew that Yeltsin would soon remove the last vestiges of power from him.

As the media began to whip up hostility towards Lebed, and the evening news on 16 October on the NTV television channel opened with a twenty-minute diatribe against him, Anatoly Kulikov accused him of plotting a 'creeping coup' and launched a bitter attack on him. He accused Lebed of planning 'anti-constitutional acts' with the aim of seizing power[50] and of preparing 'to move ahead using force instead of waiting for the next presidential election'.[51] The substance of Kulikov's allegation was absurd; that Lebed intended forcing his way to power with the support of '1,500 Chechen gunmen' and a 'Russian Legion' which he had once suggested forming to fight civil unrest was nonsense. Kulikov's accusation was so fanciful that he even suggested that the real reason Lebed had put in a request for a holiday the following week was so that he could devote himself to the organisation of his coup.[52] He dismissed Kulikov's conspiracy theory with casual disdain. 'I'm going off at this time of year because I don't like warm beer,' he said.[53]

Despite the ridiculous content of Kulikov's denunciation, it was enough to provide an appropriate context within which Yeltsin could sack Lebed. On 17 October, Yeltsin announced on television that he had decided to dismiss his security Secretary.

'Esteemed Russians,' he began. 'I would like to say a few words on the situation with General Lebed. Unfortunately the situation is not great.' Aware that recent opinion polls had shown that Lebed was now the most trusted politician in Russia, he launched straight into an attack on his reputation, accusing him of making 'a number of mistakes which were simply unacceptable for Russia'.[54]

Yeltsin's Cabinet reshuffles and occasional dismissals of his ministers have sometimes been fatuously caricatured as 'victories' or 'defeats' for 'reformers' or 'hardliners' in the Kremlin. The sacking of Lebed, however, was not an event which was susceptible to such a lazy interpretation. Intensely pro-government politicians or jittery investors might try to put that sort of gloss upon it, but as the *Financial Times* observed, it was 'hard to detect any crime Mr Lebed might have committed against the causes of democracy and market reforms'.[55] The fact was that Lebed had outlived his usefulness to the powerful group of advisers around the President. He had brought victory in the election and ended the Chechen war, but he had become difficult; he was unmanageable and beyond the control of the *apparat*.

Twenty-four hours after his dismissal, as though to suggest that the real reason had nothing to do with ideological or political differences but was simply an old-fashioned Kremlin power struggle, he set off for the theatre, accompanied by reporters, to watch a performance of *Ivan the Terrible*. When Tsar Ivan died and the *boyar* nobles failed to agree on a successor, a devastating battle for the Kremlin known as *smutnoye vremya*, 'the time of troubles', began. The audience could hardly fail to notice the parallel with modern events. As Lebed watched the scheming *boyars*, he reflected that he was the victim of similar intrigues.

Shortly after his dismissal, the German news magazine *Der Spiegel* asked him who, in his opinion, was responsible for his downfall. 'Yeltsin's head of administration, Anatoly Chubais,' he replied, unhesitatingly identifying the archetypal modern equivalent of the scheming *boyar*. 'He wants absolute power. He has already created structures to influence appointments, the army and state security. He has already taken the place of the President.' Chubais, whom Lebed accused of working closely with Yeltsin's daughter Tatyana, had 'significantly more' power than a Kremlin Chief of Staff should have. If Chubais and Yeltsin's *apparat* were responsible for Lebed's fall, they were probably acting mostly out of self-interest, trying to maintain the delicate balance of power in the Kremlin that ensured that there was no obvious successor to Yeltsin, a state of affairs that left them firmly in control.

Lebed's dismissal had some clear advantages: his hands were now free to capitalise on his popularity and prepare a team for the presidential elections which he believed would come sooner rather than later. Sensitive to criticism by his supporters that he had been duped by Yeltsin and should never have agreed to join his government, he said: 'This move was inevitable, it was just a question of when. In that entourage I was a white crow, an inconvenient man.'[56] He insisted that although he had only lasted 121 days in office, the alliance with Yeltsin had been worthwhile:

> I could only stop [the war in] Chechnya with the transfer to me of executive and administrative authority. It was impossible to give orders by the Minister of Defence from that Cabinet. I said to Yeltsin – I didn't agree with him about everything, but there was no way I was for Zyuganov. Therefore, in alliance with Yeltsin, I undertook to solve two problems: to bring an end to the military conflict in Chechnya and to investigate armed criminality. He agreed and gave me the necessary authority. Two portfolios, in particular, were united in the one post: the Secretary of the Security Council and the President's adviser on national security. The duties of the latter include management of the commission for senior military posts and appointments. This commission decides if someone will be a General or not. In that way I took over all the reins of government and solved the problems with Chechnya.[57]

Yet many of the powers that had been promised turned out to be largely illusory. Amidst the confused state of Kremlin politics in the aftermath of the presidential elections, however, and with the *apparat* in turmoil because of the crisis in Yeltsin's health, Lebed was able to find a window of opportunity to turn the illusion of power briefly into reality:

> In Russia the Security Council is a purely decorative organisation, not unlike a Potemkin village. It is an organ which doesn't work, and 90 per cent of its paper production was thrown in

the bin. In the country, people knew that such an organ existed, that the President chaired it, but in actual fact its officials were dozing in armchairs or playing chess. Only with me did we begin to create structures with the help of which it was possible to direct security . . . In general, all our constitutional system – the Duma, the Constitutional Court, the Supreme Court – all of these are inactive dummies, whose purpose is to create the illusion of democracy. They look like democratic institutions but there is no democracy.[58]

Lebed had made little effort to shore up his position, and political analysts noted elementary mistakes and a lack of experience in Kremlin intrigues as significant reasons for his dismissal. He had 'considered the votes cast for him as having a long-term significance and guaranteeing him a defence from any political collision'; he 'came to power without his own team, above all without experienced *apparatchiks*'; he 'more than over-estimated the ability of an individual to influence the decision-making process at the highest level'; he did not have 'his own effective information system, allowing him to have an objective picture of what was going on'; and he attacked 'both the government and the opposition elites. They both saw in the Security Council Secretary a figure who could destabilise not only the authorities but also the whole country, and at a certain level they united their efforts to thwart his ambitions.'[59]

Lebed is adamant that he was fully aware that the Kremlin establishment intended that he should be given little more than the appearance of power. 'My illusions had already departed by the second day after my so-called arrival in power. When I asked about the provision of a telephone for my private office, I was told, that's too expensive. Much too expensive! Then I knew that I was being treated like a blind kitten that was about to be drowned in a bucket.'[60] He claims that he had known all along that he would only have a few months in office: 'I estimated that I would hold on to power for two months, but I stayed for four in all.'[61] Although some people might have suspected that he had been used by Yeltsin, his brief period in government had not been a mistake. 'I solved the problem with Chechnya. Although I wanted to solve it from a position of honour, it was solved by bargaining; and in bargaining, one side always tries to deceive the other . . . The people are not stupid. They saw that the military conflict could be solved quickly and effectively. The people stopped losing their sons. There was an independent survey of attitudes towards my actions. Seventy-five per cent were in support, 8 per cent against, and the rest abstained.'[62]

When he was finally removed from power, Lebed was almost indifferent. 'Be in no doubt,' he told one reporter who had said he wanted to see how Lebed had taken the blow of losing power, 'I feel absolutely comfortable today. My forehead is armour-plated.'[63] He had done all he could do in the time available before power was removed from him. 'There was no power. It cannot hurt to give up something which is not even there.'[64]

Yet whilst Lebed claimed that losing power did not hurt, and political analysts suggested that he could now spend his time preparing for the next presidential elections, Lebed soon discovered that he was not simply in the wilderness; the Kremlin *apparat* wanted to ensure that he became a pariah too. The big business friends of the *apparat*, with their financial muscle and control of the media, had been used to help create Lebed's remarkable electoral success; now, they could just as easily be persuaded to dry it up by denying him the oxygen of publicity. Anatoly Chubais, who soon consolidated his grip on power, becoming both First Deputy Prime Minister and Finance Minister, did not want a surly, resentful but popular opposition leader monopolising the Russian airwaves with conspiracy theories and tales of the abuse of power by the *apparat* that were fed by Lebed's new ally, General Korzhakov. Already the target of hostile publicity after his alliance with Korzhakov, Lebed now disappeared from view in the Russian media and, before long, Boris Berezovsky, whose commercial interests include the *Nezavisimaya Gazeta* newspaper, *Ogonyok* current affairs magazine and two television stations, ORT and TV6, was made Deputy Secretary of the Security Council.

As Lebed contemplated life in the political wilderness from his modest but comfortable new offices opposite Moscow's Tretyakov Gallery, rumours and theories persisted that all was not as it seemed. There were suggestions that he had always been closer to Yeltsin than anyone imagined; he had played Blücher to Yeltsin's Wellington in both the August 1991 *putsch* and the presidential elections. Now, so the argument went, his dismissal was simply a ruse to build him up as an outsider, an opposition figure battling against the Kremlin, much as Yeltsin had done before he became President. When Yeltsin died, he would be the leading opposition figure, ready to launch himself on a sea of popular discontent. The other, less fanciful, theory was that Lebed had made a serious blunder by gambling that Yeltsin's health was much worse. He had assumed, so people said, that the President would die only a few months after his election victory, perhaps whilst Lebed was still in office. Yet, contrary to most expectations, Yeltsin had made a remarkable recovery and Lebed was left in the wilderness, gradually fading from the public's consciousness.

Worse still, as darkness appeared to descend on Lebed's political fortunes, other stars began to shine brightly. Boris Nemtsov, the highly competent young governor of Nizhny Novgorod, whose economic reforms had been widely praised, was brought into the government in March 1997 as First Deputy Prime Minister, alongside Anatoly Chubais. Yeltsin appeared delighted with Nemtsov's appointment, just as he had been with Lebed's. 'Young, energetic! It's what we need,' he said, as the press began to speculate that this was the new heir apparent.[65] Yet Nemtsov's appointment had as much to do with the intrigues of the *apparat* as with a genuine desire to bring a bright young reformer to power. In a period of tense relations between Chubais and Prime Minister Chernomyrdin, with Boris Berezovsky at the heart of the government and with other businessmen reaching for the levers of power, Nemtsov was almost certainly not being set up by the Kremlin establishment as Yeltsin's successor. Although 'President Yeltsin and his influential daughter, Tatyana Dyachenko, persuaded him to accept the ministerial job',[66] he was given responsibility for dealing with Russia's huge problem of wage arrears, which had recently provoked strikes across the country; for the fight against corruption; and for breaking up the most powerful monopolies, particularly in the energy sector. His worst enemy could hardly have arranged a portfolio more likely to set him against some of the most powerful political and commercial interests in the land. At the same time, Nemtsov was on his own in the Kremlin, as Lebed had been, without the powerful team of advisers who could have turned his position into a base from which to campaign for the presidency. 'Nemtsov has no team at all,' Lebed noted.[67]

In Moscow, an even brighter star had been shining in the firmament long before Nemtsov's arrival. Yuri Luzhkov, the city's dynamic Mayor, who claims to model himself on Mayor Daley of Chicago, is genuinely popular in the Russian capital. A short, squat barrel of energy, and like Lebed a former boxing champion, Luzhkov won 90 per cent of the vote at the Mayoral elections which were held at the same time as the presidential elections. Luzhkov's popularity, which results from his obvious success in transforming Moscow, was so widely acknowledged that, during the presidential elections, Yeltsin's advisers insisted that the President should appear on his campaign posters in the capital with the Mayor. Luzhkov is a city boss whose grandiose but rather brash construction projects have given Moscow a sense of pride and confidence in the future. A former manager in the state bio-chemical industry and an *apparatchik*, Luzhkov has perhaps played the political game more cleverly than anyone else in Russia today. Always careful to assist Yeltsin, he has nevertheless criticised Anatoly Chubais, once comparing his privatisation programme to 'the way a drunk sells his possessions in the street for nothing'.[68] With an excellent relationship with the media, particularly with his long-standing ally Vladimir Gusinsky, and a self-evident record of success in Moscow, Luzhkov has a formidable power-base from which to mount a campaign for the presidency. Yet as Lebed points out, his greatest strength, his record in Moscow, may also be his greatest weakness:

> Luzhkov has the Moscow government, which is undoubtedly strong. But Luzhkov has a range of weaknesses. The first and most decisive: Moscow was always the polar centre of Russia, where there was everything that there wasn't in other areas. In the Soviet time, for example, there were sausages only in Moscow. All Russia travelled to Moscow for sausages. Now it's the same picture. So, in Russia there is a traditional dislike of Moscow. Why have they got everything and we've got nothing, even though the whole country produces the products?[69]

In the months since his dismissal, Lebed has gathered an effective campaign team around him, founding his own political party, the Russian People's Republican Party. However, as he has been effectively denied access to the national media in Russia and, for the moment, is apparently without major financial support, his campaign has been hamstrung. There have been rumours of financial support from Korzhakov's connections, and even an exposé in Berezovsky's *Ogonyok* news magazine claiming that Lebed was being funded by the aluminium magnates, Lev and Mikhail Chyorny.[70] However, the question of funding is academic because major finance would not be needed until the start of an election campaign; Berezovsky's group of bankers only decided to support Yeltsin six months before the last election. Lebed's lack of exposure in the national media has been more worrying for him, although he denies that, at this stage, he needs the backing of a major commercial group with national media interests. 'Why Berezovsky? Who is Berezovsky?' he asked dismissively. 'Many people – 39 per cent – read the central papers in Russia, but 57 per cent read local papers. I work with them at that level . . . In the real Russia, beyond the confines of Moscow, particularly in the Urals. The business has to be done there.'[71]

Lebed has compensated for his lack of exposure in the Russian media with a concerted effort to sustain his image as the Kremlin's heir apparent in the West. High-profile visits to France, the United States and Germany have been designed to convince the West that he is still the coming man and thus, in turn, perhaps to reassure Western-oriented business interests in Russia that, when the time comes, they can feel confident in giving him their support. Americans are intrigued by the charismatic General who received a personal invitation to President Clinton's inauguration and 'sipped tea with Wall Street investors at the Harvard Club in Manhattan'.[72] He went out of his way to reassure American audiences that, as President, he would welcome foreign investment and continue the democratic process. 'I want to build a free, democratic Russia,' he told members of the United Nations Correspondents' Association in New York. 'The only thing I kill now are wars.' He appeared even more relaxed than he had been in Brussels about the prospect of NATO expansion. 'Russia should take it calmly,' he said. 'There should be no hysteria.' At one point in his visit, he even joked – albeit in poor taste – about Russia's reaction to NATO expansion: 'If the rape is unavoidable, relax and try to enjoy it.' Even Donald Trump thought he had 'a lot of wonderful ideas'.[73]

The Germans were equally enthusiastic when Lebed visited

them in February 1997. Helmut Kohl had long recognised Lebed's merits, and had even tried to persuade Yeltsin to give him more support as Security Council Secretary.[74] German support for Lebed was also substantially due to an assessment by the Bundesnachrichtendienst (BND), the federal intelligence service, that Lebed stood the best chance in the medium term of replacing Yeltsin. The BND ensured that politicians in Bonn serenaded Lebed and that 'the handshakes were a little friendlier than usual'.[75]

British policy-makers, on the other hand, seem to have been wary of Lebed. There was much more enthusiasm in the Foreign Office for Anatoly Chubais, who visited Britain shortly after Tony Blair's election victory in May 1997, and who was much in evidence during the new Prime Minister's visit to Moscow. Because of his position at the heart of the Kremlin *apparat*, British diplomats have always been quite ready to ignore the fact that Chubais has more powerful enemies than anyone else in Russian politics.

Throughout 1997, Lebed tried to reassure Western audiences that he represents a threat neither to the West's foreign policy interests nor to the prospects for democracy and stability in Russia. He neither expects nor desires major changes in Russia's policy towards the West. 'The ship is too big to turn the wheel sharply. Everything that has been arrived at and agreed upon must be fulfilled. Whatever we don't agree with must be settled by established, international procedure. There is an attitude – I've come to power and now I won't be friends with you – which we must categorically avoid.'[76]

Changes in Russian foreign policy under Lebed would be more likely to reflect new priorities rather than old antagonisms. 'Russia is an eagle with two heads. One head looks to the East, the other to the West. The head looking to the East is blind, although 60 per cent of the country's territory is in Asia. Countries such as China, Japan, Korea are considered exotic in Europe. But for us, they are neighbours . . . We are bound to build relationships with them. The eagle really must be double-headed. We shouldn't weight the scales on the side of the West alone. We need to build relationships with the East too.'[77]

Lebed sees Russia's new relations with the East as part of its traditional role defending the West. 'It has always protected the

West from military incursions from the East. Russia is a natural barrier between East and West.'[78]

Lebed's most fundamental concern, however, has always been order in Russia itself rather than foreign policy. He believes in the creation of a law-based society and has even referred to a 'dictatorship of the law'.[79] The key to such a law-based society is constitutional reform, and Lebed is convinced that the fact that Russia now has the wrong constitution is the reason for many of its recent problems:

> Today's constitution is authoritarian in form. It was built as a pyramid under one man and he is more than a President, he's a Tsar. In it, a mass of democratic institutions are absent. For example, people could elect whomever they wanted tomorrow, let's say Ivanov, but it would be impossible to get rid of this Ivanov if he dug his heels in. There is also a lack of control of relations between the authorities and the opposition. There needs to be some sort of court of arbitration so that they can't just agree on everything to their mutual advantage. They need to agree for the good of society. Moreover, this court of arbitration should be open and not secret. Open and understood by all. That's why I wrote that we needed constitutional reform. But not the usual sort that we had under Stalin, Brezhnev and Yeltsin, but a basic State Law for everyone. It should be thought through very carefully, not rushed for some holiday or other, for some sort of election or by some date. It is not a temporary thing – it is the basic law of the state.[80]

Lebed is particularly critical of both the legislature and the judiciary under the present constitution. The legislature, the State Duma, cannot control the executive, which treats it with contempt. It has failed to fulfil its function as a sensible legislature: 'Look, the fifth Duma passed more than 300 laws, the present one nearly 400. But I ask people, name me a law which works and which makes it easier to live. No one can. And laws should be for people.' Government ministers, he complains, have no respect for the Duma. 'Who is the modern minister – a faithful dog, doomed to lick the President's boots. He depends only on him, he can spit on the Duma. Taking into account the President's appalling relations with the Duma, the more the minister curses the Duma, the more the President loves him.' The judiciary is in an even worse state, according to Lebed: 'Whoever has been in our courts leaves in a state of shock. The judges sit in bad accommodation and they're paid little, which makes them take bribes.'[81]

Russia needs a constitution which guarantees a clear separation of powers, openness and accountability: 'A democratic system consists of a clear division of the appropriate functions between all three supreme authorities. Each one operates in its own sector, where there are mechanisms which pacify all the possible conflicts. We need a serious, multi-layered system, from which it is evident who appoints whom and who controls whom.'[82] Lebed is perhaps the only major presidential candidate who regards constitutional reform as an essential part of his political agenda.

Whether he will ever have the chance to translate any of his ideas into action will depend on the Russian people. Lebed's personal popularity rating has slipped during the long months since he was unquestionably the most trusted politician in Russia. A hostile press and the appearance of other figures on the nationalist right, such as General Lev Rokhlin, who might appeal to the same constituency of support, have slowed his momentum. Yet Lebed remains optimistic. He estimates that whilst the Communists can now only rely on 25 per cent of the electorate, his support remains at around 40 per cent, bolstered by a core of disaffected, desperate people in whom 'anger and resentment are boiling. They don't know where to go. They turn back and in the past not everything was bad at all.' They find themselves living now in a world where 'they feed their children with cattle feed and they don't know what to dress their children in for school'. Yet, they know that communism offers them no hope either. 'The Communist idea has outlived itself and the overflow from there is coming here, into my camp.'[83]

Lebed is convinced that his main rival for the presidency will be Yuri Luzhkov:

People think that Luzhkov paid for the [Moscow 850th anniversary] celebrations himself. So, today he is strong, but tomorrow, who knows? Nemtsov has slipped, like a cat on a fence, and now he is falling headlong – in public opinion, in the eyes of the President and the Prime Minister. Chubais has never risen. Chernomyrdin is a clever fox who always finds his way, but he is ridiculous, above all because he's tongue-tied. From my service in the army, I know that subordinates can forgive you everything: coarseness, caddishness, but to become ridiculous is fatal for your career.[84]

The truth is that there is no obvious heir apparent to Boris Yeltsin; Lebed has as good a chance as anyone of taking the Kremlin in the next presidential elections. What will be decisive, however, if the next election is anything like the last, will be the support of the great business conglomerates, which gave their allegiance to Boris Yeltsin and his chief fundraiser Anatoly Chubais in the last months of the campaign. Last time, the *apparat* made sure it got its man elected. This time, things might not be so easy. Boris Berezovsky's period of office in the Security Council was not much longer than Alexander Lebed's. When he left, however, he swore to avenge himself on the man he thought responsible for pushing him out – Anatoly Chubais. His revenge was not long in coming. Within a month, his media network was able to report gleefully that Chubais and some of his colleagues had accepted a 'publisher's advance' worth $450,000 for a book on privatisation.[85] Chubais was forced to resign his job as Finance Minister but managed to cling on to his post as First Deputy Prime Minister.

With the ice breaking so dramatically around the *apparat*, and the electoral threat from the Communists receding, Russia's political landscape is as unstable as ever. When Boris Yeltsin dismissed his entire Cabinet in a dramatic announcement on 23 March 1998, it was clear that the ill-concealed splits in the Kremlin had already penetrated deep into Russia's frozen earth. Now, the political–commercial alliance that brought Yeltsin victory has been shaken to such an extent that it has probably split beyond repair. In the next presidential elections, there will be a new pattern of alliances, no doubt creating the strangest of bedfellows. If Alexander Lebed can build a powerful enough alliance, he may finally win his battle against the Kremlin.

BIOGRAPHICAL NOTES

ACHALOV, Vladislav Alekseyevich

Born 1945. Studied at Kazan Tank Academy, Malinovsky Armoured Troops Academy and the General Staff Academy. First Deputy Commander of the 2nd Tank Army in the Western Group of Forces (Germany), 1984; Commander of the Airborne Forces, 1989–91. Colonel-General and Deputy Defence Minister to Marshal Yazov. Dismissed after his involvement in the August 1991 *putsch*. Supported Rutskoi and Khasbulatov against Yeltsin in October 1993 – Rutskoi made him his 'defence minister'. Granted an amnesty in 1994.

ANDROPOV, Yuri Vladimirovich

Born 1914. Chairman of the KGB, 1967–82. General Secretary of the CPSU, 1982–84. Chairman of the Presidium of the Supreme Soviet of the USSR, 1983–84. Died 1984.

BABICHEV, Ivan Ivanovich

Passed out of the Frunze Academy with Lebed in 1985. With rank of Major-General, commanded Western Group of Forces during the early stages of the invasion of Chechnya.

BARSUKOV, Mikhail Ivanovich

Born 1947. A graduate of the Frunze Academy, he was promoted to the rank of General. In 1992 he became head of the main security department of the Russian Federation and commandant of the Moscow Kremlin. From 1995–96 he was the Chairman of the Federal Security Service until Yeltsin sacked him after the first round of the presidential elections.

BASAYEV, Shamil

A leading Chechen field commander, who organised the raid on Budyonnovsk in June 1995. Revered in Chechnya as a daring warrior, he was despised by the Kremlin as a leading 'terrorist'. He came second in the presidential elections in Chechnya which followed Lebed's peace agreement, and agreed to serve under Aslan Maskhadov in the Chechen government.

BEREZOVSKY, Boris Abramovich

Born 1946 in Moscow. Entered Moscow State University in 1967; worked as an engineer, 1969–87. Completed a Ph.D. in physics and mathematics; his doctoral thesis was based on research conducted at the AvtoVAZ factory. In 1989, he founded LogoVAZ, which became the centre of a rapidly growing business empire that soon included interests in banking, car manufacturing and the media. In 1991, he became a correspondent member of the Russian Academy of Sciences. From 1992–93, he was a member of the Russian government's council on industry and politics. In December 1996, he was made Deputy Secretary of the Russian Security Council. He was dismissed from the post in November 1997.

BESSMERTNYKH, Alexander Alexandrovich

Born 1933. Head of the American Department of the USSR Ministry of Foreign Affairs, 1983–86. First Deputy Foreign Minister, 1988–90. Foreign Minister, 1991.

BREZHNEV, Leonid Ilyich

Born 1906. Member of the Politburo, 1957–82. Chairman of the Presidium of the USSR Supreme Soviet, 1960–64 and 1977–82. General Secretary of the Central Committee of the CPSU, 1964–82. Died 1982.

BURLAKOV, Matvey Prokopevich

Born 1935. Graduated from Omsk Military Academy, the Frunze Academy and the General Staff Academy. First Deputy Commander of Trans-Baikal military district, 1983. Commander of the South Group of Forces in Hungary, 1988. Commander of the Western Group of Forces in Germany, 1990–94. In 1994, despite widespread allegations of corruption in the Western Group of Forces, he was appointed Deputy Minister of Defence with the rank of Colonel-General. In 1995, he was dismissed for corruption.

CHERNENKO, Konstantin Ustinovich

Born 1911. Member of the Politburo, 1978–85. General Secretary of the Central Committee of the CPSU and Chairman of the Presidium of the USSR Supreme Soviet, 1984–85. Died 1985.

CHERNOMYRDIN, Viktor Stepanovich

Born 1938. Educated at Kuibyshev Polytechnic. USSR Deputy Minister of the Gas Industry, 1982–85. Head of Tyumengasprom, 1983–85. USSR Minister of the Gas Industry, 1985–89. Chairman of the board of the state gas company, Gasprom, 1989–92. From May to December 1992, Deputy Chairman of the Government of the Russian Federation, responsible for the fuel–energy complex. Since December 1992, Chairman of the Government (Prime Minister) of the Russian Federation.

CHUBAIS, Anatoly Borisovich

Born 1955. Educated at the Leningrad Institute of Engineering and Economics. First Deputy Chairman of the Leningrad City Executive Committee (Lengorispolkom), 1990–91, and then chief economic adviser to the Mayor of St Petersburg. Chairman of the State Committee of the Russian Federation on the management of state property, November 1991. Deputy Chairman of the Government of the Russian Federation, June 1992. Head of the Russian presidential administration, 1996–97. First Deputy Chairman of the Government of the Russian Federation and Minister of Finance, 1997. Dismissed as Finance Minister, November 1997.

DEMIRCHYAN, Karen Seropovich

Born 1932. First Secretary of the Communist Party of Armenia, 1974–88.

DUDAYEV, Dzhokhar Musayevich

Born 1944. Educated at Tambov Higher Military Aviation School. Graduated from the Gagarin Air Force Academy in 1977. Served in Siberia and Afghanistan, 1985–86. Served in Estonia, 1987–90. Became the first Chechen General in the Soviet Air Force. Retired in 1990 and returned to Chechnya, where he was elected President in October 1991. Led Chechen resistance to Russian intervention until April 1996, when he was reported killed in a rocket attack by the Russian Air Force.

DYACHENKO, Tatyana Borisovna

Born 1960 in Sverdlovsk. Yeltsin's daughter. Studied mathematics and cybernetics at the Moscow State University. Worked for KB Salyut, 1983–4. Worked in the Moscow branch of the Zarya Urala bank, 1994. After her crucial but unofficial role in the 1996 presidential election campaign, she was officially appointed as the President's image consultant in June 1997.

FILATOV, Sergei Alexandrovich

First Deputy Chairman of the Russian Parliament, 1991–92. Head of the Russian presidential administration, 1993–96.

GAIDAR, Yegor Timurovich

Born 1956 in Moscow. Graduated from the Economics Faculty of Moscow State University. Director of the Institute of Economic Policy at the USSR Academy of the National Economy, 1990–91. Deputy Chairman of the Government of the Russian Federation, with responsibility for economic policy, 1991–92. Minister of Finance of the Russian Federation, 1992. Acting Chairman of the Government (Prime Minister) of the Russian Federation, June–December 1992. First Deputy Chairman of the Russian Government, 1993–94. Leader of the 'Russia's Choice' group in the State Duma, 1993–95.

GORBACHEV, Mikhail Sergeyevich

Born 1931 in Stavropol. Graduated from the Law Faculty of Moscow State University. First Secretary of the Stavropol Regional Committee of the CPSU, 1970–78. Secretary of the Central Committee of the CPSU, 1978–85. General Secretary of the Central Committee of the CPSU, 1985–91. President of the USSR, 1990–91. President of the Gorbachev Foundation since 1991.

GRACHEV, Pavel Sergeyevich

Born 1948. Graduated 1969 from the Ryazan Higher Airborne Command Academy and 1981 from the Frunze Academy. Served in Afghanistan, commanding an Airborne division, 1981–83 and 1987–89. Decorated 'Hero of the Soviet Union'. In 1990, after passing out from the General Staff Academy, he was made Commander of the Airborne Forces. First Deputy Minister of Defence of the USSR, August 1991. First Deputy Commander-in-Chief of SNG joint forces, 1992. First Deputy Minister of Defence of Russian Federation, April 1992. Minister of Defence, May 1992. General of the Army. Dismissed from his post as Defence Minister in 1996.

GROMOV, Boris Vsevolodovich

Born 1943. Graduated from the Frunze Academy in 1972 and the General Staff Academy in 1984. Served in Afghanistan 1980–82, 1985–86 and 1987–89. As commander of the 40th Army, organised the Soviet withdrawal. Deputy Minister of the Interior of the USSR, 1991. Russian Deputy Minister of Defence, 1992–95. Deputy Minister of Foreign Affairs, 1995.

GUSINSKY, Vladimir

A former theatre director, Gusinsky set up the Infex co-operative in 1989 to provide foreign investors with consulting and political forecasting services. In 1990, he created and registered the Most Group in partnership with the American law firm Arnold & Porter. By 1992 Most was a wholly Russian-owned company, offering financial services and dealing in real estate. By the end of 1996, Gusinsky was ranked as Russia's top entrepreneur with a retail and commercial banking empire and expanding media interests, which include *Sevodnya* newspaper, *Itogi* magazine and NTV television.

KHASBULATOV, Ruslan Imranovich

Former Professor of Law at the Plekhanov Institute, Moscow, and corresponding member of the Russian Academy of Science. First Deputy Chairman of the Russian Parliament, 1990. Chairman (Speaker) of the Russian Parliament, 1991–93. Together with General Rutskoi, organised rebellion against Yeltsin in October 1993. Arrested but amnestied in February 1994.

KORZHAKOV, Alexander Vasilyevich

Born 1950 in Moscow. Served as an officer in the ninth directorate of the KGB, 1970–91. Head of the presidential security service, 1991–96. Dismissed by President Yeltsin in 1996 after a public row with Anatoly Chubais. Elected to the State Duma as member for Tula in February 1997.

KRAVCHUK, Leonid Makarovich

Born 1934. Secretary of the Central Committee of the Communist Party of Ukraine, 1989–90. Chairman of the Supreme Soviet of Ukraine, 1990–91. President of Ukraine, December 1991.

KRYUCHKOV, Vladimir Alexandrovich

Born 1924 in Volgograd. Graduated from the Higher Diplomatic School of USSR Foreign Ministry. Head of foreign intelligence, KGB, 1974–88. Chairman of the KGB, 1988–91. Arrested as one of the leaders of the August 1991 *putsch*. Amnestied by the State Duma in 1994.

KULIKOV, Anatoly Sergeyevich

Born 1946. Graduated from the Ordzhonikidze Higher Military Command Academy for Internal Forces of the Ministry of the USSR Interior in 1966, the Frunze Academy in 1974 and the General Staff Academy in 1990. After serving in command positions at all levels of the Interior Ministry forces, he was appointed Deputy Minister of the Interior in 1993 and Commander of the Moscow Emergency District during the 'October events'. Headed the joint command of the Federal Group of Forces in Chechnya, March–July 1995. Minister of the Interior, July 1995.

LEBED, Alexander Ivanovich

Born 1950 in Novocherkassk. Graduated from the Ryazan Higher Airborne Command Academy in 1973 and the Frunze Academy in 1985. Commanded an Airborne battalion in Afghanistan, 1981–82. Commander of the 106th Tula Guards Airborne Division, 1985. Deputy Commander of the Airborne Forces, 1991. Ordered to the White House in August 1991, where he played an important role in ensuring the failure of the *putsch*. Commander of 14th Army in Moldova, 1992. Lieutenant-General. Resigned from the army in 1995 and won a seat in the Duma as the member for Tula. Stood for President in 1996. Appointed Secretary of the Security Council of the Russian Federation by Yeltsin after the first round of the presidential elections. Signed a peace agreement with the Chechens, August 1996. Dismissed from his post by Yeltsin, October 1996.

LUZHKOV, Yuri Mikhailovich

Born 1936 in Moscow. Studied at the Gubkin Oil and Gas Institute. First Deputy Chairman of the Executive Committee of Moscow City Council, 1987–90. Chairman, 1990–91. Mayor of Moscow, 1992.

MASKHADOV, Aslan

Former Colonel of Artillery in the Soviet Army. Deputy commander of Chechen forces, 1992–94. Chief of Staff, 1994–96. Signed peace agreement with Lebed, August 1996. Elected President of Chechnya, January 1997.

NAZARBAYEV, Nursultan Abishevich

Born 1940 in Alma Ata. Graduated from Karaganda Polytechnic. Secretary of the Central Committee of the Communist Party of Kazakhstan, 1979–84. Chairman of the Council of Ministers of Kazakhstan, 1984–89. First Secretary of the Central Committee of the Kazakh Communist Party, 1989. Chairman of the Supreme Soviet of Kazakhstan, 1990. President of the Republic of Kazakhstan, 1991.

NEMTSOV, Boris Yefimovich
Born 1959. Governor of Nizhny Novgorod Region, 1991. Re-elected 1996. First Deputy Prime Minister of the Russian government, 1997.

PANKIN, Boris Dmitryevich
Born 1931. Chief editor of *Komsomolskaya Pravda*, 1965–73. Chairman of the All-Union Copyright Agency, 1973–82. USSR Ambassador to Sweden, 1982–90. USSR Ambassador to Czechoslovakia, 1990–91. USSR Foreign Minister, August–December 1991. Russian Ambassador to the United Kingdom, 1992–94.

PODKOLZIN, Yevgeny Nikolayevich
Born 1936. Educated at the Alma Ata Airborne Service School and the Frunze Academy. Graduated from the General Staff Academy, 1982. First Deputy Chief of Staff, Airborne Forces, 1982. Chief of Staff and First Deputy Commander, Airborne Forces, 1986. Commander, Airborne Forces, August 1991.

PUGO, Boris Karlovich
Born 1937. Chairman of the Latvian KGB, 1980–84. USSR Minister for Internal Affairs, 1990–91. Committed suicide after the failure of the *putsch* in August 1991.

PULIKOVSKY, Konstantin
Russian commander in Chechnya with rank of Lieutenant-General.

RADUYEV, Salman
Chechen field commander who led hostage-taking raids on Kizlyar and Pervomaiskoye in January 1996. Married to General Dudayev's niece.

ROKHLIN, Lev
General commanding Northern Group of Forces in Chechnya, 1994–95. Captured Grozny. Entered the State Duma in 1995 as a member of Chernomyrdin's 'Our Home is Russia' Party but quarrelled with the leadership. Chairman of the Duma Defence Committee.

SHAPOSHNIKOV, Yevgeny Ivanovich

Born 1942. Educated at the Kharkov Higher Aviation School and the Gagarin Air Force Academy. Graduated from the General Staff Academy in 1984. Commanding Officer, Aviation for Western Group of Forces (Germany), 1987–88. First Deputy Commander-in-Chief, Soviet Air Forces, 1988–90. Commander-in-Chief, Air Forces, and Deputy Minister of Defence, 1990–91. Appointed USSR Minister of Defence, August 1991. Commander-in-Chief, SNG joint armed forces, 1992. Secretary of Security Council, 1993. Presidential representative to Rosvooruzhenie, 1994. Chairman of Aeroflot, 1995.

SHUMEIKO, Vladimir Filippovich

First Deputy Chairman of the Council of Ministers, 1992–94. Chairman of the Federation Council (upper house) of the Russian Duma, 1994.

SHUSHKEVICH, Stanislav Stanislavovich

President of the Belorussian State University, 1986–90. Chairman of the Supreme Soviet of the Republic of Belarus, 1991–94.

SOSKOVETS, Oleg Nikolayevich

Born 1949 in Kazakhstan. Completed training as an engineer at the Karaganda metallurgical plant, 1971. Member of the Communist Party, 1972–91. President of the Kazakhstan union of industrialists and entrepreneurs, 1992. Chairman of the Russian Federation Committee on the metallurgical industry, 1992–93. First Deputy Chairman of the Government of the Russian Federation and Chairman of the Russian Export Control Commission, 1993. Chairman of the military–technical commission for co-operation with foreign countries, 1994. President Yeltsin's special representative in the Chechen republic, 1995.

STEPASHIN, Sergei Vadimovich

Born 1952 in Port Arthur, the son of a naval officer. Educated at the political academy of the USSR Ministry of the Interior (MVD). Served in the Interior Ministry forces, 1973–90. Served in Baku, Fergana, Nagorny Karabakh and Sukhumi, 1987–90. Deputy Minister of Security of the Russian Federation, 1992. First

Deputy Minister of Security, 1993. Director of the Federal Counter-Intelligence Service of the Russian Federation, 1994. Resigned from his post in 1995 after the Chechen attack on Budyonnovsk. Subsequently appointed by Yeltsin to a position in a government administration department.

TARASOV, Artyom Mikhailovich

Born 1950. Member of the State Duma, 1993–95. The Central Electoral Commission refused to register his candidature in the 1996 presidential elections.

USTINOV, Dmitry Fyodorovich

Born 1908. USSR Minister of Defence and member of the Politburo, 1976–84. Marshal of the Soviet Union. Died 1984.

VOROBYOV, Eduard Arkadyevich

Born 1938. Educated at the Baku Combined Arms School and the Frunze Academy. Graduated from the General Staff Academy, 1981. Commanding Officer, Central Group of Forces (Czechoslovakia), 1987. As Colonel-General and First Deputy Commander-in-Chief of ground troops, transferred to reserves in 1995 for refusal to accept command of invasion forces in Chechnya.

YANAYEV, Gennady Ivanovich

Born 1937. Chairman of the USSR Committee for Youth Organisations, 1968–80. Deputy Chairman of the Soviet Union of Friendship Societies, 1980–86. Chairman of the All-Union Central Council of Trade Unions, 1989–90. Secretary of the Central Committee of the CPSU and member of the Politburo, 1990–91. Vice-President of the USSR. Arrested for his part in the August 1991 *putsch*. Released from prison, 1993. Amnestied by the State Duma, 1994.

YANDARBIYEV, Zelimkhan

Vice-President of Chechnya, 1993–96. President of Chechnya, 1996–97.

YAVLINSKY, Grigory Alexandrovich

Born 1952. Deputy Chairman of the RSFSR Council of Ministers, 1990. An economist, he was the co-author of the

'Shatalin Plan' for a 500-day transition to a market economy. Chairman of the Centre for Economic and Political Research. Leader of the 'Yabloko' bloc, 1991. Elected to the State Duma, 1993.

YAZOV, Dmitry Timofeyevich

Born 1923. Commanding Officer of the Central Asian military district, 1980–84. CO, Far East Military District, 1984–86. USSR Minister of Defence, 1987–91. Member of the State Emergency Committee, August 1991.

YELTSIN, Boris Nikolayevich

Born 1931. First Secretary of the Sverdlovsk Communist Party Committee, 1976–85. Head of the Construction Department of the CPSU Central Committee and Secretary of the Central Committee, 1985. First Secretary of the Moscow Party, 1985–87. First Deputy Chairman of the USSR State Construction Committee (Gosstroi), 1987–89. Chairman of the Supreme Soviet of the RSFSR, 1990. Elected President of Russia, 1991. Re-elected 1996.

YERIN, Viktor Fyodorovich

Born 1944 in Kazani. Educated at the Higher Interior Ministry school. Director of the Criminal Investigation Department in the Tartar Autonomous Republic, 1980–83. First Deputy Minister of Internal Affairs of Armenia, 1988–90. Deputy Minister of the Interior of the RSFSR and head of the criminal police, 1990–91. First Deputy Minister of the Interior of the USSR, September–December 1991. Minister of the Interior of Russia, 1992. Awarded the title of 'Hero of the Russian Federation' in October 1993 for his part in suppressing the rebellion by Rutskoi and Khasbulatov. Resigned his post in 1995 after the Chechen attack on Budyonnovsk.

ZHIRINOVSKY, Vladimir Volfovich

Born 1946. According to him, his mother was a Russian, his father was a 'lawyer'. Leader of the Liberal Democratic Party of Russia, 1990. Ran for President, 1991. Elected to the State Duma, 1993. Re-elected 1995. Ran again for President, 1996.

ZYUGANOV, Gennady Andreyevich
   Born 1944. Secretary of the Central Committee of the Russian Communist Party and member of the Politburo, 1990–91. Head of the Communist Party of the Russian Federation, 1993.

NOTES

Further publication and source details are provided in the Bibliography.

PREFACE

1 Leskov, 'A Winter's Day' in *Lady Macbeth of Mtsensk and Other Stories*, translated by David McDuff.

I: NOVOCHERKASSK

1 Lermontov, 'Kazachya Kolybel'naya Pyesnya' in *Izbrannye Sochineniya*.
2 Lebed, *Za Derzhavu Obidno*.
3 Ibid.
4 Ibid.
5 Yeltsin, *The View from the Kremlin*.
6 Lebed, op. cit.
7 *Guardian*, 15 July 1988.
8 Hosking, *A History of the Soviet Union*.
9 *Guardian*, 15 July 1988.
10 Ibid.
11 *Izvestiya*, 4 June 1994.

12   Ibid.
13   *Guardian*, 3 June 1989.
14   Ostrogorski, *Lebed. Der Weg zur Macht.*
15   Ibid.
16   Lebed, op. cit.
17   Ibid.
18   Ibid.
19   Ibid.
20   Ibid.
21   Ibid.

2: RYAZAN

1   Yevtushenko, 'The Heirs of Stalin' in *The Poetry of Yevgeny Yevtushenko*, translated by George Reavey.
2   Zaloga, *Inside the Blue Berets.*
3   Suvorov, *Inside the Soviet Army.*
4   Ericksson, 'Soviet Military Power'.
5   Lebed, *Za Derzhavu Obidno.*
6   Ericksson, op. cit.
7   *The Officer's Handbook.* The quote from Brezhnev is taken from Brezhnev, *50 Let Velikogo Sotsializma.*
8   *Financial Times*, 6 September 1994.
9   Ostrogorski, *Lebed. Der Weg zur Macht.* The incident referred to actually happened slightly later in Lebed's time at Ryazan, during a period when the battalion political officer was on leave and Lebed briefly took his place.
10   Lebed, op. cit.
11   Ibid.
12   Ibid.
13   Ibid.
14   Ibid.
15   Laqueur, *The Dream That Failed.*

3: AFGHANISTAN

1   Kipling, *Rudyard Kipling's Verse, 1885–1918.*
2   Quoted in Galeotti, *Afghanistan: The Soviet Union's Last War.*
3   Hosking, *A History of the Soviet Union.*
4   Gromov, *Ogranichenny Kontingent.*
5   Baumann, *Russian–Soviet Unconventional Wars in the Caucasus, Central Asia and Afghanistan.*

6 Galeotti, op. cit.
7 Zaloga, *Inside the Blue Berets*.
8 Quoted in Zaloga, op. cit.
9 A detailed description appears in Zaloga, op. cit.
10 Hopkirk, *The Great Game*.
11 Lebed, *Za Derzhavu Obidno*.
12 Lermontov, *Izbrannye Sochineniya*.
13 Lebed, op. cit.
14 Ibid.
15 Ibid.
16 Baumann, op. cit.
17 Ibid.
18 Lebed, op.cit.
19 Ibid.
20 Petrov, 'An Airborne Battalion Searches Sherkhankel Village, March 1982'.
21 Lebed, op. cit.
22 Ibid.
23 Galeotti, op. cit.
24 Lebed, op. cit.
25 Zaloga, op. cit.
26 Lebed, op. cit.
27 Ibid.
28 Ibid.
29 Ibid.
30 Ibid.

4: THE FRUNZE ACADEMY

1 Tolstoy, *The Death of Ivan Ilyich*, translated by Rosemary Edmonds.
2 Lebed, *Za Derzhavu Obidno*.
3 Ibid.
4 Hosking, *A History of the Soviet Union*.
5 Lebed, op. cit.
6 Ibid.
7 Ibid.
8 Ibid.
9 Ibid.
10 Ibid.
11 Doder, *Shadows and Whispers*.
12 Lebed, op. cit.

13   Ibid.

14   Hopkins, 'Unchained Reactions: The Strained Evolution of Glasnost'.

5: THE CAUCASUS

1   Turgenev, *On the Eve*, translated by Gilbert Gardiner.

2   Gorbachev, *Memoirs*.

3   Ibid.

4   Ibid.

5   Suny, *The Revenge of the Past*.

6   Lebed, *Za Derzhavu Obidno*.

7   Ibid.

8   Ibid.

9   Gorbachev, op. cit.

10   Ibid.

11   Lebed, op. cit.

12   Ibid.

13   Ibid.

14   Ibid.

15   Ibid.

16   Gorbachev, op. cit.

17   Ibid.

18   Lebed, op. cit.

19   Hosking, *A History of the Soviet Union*.

20   Lebed, op. cit.

21   Gorbachev, op. cit.

22   Hosking, op. cit.

23   Goldenberg, *The Pride of Small Nations*.

24   Ibid.; and O'Ballance, *Wars in the Caucasus*. Also mentioned by Zaloga in *Inside the Blue Berets*.

25   Lebed, op. cit.

26   Gorbachev, op. cit.

27   Lebed, op. cit.

28   Gorbachev, op. cit.

29   Holoboff, 'The Crisis in Soviet Military Reform'.

30   Ibid.

31   Plater-Zyberk, 'The Soviet Withdrawal from Central Europe'.

32   US Department of Defense, *Soviet Military Power, 1990*.

33   Dick Cheney, Introduction to *Soviet Military Power, 1990*, op. cit.

34   Ibid.

35   Suny, op. cit.

36 Lebed, op. cit.
37 Ibid.
38 Gorbachev, op. cit.
39 O'Ballance, op. cit.
40 Zaloga, op. cit.
41 O'Ballance, op. cit.
42 Gorbachev, op. cit.
43 Holoboff, op. cit.
44 Lebed, op. cit.
45 Ibid.
46 Gorbachev, op. cit.
47 Hosking, op. cit.
48 Suny, op. cit.
49 Zaloga, op. cit.
50 Lebed, op. cit.
51 Gorbachev, op. cit.
52 Ibid.
53 Ibid.

6: MOSCOW – AUGUST 1991

1   Pushkin, 'The Storm' in *Sochineniya*.
2   Zaloga, *Inside the Blue Berets*.
3   Lebed, *Za Derzhavu Obidno*.
4   Lambeth, *The Warrior Who Would Rule Russia*.
5   Lebed, op. cit.
6   Ibid.
7   Korzhakov, *Ot Rassveta Do Zakata*.
8   Yeltsin, *The View from the Kremlin*.
9   Gorbachev, *Memoirs*.
10 Ibid.
11 Author's interview with Gennady Yanayev, 1997.
12 Ibid.
13 Ibid.
14 Ibid.
15 Author's interview with Boris Pankin, 1997.
16 Interview with Yanayev, op. cit.
17 Gorbachev, op. cit.
18 Interview with Yanayev, op. cit.
19 Gorbachev, op. cit.
20 Interview with Yanayev, op. cit.
21 O'Ballance, *Wars in the Caucasus*.

22   Interview with Yanayev, op. cit.
23   Ibid.
24   BBC, 'Summary of World Broadcasts', 20 August 1991.
25   Interview with Yanayev, op. cit.
26   Ibid.
27   Schofield, *The Russian Elite*.
28   Gorbachev, op. cit.
29   Interview with Yanayev, op. cit.
30   *Financial Times*, 19 August 1991.
31   *Independent*, 20 August 1991.
32   Zaloga, op. cit.
33   Korzhakov, op. cit.
34   Yeltsin, op. cit.
35   Korzhakov, op. cit.
36   Yeltsin, op. cit.
37   Interview with Yanayev, op. cit.
38   Schofield, op. cit.
39   Ibid.
40   BBC, op. cit.
41   Interview with Yanayev, op. cit.
42   BBC, op. cit.
43   Interview with Yanayev, op. cit.
44   Yeltsin, op. cit.
45   Ibid.
46   Korzhakov, op. cit.
47   Interview with Yanayev, op. cit.
48   Korzhakov, op. cit.
49   Ibid.
50   Yeltsin, op. cit.
51   Yeltsin, *Against the Grain*.
52   Yeltsin, *The View from the Kremlin*.
53   Korzhakov, op. cit.
54   Lebed, op. cit.
55   *Financial Times*, 21 August 1991.
56   Schofield, op. cit.
57   Ibid.
58   Lebed, op. cit.
59   Author's interview with Alexander Lebed, 1997.
60   Lebed, *Za Derzhavu Obidno*.
61   Korzhakov, op. cit.
62   Ibid.
63   Lebed, op. cit.

64 Interview with Yanayev, op. cit.
65 Lebed, op. cit.
66 Zaloga, op. cit.
67 Interview with Yanayev, op. cit.
68 Schofield, op. cit.
69 Ibid.
70 Ibid.
71 Interview with Yanayev, op. cit.
72 *Financial Times*, 21 August 1991.
73 Interview with Yanayev, op. cit.
74 Ibid.
75 Ibid.
76 Ibid.
77 Ibid.
78 Lebed, op. cit.
79 Gorbachev, op. cit.
80 Interview with Pankin, op. cit.
81 Interview with Lebed, op. cit.

7: THE RIVER DNIESTER

1   Gogol, *Dead Souls*, translated by David Magarshack.
2   Gorbachev, *Memoirs*.
3   Author's interview with Alexander Lebed, 1997.
4   Lebed, *Za Derzhavu Obidno*.
5   Schofield, *The Russian Elite*.
6   Lebed, op. cit.
7   Ibid.
8   Plater-Zyberk, 'The Soviet Withdrawal from Central Europe'.
9   Ibid.
10 Mathers, 'Corruption in the Russian Armed Forces'.
11 Ibid.
12 Starr, *The New Military in Russia*.
13 Pleines, 'Organised Crime and Corruption in Russia Since 1987'.
14 Zhilin, 'Lebed and Grachev'.
15 Dima, *From Moldavia to Moldova*.
16 Zhilin, op. cit.
17 Ostrogorski, *Lebed. Der Weg zur Macht*.
18 Zhilin, op. cit.
19 Lebed, op. cit.
20 Ibid.
21 Zhilin, op. cit.

22 Lebed, op. cit.
23 Ibid.
24 Ibid.
25 Zhilin, op. cit.
26 Lebed, op. cit.
27 Ibid.
28 *Daily Telegraph*, 16 March 1993.
29 Clark, *An Empire's New Clothes*.
30 *Daily Telegraph*, 22 March 1993.
31 Ibid.
32 Ibid.
33 Clark, op. cit.
34 Yeltsin, *The View from the Kremlin*.
35 Simonsen, 'Going His Own Way: A Profile of Alexander Lebed'.
36 Ibid.
37 Zaloga, *Inside the Blue Berets*.
38 Galeotti, 'Another Shtorm – Forces of the 1993 Moscow Coup'.
39 Clark, op. cit.
40 Ibid.
41 Quoted in Yeltsin, op. cit.
42 Korzhakov, *Ot Rassveta Do Zakata*.
43 Ibid.
44 Simonsen, op. cit.
45 Ibid.
46 Ibid.
47 Ibid.
48 Zhilin, op. cit.
49 Ibid.
50 Simonsen, op. cit.
51 Sergei Bychkov of *Moskovsky Komsomolets* for *Moscow News*, 21 October 1994.
52 *Moscow News*, 3 November 1994.

8: CHECHNYA

1 Lermontov, 'Kazachya Kolybel'naya Pyesnya' in *Izbrannye Sochineniya*.
2 Author's interview with *boyeviki*, 1997.
3 From Baddeley, *The Russian Conquest of the Caucasus*. Quoted in Gammer, 'Russian Strategies in the Conquest of Chechnia and Daghestan, 1825–1859'.
4 Ibid.

5 Quoted by Blanch in *Sabres of Paradise*.

6 Ibid.

7 Gammer, op. cit.

8 Ibid.

9 Quoted in Hosking, *A History of the Soviet Union*.

10 Ibid.

11 Avtorkhanov, 'The Chechens and Ingush During the Soviet Period and Its Antecedents'.

12 Ibid.

13 Ibid.

14 An event described to the author by Chechen sources during a visit to the area in 1997. Also mentioned by Benningsen Broxup in 'Tchétchènie: Une Guerre Coloniale'.

15 Avtorkhanov, op. cit.

16 Quoted by Avtorkhanov, op. cit.

17 Information provided to the author by Chechen sources, 1997.

18 Ostrogorski, *Lebed. Der Weg zur Macht*.

19 Author's interview with Dzhokhar Dudayev, 1995.

20 Quoted by Benningsen Broxup in 'After the Putsch'.

21 Ibid.

22 Ibid.

23 From Alexander Snopov, 'Highlanders' Judgment: Yeltsin Whipping Up Second Caucasus War' in *Komersant*. Quoted in Panico, *Conflicts in the Caucasus*.

24 Quoted in Panico, op. cit.

25 Schneider, 'Moscow's Decision for War in Chechenia'.

26 The International Alert Mission is mentioned in Shah-Kazemi, 'Crisis in Chechnia: Russian Imperialism, Chechen Nationalism and Militant Sufism'.

27 Author's interview with residents of Grozny, 1993.

28 Schneider, op. cit.

29 Broxup, 'After the Putsch', op. cit.

30 Author's interview with Dzhokhar Dudayev, 1993.

31 Author's interview with Dzhaba Ioseliani, 1993.

32 Author's interview with Shamseddin Yusuf, 1993.

33 Interview with Dudayev, op. cit.

34 Shah-Kazemi, op. cit.

35 Schneider, op. cit., quoting *Izvestiya*, 10 January 1995, as source.

36 Articles in *Moscow Tribune* and *Moscow Times*, 4 July 1997.

37 Author's interview, 1995.

38 Author's interview.

39 Author's interview with members of Dudayev's circle, 1995.

40   Author's interview with Boris Pankin, 1997.
41   Ibid.
42   Mau, 'Yeltsin's Choice: Background to the Chechnya Crisis'.
43   Schneider, op. cit.
44   Quoted in Panico, op. cit.
45   Ibid.
46   Report quoted by Kinichkin in 'Rossiyskaya "Operatsiya Gleiwitz"
     V Ispolnenii Federalnoi Sluzhby Kontrrazvedki'.
47   *Izvestiya*, 29 November 1994, quoted in Panico, op. cit.
48   Kinichkin, op. cit.
49   *Daily Telegraph*, 18 November 1994.
50   Evidence given by Kovalev.
51   Author's interview with member of Dudayev's circle.
52   Kovalev, op. cit.
53   *The Economist*, 7 January 1995.
54   Gaidar, *Dni Porazhenii I Pobed*.
55   Ibid.
56   Kovalev, op. cit.
57   *The Times*, 17 December 1994.
58   Quotation from Interfax, 28 December 1994, in Lambeth, *The
     Warrior Who Would Rule Russia*.
59   *Daily Telegraph*, 23 December 1994.
60   *Daily Telegraph*, 30 December 1994.
61   Kovalev, op. cit.
62   Yakunin, 'Testimony of a Deputy'.
63   Ibid.
64   Kovalev, op. cit.
65   *Argumenty I Fakty*, April 1995, quoted in Lambeth, op. cit.
66   Author's interview with Alexander Lebed, 1997.
67   Rogachy, 'K Vizitu Generala Lebedya V Parizh'.
68   Ibid.
69   Author's interview with residents of Grozny (who also showed
     gruesome photographs), 1995.
70   *Daily Telegraph*, 21 February 1995.
71   Author's interview with rebel fighter and close colleague of Basayev,
     1997.
72   *Daily Telegraph*, 21 February 1995.
73   Author's interview with Russian deserters, 1995.
74   Author's interview with Alexander Lebed, 1996.
75   Author's interview with rebel fighter, 1997.
76   Author's interview with former inmate of filtration camp, 1995.
77   *Daily Telegraph*, 21 February 1995.

78   Evidence given by Shabad.
79   *Financial Times*, 27 January 1995.
80   *Paris Match*, 9 February 1995. Quoted in Lambeth, op. cit.
81   Author's interview with Dzhokhar Dudayev, 1995.
82   Ibid.
83   *Daily Telegraph*, 22 June 1995.
84   *Daily Telegraph*, 27 October 1995.

9: THE STATE DUMA

1   Tolstoy, *War and Peace*, translated by Constance Garnett.
2   Author's interview with Alexander Lebed, 1997.
3   Radio Free Europe/Radio Liberty Daily Report: No. 172, 9
     September 1994.
4   Simonsen, 'Going His Own Way: A Profile of Alexander Lebed'.
5   Ibid.
6   Interview with Lebed, op. cit.
7   *Soldat Otyechestva*, 13 March 1994.
8   Quoted in Simonsen, op. cit.
9   Lambeth, *The Warrior Who Would Rule Russia*.
10   Itar-Tass, 2 July 1996.
11   *Moscow News*, 26 May 1995.
12   *Moscow News*, 15 September 1995.
13   *Moscow News*, 6 October 1995.
14   *Moscow News*, 20 October 1995.
15   Ibid.
16   *The Times*, 28 October 1995.
17   *Independent*, 4 December 1995.
18   Ibid.
19   *Independent*, 5 November 1995.
20   *Financial Times*, 8 November 1995.
21   *The Times*, 13 November 1995.
22   *Independent Magazine*, 2 April 1994.
23   *Sunday Times*, 17 July 1995.
24   Quoted in Lambeth, op. cit.
25   Lambeth, op. cit., quoting interview with Alexander Prokhanov in
     Zavtra, August 1995.
26   Interview with Lebed, op. cit.
27   *Izvestiya*, 8 August 1995.
28   *The Times*, 28 October 1995.
29   *Independent*, 28 October 1995.
30   *Sunday Times*, 29 October 1995.

31 Ibid.
32 *Sunday Times*, 17 September 1995.
33 *The Times*, 5 December 1995.
34 *Independent*, 25 November 1995.
35 *Financial Times*, 19 December 1995.
36 Korzhakov, *Ot Rassveta Do Zakata*.
37 Ibid.
38 Ibid.
39 *The Economist*, 8 November 1997.
40 Author's interview with Artyom Tarasov, 1997.
41 *Russia Review*, 3 November 1997.
42 Korzhakov, op. cit.
43 Interview with Tarasov, op. cit.
44 Korzhakov, op. cit.
45 *Obshchaya Gazeta*, 4 July 1996. Quoted in Morvant, 'Soldier Turned Politician in Russia'.
46 *The Times*, 20 June 1996.
47 Ibid.
48 *Nezavisimaya Gazeta*, 3 April 1996.
49 *Paris Match*, interview quoted in Lambeth, op. cit.
50 Author's interview with S. Poumpianskaya, 1997.
51 *Irish Times*, 22 June 1996.
52 *Independent*, 17 June 1996.
53 *The Times*, 18 June 1996.
54 *The Times*, 19 June 1996.
55 *Independent*, 22 June 1996.
56 *The Times*, 22 June 1996.
57 *Sovietskaya Rossiya*, 27 July 1996, quoting the full text of an interview by Chubais with Radio Svoboda.
58 *Sovietskaya Rossiya*, ibid.
59 *Sunday Times*, 23 June 1996.
60 Ibid.
61 *Daily Telegraph*, 22 June 1996.

10: THE KREMLIN

1 Gogol, 'The Overcoat' in *Shinyel*.
2 Turgenev, *Rudin*, translated by Constance Garnett.
3 *Financial Times*, 24 April 1996.
4 *Guardian*, 24 April 1996.
5 *Observer*, 28 April 1996.
6 *The Economist*, 27 April 1996.

7   Author's interview with a member of Dudayev's circle.
8   *Sunday Times*, 28 April 1996.
9   *The Times*, 28 May 1996.
10 *The Economist*, 1 June 1996.
11 *The Times*, 28 May 1996.
12 *Financial Times*, 3 June 1996.
13 When I met him in Gekhi in late 1995, Makhaiev insisted that things had already gone too far for compromise – without independence there would be no peace.
14 *Financial Times*, 3 June 1996.
15 *Moscow News*, 19 August 1996.
16 Author's interview with Lechi Makhaiev, 1997.
17 *Guardian*, 12 July 1996.
18 *The Times*, 13 August 1996.
19 Author's interview with member of Maskhadov's government, 1997.
20 *Izvestiya*, 21 August 1996.
21 *The Times*, 13 August 1996.
22 *Independent*, 15 August 1996.
23 *Independent*, 17 August 1996.
24 Ibid.
25 *Daily Telegraph*, 17 August 1996.
26 *Izvestiya*, 21 August 1996.
27 Ibid.
28 *Independent*, 23 August 1996.
29 Gall and de Waal, *Chechnya: A Small Victorious War*.
30 *Moscow News*, 4 September 1996.
31 Ibid.
32 Ibid.
33 Ibid.
34 *Izvestiya*, 4 September 1996.
35 *Independent*, 23 August 1996.
36 *Moscow News*, 4 September 1996.
37 *Izvestiya*, 3 September 1996.
38 *Der Spiegel*, 9 September 1996.
39 *Guardian*, 24 August 1996.
40 Quotation from Interfax, 2 July 1996, in Lambeth, *The Warrior Who Would Rule Russia*.
41 Quotation from Mayak radio network, 27 July 1996, in Lambeth, op. cit.
42 *Financial Times*, 30 September 1996.
43 Lambeth, op. cit.
44 *Moscow News*, 25 September 1996.

45   *Guardian*, 4 October 1996.
46   *Guardian*, 7 October 1996.
47   *Daily Telegraph*, 8 October 1996.
48   *Guardian*, 8 October 1996.
49   *Daily Telegraph*, 14 October 1996.
50   *Sevodnya*, 17 October 1996.
51   *Daily Telegraph*, 17 October 1996.
52   *Sevodnya*, 17 October 1996.
53   *Daily Telegraph*, 17 October 1996.
54   *Daily Telegraph*, 18 October 1996.
55   *Financial Times*, 20 October 1996.
56   *Financial Times*, 18 October 1996.
57   Interview with Lebed, op. cit.
58   Ibid.
59   *Nezavisimaya Gazeta*, 24 December 1996.
60   Lebed, interview with Jörg Mettke of *Der Spiegel*, quoted in Lebed, *Russlands Weg*.
61   *Moskovskaya Pravda*, 15 January 1997.
62   Interview with Lebed, op. cit.
63   *Moskovskaya Pravda*, 15 January 1997.
64   Lebed, *Russlands Weg*.
65   *Sunday Times*, 31 March 1997.
66   *The Times*, 7 April 1997.
67   Interview with Lebed, op. cit.
68   Durden-Smith, 'Moscow Dynamo'.
69   Interview with Lebed, op. cit.
70   *Ogonyok*, No. 3, January 1997.
71   Interview with Lebed, op. cit.
72   *New York Times International*, 23 January 1997.
73   Ibid.
74   *Komsomolskaya Pravda*, 21 September 1996.
75   Ulfkotte, *Verschlußsache BND*.
76   Interview with Lebed, op. cit.
77   Ibid.
78   Ibid.
79   *Izvestiya*, 17 February 1996.
80   Interview with Lebed, op. cit.
81   Ibid.
82   Ibid.
83   Ibid.
84   Ibid.
85   *The Economist*, 22 November 1997.

BIBLIOGRAPHY

BOOKS

Baumann, R. F., *Russian–Soviet Unconventional Wars in the Caucasus, Central Asia and Afghanistan* (Kansas: Leavenworth Papers, Combat Studies Institute, US Army Command and General Staff College, 1993).

Baddeley, J. F., *The Russian Conquest of the Caucasus* (London: 1908).

Benningsen Broxup, M. (ed.), *The North Caucasus Barrier* (New York: St Martin's Press, 1992).

Blanch, L., *Sabres of Paradise* (New York: 1960).

Brezhnev, L. I., *50 Let Velikogo Sotsializma* (Moscow: Polizdat, 1967).

Brook, S., *Claws of the Crab: Georgia and Armenia in Crisis* (London: Pan, 1993).

Clark, B., *An Empire's New Clothes: The End of Russia's Liberal Dream* (London: Vintage, 1995).

Cordovez, D., and Harrison, S., *Out of Afghanistan: The Inside Story of the Soviet Withdrawal* (Oxford: OUP, 1995).

Dima, N., *From Moldavia to Moldova: The Soviet–Romanian Territorial Dispute* (Boulder, CO: East European Monographs, 1991. Distributed by Columbia University Press, New York).

Doder, D., *Shadows and Whispers: Power Politics Inside the Kremlin from Brezhnev to Gorbachev* (London: Harrap, 1987).

Gaidar, Y., *Dni Porazhenii I Pobed* (Moscow: Vagarius, 1997).

Galeotti, M., *Afghanistan: The Soviet Union's Last War* (London: Frank Cass, 1995).

——, *The Kremlin's Agenda* (Surrey: Jane's Intelligence Review, 1995).

Gall, C., and de Waal, T., *Chechnya: A Small Victorious War* (London: Pan, 1997).

Gogol, N. V., *Dead Souls* (London: Penguin, 1961).

——, *Shinyel* (Moscow: Izdatel'stvo 'Dyetskaya Literatura', 1979).

Goldenberg, S., *The Pride of Small Nations: The Caucasus and Post-Soviet Disorder* (London and New Jersey: Led Books, 1994).

Gorbachev, M. S., *Memoirs* (New York: Doubleday, 1995).

Gouliev, R., *Oil and Politics* (New York: Liberty Publishing House, 1997).

Gromov, B., *Ogranichenny Kontingent* (Moscow: Progress, 1990).

Halfon, R., *Retreat or Reform? Russia's Struggle for Democracy* (London: Institute for European Defence and Strategic Studies, 1995).

——, *Russia After the Elections: Impact for Investors* (London: Centre for Transition Economies, 1996).

Hiden, J., and Salmon P., *The Baltic Nations and Europe: Estonia, Latvia and Lithuania in the Twentieth Century* (London: Longman, 1991).

Hopkins, A. T., *Unchained Reactions – Chernobyl, Glasnost and Nuclear Deterrence* (n.d.).

Hopkirk, P., *The Great Game: On Secret Service in High Asia* (Oxford: OUP, 1991).

Hosking, G., *A History of the Soviet Union, 1917–1991* (London: Fontana, 1992).

Khan, M. I., *The Muslims of Chechnya: Struggle for Independence* (Leicester: The Islamic Foundation, 1995).

Kipling, R., *Rudyard Kipling's Verse, 1885–1918* (London: Hodder & Stoughton, n.d.).

Korzhakov, A., *Ot Rassveta Do Zakata* (Moscow: Izdatel'stvo 'Interbuk', 1997).

Lacquer, W., *The Dream That Failed: Reflections on the Soviet Union* (Oxford: OUP, 1994).

Lambeth, B. S., *The Warrior Who Would Rule Russia* (Santa Monica, CA: RAND, 1996).

Lebed, A. I., *Spektakl Nazyvalsya Putsch* (Tiraspol: LADA, 1993).

——, *Za Derzhavu Obidno* (Moscow: Gregori-Peidzh/Redaktsiya Gazety 'Moskovskaya Pravda', 1995).

——, *Russlands Weg* (Hamburg: Hoffmann und Campe, 1997).

Lermontov, M. Y., *Izbrannye Sochineniya* (Moscow: Khudozhestvennaya Literatura, 1983).

Leskov, N. S., *Lady Macbeth of Mtsensk and Other Stories* (London: Penguin Books, 1987).

Mackintosh, M., *The New Russian Revolution: The Military Dimension* (London: Research Institute for the Study of Conflict and Terrorism, 1992).

McGwire, M., *Perestroika and Soviet National Security* (Washington: Brookings Institute, 1991).

Nemtsov, B., *Provintsial* (Moscow: Bagrius, 1997).

Novichkov, N. N., et al., *Rossiskiye Vooruzhennye Sily v Chechenskom Konflikte: Analiz, Itogi, Vyvody* (Paris and Moscow: Kholveg-Infoglob/Trivola, 1995).

O'Ballance, E., *Wars in the Caucasus, 1990–1995* (New York: 1997).

Ostrogorski, V., *Lebed. Der Weg zur Macht* (Berlin: Brandenburgisches Verlagshaus, 1996).

The Officer's Handbook (Moscow: 1971).

Panico, C., *Conflicts in the Caucasus: Russia's War in Chechnya* (London, Research Institute for the Study of Conflict and Terrorism, 1995).

Pankin, B., *The Last Hundred Days of the Soviet Union* (London: I. B. Tauris, 1996).

Polushin, V., *General Lebed – Zagadka Rossii* (Moscow: Vneshtorgizdat, 1996).

Pushkin, A. S., *Sochineniya* (Moscow: Khudozhestvennaya Literatura, 1978).

Pyataya Rossiskaya Gosudarstvennaya Duma (Moscow: Izvestiya, 1994).

Saikal, A., and Maley, W., *The Soviet Withdrawal from Afghanistan* (Cambridge: CUP, 1989).

Schofield, C., *The Russian Elite* (London: 1996).

Shearman, P., *Russian Foreign Policy Since 1990* (Boulder, CO: Westview Press, 1995).

Simis, K., *USSR: Secrets of a Corrupt Society* (London: Dent, 1982).

Starr, R. F., *The New Military in Russia: Ten Myths That Shape the Image* (Annapolis, MD: Naval Institute Press, 1996).

Suny, R. G., *The Revenge of the Past: Nationalism, Revolution and the Collapse of the Soviet Union* (Stanford, CA: Stanford University Press, 1993).

Suvorov, V., *Inside the Soviet Army* (New York: 1982).

The Soviet Weapons Industry: An Overview (Washington, DC: Directorate of Intelligence, 1986).

Tolstoy, L. N., *The Death of Ivan Ilyich* (London: Penguin, 1979).

——, *War and Peace* (London: Pan, 1972).

Turgenev, I. S., *On the Eve* (London: Penguin, 1977).

——, *Rudin* (London: William Heinemann, 1911).

Ulfkotte, U., *Verschlußsache BND* (Munich and Berlin: Köhler & Amelang, 1997).

US Department of Defense, *Soviet Military Power, 1990* (Washington DC: 1990).

Yelstin, B. N., *Against the Grain* (London: Pan, 1991).
——, *The View from the Kremlin* (London: HarperCollins, 1994).
Yevtushenko, Y., *The Poetry of Yevgeny Yevtushenko* (London: Calder & Boyars, 1969).
Zaloga, S. J., *Inside the Blue Berets: A Combat History of Soviet and Russian Airborne Forces, 1930–1995* (Novato, CA: Presidio Press, 1995).

ARTICLES

Andreyev, N., 'Vylupitsya Li Iz Lebedya Rutskoi' in *Moskovskaya Pravda*, 2 October 1996.
Avtorkhanov, A., 'The Chechens and Ingush During the Soviet Period and Its Antecedents' in Benningsen Broxup (ed.), *The North Caucasus Barrier* (New York: St Martin's Press, 1992).
Aris, B., 'Demistifying the Magnificent 7' in *Russia Review*, 3 November 1997.
Benningsen Broxup, M., 'Tchétchènie: Une Guerre Coloniale' in *Politique Internationale*, Spring 1995.
Bershin, Y., 'V Politiku Menya Ne Prosto Priveli – Zagnali' (interview with Lebed) in *Literaturnaya Gazeta*, 17 May 1995.
Bovkun, Y., 'Nemtsy Zaputalis V Aforizmakh Lebedya', 17 January 1997.
Bradley, B., 'Eurasia Letter: A Misguided Russia Policy' in *Foreign Policy*, No. 101, Winter 1995.
Chelnokov, A., 'Okruzheniye Lebedya' in *Izvestiya*, 11 July 1996.
Chudakova, M., 'Alexander Lebed – Novaya Metla Ili Novy Etap?' in *Izvestiya*, 25 June 1996.
Cohen, A., 'Who's Who in the Russian Presidential Elections' in *Heritage Foundation Backgrounder*, June 1996.
Durden-Smith, J., 'Moscow Dynamo' in the *Sunday Telegraph Magazine*, 30 November 1997.
Ericksson, J., 'Soviet Military Power' in *RUSI*, 1971.
Foye, S., 'Confrontation in Moscow: The Army Backs Yeltsin, for Now' in *RFE/RL Research Report*, Vol 2, No. 42, October 1993.
——, 'Civilian and Military Leaders in Russia's "New" Political Arena' in *RFE/RL Research Report*, Vol. 3, No. 15, April 1994.
Galeotti, M., 'Another Shtorm – Forces of the 1993 Moscow Coup' in *Jane's Intelligence Review*, December 1993.
——, 'General Lebed: The Voice of Russia's Soldiers' in *Jane's Intelligence Review*, January 1995.
——, 'Decline and Fall: Russia After Yeltsin' in *Jane's Intelligence Review*, September 1995.

Gammer, M., 'Russian Strategies in the Conquest of Chechnia and Daghestan, 1825–1859' in Benningsen Broxup (ed.), *The North Caucasus Barrier* (New York: St Martin's Press, 1992).

Gamova, S., 'Alexander Lebed: Sama Zhizn Zastavlyaet Generalov Zanimatsya Politikoi' in *Izvestiya*, 20 July 1994.

Gerol, I., 'Dembel Generala' in *Novoye Vremya*, No. 27, 1996.

Golubev, V., 'Alexander Lebed Vozvrashchaetsya' in *Nezavisimaya Gazeta*, 24 December 1996.

——, 'Alexander Lebed: Lider ili Politik Vtorogo Eshelona?' in *Nezavisimaya Gazeta*, 1 August 1997.

Golyshev, B., 'Stavka Bolshe, Chem Chest' in *Pravda*, 20 June 1996.

Halfon, R., 'Russia's Democratic Bypass' in *Jane's Intelligence Review*, February 1997.

Herspring, D., 'The Russian Military: Three Years On' in *Communist and Post-Communist Studies*, Vol. 28, No. 2, 1995.

Holoboff, E. M., 'The Crisis in Soviet Military Reform' (London: Brassey's/Centre for Defence Studies, 1991).

Karaganov, S., 'Russia: The New Foreign Policy and Security Agenda: A View from Moscow' (London: Brassey's/Centre for Defence Studies, 1992).

Kinichkin, A., 'Rossiyskaya "Operatsiya Gleiwitz" V Ispolnenii Federalnoi Sluzhby Kontrrazvedki' in *Report of VI Round Table of Glasnost Foundation*, 1995.

Kipp, J., 'The Political Ballet of General Aleksandr Lebed' in *Problems of Post-Communism*, July–August 1996.

Kishkin, N., et al., 'Khotel I Khochu Byt Prezidentom Gosudarstva Rossiiskogo' in *Trud*, 22 October 1996.

Kolchanov, R., 'Alexander Lebed: U Nas Nikogda Ne Bylo Demokratii' in *Trud*, 18 January 1997.

Konovalov, V., 'Postavlena Tochka V Rassledovanii Novocherkasskikh Sobytii 1962 Goda' in *Izvestiya*, 4 July 1994.

Kovalev, S.: evidence given to the International Non-Governmental Tribunal on Crimes Against Humanity and War Crimes in the Chechen Republic, published by the Glasnost Foundation, Moscow, February 1996.

Kozyrev, A., 'Partnership or Cold Peace' in *Foreign Policy*, No. 99, Summer 1995.

Krumm, R., and Mettke, J., 'Sie Schotten Jelzin ab: General Alexander Korschakow, Ex-Leibwachter Boris Jelzins, uber den kranken Prasidenten und den Moskauer Machtkampf' in *Der Spiegel*, No. 44, 1996.

Ladny, V., 'A Pochemu U Generala Lebedya Takoi Golos?' (interview with Lebed's mother, Yekaterina Grigoryevna) in *Komsomolskaya Pravda*, 12 July 1996.

Lambeth, B. S., 'Russia's Wounded Military' in *Foreign Affairs*, Vol. 74, No. 2, March–April 1995.

Lebed, A., 'Pobezhdat Dano Kholodnym I Paschyotlivym' in *Argumenty I Fakty*, No. 43, 1996.

——, 'Znaiu Chto Delat. Znaiu Kak Delat' in *Trud*, 28 June 1996.

——, 'Ya Reshil Stat Samym Trezvym Chelovekom V Rossii' in *Komsomolskaya Pravda*, 17 September 1996.

——, 'Ya Prishel Sluzhit Gosudarstvu' in *Izvestiya*, 26 September 1996.

Lebed, A., and Maskhadov, A., 'Zayavlenie' in *Izvestiya*, 3 September 1996.

Levina, Y., 'Moi Muzh General-Leitenant, A Ya General-Polkovnik' (interview with Inna Lebed) in *Komsomolskaya Pravda*, 10 May 1996.

Mackintosh, M., 'Reform in the Russian Armed Forces' in *Jane's Intelligence Review*, December 1994.

Mathers, J., 'Corruption in the Russian Armed Forces' in *The World Today*, August–September 1995.

Mau, V., 'Yeltsin's Choice: Background to the Chechnya Crisis' in *Social Market Foundation Memorandum*, No. 12, February 1995.

McFaul, M., 'Eurasia Letter: Russian Politics after Chechnya' in *Foreign Policy*, No. 99, Summer 1995.

Nadyein, V., 'Kakim Uvidela Lebedya Amerika' in *Izvestiya*, 28 November 1996.

Malkina, T., 'Alexander Lebed Gotovit Myatezh' in *Sevodnya*, 17 October 1996.

Maslov, S., 'Chto Helmut Kohl Skazal "Drugu Borisu" Bez Svidetelyei', 21 September 1996.

Mettke, J., 'Ein Sieg war unmoglich: Russlands Sicherheitsberater Alexander Lebed uber seine Friedensmission in Tschetschenien' in *Der Spiegel*, No. 37, 1996.

——, 'Ich sehe mich als Prasident: Der russische General a.D. Alexander Lebed uber seinen Bruch mit Boris Jelzin und seine Absetzung' in *Der Spiegel*, No. 43, 1996.

Morvant, P., 'Soldier Turned Politician in Russia' in *Transition*, 23 August 1996.

Morzharetto, I., and Perushkin, V., 'Alexander Lebed: "Ya Sluzhu Tak, Kak Schitayu Nuzhnym"' in *Argumenty I Fakty*, No. 14, 1995.

Ogurtsov, V., 'Novocherkassk Pomnit' in *Moskovskaya Pravda*, 8 August 1992.

Oleynik, I., 'Lebed Bezhit Rovno' in *Dyelovye Lyudi*, August 1997.

Petrov, Major S. N., 'An Airborne Battalion Searches Sherkhankel Village, March 1982' in *Combat Actions of Soviet Forces in the Republic of Afghanistan* (Moscow: Frunze Academy Press), published in London in the *Journal of Slavic Military Studies*, Vol. 7, No. 3, September 1994, by Frank Cass.

Plater-Zyberk, H., 'The Soviet Withdrawal from Central Europe' (London: Brassey's/Centre for Defence Studies, n.d.).

Pleines, H., 'Organised Crime and Corruption in Russia Since 1987' in *Russia and the Successor States Briefing Service*, Vol. 3/5, October 1995.

Pogorzhelsky, D., 'Alexander Lebed Pokoryaet Germaniyu' in *Sevodnya*, 17 January 1997.

Pridotkas, A., 'Aleksandr Lebed in Defense of the Motherland' in *Post-Soviet Prospects*, Vol. IV, 5 April 1996.

Radzikovsky, L., 'Komu Podchinyaetsya Armiya?' in *Ogonyok*, No. 42, October 1996.

Rogachy, I., 'K Vizitu Generala Lebedya V Parizh' in *Russkaya Mysl*, No. 4162, 20–26 February 1997.

Schneider, E., 'Moscow's Decision for War in Chechenia' in *Aussen-politik*, February 1995.

Schofield, C., 'Anti-Coup Leaders: The Men of the Future?' in *Jane's Intelligence Review*, October 1991.

Shabad, A.: evidence given to the International Non-Governmental Tribunal on Crimes Against Humanity and War Crimes in the Chechen Republic, published by the Glasnost Foundation, Moscow, February 1996.

Shah-Kazemi, R., 'Crisis in Chechnia: Russian Imperialism, Chechen Nationalism and Militant Sufism' in *Islamic World Report*, 1995.

Shakina, M., 'The Nemtsov Myth' in *New Times*, July 1997.

Shevtsova, L., 'Rossiyskaya Vlast Opyat Na Pereputye' in *Nezavisimaya Gazeta*, 25 February 1997.

Simonsen, S. G., 'Going His Own Way: A Profile of Alexander Lebed' in the *Journal of Slavic Military Studies*, Vol. 8, No. 3, September 1995.

Stepovoi, A., 'Lebed Poidyot Po Tretyemu Puti' in *Izvestiya*, 31 December 1996.

Tarasov, A., 'Chernye Lebedi' in *Ogonyok*, No. 3 (4486), January 1997.

Taylor, H. J., 'The Origins and Development of Chechen Separatism' in *War Studies Journal*, Vol. 2, No. 2, Spring 1997.

Timakova, N., and Budberg, A., 'Tsirkach Bolshoi Politiki' in *Moskovsky Komsomolets*, 28 November 1996.

Trushkov, V., 'Lebed Menyaet Operenie' in *Pravda*, 20 June 1996.

Urigashvili, B., 'General Pulikovsky Vzyvaet K Bogu' in *Izvestiya*, 21 August 1996.

Vandenko, A., 'Krutye Gorki Alexandra Lebedya' in *Moskovskaya Pravda*, 15 January 1996.

Yakunin, G., 'Testimony of a Deputy' in *Report of VI Round Table of Glasnost Foundation*, 1995.

Yavlyansky, I., 'Kak U Lyudyei Zakonchatsya Zapasy Kartoshki, Tak I Nachnyotsya Krizis' in *Komsomolskaya Pravda*, 18 January 1997.

Zaripov, R., et al., 'Ya Ne Karatel, Ya Soldat' (interview with Lebed) in *Komsomolskaya Pravda*, 19 March 1996.

Zhilin, A., 'Lebed and Grachev' at <http://www.spb.su/times/175-176/battle.html>.

——, 'Bizness Generalov' in *Moskovskie Novosti*, No. 24, 1994.

——, 'Ya Ne Politichesky Killer' (interview with Lebed) in *Moskovskie Novosti*, No. 25, 1996.

Zimin, N., 'Alexander Lebed Litsom K Litsu S Amerikoi' in *Sevodnya*, 26 November 1996.

INDEX